SOME PHYSICAL CONSTANTS

Speed of light	c	3.00×10^8 m/s
Gravitational constant	G	6.67×10^{-11} J·m/kg^2
Coulomb constant	k	8.99×10^9 J·m/C^2
Planck constant	h	6.63×10^{-34} kg·m^2/s
Boltzmann's constant	k_B	1.38×10^{-23} J/K
Proton charge	e	1.60×10^{-19} C
Electron mass	m_e	9.11×10^{-31} kg
Proton mass	m_p	1.67×10^{-27} kg
Neutron mass	m_n	1.68×10^{-27} kg

STANDARD METRIC PREFIXES
For Powers of Ten

Power	Prefix	Symbol
10^{18}	exa-	E-
10^{15}	peta-	P-
10^{12}	tera-	T-
10^{9}	giga-	G-
10^{6}	mega-	M-
10^{3}	kilo-	k-
10^{-2}	centi-	c-
10^{-3}	milli-	m-
10^{-6}	micro-	μ-
10^{-9}	nano-	n-
10^{-12}	pico-	p-
10^{-15}	femto-	f-
10^{-18}	atto-	a-

COMMONLY-USED PHYSICAL DATA

Gravitational Field Strength g	9.80 m/s^2
Mass of the Earth M_e	5.98×10^{24} kg
Radius of the Earth R_e	6,380 km (equatorial)
Mass of the Sun M_s	1.99×10^{30} kg
Radius of the Sun R_s	696,000 km
Distance to Moon	3.84×10^8 m
Distance to Sun	1.50×10^{11} m
Density of Water	1000.0 kg/m^3 = 1 g/cm^3 *
Density of Air	1.2 kg/m^3 *
Absolute Zero	0 K = –273.15 °C = –459.67 °F
Freezing point of water **	273.15 K = 0 °C = 32 °F
Room Temperature	295 K = 22 °C = 72 °F
Boiling point of water **	373 K = 100 °C = 212 °F

** at normal atmospheric pressure   * at normal pressure and at 20 °C

USEFUL CONVERSION FACTORS

1 meter = 1 m = 100 cm = 39.4 inches = 3.28 ft
1 mile = 1 mi = 1609 m = 1.609 km = 5280 ft
1 inch = 2.54 cm
1 light-year = 1 ly = 9.46 Pm = 0.946×10^{16} m

1 hour = 1 h = 60 min = 3600 s
1 day = 1 d = 24 h = 86.4 ks = 86,400 s
1 year = 1 y = 365.25 d = 31.6 Ms = 3.16×10^7 s

1 J = 1 kg·m^2/s^2 = 0.239 cal
1 cal = 4.186 J
1 W = 1 J/s
1 kWh = 3.6 MJ

1 K (temperature difference) = 1 °C = 1.8 °F

$$T \text{ (in K)} = \left(\frac{1\,\text{K}}{1°\text{C}}\right)[T \text{ (in °C)} + 273.15°\text{C}]$$

1.0 radian = 57.3° = 0.1592 rev

1 m/s = 2.24 mi/h
1 mi/h = 1.61 km/h
1 ft^3 = 0.02832 m^3
1 gallon = 1 gal = 3.79×10^{-3} m^3 ≈ 3.8 kg H$_2$O

1 N = 1 kg·m/s^2 = 1 J/m = 0.225 lb
1 lb = 4.45 N
weight of 1-kg object near earth = 9.8 N = 2.2 lbs

1 cal = energy to raise temp. of 1 g of H$_2$O by 1 K
1 food calorie = 1 Cal = 1 kcal = 1000 cal
1 horsepower = 1 hp = 746 W

$$T \text{ (in °C)} = (5°\text{C}/9°\text{F})[T \text{ (in °F)} - 32 °\text{F}]$$

$$T \text{ (in K)} = \left(\frac{5\,\text{K}}{9°\text{F}}\right)[T \text{ (in °F)} + 459.67°\text{F}]$$

1 rev = 360° = 2π radians = 6.28 radians

SYMBOLS AND THEIR MEANINGS

$=$	is equal to
$\neq$	is not equal to
$\approx$	is approximately equal to
$>$	is greater than
$<$	is less than
$>>$	is much greater than
$<<$	is much less than
$\equiv$	is defined to be
$\propto$	is proportional to
$\Rightarrow$	implies or therefore
$\Leftrightarrow$	if and only if (implication goes both ways)
∞	infinity
$\cdot$	indicates a dot product of vectors OR product of units OR general multiplication of scalars
$\times$	indicates a cross product of vectors OR multiplication by a power of 10 (as in 5×10^6)
i.e.	*id est* "that is"
e.g.	*exempli gratia* "for example"
etc.	*etcetera* "and so on"
Q.E.D.	*quod erat demonstrandum* "which was to be demonstrated"
$|x|$	absolute value of x
mag()	magnitude of a vector
α, θ, ϕ	angles
Δ	(as prefix) a largish change in the variable whose symbol follows
ρ	mass density
Σ	indicates a sum
$\vec{\omega}$	angular velocity (magnitude $= \omega$)
$\vec{a}, \vec{b}, \vec{c}$	(in this unit) arbitrary vectors
b	generally used as a scalar constant
c	speed of light OR magnitude of vector $\vec{c}$ OR specific heat* (especially if with a subscript)
C	arbitrary constant
C	(not italic) coulomb, the SI unit of charge
cal, Cal	units of energy
CM	(not italic, often as subscript) center of mass
d, D	distance OR sometimes depth
d	(as a prefix): a tiny change in the variable whose symbol follows
$đ$	(as a prefix): one contribution to a tiny change in the variable following
deg	degree, a unit of angle
$d\vec{r}$	tiny displacement
dK	tiny energy transfer
$d\vec{p}$	tiny momentum transfer
$\vec{F}$	force
g	gravitational field strength
G	universal gravitational constant
h	height OR Planck constant
i	(as a subscript) means "initial" OR represents an index in a sum
I	moment of inertia OR intensity
j	(as a subscript) indicates an index in a sum

J	(not italic) joule, the SI unit of energy
k	Coulomb constant
k_B	Boltzmann constant
k_s	spring (stiffness) constant
K	kinetic energy
K^{rot}	rotational kinetic energy
K^{cm}	translational kinetic energy of an object's CM
K	(not italic) kelvin, the SI unit of temperature
KE	(not italic) kinetic energy
L	length OR magnitude of angular momentum OR latent heat* (in C11)
$\vec{L}$	angular momentum
$\vec{L}^{rot}$	angular momentum of an object around its CM
$\vec{L}^{cm}$	angular momentum associated with the translational motion of an object's CM
m	mass
M	mass (usually of a system or large object)
n	an arbitrary or unknown integer
N	number of particles in a system
N	(not italic) newton, the SI unit of force
0	(as a subscript) means original or initial
O	origin of a reference frame
$\vec{p}$	momentum OR arbitrary vector (in C3)
P	power
PE	(not italic) potential energy
q	electrical charge OR an arbitrary scalar
$\vec{q}$	arbitrary vector (in C3) or particle's position relative to the system's CM (in C9)
Q	heat
$\vec{r}$	a position vector
r	a radius OR separation OR mag($\vec{r}$)
rad	radian, the SI "unit" of angle
R	radius (often the fixed outer radius of some object or a radius distinct from r)
s	arclength
t	time
T	temperature
$\vec{u}$	arbitrary vector OR velocity of a particle relative to a system's CM (in C9)
U	internal energy OR thermal energy (in C10)
U^{th}	thermal energy
U^{la}	latent energy
U^{ch}	chemical energy
U^{nu}	nuclear energy
U^{el}	electrical energy
U^{sw}	energy in sound waves
U^{em}	energy in electromagnetic waves
$\vec{v}$	velocity (speed $\equiv$ mag($\vec{v}$) $= v$)
V	potential energy
$\vec{w}$	an arbitrary vector
W	(in thermal physics) work
W	(not italic) watt, the SI unit of power
x, y, z	position coordinates
x, y, z	(as a subscript) indicates a component of a vector quantity
$x\text{-}, y\text{-}, z\text{-}$	(as a prefix) indicates a component of a vector quantity

SIX IDEAS THAT SHAPED PHYSICS

Unit C: Conservation Laws
Constrain Interactions

(a)

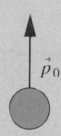

$\vec{p}_0$

INITIAL

(b)

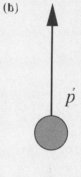

$\vec{p}'$

$\vec{p}_2$

FINAL

Thomas A. Moore
Pomona College

**WCB
McGraw-Hill**

Boston   Burr Ridge, IL   Dubuque, IA   Madison, WI   New York   San Francisco   St. Louis
Bangkok   Bogotá   Caracas   Lisbon   London   Madrid
Mexico City   Milan   New Delhi   Seoul   Singapore   Sydney   Taipei   Toronto

For all my family, near and far,
(and in memory of Anne Moore),
whose love has conserved what is best.

WCB/McGraw-Hill
A Division of the McGraw-Hill Companies

SIX IDEAS THAT SHAPED PHYSICS/
UNIT C: CONSERVATION LAWS CONSTRAIN INTERACTIONS

This book is printed on recycled, acid-free paper containing 10% postconsumer waste.

4 5 6 7 8 9 0 QPD/QPD 9 0 9

ISBN 0-07-043049-7

Vice president and editorial director: *Kevin T. Kane*
Publisher: *James M. Smith*
Sponsoring editor: *John Paul Lenney*
Developmental editor: *Donata Dettbarn*
Marketing manager: *Lisa L. Gottschalk*
Project managers: *Larry Goldberg, Sheila Frank*
Production supervisor: *Mary E. Haas*
Cover designer: *Jonathan Alpert/SCRATCHworks Creative*
Compositor: *Thomas A. Moore*
Typeface: *9/10 Times Roman*
Printer: *Quebecor Printing Book Group/Dubuque*

Cover photo: © Corel

Library of Congress Catalog Card Number: 97-62246

www.mhhe.com

CONTENTS

PREFACE

1. INTRODUCTION

This volume is one of six that together comprise the PRELIMINARY EDITION of the text materials for *Six Ideas That Shaped Physics,* a fundamentally new approach to the two- or three-semester calculus-based introductory physics course. This course is still very much a work in progress. We are publishing these volumes in preliminary form so that we can broaden the base of institutions using the course and gather the feedback that we need to better polish both the course and its supporting texts for a formal first edition in a few years. Though we have worked very hard to remove as many of the errors and rough edges as possible for this edition, we would greatly appreciate your help in reporting any errors that remain and offering your suggestions for improvement. I will tell you how you can contact us in a section near the end of this preface.

Much of this preface discusses features and issues that are common to all six volumes of the *Six Ideas* course. For comments about this specific unit and how it relates to the others, see section 7.

Six Ideas That Shaped Physics was created in response to a call for innovative curricula offered by the Introductory University Physics Project (IUPP), which subsequently supported its early development. IUPP officially tested very early versions of the course at University of Minnesota during 1991/92 and at Amherst and Smith Colleges during 1992/93. In its present form, the course represents the culmination of over eight years of development, testing, and evaluation at Pomona College, Smith College, Amherst College, St. Lawrence University, Beloit College, Hope College, UC-Davis, and other institutions.

We designed this course to be consistent with the three basic principles articulated by the IUPP steering committee in its call for model curricula:

1. **The pace of the course should be reduced** so that a broader range of students can achieve an acceptable level of competence and satisfaction.
2. **There should be more 20th-century physics** to better show students what physics is like at the present.
3. **The course should use one or more "story lines"** to help organize the ideas and motivate student interest.

The design of *Six Ideas* was also strongly driven by two other principles:

4. **The course should seek to embrace the best of what educational research has taught us** about conceptual and structural problems with the standard course.
5. **The course should stake out a middle ground** between the standard introductory course and exciting but radical courses that require substantial investments in infrastructure and/or training. This course should be useful in fairly standard environments and should be relatively easy for teachers to understand and adopt.

In its present form, *Six Ideas* course consists of a set of six textbooks (one for each "idea"), a detailed instructor's guide, and a few computer programs that support the course in crucial places. The texts have a variety of innovative features that are designed to (1) make them more clear and readable, (2) teach you *explicitly* about the processes of constructing models and solving complex problems, (3) confront well-known conceptual problems head-on, and (4) support the instructor in innovative uses of class time. The instructor's manual is much

---

Margin notes:

Opening comments about this preliminary edition

The course's roots in the Introductory University Physics Project

The three basic principles of the IUPP project

My additional working principles

A summary of the course's distinctive features

more detailed than is normal, offering detailed suggestions (based on many teacher-years of experience with the course at a variety of institutions) about how to structure the course and adapt it to various calendars and constituencies. The instructor's manual also offers a complete description of effective approaches to class time that emphasize active and collaborative learning over lecture (and yet can still be used in fairly large classes), supporting this with day-by-day lesson plans that make this approach much easier to understand and adopt.

In the remainder of this preface, I will look in more detail at the structure and content of the course and briefly explore *why* we have designed the various features of the course the way that we have.

2. GENERAL PHILOSOPHY OF THE COURSE

Problems with the traditional intro course

The current standard introductory physics course has a number of problems that have been documented in recent years. (1) There is so much material to "cover" in the standard course that students do not have time to develop a deep understanding of any part, and instructors do not have time to use classroom techniques that would help students really learn. (2) Even with all this material, the standard course, focused as it is on *classical* physics, does not show what physics is like *today*, and thus presents a skewed picture of the discipline to the 32 out of 33 students who will never take another physics course. (3) Most importantly, the standard introductory course generally fails to *teach physics*. Studies have shown that even students who earn high grades in a standard introductory physics course often cannot

1. apply basic physical principles to realistic situations,
2. solve realistic problems,
3. perceive or resolve contradictions involving their preconceptions, or
4. organize the ideas of physics hierarchically.

What students in such courses *do* effectively learn is how to solve highly contrived and patterned homework problems (either by searching for analogous examples in the text and then copying them without much understanding, or by doing a random search through the text for a formula that has the right variables.) The high pace of the standard course usually drives students to adopt these kinds of non-thinking behaviors even if they don't want to.

The goal: to help students become competent in using the skills listed above

The goal of *Six Ideas* is to help students achieve a meaningful level of competence in each of the four thinking skills listed above. We have rethought and restructured the course from the ground up so that students are goaded toward (and then rewarded for) behaviors that help them develop these skills. We have designed texts, exams, homework assignments, and activity-based class sessions to reinforce each other in keeping students focused on these goals.

The focus is more on skills than on specific content

While (mostly for practical reasons) the course does span the most important fields of physics, the emphasis is *not* particularly on "covering" material or providing background vocabulary for future study, but more on developing problem-solving, thinking, and modeling skills. Facts and formulas evaporate quickly (particularly for those 32 out of 33 that will take no more physics) but if we can develop students' abilities to think like a physicist in a variety of contexts, we have given them something they can use throughout their lives.

3. TOPICS EXPLORED IN THE COURSE

The six-unit structure

Six Ideas That Shaped Physics is divided into six units (normally offered three per semester). The purpose of each unit is to explore in depth a single idea that has changed the course of physics during the past three centuries. The list below describes each unit's letter name, its length (1 d = one day $\equiv$ one 50-minute class session), the idea, and the corresponding area of physics.

First Semester (37 class days excluding test days):
Unit C (14 d) *Conservation Laws Constrain Interactions* (conservation laws)
Unit N (14 d) *The Laws of Physics are Universal*   (forces and motion)
Unit R   (9 d) *Physics is Frame-Independent*   (special relativity)

Second Semester (42 class days excluding test days):
Unit E (17 d) *Electromagnetic Fields are Dynamic*   (electrodynamics)
Unit Q (16 d) *Particles Behave Like Waves*   (basic quantum physics)
Unit T   (9 d) *Some Processes are Irreversible*   (statistical physics)

(Note that the spring semester is assumed to be longer than fall semester. This is typically the case at Pomona and many other institutions, but one can adjust the length of the second semester to as few as 35 days by omitting parts of unit Q.)

Dividing the course into such units has a number of advantages. The core idea in each unit provides students with motivation and a sense of direction, and helps keep everyone focused. But the most important reason for this structure is that it makes clear to students that some ideas and principles in physics are more important than others, a theme emphasized throughout the course.

The non-standard order of presentation has evolved in response to our observations in early trials. **[1]** Conservation laws are presented first not only because they really are more fundamental than the particular theories of mechanics considered later but also because we have consistently observed that students understand them better and can use them more flexibly than they can Newton's laws. It makes sense to have students *start* by studying very powerful and broadly applicable laws that they can also understand: this builds their confidence while developing thinking skills needed for understanding newtonian mechanics. This also delays the need for calculus. **[2]** Special relativity, which fits naturally into the first semester's focus on mechanics and conservation laws, also ends that semester with something both contemporary and compelling (student evaluations consistently rate this section very highly). **[3]** We found in previous trials that ending the second semester with the intellectually demanding material in unit Q was not wise: ending the course with Unit T (which is less demanding) and thus more practical during the end-of-year rush.

Comments about the non-standard order

The suggested order also offers a variety of options for adapting the course to other calendars and paces. One can teach these units in three 10-week quarters of two units each: note that the shortest units (R and T) are naturally paired with longest units (E and Q respectively) when the units are divided this way. While the first four units essentially provide a core curriculum that is difficult to change substantially, omitting either Unit Q or Unit T (or both) can create a gentler pace without loss of continuity (since Unit C includes some basic thermal physics, a version of the course omitting unit T still spans much of what is in a standard introductory course). We have also designed unit Q so that several of its major sections can be omitted if necessary.

Options for adapting to a different calendar

Many of these volumes can also stand alone in an appropriate context. Units C and N are tightly interwoven, but with some care and in the appropriate context, these could be used separately. Unit R only requires a basic knowledge of mechanics. In addition to a typical background in mechanics, units E and Q require only a few very basic results from relativity, and Unit T requires only a very basic understanding of energy quantization. Other orders are also possible: while the first four units form a core curriculum that works best in the designed order, units Q and T might be exchanged, placed between volumes of the core sequence, or one or the other can be omitted.

Using the volumes alone or in different orders

Superficially, the course might seem to involve quite a bit *more* material than a standard introductory physics course, since substantial amounts of time are devoted to relativity and quantum physics. However, we have made substantial cuts in the material presented in the all sections of the course compared to a standard course. We made these cuts in two different ways.

The pace was reduced by cutting whole topics...

First, we have omitted entire topics, such as fluid mechanics, most of rotational mechanics, almost everything about sound, many electrical engineering topics, geometric optics, polarization, and so on. These cuts will no doubt be intolerable to some, but *something* has to go, and these topics did not fit as well as others into this particular course framework.

... and by streamlining the presentation of the rest

Our second approach was to simplify and streamline the presentation of topics we *do* discuss. A typical chapter in a standard textbook is crammed with a variety of interesting but tangential issues, applications, and other miscellaneous factons. The core idea of each *Six Ideas* unit provides an excellent filter for reducing the number density of factons: virtually everything that is not *essential* for developing that core idea has been eliminated. This greatly reduces the "conceptual noise" that students encounter, which helps them focus on learning the really important ideas.

Because of the conversational writing style adopted for the text, the total page count of the *Six Ideas* texts is actually similar to a standard text (about 1100 pages), but if you compare typical chapters discussing the same general material, you will find that the *density* of concepts in the *Six Ideas* text is much lower, leading to what I hope will be a more gentle perceived pace.

Choosing an appropriate pace

Even so, this text is *not* a "dumbed-down" version of a standard text. Instead of making the text dumber, I have tried very hard to challenge (and hopefully enable) students to become *smarter*. The design pace of this course (one chapter per day) is pretty challenging considering the sophistication of the material, and really represents a maximum pace for fairly well-prepared students at reasonably selective colleges and universities. However, I believe that the materials *can* be used at a much broader range of institutions and contexts at a lower pace (two chapters per three sessions, say, or one chapter per 75-minute class session). This means either cutting material or taking three semesters instead of two, but it can be done. The instructor's manual discusses how cuts might be made.

Part of the point of arranging the text in a "chapter-per-day" format is to bee clear about how the pace should be *limited*. Course designs that require covering *more* than one chapter per day should be strictly avoided: if there are too few days to cover the chapters at the design pace, than chapters will *have* to be cut.

4.   FEATURES OF THE TEXT

The texts are designed to serve as students' primary source of new information

Studies have suggested that lectures are neither the most efficient nor most effective way to present expository material. One of my most important goals was to develop a text that could essentially replace the lecture as the primary *source* of information, freeing up class time for activities that help students *practice* using those ideas. I also wanted to create a text that not only presents the topics but goads students to develop model-building and problem-solving skills, helps them organize ideas hierarchically, encourages them to think qualitatively as well as quantitatively, and supports active learning both inside and outside of class.

A list of some of the texts' important features

In its current form, the text has a variety of features designed to address these needs, (many of which have evolved in response to early trials):

1. **The writing style is expansive and conversational**, making the text more suitable to be the primary way students learn new information.
2. **Each chapter corresponds to one (50-minute) class session**, which helps guide instructors in maintaining an appropriate pace.
3. **Each chapter begins with a unit map and an overview** that helps students see how the chapter fits into the general flow of the unit.
4. **Each chapter ends with a summary** that presents the most important ideas and arguments in a hierarchical outline format.
5. **Each chapter has a glossary** that summarizes technical terms, helping students realize that certain words have special meanings in physics.

6. **The book uses "user-friendly" notation and terminology** to help students keep ideas clear and avoid misleading connotations.

7. **Exercises embedded in the text** (with provided answers) help students actively engage the material as they prepare for class (providing an active alternative to examples).

8. **Wide outside margins** provide students with space for taking notes.

9. **Frequent *Physics Skills* and *Math Skills* sections** explicitly explore and summarize generally-applicable thinking skills.

10. **Problem-solving frameworks** (influenced by work by Alan van Heuvelen) help students learn good problem-solving habits.

11. **Two-minute problems** provide a tested and successful way to actively involve students during class and get feedback on how they are doing.

12. **Homework problems** are generally more qualitative than standard problems, and are organized according to the general thinking skills required.

5. ACTIVE LEARNING IN AND OUT OF CLASS

The *Six Ideas* texts are designed to support active learning both inside and outside the classroom setting. A properly designed course using these texts can provide to students a rich set of active-learning experiences.

The *two-minute exercises* at the end of each chapter make it easy to devote at least part of each class session to active learning. These mostly conceptual questions do not generally require much (if any) calculation, but locating the correct answer does require careful thinking, a solid understanding of the material, and (often) an ability to apply concepts to realistic situations to answer correctly. Many explicitly test for typical student misconceptions, providing an opportunity to expose and correct these well-known stumbling blocks.

Active learning using two-minute exercises

I often begin a class session by asking students to work in groups of two or three to find answers for a list of roughly three two-minute problems from the chapter that was assigned reading for that class session. After students have worked on these problems for some time, I ask them to show me their answers for each question in turn. The students hold up the back of the book facing me and point to the letter that they think is the correct answer. This gives me instant feedback on how well the students are doing, and provides me with both grist for further discussion and a sense where the students need the most help. On the other hand, students cannot see each others' answers easily, making them less likely to fear embarrassment (and I work very hard to be supportive).

Once everyone gets the hang of the process, it is easy to adapt other activities to this format. When I do a demonstration, I often make it more active by posing questions about what will happen, and asking students to respond using the letters. This helps everyone think more deeply about what the demonstration really shows and gets the students more invested in the outcome (and more impressed when the demonstration shows something unexpected).

Active demonstrations

The in-text exercises and homework problems provide opportunities for active learning *outside* of class. The exercises challenge students to test their understanding of the material as they read it, helping them actively process the material and giving them instant feedback. They also provide a way to get students through derivations in a way that actively involves them in the process and yet "hides" the details so that the structure of the derivation is clearer. Finally, such exercises provide an active alternative to traditional examples: instead of simply displaying the example, the exercises encourage students to work through it.

The exercises support active reading

The homework problems at the end of each chapter are organized into four types. *Basic* problems are closest to the type of problems found in standard texts: they are primarily for practicing the application of a single formula or concept in a straightforward manner and/or are closely analogous to examples in the text. *Synthetic* problems generally involve more realistic situations, require

The types of homework problems

students to apply *several* concepts and/or formulas at once, involve creating or applying models, and/ or require more sophisticated reasoning. ***Rich-Context*** problems are synthetic problems generally cast in a narrative framework where either too much or too little information is given and/or a non-numerical question is posed (that nonetheless requires numerical work to answer). ***Advanced*** problems usually explore subtle theoretical issues or mathematical derivations beyond the level of the class: they are designed to challenge the very best students and/or remind instructors about how to handle subtle issues.

Collaborative recitation sessions

The rich-context problems are especially designed for collaborative work. Work by Heller and Hollenbaugh has shown that students solving standard problems rarely collaborate even when "working together", but that a well-written rich-context problem by its very open-ended nature calls forth a discussion of physical concepts, requiring students to work together to create useful models. I typically assign one such problem per week that students can work in a "recitation" section where can they work the problem in collaborative groups (instead of being lectured to by a TA).

The goal of the course is that the majority of students should ultimately be able to solve problems at the level of the *synthetic* problems in the book. Many of the rich-context problems are too difficult for individual students to solve easily, and the advanced problems are meant to be beyond the level of the class.

The way that a course is structured can determine its success

In early trials of *Six Ideas*, we learned that whether a course succeeds or fails depends very much the details of how the course is *structured*. This text is designed to more easily support a productive course structure, but careful work on the course design is still essential. For example, a "traditional" approach to assigning and grading homework can lead students to be frustrated (rather than challenged) by the richer-than-average homework problems in this text. Course structures can also either encourage or discourage students from getting the most out of class by preparing ahead of time. Exams can support or undermine the goals of the course. The instructor's manual explores these issues in much more depth and offers detailed guidance (based on our experience) about how design a course that gets the most out of what these books have to offer.

6. USE OF COMPUTERS

Using computers

The course, unlike some recent reform efforts, is *not* founded to a significant degree on the use of computers. Even so, a *few* computer programs are deployed in a few crucial places to support a particular line of argument in the text, and unit *T* in particular comes across significantly better when supported by a relatively small amount of computer work.

The most current versions of the computer programs supporting this course can be downloaded from my web-site or we will send them to you on request (see the contact information in section 8 below).

7. NOTES ABOUT UNIT *C*

This unit is the foundation on which the rest of the *Six Ideas* course is constructed. The current structure of the course assumes that unit *C* will be taught first and will be immediately followed by unit *N*.

Why study conservation laws first?

Why study conservation laws *before* newtonian mechanics? The most important reasons have already been mentioned in section 3 above: (1) conservation laws are easy to understand and use, which helps build student confidence at the beginning of the course, (2) using conservation laws does not require calculus, thus delaying the introduction of calculus for several weeks, (3) studying conservation of momentum and angular momentum *does* require vectors, allowing vector concepts to be developed for several weeks in simple contexts before getting into vector calculus, and (4) conservation laws really are more fundamental than even newtonian mechanics, so it is good to start the course with physical concepts that are crucially important and will be useful throughout the course.

We did not intuit these benefits at first: the earliest versions of *Six Ideas* presented mechanics in the standard order. Rather, this inversion emerged naturally as a consequence of observations of student learning and some reflection about the logic of the course. (Interestingly, a number of people interested in reforming the course have independently come to the same conclusion.)

Inverting the order *can* be a challenge (in both the positive and negative sense) for the student who has already had some mechanics. Studying mechanics "backwards" this way can actually be very good for such a student, because it makes them really *think* about the subject again and the new perspective gives them greater flexibility. The instructor can play a key role in helping such students appreciate this by emphasizing the power and breadth of the conservation-law approach and its importance in contemporary physics, as well as celebrating with them the strength that one gains by being able to look at a situation from multiple perspectives.

This approach can be very good for knowledgeable students

The momentum-transfer model of interactions (which is introduced in chapter C4) is really what makes it possible to talk about conservation laws without starting with Newton's laws. This model will be a new and challenging idea to almost everyone. Instructors should work carefully with students, giving them enough practice with the model to *ensure* that they understand it and can talk about it correctly. The payoff is that when students really grasp this model, it by its very nature helps them avoid many of the standard misconceptions that tend to plague students in introductory courses. It takes a little work to get use to the new language, but I think that you will find it worth the effort.

Some unusual features of the approach in this unit

Instructors should also note that I have deliberately avoided both the term and concept of *work* (except in the thermal physics sense). A number of physicists have recently pointed out the contradictory ways that we define and use this term. I have tried to be very careful to define and use *energy transfer* to mean strictly what might be called "center-of-mass work": this is the form of work that appears in the standard work-energy theorem and which has the most fundamental meaning. Students that are going on in physics need to understand that this idea is traditionally called *work*, but that I am renaming and more sharply defining it to avoid confusion with the thermodynamic concept and the idea of "a force acting through a distance," both of which are very different concepts.

Many of the chapters of this unit begin with a "puzzle" about the behavior of interacting objects. The pedagogical effectiveness of these puzzles can be greatly enhanced if they are demonstrated and discussed in class *before* students do the assigned reading. This helps students connect the puzzle with the real world and gives them a chance to "discover" the issue actively before they passively read about it. The instructor's guide offers suggestions about how one can do these demonstrations in a way that actively engages the students.

Taking advantage of the "puzzles" that begin many chapters

Please also see the instructor's guide for more detailed information about this unit and suggestions about how to teach it.

Almost every chapter in this unit is essential preparation or background for other parts of the course (indeed, most chapters have been deliberately pared down so that only what is essential remains). If one is desperate for something to cut, one might omit chapter C12 (which looks at some interesting and contemporary applications of conservation of energy as well as studying elastic and inelastic collisions). The rest of the unit is pretty much an indivisible whole.

There is not much one can cut in this unit

8. HOW TO COMMUNICATE SUGGESTIONS

As I said at the beginning of this preface, this is a preliminary edition that represents a snapshot of work in progress. I would greatly appreciate your helping me make this a better text by telling me about errors and offering suggestions for improvement (words of support will be gratefully accepted too!). I will also try to answer your questions about the text, particularly if you are an instructor trying to use the text in a course.

Please help me make this a better text!

The *Six Ideas* bulletin board

McGraw-Hill has set up an electronic bulletin board devoted to this text. This is the primary place where you can converse with me and/or other users of the text. Please post your comments, suggestions, criticisms, encouragement, error reports, and questions on this bulletin board. I will check it often and respond to whatever is posted there. The URL for this bulletin board is:

`http://mhhe.com/physsci/physical/moore`

The *Six Ideas* web site

Before you send in an error or ask a question, please check the error postings and/or FAQ list on my *Six Ideas* web site. The URL for this site is:

`http://pages.pomona.edu/~tmoore/sixideas.html`

Visiting this site will also allow you to read the latest information about the *Six Ideas* course and texts on this site, download the latest versions of the supporting computer software, and visit related sites. You can also reach me via e-mail at `tmoore@pomona.edu`.

How to get other volumes or ancillary materials

Please refer questions about obtaining copies of the texts and/or ancillary materials to your WCB/McGraw-Hill representative or as directed on the *Six Ideas* web-site.

9. APPRECIATION

Thanks!

A project of this magnitude cannot be accomplished alone. I would first like to thank the others who served on the IUPP development team for this project: Edwin Taylor, Dan Schroeder, Randy Knight, John Mallinckrodt, Alma Zook, Bob Hilborn and Don Holcomb. I'd like to thank John Rigden and other members of the IUPP steering committee for their support of the project in its early stages, which came ultimately from an NSF grant and the special efforts of Duncan McBride. Early users of the text, including Bill Titus, Richard Noer, Woods Halley, Paul Ellis, Doreen Weinberger, Nalini Easwar, Brian Watson, Jon Eggert, Catherine Mader, Paul De Young, Alma Zook, and Dave Dobson have offered invaluable feedback and encouragement. I'd also like to thank Alan Macdonald, Roseanne Di Stefano, Ruth Chabay, Bruce Sherwood, and Tony French for ideas, support, and useful suggestions. Thanks also to Robs Muir for helping with several of the indexes. My editors Jim Smith, Denise Schanck, Jack Shira, Karen Allanson, Lloyd Black, and JP Lenney, as well as Donata Dettbarn, Larry Goldberg, Sheila Frank, Jonathan Alpert, Zanae Roderigo, Mary Haas, Janice Hancock, Lisa Gottschalk, and Debra Drish, have all worked very hard to make this text happen, and I deeply appreciate their efforts. I'd like to thank reviewers Edwin Carlson, David Dobson, Irene Nunes, Miles Dressler, O. Romulo Ochoa, Qichang Su, Brian Watson, and Laurent Hodges for taking the time to do a careful reading of various units and offering valuable suggestions. Thanks to Connie Wilson, Hilda Dinolfo, and special student assistants Michael Wanke, Paul Feng, and Mara Harrell, Jennifer Lauer, Tony Galuhn, Eric Pan, and all the Physics 51 mentors for supporting (in various ways) the development and teaching of this course at Pomona College. Thanks also to my Physics 51 students, and especially Win Yin, Peter Leth, Eddie Abarca, Boyer Naito, Arvin Tseng, Rebecca Washenfelder, Mary Donovan, Austin Ferris, Laura Siegfried, and Miriam Krause, who have offered many suggestions and have together found many hundreds of typos and other errors. Finally, very special thanks to my wife Joyce and to my daughters Brittany and Allison, who contributed with their support and patience during this long and demanding project. Heartfelt thanks to all!

Thomas A. Moore
Claremont, California
November 24, 1997

INTRODUCTION

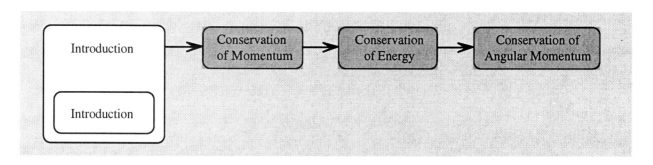

C1.1 OVERVIEW

Welcome to *Six Ideas that Shaped Physics*! This introductory chapter presents overviews of physics as a discipline, the *Six Ideas* text and course, and this particular unit of the text. The purpose of these overviews is to provide you with some background information and a sense of where we are going in the course.

This chapter also discusses various unusual features of the text and the importance of active reading. Be sure to read section C1.7 very carefully: this section describes things that you *must* understand to use this text effectively.

At the top of this page, you will find a unit map: such a map appears at the beginning of each chapter. The map helps you see at a glance how the chapter fits into the sequence of ideas presented in the unit. The boxes on the top row represent the major subunits in the unit: the current subunit is shown in white. The boxes in the second row show the chapters in the current subunit (note that there is only one chapter in this particular subunit), and again, the current chapter is shown in white. This map is a collapsed version of the entire unit map shown in Figure C1.3 in section C1.6.

The following is an overview of the sections of this chapter. A list like this will appear at the beginning of each chapter to give you a sense of exactly what will be discussed in that chapter and how that discussion will progress.

C1.2 *SCIENTISTS ARE MODEL-MAKERS* discusses how the basic task of science is to create *models* of natural phenomena that present simplified stories or pictures of the world that are small enough to understand.

C1.3 *THE NATURE OF SCIENCE* describes science as a *process* that efficiently produces powerful models, and distinguishes science from other disciplines that create stories about the world.

C1.4 *THE CURRENT STRUCTURE OF PHYSICS* gives an overview of the historical development of physics and its current conceptual structure.

C1.5 *SIX IDEAS THAT SHAPED PHYSICS* provides an overview of the structure of this six-unit introductory course.

C1.6 *AN OVERVIEW OF UNIT C* presents an overview of the structure of Unit C and how it fits into the course as a whole.

C1.7 *USING THIS TEXT* discusses the unusual features of this text, why these features exist, and how you can take advantage of these features to learn from the text most effectively.

C1.2 SCIENTISTS ARE MODEL-MAKERS

To explain is human

It is part of human nature that we strive to discern order lying behind what we experience and love to tell each other stories that *explain* the order that we find in terms of concepts and ideas common to our experience. For example, ancient observers noted that the stars maintained fixed positions relative to each other, but the whole array of stars seemed to rotate around the earth once a day. Early western storytellers offered the explanation that the stars were lamps fixed to the inside of a solid bowl that rotated daily around the earth (which is called the *raqia'* or "firmament" in the creation story in the Bible). This story explained the ordered behavior of the stars in terms of objects (lamps and bowls) that were a part of the listeners' common experience.

Scientists continue in this long tradition by constructing **conceptual models** of the natural world. These models bear roughly the same relation to real physical phenomena as a model airplane does to a real airplane. An artfully imagined physical model captures the *essence* of a phenomenon while remaining small and simple enough to hold in your mind (the way a model plane can be held in your hand). Model-building is an essential aspect of science because reality is much too complicated for us to understand completely: models compress complex and detailed experiences into simpler bite-sized chunks that can be digested by finite minds.

Because models are necessarily simpler than reality, they are also necessarily only *partly* true or accurate. The ancient model of the universe, for example, successfully explains why the stars shine even when it is dark and why they seem to wheel together around the earth. But if we examine the model more closely, it breaks down: the spectrum of stars is different from the spectrum of oil lamps, accurate measurements in this century show that certain stars move discernibly relative to other stars, and so on. The ancient model cannot explain such observations, and so has long since been replaced by a more sophisticated model where stars are objects like our sun that are enormously far away and follow huge individual orbits around the center of our galaxy.

The modern model is better than the ancient model in that it is consistent with more observations, but like the ancient model, it is *still* a simplification, with its own rough edges and puzzles. The modern model also has the disadvantage of being much more complicated and distant from daily experience, so that a person needs years of training to understand it completely.

The task of science is to create good models

The task of science, no matter what you may have been told, is not to uncover "the Truth": the complete truth about our infinite universe is too large for a human mind to hold. The basic task of science is rather to ask questions of nature, compile evidence, and then *invent models* that are as *simple* as possible, and yet logically *consistent* with everything known. Inventing a model is less an act of discovery than it is an act of *imagination* akin to creating a work of art: a good model is a vivid *story* about reality that creatively ignores complexity.

Model-making in science happens continually at all levels. Grand models that are able to embrace a huge range of phenomena are usually called **theories** and are for science what great novels are for literature: rare and extraordinary works of imagination that we strive to understand and cherish. But in order to apply these great models to a real-life situation, we must construct a smaller model of the situation itself, simplifying and making approximations so that we can understand it well enough to connect it correctly to a grand model that explains it. Scientists do this kind of model-making all the time.

This text is about models and model-building

This text is thus primarily about *models* of physical phenomena. My purpose is only *partly* to help you understand and appreciate the grand models (theories) of physics: my more important (and difficult) goal is to teach you how to build smaller models *yourself* (an essential skill for any scientist). We will return again and again to the theme of understanding and building models as the text progresses.

C1.3 THE NATURE OF SCIENCE

If science is based on models, which in turn are simply imaginative stories that we construct about the universe, then what (if anything) makes science different from mythology, religious creeds, philosophy, or literature? To make sense of the difference, you must understand that **science** is emphatically *not* a set of facts or even models concerning the physical world, but rather a *process* for generating and evaluating such models, a process that has proved to be a prolific producer of rich and powerfully predictive conceptual models.

Physics itself is a good case in point. People had been constructing models about the physical world for thousands of years without much discernible agreement or progress in terms of the models' predictive abilities. In the middle of the 17th century, something happened that converted physics from an obscure branch of philosophy into a vigorous producer of effective and useful models. Less than three hundred years later, people were standing on the moon. What happened?

I believe that at least four distinct elements are necessary to make a discipline a science. (1) There must exist a sufficiently large *community* of scholars, who agree to accept (2) *logical consistency* as the basic principle for constructing models and (3) *reproducible experiments* as the standard for testing models, and, finally, (4) a *basic theory* rich and broad enough to embrace a substantial part of the discipline and generate a variety of questions for further exploration.

The ancient Greeks began the process by exploring and refining the thinking skill that we call logical reasoning and by inspiring a core community of intellectuals that appreciated the power of this mode of thought in helping people refine and share knowledge. In fact, that community found the power of logical reasoning so liberating that it imagined for nearly two thousand years that pure reason should be *sufficient* for completely understanding the world. This held up the development of science because the community did not believe that experimental verification was necessary.

The specific idea that formal experiments might be used to test models did not gain full expression until the 13th century, and even then several more centuries passed before western thinkers commonly began to accept this as being a *necessary* adjunct to pure logic. But eventually, people began to realize that our human desire to order our experience is so strong that one of the most difficult tasks facing any thinker is to distinguish the order that really exists in the world from that which only *seems* to exist. Reproducible experiments make what would otherwise be individual experience available to a wider community. Models consistent with such experiments are thus anchored to reality in a way that makes them far less subject to the variability of individual experience. Galileo Galilei (1564-1642) was an energetic proponent of the experimental approach. He used the newly-invented telescope to discern features of heavenly bodies that were completely unimagined in any models of the time. To the most thoughtful of his contemporaries, this vividly underlined his point about the inadequacy of pure reason and the importance of experiment and observation.

If only the first three elements are present, the prescientific community may agree on certain experimental data, but is fragmented into schools, each exploring its own model. Some progress is made, but at a much slower rate than when the whole community is able to work together. This was the situation of physics in the decades following Galileo.

In 1686, Isaac Newton published the first comprehensive model of physics broad enough to embrace both terrestrial and celestial phenomena. His ideas were such an amazing step forward that they captured the imagination of the whole physics community, and as this happened, physics in a real sense became a science. The focus of the physics community shifted from arguing about smaller partial models to working *together* to refine, test, and extend Newton's extraordinarily rich model, in the confidence that ultimately it would be shown to be completely true.

Science as an *process* for producing powerful models

Four features of any scientific discipline

How physics became a science

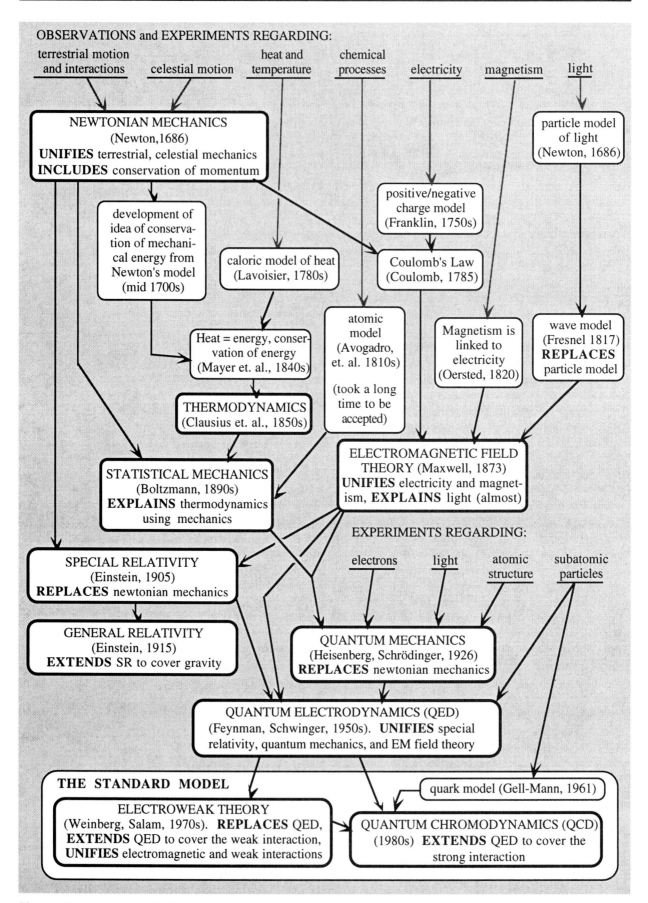

Figure C1.1: A schematic history of physics.

The irony is that the community that believed wholeheartedly in Newton's model and strove to extend it to cover everything eventually amassed the evidence needed to prove it *false*! Only a community that is *devoted* to exploring a powerful model can collect the kind of detailed and careful evidence necessary to prove it false and thus move to better models. This paradox is the engine that drives science, making it a prolific producer of powerful and effective models.

The paradox at the heart of science

C1.4 THE CURRENT STRUCTURE OF PHYSICS

Figure C1.1 summarizes the history of physics after Newton. Each box describes the development of an important physical model or idea: its vertical position roughly represents its place in time (lower being later). The boxes with dark outlines and titles in capital letters represent the major comprehensive theories of physics. Arrows are used to represent some flow of ideas between the theories. Gray arrows in certain subject areas represent prescientific periods when people made and recorded quantitative observations but had no comprehensive theory to explain those observations.

A one-page history of physics as a science

Near its bottom, the diagram refers to **weak** and **strong interactions**: these represent two ways that subatomic particles can interact (physicists discovered these interactions in the 1930's). Unlike the gravitational, electric, and magnetic interactions, these interactions are insignificant between particles separated by more than about the width of a proton, and so are impossible to observe between objects of normal size. We will see in unit Q that the existence of these modes of interaction have important implications for the structure and behavior of large objects even if the interactions cannot be observed directly.

Such a schematic diagram is necessarily simplified, and thus does little justice to the wonderful complexity of the history of physics. As the dates in the boxes indicate, development of many of the most important ideas in physics took many years and involved many collaborators. Even in the cases where a single person presented a significantly new model at a definite time, one finds that the model stands on the shoulders of decades of work done by scores of people.

The most important thing to note about this diagram is that the basic movement of physics is toward increasing *unification*. Newtonian mechanics unifies terrestrial and celestial physics. Statistical mechanics absorbs thermal physics into the newtonian model. Maxwell's electromagnetic field theory presents an explanation of electric, magnetic, and optical phenomena in terms of a single, dynamic *electromagnetic field*. Quantum electrodynamics unifies special relativity, quantum mechanics, and electromagnetic field theory. Electroweak theory shows that electricity, magnetism, and the weak nuclear interaction are all manifestations of a single *electroweak* interaction. As history progresses, the models created by physicists have become more powerful and all-embracing. At present, the two **relativistic quantum field theories** (the electroweak theory and quantum chromodynamics, which together comprise what is called the **standard model** of particle physics) and the theory of **general relativity** (which is our current best theory of gravitation) cover essentially all known phenomena.

The basic movement of physics toward unification

The success of this program of unification has led physicists in this century to hope that all physical phenomena might eventually be embraced by a single model, a "theory of everything." Physicists are currently searching for a **grand unified theory** (GUT) that will present a unified explanation of the electroweak and strong interactions, and then ultimately for some kind of theory that will unify the GUT with gravity. (So far, the search has been without success.)

Figure C1.2 illustrates the current conceptual structure of physics, with the most fundamental ideas and models appearing at the top, and models that represent simplified approximations to the fundamental models appearing below. (The two quantum field theories and general relativity appear to be valid and accurate in all circumstances so far examined, though there are some open questions that cast doubt in some physicists' minds about their ultimate validity.)

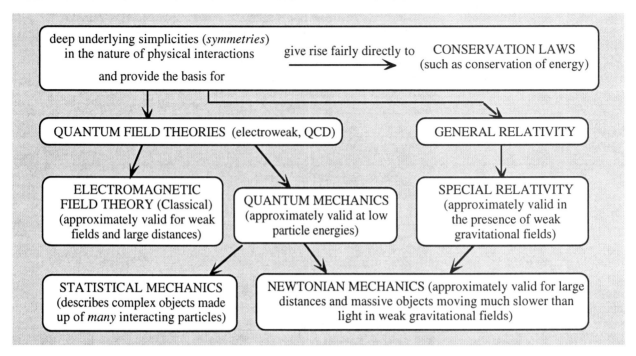

Figure C1.2: The current conceptual structure of physics.

The importance of symmetries in current physics

One of the most interesting things about Figure C1.2 is its top line. Since roughly the 1960s, physicists have become increasingly aware of the importance of **symmetries** in physics, understanding that even an almost obvious assumption like "the laws of physics should be the same now as at any time in the past or future" can have important and interesting consequences. In the early part of this century, the mathematician Emmy Noether showed that, within a very broad range of possible physical theories, each such symmetry implies a **conservation law.** For example, the time-independence of the laws of physics (again, within a wide range of possibilities for what those specific laws might be) implies that *energy* must be conserved (that is, the total energy in an isolated system has a value that does not change as time passes). Thus we now understand that conservation laws stand in a certain sense *above* the particular models of physics: conservation of energy is a feature of newtonian mechanics, electromagnetic field theory, general relativity, QCD, and so on because *all* these theories assume that the basic laws of physics are time-independent (and also happen to have the right form to satisfy the requirements of Noether's theorem).

Moreover, our current fundamental theories (electroweak, QCD, and general relativity) are similar in that they propose *new*, non-obvious symmetries and then unfold their consequences. Thus a thoughtful exploration of the consequences of symmetries lies at the very foundation of contemporary physics.

C1.5 SIX IDEAS THAT SHAPED PHYSICS

Why not start studying our best available models?

It might seem at first glance to be logical to start a course like this with the most fundamental models (general relativity and the quantum field theories) and then work downward to the approximations and applications that appear below them in Figure C1.2. However, this is impractical. The historical movement of physics toward unification means that as our models become more powerful and all-embracing, they also become more abstract and mathematical. General relativity and relativistic quantum field theory are indeed *founded* on very simple symmetry ideas, and are breathtaking in their ability to embrace so many different kinds of phenomena using these simple ideas. But actually *using* these models involves such difficult mathematics that physicists rarely learn these theories before graduate school. Even setting aside the mathematics, these theories are often difficult to apply to situations of interest in everyday life. The earlier (approximate) models are in practice much easier both to understand and to use.

Moreover, the physicists who invented our current best theories were fully conversant with earlier models, and so used many of the concepts and much of the language found in those models. Therefore, whether one hopes to study advanced physics or apply physics to the everyday world, it is essential to begin with the historical models that have brought us to where we stand today.

This is the first of a series of text modules that together comprise an introductory physics course called *Six Ideas That Shaped Physics*. As the name suggests, the course is divided into six units, each of which explores a *single* crucial idea that has shaped the progress of physics in the past three hundred years. These ideas have been chosen to give you a solid introduction to each of the five basic historical models at the bottom of Figure C1.2. Studying these models will give you both the basic tools to apply physical reasoning to your own experience and a foundation for future study in physics. Even so, this course is not meant to be a superficial *survey* of physics: rather, it is meant to guide you in a deep and focused exploration of the following *specific* ideas.

Conservation Laws Constrain Interactions (Unit C). The deepest symmetries in the laws of physics imply that when objects interact, they do so in such a manner as to conserve the values of certain quantities, which we call *energy, momentum,* and *angular momentum.* Since these conservation laws provide a framework within which all current theories and models of physics reside, it is appropriate to begin the course with a discussion of these laws. (We will, however discuss them in the specific context of the newtonian model to begin with.)

The Laws of Motion are Universal (Unit N). In this unit, we will learn how to use the theory of *newtonian mechanics* to predict how an object moves in response to its interaction with other objects. Our ultimate goal is to understand how Newton's mechanics explains not only the behavior of terrestrial bodies but also the motion of the planets and thus appreciate the intellectual triumph that gave birth to physics as a science.

Physics is Frame-Independent (Unit R). In 1905, Albert Einstein published a paper outlining the *special theory of relativity* in which he argued that *the laws of physics should be the same for all observers*, even observers uniformly moving relative to each other. The purpose of this unit is to explore the strange and fascinating consequences of this simple idea.

Electromagnetic Fields are Dynamic (Unit E). Electrically charged objects interact by exerting electric and/or magnetic forces on each other. The theory of special relativity implies that we need to describe these interactions in terms of electric and magnetic *fields*. The purpose of this unit is to discuss this field model and explore the consequences of *Maxwell's equations* (which specify how the fields change in time), consequences that include the existence of traveling electromagnetic waves (which we experience as *light*).

Matter Behaves Like Waves (Unit Q). Experiments in the early 20th century showed that light does indeed behave like a wave (consistent with Maxwell's model) in some cases but like a stream of particles in others. This puzzle led to the development of *quantum mechanics,* which replaced newtonian mechanics and reconciled the wave and particle-like character of all forms of matter and energy. The purpose of this unit is to discuss how the wavelike nature of matter implies that the energy of a system will be quantized, and what energy quantization means for the structure and behavior of atomic nuclei.

Some Energy Flows are Irreversible (Unit T). Thermal energy flows from a hot object to a cold object, but never the other way (even though conservation of energy would allow this). Why? It turns out that there is a fairly simple answer to this question. Our purpose in this unit is to find that answer, along the way developing a deeper understanding of the concepts of *temperature, heat,* and *entropy* using the methods and concepts of statistical mechanics.

**An overview of each of the
six units in this course**

C1.6 AN OVERVIEW OF UNIT *C*

Three basic conservation laws appear in all current theories of physics

We begin our study of physics by focusing on the conservation laws that lie at the foundation of *all* current physical theories. When an isolated set (or **system**) of objects interact with each other, we find that (no matter how the objects interact) certain quantities (which we call the system's total **energy, momentum**, and **angular momentum**) are *conserved* (that is, have values that do not change with time). Conservation laws provide very general tools for analyzing the behavior of a system of interacting objects without having to delve into the detailed physical laws describing those interactions.

Noether's theorem asserts that these three conservation laws are manifestations of three basic symmetry principles: that the laws of physics are independent of (1) *time*, (2) *place*, and (3) *orientation* respectively (meaning, for example, that an experiment done on an isolated system of objects will yield the same result whether one does it today or tomorrow, here or on the moon, or facing west or east). These principles (as well as the other assumptions going into Noether's theorem) are so basic that many physicists believe that even physical theories yet unimagined will almost certainly be consistent with them. Since proving Noether's theorem (alas!) requires mathematics beyond our means, we will in this course take the conservation laws themselves as our starting point.

We will see (particularly in unit *R*) that while the same conservation laws appear in all current theories of physics, the exact *definitions* of energy, momentum, and angular momentum are somewhat different in different theories. In this unit, we will start with the definitions of these quantities used in newtonian mechanics. We will see that with these definitions, the rest of the laws of newtonian mechanics emerge fairly naturally from the conservation laws.

The structure of unit *C*

The remainder of this unit is divided into three subunits. The first discusses the law of conservation of momentum and the most fundamental principles about interactions between objects. The second subunit looks at conservation of energy, one of the richest and most far-reaching ideas of physics. The third explores the laws of rotational motion and the conservation of angular momentum.

Figure C1.3 is a map of the unit. The four boxes with bold outlines in the top row correspond to the four subunits of this unit. The boxes strung in columns below each subunit box show the topics covered by each *chapter* in the subunit (note that the first and last subunits are only one chapter long!).

Figure C1.3: A schematic map describing the structure of unit *C*.

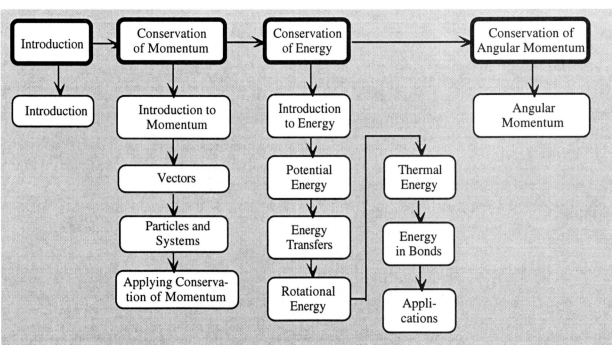

C1.7   HOW TO USE THIS TEXT EFFECTIVELY

This text is different than any science text you are likely to have encountered so far (that is, virtually all high-school science texts and most introductory college texts). As such, it requires different study strategies to use effectively. How and why is it different?

The accepted model of physics education in the 1960s was that physics was a collection of facts that a teacher transmits to a student. But research done during the past two decades on how students learn physics has made it clear that this model is inadequate. We now understand that the physics is less a collection of facts than it is a set of thinking skills, and that you cannot learn such skills by listening to lectures any more than you can learn to play the piano by going to concerts. To master the skills of physics, you have to *practice* using them.

Because of this, studies of physics learning have repeatedly shown that a typical lecture class is generally ineffective at helping most people learn physics (quite independent of the lecturer!). This has greatly and unnecessarily contributed to the reputation of physics as being impossible: while physics is not *easy*, studying it in ineffective ways doesn't help!

How should physics be studied, then? Research on physics learning consistently shows that activities in class and out of class that have students *practice* applying their knowledge to realistic situations do much better at helping them develop and internalize physics thinking disciplines and model-building skills. Therefore, this text has a variety of features that (1) make it easier to use as the *primary place* where you learn new material (so that you can spend class time doing things that are more effective and interesting than sitting through a lecture), and (2) provide tools for active learning both inside and outside of class.

First and foremost, this text is designed to be read *actively*. While I have deliberately worked toward a clear but more expansive and conversational writing style than is typical for a text (so that this text is more suitable as the primary place where you learn new material), passively reading a text is no better than passively listening to a lecture. **Active reading** is a crucial study skill for effectively learning from this text (and higher-level physics texts and most technical literature as well). Active reading primarily means really *wrestling* with ideas as one reads. An active reader stops frequently to ask questions like: *Does this make sense? Is this consistent with my experience? Am I following the logic here? Do I see how I might use this idea in realistic situations?*

This text provides two important tools to make it easier for you to do this: *wide outside margins* and *in-text exercises*. If you have a question about a passage, you can write it immediately in the margin, and when you find the answer (either by thinking about it or asking someone), you can write *that* in the margin so that you don't forget. You can also use the margin to highlight something important or record an insight. Doing these things helps keep your mind actively engaged as you read, and your marginal comments are also generally very helpful as you review. The *in-text exercises* help goad you to develop the crucial active-reading skill of habitually filling in the gaps in mathematical or logical arguments whenever such gaps appear, and also give you an excuse to practice using the ideas you are reading about. Answers to the exercises appear at the end of each chapter, so you can get immediate feedback on your efforts, feedback that might highlight issues you should raise in class. Doing at least some of the exercises as you read is probably the *single most important thing you can do* to become an effective active reader of this text.

Active reading takes time and effort. You might be able to run your eyes over a typical chapter in this text in 45 minutes: active reading might take twice as long. But if you read a chapter actively *once* and get your questions answered (and so firmly seat the ideas in your mind), you will not have to search the chapter so often when doing homework or reread it so carefully when you review for a test. You will ultimately save time *and* do better in the class (trust me!).

This text is different

Like the piano, you learn physics by *practicing* it

The features of this text

Becoming an active reader

Wide outside margins and in-text exercises help make this easier

Active reading is worth the effort (trust me!)

(I personally find active reading tiring, and I often "blow a fuse" after about 20 minutes. If you find this to be true for you too, don't feel badly about taking short breaks so that you can return to the text refreshed and ready to learn.)

Text features for helping you with technical terms

The text provides other helpful features as well. One of the most difficult things about learning physics is learning its technical language (which mostly consists of English words that do *not* have their common English meaning!). I always flag such technical terms (using bold sans-serif type like **this**) when they first appear and immediately offer a definition in the text. The technical terms introduced in a chapter are also collected in a *glossary* at the end of that chapter.

Text features that help you understand how the text is organized

Students often find that standard texts offer insufficient guidance about the flow of the text's argument and which concepts are more important than others. Each chapter of this text begins with a *unit map* to help you see at a glance where the chapter fits into the unit. The *overview* that follows describes the purpose of the chapter in that context, and then summarizes the contents of each of the chapter's sections to give you an overview of how this purpose is worked out. The chapter's most crucial ideas are then reviewed in the *summary* following the chapter text. If a concept or formula is really important, it will be found here! This summary is presented in an outline format, so that you can see more clearly the skeleton of the chapter's argument and the hierarchical relationships between the ideas presented. These three features are my way of following the old advice that I should tell you what I am going to say (in the overview), say it (in the chapter text), and then tell you what I said (in the summary).

The various types of problems appearing in the text

The problems appearing at the end of each chapter (following the summary and glossary) provide important opportunities for practice both in and out of class. These problems are organized into categories that reflect somewhat different purposes. *Two-minute problems* are short, concept-oriented, multiple-choice problems that are primarily meant to be used *in* class as a way of practicing the ideas and/or exposing pernicious conceptual problems for further discussion. Your instructor will discuss with you how these problems will be used in your course. The other types are primarily meant for use as homework outside of class. *Basic* problems offer straightforward practice in applying a single formula or concept discussed in the chapter. *Synthetic* problems are more realistic problems whose solutions typically require the synthesis of several ideas (perhaps even some from different chapters) and provide crucial practice in the process of constructing models. *Rich-Context* problems are more challenging synthetic-type problems primarily for use in group problem-solving sessions. These problems are usually stated as narratives, and often (as synthetic problems occasionally) provide too much information (requiring you to decide what is relevant) and/or too little (requiring you to make estimates or approximations). Since real life usually presents physics applications this way, doing such problems is essential practice for learning how to use your physics knowledge in real life. *Advanced* problems ask for more than I would expect from a typical student: they are meant to provide special challenges (and explore subtle issues) for the benefit of extraordinarily well-prepared students. Typically you will spend the bulk of your homework time doing synthetic and rich-context problems. Learning to solve such problems effectively should be your major goal in the course.

It is very important to read the text before class

I want to emphasize in closing that it is *essential* in this course that you read the assigned chapter *before* coming to class (this is likely to be *much* more important than in science courses you may have taken before)! The design of this course *assumes* that you will spend class time in activities where you practice using the ideas in the assigned reading. This only works if people are prepared!

Be sure to get your questions answered

Class time provides a wonderful opportunity to get answers to questions you have about the material. Getting your questions answered (one way or another) is one of the most important things you can do after reading the text, so preparing these questions ahead of time can really pay off handsomely.

In summary, to use this text *most* effectively you should (1) read it *actively* (using the margins and doing at least some exercises), (2) understand and take advantage of its other features of the text, and (3) come to class fully prepared to practice the ideas and get your questions answered.

SUMMARY

I.   SCIENTISTS ARE MODEL-MAKERS
     A.   Human beings have always liked to tell stories about the order found in nature: scientists continue this long tradition by building *models*
     B.   This text is primarily about models
          1.   about the power (and limitations) of the great models of physics
          2.   about small-scale model making (necessary skill for all scientists)

II. THE NATURE OF SCIENCE
     A.   Science is a process for rapidly developing powerful conceptual models
     B.   Four elements seem necessary to make a discipline a science
          1.   A sufficiently large community that believe the following:
          2.   Logical consistency is the standard for constructing all models
          3.   Reproducible experiments are the standard for testing all models
          4.   We accept an overarching theory that embraces the discipline.
     C.   The historical path toward making physics a science
          1.   Greek philosophy created a community devoted to logical reasoning
          2.   Early Renaissance thinkers championed the value of experiment
          3.   Newtonian mechanics provided the overarching model

III. THE HISTORICAL DEVELOPMENT AND STRUCTURE OF PHYSICS
     A.   Physics has historically moved toward unification (see Figure C1.1):
          1.   Newer models typically embrace more and more
          2.   This has lead to the current quest for the "theory of everything"
     B.   The current conceptual structure of physics (see Figure C1.2)
          1.   General relativity and the "standard model" are our best models now
          2.   Historical models are approximations true in various contexts
     C.   *Symmetry* is very important in contemporary physics
          1.   Conservation laws reflect very basic symmetries
          2.   Symmetry principles can also be used to generate *new* models

IV. SIX IDEAS THAT SHAPED PHYSICS
     A.   Historical approximate models serve two important purposes
          1.   They provide crucial background for understanding current models
          2.   They are often easier to understand and use than current models
     B.   Course has six units, each focused on a single crucial historical idea
          1.   Unit *C*: *Conservation Laws Constrain Interactions*
          2.   Unit *N*: *The Laws of Motion are Universal*
          3.   Unit *R*: *Physics is Frame-Independent*
          4.   Unit *E*: *Electromagnetic Fields are Dynamic*
          5.   Unit *Q*: *Matter Behaves Like Waves*
          6.   Unit *T*: *Some Processes are Irreversible*

V.   STRUCTURE OF UNIT *C* (see Figure C1.3)
     A.   Conservation of energy, momentum, and angular momentum
          1.   These laws apply in all of the current theories of physics
          2.   These laws therefore provide a good place to begin!
     B.   We will explore each of these conservation laws in turn in this unit

VI. READING THE TEXT
     A.   A typical course structure based purely on lectures is not effective
     B.   The various features of the *Six Ideas* texts are designed to:
          1.   enable the text to serve as a primary source of information
          2.   provide tools for active learning in and outside of class
     C.   *Active reading* is necessary to use this text effectively:
          1.   Write comments and questions in the margin as you read
          2.   Do exercises provided in the text
          3.   Come to class prepared to learn and ask questions

GLOSSARY

conceptual model: a simplified mental image of a natural phenomenon or process that helps us understand and predict things about the process.

theory: an especially comprehensive model that embraces a whole range of phenomena.

science: a process that has proved to be a prolific producer of powerful and predictive conceptual models. A discipline is a science if (1) it involves a *community* of scholars who communally accept (2) *logical consistency* as a basic principle for constructing models and (3) *reproducible experiments* as the standard for testing models, and (4) a *basic theory* that provides a framework for the discipline and generates questions for further research.

weak and strong interactions: two ways that subatomic particles can interact. These interactions, the gravitational interaction, and the electromagnetic interaction represent the four known fundamental interactions.

relativistic quantum field theories: theories that unify relativity with quantum mechanics and the theory of fields. *Electroweak* theory and *quantum chromodynamics* (QCD) are the most comprehensive relativistic quantum field theories available to us at the present.

standard model: the combination of quantum field theories for the electroweak and strong interactions (and supporting ideas) that comprise our currently-accepted theory of elementary particle physics.

general relativity: the currently accepted comprehensive theory of gravitation.

grand unified theory (GUT): a hypothetical theory that would show that the electromagnetic, weak, and strong interactions are simply different manifestations of the same basic interaction. No one has yet produced a satisfactory grand unified theory.

symmetry: a statement such as "the laws of physics do not change with time" that expresses a basic simplifying assumption about physics that is independent of the particular laws in question. Each such symmetry statement is linked by Noether's theorem to a conservation law.

conservation law: a law that asserts that for an isolated set of interacting object, the total value of some quantity (for example, energy) does not change with time.

system: a well-defined set of interacting objects.

energy, momentum, and angular momentum: quantities that are conserved because the laws of physics do not depend what time it is, where you are located, and how you are oriented (respectively). Note that the quantity called *momentum* is sometimes called *linear momentum* to distinguish it from angular momentum, but in cases where there is no ambiguity the qualifier is usually dropped.

active reading: a study skill that involves writing marginal notes, filling in missing steps in an argument, and other activities that helps you to *think* as you read.

TWO-MINUTE PROBLEMS

C1T.1 According to the definition of science given in this chapter, *astrology* is not a science. What does it lack?
A.   a community of scholars devoted to its study
B.   agreement that models must be logically consistent
C.   reliance on reproducible experiments to test models
D.   a fundamental theory embracing the discipline

C1T.2 According to the definition of *science* given in the chapter, which of the following do you think are sciences? Answer T if you think it is and F if not. Be ready to defend your answer. (Answers may be open to debate here!)
(1) Geology   (4) Economics
(2) Psychology   (5) Political Science
(3) Anthropology   (6) Philosophy

HOMEWORK PROBLEMS

SYNTHETIC

C1S.1 The existence of "free will" cannot be verified scientifically. Why not? Does this mean that free will does not exist? Why or why not?

C1S.2 According to the definition of science given in this chapter, is astronomy a science? Are there any aspects of the definition that are troublesome when applied to astronomy? How might such aspect(s) be rephrased or interpreted to make it clear that astronomy is a science?

C1S.3 The very definition of science given in this chapter means that the range of issues that can be investigated

scientifically is limited. Why? List some questions or issues that (at least at present) *cannot* be investigated scientifically. Does this mean that it is fruitless to discuss these questions? Defend your response.

ADVANCED

C1A.1 Pick either biology or chemistry and make a case for when and how your selected discipline became a science according to the definition given in this chapter, focusing on the last of the four elements to fall into place for your selected discipline. (You may have to do a bit of reading in the history of the discipline to answer this question.)

ANSWERS TO EXERCISES

(There were no exercises in this chapter.)

INTRODUCTION TO MOMENTUM

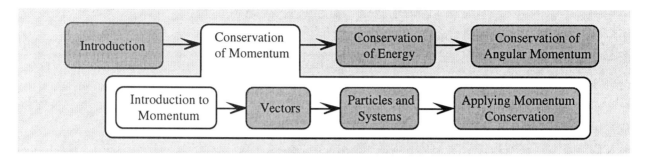

C2.1 OVERVIEW

This chapter begins a four-chapter subunit exploring the law of conservation of momentum. Our goal in the subunit is to develop a conceptual and mathematical model that describes what momentum is and how it behaves, which in turn will provide a basic foundation on which we can build the rest of the unit.

After a brief look at common-sense models of physics and the difficulties they can present, the chapter then moves on to its main business of looking at a series of experimental puzzles that help us see how to build a useful model of momentum conservation. The final puzzle in the chapter will help us see why momentum must be a vector quantity, launching us into the next chapter.

(We will continue as the unit develops to use puzzles that express seeming contradictions to our model as a means of pushing us forward. Such puzzles are very useful for exposing any incomplete parts of a model, and polishing a model by resolving such puzzles is a basic part of theoretical science in any field.)

Here is an overview of the sections of this chapter.

C2.2 *COMMON SENSE MODELS OF MOTION* looks at how experience leads us all toward common-sense models of motion that are less broad and powerful than the newtonian model. The basic point is that we have to examine models carefully and be very suspicious of our intuition.

C2.3 *INTERACTIONS AND MOTION* examines the weaknesses of one such common-sense model (the idea that "motion is caused by forces") and lays the foundations for a more sophisticated newtonian model for looking at how interactions between objects affect their motion.

C2.4 *SPEED* defines a quantity that will help us quantify "motion."

C2.5 *SOME COLLISION EXPERIMENTS* look at some simple experiments that help us toward a definition of momentum. Along the way, we will see that *mass* must play a crucial role in that definition.

C2.6 *MASS AND WEIGHT* more formally defines the concept of mass and contrasts it with the idea of *weight*.

C2.7 *MOMENTUM ALSO INVOLVES DIRECTION* looks at an experiment that shows that momentum must also take account of an object's direction of motion, pointing to the need for definition of momentum based on *vectors* (the topic of the next chapter).

**** *PHYSICS SKILLS: TECHNICAL TERMS* discusses the importance of technical terms in physics and how to learn them effectively.

**** *PHYSICS SKILLS: UNITS* discusses the standard scientific unit system (SI units), and how to convert units.

C2.2 COMMON-SENSE MODELS OF MOTION

One cannot live in the world very long without developing a set of mental models about how objects react to the pushes and pulls we call "forces." These common-sense models are typically intuitive and difficult to describe verbally without running into contradictions, but a person cannot survive very long without developing models that are at least pretty good at predicting the behavior of objects in common situations. Everyone is an embryonic physicist in this sense.

The common-sense models that people develop naturally tend to be large in number and small in scope, each working well in only in a narrow range of situations. This is acceptable in most everyday circumstances, but in unusual situations, a person relying on common-sense models will often make incorrect predictions. Moreover, when examined closely, common-sense models are often incompatible with one another and are sometimes even self-contradictory.

In 1686, Isaac Newton showed the world that it was possible to replace this mess of incoherent common-sense models about force and motion with a *single*, simple, logically consistent, and powerfully predictive model. This *newtonian model* of force and motion liberated scientists from the confusing morass of their own common sense, and still is the foundation on which all of physics is built.

The problem is that Newton's model is in certain ways *counterintuitive*. (This should not be surprising: if this model were intuitive, people would naturally develop it instead of common-sense models.) This means that people learning newtonian physics for the first time have to work *against* the common sense that they have developed during their lifetime. This is not easy and takes time.

You have probably already learned bits and pieces of the newtonian model in school or from reading. In particular, you have probably heard or read the newtonian words "force," "momentum," "speed," "inertia," and "gravity" used in explanations of the physical behavior of objects. But how much of the newtonian perspective have you really absorbed so far? Try the following exercises to find out. (You can find the answers at the end of the chapter.)

Exercise C2X.1: A bicyclist coasts without pedaling on a level road. Why does the cyclist eventually come to rest?
A. all moving objects naturally come to rest   E. *D* and *B*
B. friction forces steadily slow the bike down   F. *D* and *C*
C. friction forces eventually overcome the bike's force of motion
D. the force of the bike's initial motion eventually wears out

---

Exercise C2X.2: A child throws a baseball into the air. *After* the ball leaves the child's hand, it moves vertically upward for a while, reaches a certain maximum height, and then falls back toward the ground. Ignoring air resistance, the force(s) acting on the ball during this time is (are)
A. The constant downward force of gravity alone.
B. The constant force of gravity and a steadily decreasing upward force.
C. The constant force of gravity and a steadily decreasing upward force that acts only until the ball reaches its maximum height.
D. A decreasing upward force before the ball reaches its maximum height, and an increasing downward force of gravity afterward.
E. No forces act on the ball: it returns to the ground naturally.

Exercise C2X.3: Imagine that you throw a rock eastward at a speed of 10 m/s from the top of a high cliff. It falls for a long time before hitting the water. If we ignore air friction, what is the rock's eastward speed when it hits the water?
A. The rock's motion is entirely downward; it does not move eastward at all.
B. The rock is moving eastward much slower than 10 m/s when it hits.
C. The rock is still moving eastward at exactly 10 m/s when it hits.
D. Since it has picked up speed, the rock is moving faster than 10 m/s eastward

---

Exercise C2X.4: A hockey puck sliding due north on a frictionless plane of ice is given a very brief eastward "tap" by a hockey player. What path on Figure C2.1 will the hockey puck follow after the tap is over (circle one)?

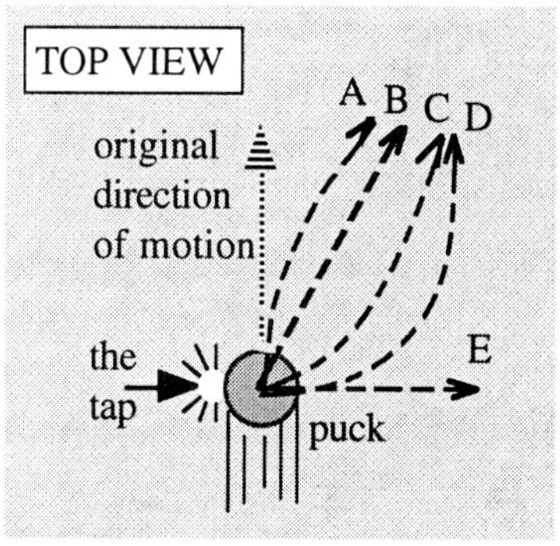

Exercise C2X.5: Imagine that a small car rear-ends a large truck that is initially at rest. During the collision, the force that the *truck* exerts on the car is
A. zero (the truck is just sitting there)
B. smaller than the force the *car* exerts on the truck.
C. equal to the force the *car* exerts on the truck.
D. greater than the force the *car* exerts on the truck.

Figure C2.1.

How did you do? If you answered 4 or 5 of these questions correctly you have absorbed the newtonian model unusually well at this stage. Scores ranging from 1 to 3 are normal for someone beginning an introductory physics course, but indicate that common-sense models are exerting a significant influence.

The point of this quiz is not to be discouraging but make it clear that one of our tasks during units *C* and *N* will be to expose and critique these common-sense models so that you can develop a clearer understanding (and appreciation!) of the newtonian model. This will take some time and effort, but after you finish unit *N* (some 10 weeks from now), you will do *much* better on a quiz like this.

The point: one of our main tasks will be to root out common-sense models

C2.3 INTERACTIONS AND MOTION

One of the most tenacious common-sense models about motion asserts that *motion is caused by forces* (**force** here having its everyday definition as some push or pull). According to this model, if you push on an object, it moves; if you push harder, it moves faster; and if you stop pushing, it comes to rest. (If you answered anything but *B* to exercise C2X.1, anything but *A* or *E* to exercise C2X.2, or anything but *A* or *B* to question C2X.4, you are at least being unconsciously influenced by this particular model.)

One common-sense model and its weaknesses

This common-sense model seems intuitively sound and certainly is consistent with much of daily experience. But from a modern perspective, this model works at all only because familiar moving objects commonly encounter significant amounts of friction. Thus the model gets into serious trouble in situations when frictional effects are small. For example, consider a child in a wagon coasting along a level road after being pushed by a friend. We know from experience that a wagon with well-greased wheels can coast for a very long time without any additional effort from the friend. So if motion is caused by force, what force pushes the wagon along as it coasts?

A common-sense answer (believed intuitively by many people and actually articulated by some pre-newtonian scholars) is that the coasting wagon is pushed by a force that is a kind of memory of the original push, as if the push continues to act long after the friend has let go. But here the model begins to dissolve into unanswerable puzzles and contradictions. Why is this "remembered force" forgotten faster if the wheels have more friction? Why doesn't this "remembered force" feel anything like the friend's original shove? Why, in fact, is there absolutely no corroborating physical evidence for this "remembered force" other than the continued motion of the wagon itself? A sign of a weak model is that we can extend it to new situations only by patching it up in awkward and unsupported ways that lead to intellectual dead ends instead of new insight.

The newtonian model, in contrast, provides simple and logical explanations not only of wagons coasting but many other phenomena using a mere handful of simple ideas. These ideas are so powerful that, when stated *qualitatively* (as I am about to do), they remain true even in the context of our best current theories: they thus provide an excellent starting place for any study of physics.

The following qualitative newtonian ideas still apply to current theories

I will state these core ideas in the form of four qualitative assertions. The first draws our attention to the link between forces and interactions:

**The first assertion:
the connection between
forces and interactions**

Any force (push or pull) acting on an object is *always* a result of that object's current participation in an *interaction* with another object.

For example, forces on an object can arise from, say, direct physical contact with something else, but *never* from a memory of a past interaction (as in the common-sense model just discussed) or from any internal characteristic or property of the object itself (as some other common-sense models claim).

What exactly is an "interaction" here? The second assertion clarifies the meaning of this term by listing and categorizing known interactions:

**The second assertion:
what is an interaction?**

An **interaction** is a physical relationship between two objects that allows them to influence each other's motion. The only known physical interactions between two **macroscopic** objects (objects significantly larger than atoms) are either:

1. **contact** interactions (including friction) that arise only when the two objects are in direct physical contact, or
2. **long-range** interactions that act over a distance, which are either
   a. gravitational (which act between all objects)
   b. electromagnetic (which involve charged objects and/or magnets)

While *all* objects participate in gravitational interactions, these interactions are usually weak enough to be ignored unless one of the two participating objects is very large (the size of a planet or bigger). We will see why we group electric and magnetic interactions together when we get to unit *E*. We will consider additional possible interactions between *microscopic* objects in unit *Q*.

The remaining assertions describe how interactions are related to motion:

**The third assertion:
The motion of an isolated
object does not change**

When an object is **isolated** (that is, it participates in no interactions), *its motion does not change* (if it is at rest, it remains at rest; if it is moving, it continues to move in the same direction at the same speed).

**The fourth assertion:
Interactions act to *change*
an object's motion**

Interactions therefore generally act to *change* an object's motion. When an object participates in a *single* interaction with another object, the interaction *always* changes its motion (though the effect may be small). When an object participates in multiple interactions, the effects of the interactions *may* cancel each other out, resulting in no net effect.

(The first of these last two assertions is called **Newton's first law**.)

These ideas are the foundation upon which we will build the rest of the course. In fact, almost all our efforts in this unit and the next will be directed toward making the last statement more precise and quantitative and exploring its rich implications and applications.

**Why the newtonian model
is better than the common-
sense model**

Even with our current qualitative understanding of this model, we can get a sense of how much more powerful it is than common-sense models. For example, this model explains the behavior of the coasting wagon very naturally. From the newtonian perspective, though, the question is not why the wagon *continues* to move (this is what moving objects *naturally* do according to the third assertion!), but rather why it eventually comes to *rest*. The answer is that friction in the wheel bearings and friction with the surrounding air (which are both contact interactions acting on different parts of the wagon) exert effects on the wagon that oppose its continued motion, and these effects thus steadily *change* the wagon's forward motion by slowing it down. Reducing the strength of these friction interactions (by greasing the wheels, for example) *should* reduce their opposing effect and thus increase the time it takes the wagon to slow down (and we know from experience that this is true). To keep moving at a constant rate, the wagon must participate in some additional interaction that cancels the effects of friction: we should be able to arrange this by having the friend continue to push the wagon gently forward (again, this is corroborated by experience).

Perhaps you can see how naturally this model not only explains the behavior of the coasting wagon but also makes new predictions about what happens when we change the situation, predictions that are supported by experiment. This is one sign of a healthy and vibrant model!

All the same, you should clearly understand that it is nothing *more* than a model. These assertions paint a nice and pretty mental picture of a complicated reality. Real interactions (when examined in more detail) chafe at the boundaries of the clear-cut categories in the second assertion. Real objects can never be truly isolated, so the third assertion as stated is an idealization that reality can only approach imperfectly.

Once we understand that this *is* still a model, the question becomes, "Is it a *good* (helpful, useful) model?" Throughout the rest of the course, these four ideas will come up again and again, and indeed provide the foundation for additional successful and powerful models that cover an enormous range of phenomena. I think that you will see very vividly that the answer is "Yes!"

Exercise C2X.6: A friend tells you that the "force of inertia" is what keeps a baseball moving after it is thrown by the pitcher. Is this idea a consequence of the newtonian model, or is it an idea from a common-sense model? Explain.

Exercise C2X.7: A soccer ball sitting at rest on a level playing field is suddenly kicked by a player, and rolls quite a distance before coming to rest. According to the newtonian model, what interactions (if any) (**a**) get the ball moving initially, (**b**) keep it moving after the kick, and (**c**) eventually bring it to rest?

C2.4 SPEED

The first step in making the newtonian model more quantitative is to find a way of quantifying an object's motion. An object's **speed** v expresses the rate at which it moves as a numerical quantity defined as follows:

$$v \equiv \frac{|dr|}{dt} \qquad\qquad \text{(C2.1)}$$

Definition of speed

where " $\equiv$ " means "is defined to be," dt is a time interval (which must be short enough that the object's speed doesn't change significantly during that interval), and $|dr|$ is the distance that the object travels during that interval.

Physicists informally interpret the symbol d before a variable as indicating a "tiny" *change* in the variable's value. Thus we would interpret dt here as being a tiny change in time, and (since r is a standard symbol for position) dr represents a tiny change in position, and thus $|dr|$ (the absolute value ensuring that the quantity is positive) stands for the tiny distance traveled. When the symbol d is used this way, we need to define what we consider "tiny": in this case (as stated) we mean tiny compared to how far or long the object has to move before its speed changes by an amount we consider appreciable. The symbol Δ is commonly used for changes that *cannot* be considered tiny in this sense. (Note that a list of symbols and their meanings appears on the inside back cover of the text.)

The meaning of the symbols d and Δ

In the accepted international system of scientific units (called the *Système International* or **SI units**) distances are measured in *meters* and time intervals in *seconds*. Since equation C2.1 defines speed as the ratio of a tiny distance to a tiny time interval, the SI units of speed are *meters per second* (abbreviated "m/s"). You probably have a better intuitive feeling for speeds in *miles per hour* but you can easily convert a speed in m/s to mi/h (or vice versa) if you remember that 1 m/s = 2.24 mi/h. See the *Physics Skills* section at the end of the chapter for discussion of the SI system and how to convert units.

Units for speed

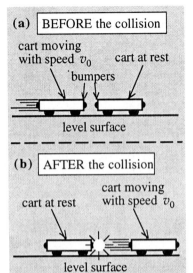

Figure C2.2: An example collision between identical carts. (The final speeds are the actual experimental results in this situation.)

C2.5 SOME COLLISION EXPERIMENTS

One of our goals in this unit is to understand the law of **conservation of momentum**, which we are taking as a basic principle of physics. (Study of this law will also eventually show us how to make the fourth newtonian assertion in section C2.3 more quantitative.) One way to express this law is as follows:

Any interaction between two objects always acts on them in such a way as to keep the value of their total momentum fixed.

But what do we mean by "total momentum" here? Our task in the next few chapters will be to uncover the definition of momentum by experimenting with various definitions until this law fits as broad a range of circumstances as possible.

We will begin by considering experiments where we collide two carts. The interaction that is supposed to conserve momentum is the carts' contact interaction during the collision. (If the carts roll essentially without friction on a level surface, the effects of other interactions involving the carts will be minimal.)

Consider the experiment shown in Figure C2.2. Here a cart moving with a certain initial speed v_0 collides with an identical cart at rest. If you actually do the experiment (and the carts' bumpers are sufficiently "springy"), you will find that the collision interaction affects the carts' motion by bringing the first to rest and sending the second away with the same speed as the first had initially.

In this collision, we see that the sum of the *speeds* of the two carts is preserved in this interaction (the sum is v_0 in both cases). So is momentum perhaps equivalent to speed? In a certain sense, this coincides with the way *momentum* is used in everyday English. We say that something that is moving has momentum, and we usually imagine that if it moves faster it has more momentum.

Let's check this hypothesis by looking at another experiment. Consider the experiment shown in Figure C2.3. The initial situation in this experiment looks just like that shown in Figure C2.2, except that the initially moving cart is now twice as massive as the first cart. If you do this experiment (and if the bumpers are sufficiently springy), you would find this time that the initially moving cart is *not* brought to rest by the collision interaction, but rather continues to move forward with about one-third of its original speed v_0. The lighter cart, on the other hand, bounds away from the collision with a speed of about $\frac{4}{3}v_0$.

This experimental result is the death knell for our initial hypothesis that *momentum* is equivalent to *speed*: the sum of the carts' speeds before the collision is equal to the moving cart's initial speed v_0, but the sum of the carts' final speeds is $\frac{1}{3}v_0 + \frac{4}{3}v_0 = \frac{5}{3}v_0$. The sum of the carts' speeds is therefore *not* preserved in this experiment, meaning that if the carts' total momentum *is* really conserved in this situation, it cannot be the same as their total speeds.

How might we define momentum differently? We can again take a clue from the way *momentum* is used in everyday English. Judging from common usage, which do you think has more momentum, a small car moving at 60 mi/h or a large truck moving at the same speed? Most people would say that the truck has more momentum, because it is more relentless in its motion (meaning that it is harder to stop). This suggests that an object's momentum might be proportional to the object's mass as well as its speed.

So let's propose a *new* hypothesis. Perhaps an object's momentum p is equal to the object's mass m *times* its speed v: $p \equiv mv$ (for historical reasons, p is the standard symbol for momentum in physics). Does this explain the results of our second experiment? If we define the mass of the lighter cart to be m, and the initial speed of the other cart to be v_0, then the carts' total momentum before the collision is $(2m)v_0 + 0 = 2mv_0$ (since the lighter cart is at rest), while the carts' total momentum after the collision is

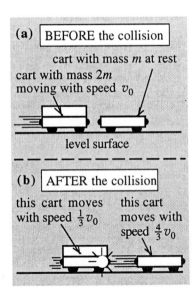

Figure C2.3: An example collision where one cart is twice as massive as the other. (The final speeds are the actual experimental results in this situation.)

$$(2m)(\tfrac{1}{3}v_0) \ + \ m(\tfrac{4}{3}v_0) \ = \ mv_0(\tfrac{2}{3} + \tfrac{4}{3}) \ = \ \tfrac{6}{3}mv_0 \ = \ 2mv_0 \qquad \text{(C2.2)}$$

as well. Thus momentum defined this way *is* conserved in this interaction.

Exercise C2X.8: When we change a model to fit new data like this, it is important that we make sure that the revised model still successfully explains previously-known results. Check that the carts' total momentum defined the new way is *still* conserved in the collision shown in Figure C2.2.

C2.6 MASS AND WEIGHT

In physics, we in fact *define* mass in terms of momentum. Consider the collision experiment shown in Figure C2.4. In this case, we take an object of known mass m_0 (shown generically as a spherical ball), give it a modest initial speed v_0, and allow it to collide with an object with unknown mass m (also shown as a generic ball). We use velcro or glue to ensure that the two objects stick together after the collision and measure the combined objects' final speed v_f. Our current hypothesis about momentum implies that the objects' total initial momentum $m_0v_0 + 0 = m_0v_0$ must be equal to their total final momentum $m_0v_f + mv_f = (m_0 + m)v_f$, meaning that:

$$m_0v_0 = (m_0 + m)v_f \qquad \Rightarrow \qquad \frac{m}{m_0} = \frac{v_0}{v_f} - 1 \qquad (C2.3)$$

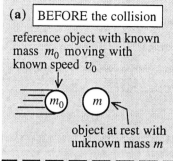

(a) BEFORE the collision

reference object with known mass m_0 moving with known speed v_0

object at rest with unknown mass m

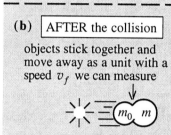

(b) AFTER the collision

objects stick together and move away as a unit with a speed v_f we can measure

Figure C2.4: An experiment we can use to determine an object's unknown mass m in terms of a known mass m_0.

Exercise C2X.9: Fill in the steps of algebra that are missing in equation C2.3. Note that the symbol "$\Rightarrow$" is short for "implies that." (*Hint:* Divide both sides of the equation on the left by m_0v_f.)

We therefore *define* an object's **mass** as follows:

> An object's mass can be determined by using the object as the initially stationary object in the experiment described by Figure C2.4. The value of its mass m is then defined to be equal to $m_0[(v_0 / v_f) - 1]$.*

A definition of *mass*

This kind of experiment therefore allows us (at least in principle) to measure any unknown mass m in terms of a known standard mass m_0.

The SI unit of mass is the **kilogram** (abbreviated "kg"): the reference object defined to have that mass is a certain platinum-iridium cylinder kept in a controlled environment at the International Bureau of Weights and Measures near Paris. In principle, you could borrow this object to use as the reference mass in the experiment above: this would enable you to find the unknown object's mass directly in kilograms. (In practice, one uses a *copy* of the standard kilogram.)

The SI unit of mass

Why not just *weigh* the object using a scale instead of going through this complicated process? In physics, **weight** is not the same as *mass*: it instead expresses *the strength of the force gravity exerts on the object*. While experiments show that an object's *mass* is an intrinsic and invariant property of that object (its value remaining fixed as long as the object maintains its integrity), an object's *weight* at a given location depends on the strength of the gravitational field at that location. For example, an object's *weight* on the surface of the moon is only about 1/6 of what it is on earth, but its *mass* is the same both places.

The difference between *mass* and *weight*

We see that *weight* and *mass* are completely distinct ideas in physics: there is no *logical* reason to suspect that these quantities should even be related! Since equation C2.3 *defines* an object's mass in terms of a collision experiment without referring to weight in any way, we can use it to investigate the connection between an object's weight and its mass. *It turns out* that at a given location in a specific gravitational field (say, at the earth's surface), an object's weight is

But mass is proportional to weight in a given gravitational field

*Technically, we should determine this value *in the limit that v_0 approaches zero* to be completely consistent with the theory of relativity. This is not much of a concern in normal circumstances, though: the definition as it stands is quite accurate unless v_0 is a significant fraction of the speed of light.

strictly proportional to its mass. This is why it is so easy to confuse these ideas. Considering how different the *concepts* of weight and mass are, this is surprising, but it appears to be true. (One strength of the theory of general relativity is that offers a straightforward *explanation* for this.)

Units for weight

Because weight expresses the strength of a gravitational *force*, it is measured in units of force. The SI unit of force is the **newton**, which we will define later in the course. You are probably more familiar with the **pound**, the unit of weight (and thus force) most commonly used in the United States. Near the surface of the earth, an object with a *mass* of 1.0 kg *weighs* roughly 2.2 lbs.

Exercise C2X.10: A specification sheet for a certain car states that its "curb weight is 1250 kg." Why might a physicist grumble at such a statement?

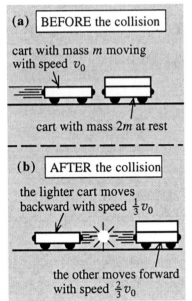

Figure C2.5: An example collision where the cart at rest is more massive than the other. The speeds shown after the collision are actual experimental results (which you can check).

C2.7   MOMENTUM ALSO INVOLVES DIRECTION

Our current hypothesis is that an object's *momentum* is a numerical quantity equal to its *mass* times its *speed*. This hypothesis satisfies all of the experiments we have considered thus far. Let's test this hypothesis by considering one more experiment. Consider the collision shown in Figure C2.5. This is like the experiment illustrated in Figure C2.3 except that now it is the cart at *rest* that is twice as massive as the other. If you do the experiment (and the bumpers are sufficiently springy), you will find that after the collision the more massive cart moves forward with a speed of about $\frac{2}{3}v_0$, while the lighter cart actually moves *backward* with a speed of about $\frac{1}{3}v_0$.

Is momentum (as we have currently defined it) conserved in this collision? The total momentum before the collision is $mv_0 + 0 = mv_0$, but the total momentum after the collision is $m(\frac{1}{3}v_0) + (2m)(\frac{2}{3}v_0) = \frac{5}{3}mv_0$, so momentum according to our current definition is *not* conserved, as it should be.

What if momentum is an *arrow* instead of a number?

What could possibly be wrong *this* time? The only thing that is qualitatively different about this experiment compared to the others we have studied is that after the collision, one cart moves *backward* compared to the other motions involved. Maybe an object's momentum is somehow connected to the *direction* of that object's motion as well as to its speed and mass.

How might we represent a quantity that has a direction as well as a numerical magnitude? Suppose that instead of treating momentum as a numerical quantity $p = mv$, we think of it as an *arrow* with a *length* that is proportional to mv. Such an arrow links the numerical definition of momentum that we have used previously with a clearly-defined direction.

If we think of momentum as being an arrow, how can we define the *total* momentum of two objects (that is, the sum of two momentum arrows)? For the sake of argument, let's define the sum of two arrows to be the arrow that we get if we place the two arrows in sequence (so that the tail of the second coincides with the front end of the first) and then draw an arrow from the tail of the first to the head of the second. This definition certainly makes sense when the arrows all point in the same direction (see Figure C2.6a). To see that this definition also makes sense if the arrows point in opposite directions, imagine that you walk along the first arrow (from tail to tip) and then along the second arrow (from tail to tip). Someone who starts at the same place you did and walks along the sum arrow (see Figure C2.6b) ends up at the same place that you do. The sum therefore represents your total effective journey from your starting point.

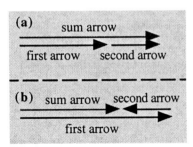

Figure C2.6: How to sum arrow quantities. (The arrows are displaced a little apart vertically to make them easier to see.)

Never mind how anyone could come up with such a model for momentum: the question is, *does it work* for the collision shown in Figure C2.5? Since the massive cart is at rest initially, the two carts' total momentum before the collision is simply equal to the momentum of the moving cart, which is a rightward arrow whose length is mv_0. After the collision, the carts' total momentum is the sum of a rightward arrow whose length is $(2m)\frac{2}{3}v_0 = \frac{4}{3}mv_0$ and a leftward arrow whose length is $\frac{1}{3}mv_0$. Figure C2.7 shows that these arrows do indeed sum to a rightward arrow whose length is mv_0, just as we had in the beginning!

Exercise C2X.11: Show that the arrow model of momentum also implies that momentum is conserved in the collisions shown in Figures C2.2 and C2.3.

In short, we see that the arrow model of momentum is the only one that is powerful enough to embrace all of the cases we have considered thus far. The arrow model also *promises* to be able to handle in a natural way collisions where the objects do *not* all move along the same line (since the definition of the sum of arrows makes sense even if the arrows do not lie on the same line).

In closing, let me point out how the arrow model of momentum nicely illustrates features of many good physical models. Quantitative physical models often come in two parts: a *conceptual* model and a *mathematical* model. The conceptual model creates a simplified picture of reality by stating a simile, saying (in effect) "the universe in this situation behaves *like* this..." (This part of our momentum model says basically that "momentum behaves like an arrow"). The mathematical model links the elements of the conceptual model to mathematical objects and processes (here, it defines exactly how we add arrows and provides other tools for calculating quantities of interest using the arrows).

To understand the full power of this model, therefore, we need work more with the mathematical part of this model, learning how to do calculations with arrow-quantities like momentum (which are called *vectors*) in one, two, and three dimensions. This will be our focus in the next chapter.

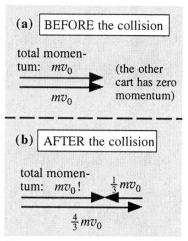

Figure C2.7: The arrow model of momentum succeeds (where simpler models fail) in conserving momentum in the collision shown in Figure C2.5.

In order to clearly and concisely communicate ideas to one another, physicists (like any close-knit community) have over time developed a community language involving **technical terms** with special meanings. We have seen a number of such terms introduced in this chapter.

In physics, these technical terms are usually English words or phrases. This means that English-speakers may *think* that they understand what they hear or read in a discussion of physics, but if they are not familiar with the *special* meanings that certain words have to physicists, they can become quickly lost.

Velocity, force, inertia, mass, weight, energy, and *momentum* are all words that mean different things in physics than they do in common English. For example, *weight* is equivalent to *mass* in everyday discourse, but not in physics (as we have seen). A sentence like "the force of its momentum keeps the ball moving" makes sense in common English, but it is nonsense in physics: *force* and *momentum* are being used in ways inconsistent with their technical meanings.

Correct use of technical terms is more than just a matter of good style. The precise and unambiguous definitions of these terms make it both easier to express physical ideas clearly and *think* about them correctly. In my experience, careless use of technical terms (usually arising from mixing in meanings from common English) is a leading cause of confusion among introductory students.

Part of your task in this course is to learn the language of practicing physicists. The key is to realize that you *are* learning a new language and thus should treat technical terms as you would vocabulary in a foreign language! Specifically, you have to (1) learn to *recognize* technical terms, and (2) *memorize* their definitions (using flash cards or whatever aids help). When you later use the term, always pause to *think* about whether you are using it correctly: be particularly aware that connotations from everyday English may creep in.

It will help you identify and study these terms if you remember that I highlight each technical term in **boldface** when it is first introduced, define the term clearly nearby, and then *restate* the definition in the glossary at the end of the chapter. If you make *sure* that you know the technical meaning of each term in the glossary, you will greatly reduce opportunities for confusion.

PHYSICS SKILLS:
Technical Terms

PHYSICS SKILLS: Units

STANDARD PREFIXES

Power	Prefix	Symbol
10^{18}	exa	E
10^{15}	peta	P
10^{12}	tera	T
10^9	giga	G
10^6	mega	M
10^3	kilo	k
10^{-2}	centi	c
10^{-3}	milli	m
10^{-6}	micro	μ
10^{-9}	nano	n
10^{-12}	pico	p
10^{-15}	femto	f
10^{-18}	atto	a

Figure C2.8: Standard SI prefixes for powers of 10.

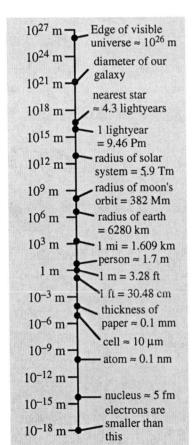

Figure C2.9a: Benchmarks for distances in meters.

Units attach physical meaning to bare numbers. If you catch a fish and brag to your friends that it was "3" long, they are not going to know how to react. On the other hand, if you say "3 meters", "3 feet", or "3 cm", this clearly communicates the physical meaning of your feat. In order to clearly and precisely communicate the magnitude of a measured quantity to someone, we must state it in terms of a previously agreed-upon standard unit for that quantity. The purpose of a **system of units** is to define such standards.

Standard SI units and Prefixes

An international committee has been working since 1960 to provide clear and reproducible definitions of standard units to help scientists communicate results more precisely. The system of units adopted by the committee as the standard for all scientific communication is an adaptation of what used to be called the *metric* system: the units are now called **SI units** (from the French *Système Internationale*). This system defines seven units to be fundamental: the **meter** (for distance), the **second** (for time), the **kilogram** (for mass), the **kelvin** (for temperature), the **mole** (a conveniently large unit for counting molecules), the **ampere** (for electrical current) and the **candela** (a unit of luminous intensity that we will not use in this course). The committee has carefully defined most of these basic units so that scientists can easily recreate the unit in their own laboratories. For example, the *second* is currently defined to be 9,192,631,770 oscillations of the radio waves emitted by a cesium-133 atom under certain well-defined conditions. A scientist anywhere in the world can thus create a cesium-based atomic clock that measures time in standard seconds.

Each of these units has a standard single-letter abbreviation. For the units that we will use in this course, the abbreviations are "m" for the meter, "s" for the second, "g" for 10^{-3} kilogram, "K" for the kelvin, and "A" for the ampere.

In addition to these basic units, the SI committee has defined a set of **derived units** that are combinations of these basic units. The most important of these formally defined derived units are the **joule** ($1\text{ J} \equiv 1\text{ kg·m}^2/\text{s}^2$) for energy, the **watt** ($1\text{ W} \equiv 1\text{ J/s}$) for power, the **newton** ($1\text{ N} \equiv 1\text{ kg·m/s}^2$) for force, the **pascal** ($1\text{ Pa} \equiv 1\text{ N/m}^2$) for pressure, the **coulomb** ($1\text{ C} = 1\text{ A·s}$) for electrical charge, the **volt** ($1\text{ V} = 1\text{ J/C}$) for electrical energy per unit charge, and the **ohm** ($1\text{ }\Omega = 1\text{ V/A}$) for electrical resistance. Future chapters will explore the reasons behind the definitions of these other derived units.

The SI committee has also defined a set of standard prefixes and prefix abbreviations (see Figure C2.8) that one attaches to a unit to multiply it by various powers of 10. Thus a *millimeter* (abbreviation: "mm") is equal to 10^{-3} m, a *gigajoule* (abbreviation: "GJ," which is pronounced with a hard *g* as in *get*) is 10^9 J, a *nanosecond* (abbreviation: "ns") is 10^{-9} s, and so on.

Units for angles (the *radian* and the *degree*) are standard but (for historical reasons) are not treated as formal SI units. We will also occasionally refer to English units like the *mile*, the *foot*, and the **pound** (a unit of force).

Developing an Intuitive Feel for the Units

Technical definitions are fine and good, but they lack intuitive meaning. How big is a "megameter"? How much energy is a "microjoule"? You probably do not have an intuitive feeling for such quantities. There are two things that you can do to feel more at home with SI units: (1) *memorize the prefixes*, and (2) *learn some benchmarks*.

The SI prefixes are used frequently in physics literature, and increasingly are creeping into everyday usage (as in "a gigabyte disk drive"). It will slow you down considerably if you do not at *least* memorize the prefixes between 10^{-12} and 10^{+12}. Particularly difficult for speakers of U.S. English is the prefix "milli" (which means "one-*thousandth*", *not* "one-millionth") and "micro" (which *does* mean "one-millionth").

The best way to get a feeling for large multiples and small divisions of the basic SI units is to study the benchmark charts shown in Figures C2.9. Knowing these charts can help you to flag absurd answers when you solve problems (for example, if a problem asks you to compute how high you can throw a ball, and your answer comes out to be larger than the size of the solar system, you can assume that you have made a mistake somewhere).

Conversion of Units

Often in this course you will need to convert a quantity expressed in one unit to the equivalent quantity expressed in another unit. For example, imagine that we are told that the distance to a nearby town is 23 mi, and we want to convert this to a distance in meters. We start by writing down the equation that defines the relationship between the units:

$$1 \text{ mi} = 1609 \text{ m} \tag{C2.4a}$$

Since a mile is *equivalent* to 1609 m, the ratio of these quantities is one:

$$\left(\frac{1609 \text{ m}}{1 \text{ mi}} \right) = 1 \tag{C2.4b}$$

Such a ratio of equivalent units is called a **unit operator.** Since we can always multiply a quantity by 1 without changing it, we can multiply our original distance of 23 miles by 1 in the form of the unit operator to get:

$$(23 \text{ mi})(1) = (23 \text{ mi}) \left(\frac{1609 \text{ m}}{1 \text{ mi}} \right) \tag{C2.4c}$$

Note that we cancel the unit of "mi" that appears in the numerator and denominator exactly as if it were an algebraic symbol. In general, when writing equations involving units, you should treat the units as if they were algebraic symbols, carrying any uncanceled units through to the right side.

This method amounts to being a useful mnemonic device that helps you do unit conversions correctly. When you multiply a quantity by one or more unit operators and cancel any units that appear in both the numerator and denominator, then if the units that remain are the final units that you wanted, you can be assured that your quantity has been correctly converted.

Let us consider another example that illustrates how to treat powers of units. Consider a rock whose density of 3000 kg/m³ and volume is 10 cm³. What is its mass? Since density $\rho \equiv m/V$ (where m is the object's mass and V is its volume), $m = \rho V$. When we multiply ρ and V, we have to include *three* powers of the unit operator converting meters to centimeters in order to get the units to come out to be simply kilograms:

$$(3000 \frac{\text{kg}}{\text{m}^3})(10 \text{ cm}^3) \left(\frac{1 \text{ m}}{100 \text{ cm}} \right) \left(\frac{1 \text{ m}}{100 \text{ cm}} \right) \left(\frac{1 \text{ m}}{100 \text{ cm}} \right) = 0.03 \text{ kg}. \tag{C2.5}$$

Unit Consistency

Any equation relating physical quantities *must* have the same units on both sides of the equation. For example, the definition of speed is $v = |d\mathbf{r}|/dt$: since $d\mathbf{r}$ is measured in meters and dt in seconds, the quantity v *must* have units of meters per second (m/s). Note also that it is possible to multiply or divide quantities having different units, but two quantities being added or subtracted must have the *same* units (for example, adding 10 m to 2.3 s is nonsense!).

Unit consistency provides a very useful way to check algebraic work or other calculations: correct manipulations should yield the correct final units!

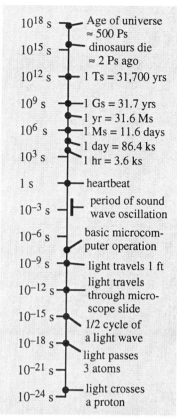

Figure C2.9b: Benchmarks for times in seconds.

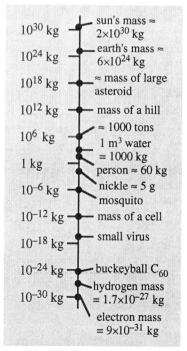

Figure C2.9c: Benchmarks for masses in kilograms.

SUMMARY

I. COMMON-SENSE MODELS OF MOTION
A. People intuitively develop common-sense models from experience
   1. Such models tend to be large in number but small in scope
   2. They are often incompatible and/or even self-contradictory
B. The newtonian model
   1. provides a *single* powerful and logically consistent model
   2. but is also somewhat counterintuitive (so learning it takes effort)

II. INTERACTIONS AND MOTION
A. A tenacious common-sense model: *motion is caused by force*
   1. This model works fine when friction is significant
   2. But it runs into difficulties when friction is small
B. The newtonian model is built on four qualitative assertions
   1. *Forces* always arise from *interactions* between two objects
   2. An *interaction* is a physical connection between two objects that allows them to influence each other's motion. The only known interactions between macroscopic objects are either
      a) *contact* interactions (involving direct physical contact)
      b) *long-range* interactions, which are either
         (1) gravitational interactions or
         (2) electromagnetic interactions
   3. The motion of an *isolated* object does not change
   4. Interactions cause *changes* in an object's motion
C. These assertions apply (qualitatively at least) to all current theories
D. The newtonian model successfully and naturally explains situations where the common-sense model fails or is awkward

III. SPEED
A. An object's speed v quantifies how fast it is moving
B. Mathematical definition: $v \equiv |dr| / dt$
   1. dt is a tiny time interval (so $v \approx$ constant during it)
   2. $|dr|$ is the *distance* that the object moves during dt
C. Standard units: m/s (1 m/s = 2.24 mi/h)

IV. MASS AND WEIGHT
A. A study of some example collisions suggests that if the colliding objects' total momentum is conserved, its magnitude for an object must be equal to that object's speed times its *mass*
B. In physics, we in fact *define* mass in terms of momentum. An experiment to determine an object's unknown mass m looks like this (the objects in question are assumed to be isolated from other interactions):
   1. Give an object of known mass m_0 a known speed v_0
   2. Allow it to collide with the unknown mass at rest and stick to it
   3. Measure the final speed v_f of the combined objects
   4. Calculate $m = m_0(v_0 / v_f - 1)$
C. The standard unit of mass is the *kilogram* (= mass of an object in Paris)
D. *Weight* is not the same thing as *mass* in physics
   1. Weight expresses the *force* that gravity exerts on an object
   2. An object's weight thus depends on the nature of the surrounding gravitational field (and so is different on the moon than on earth)
   3. Mass, by contrast, is an intrinsic, fixed characteristic of an object

V. AN ARROW MODEL OF MOMENTUM
A. Consideration of another example experiment shows that we must model an object's momentum as if it were an *arrow*, where:
   1. The direction of the arrow is the object's direction of motion
   2. The length of the arrow is proportional to mv
   3. We add arrows by placing them head-to-tail in sequence
B. The next chapter develops the mathematical side of this model

GLOSSARY

technical term: a word or phrase that has a specific technical meaning in physics, which may be *different* its meaning of the word or phrase in common English.

macroscopic (object): an object larger than a few thousand atoms. This category is important because Newtonian mechanics adequately describes the behavior of such objects: quantum mechanics is usually necessary to describe the behavior of objects that are smaller.

interaction: a physical relationship between two objects that allows them to change each other's motion.

contact (interaction): an interaction between two macroscopic objects arising from direct physical contact.

long-range (interaction): an interaction between two objects that affects their motion even when they are not in direct contact. The *only* types of long-range interactions that are relevant for macroscopic objects are **gravitational** interactions (which act between all objects), **electrostatic** interactions (which involve at least one electrically charged object) and **magnetic** interactions (which involve at least one magnet).

force: informally defined in this chapter as being some kind of push or pull. (We will define force more precisely in a future chapter.) In the newtonian model, forces are always manifestations of interactions.

isolated (object): an object is isolated if it does not participate in any interactions with other objects.

Newton's first law: a law of physics stating that the motion of an isolated object does not change.

speed v: a numerical quantity that specifies how fast an object is moving, defined to be the *distance* $|dr|$ that the object covers in a certain time interval divided by the *duration* dt of that interval: $v = |dr|/dt$. This definition applies only if dt is small enough so that v is (at least nearly) constant during that time interval.

mass m: an intrinsic characteristic of an object or system expressing its resistance to changes in motion. An object's mass can be determined by colliding it with a reference mass, as discussed in section C2.6.

weight: the gravitational *force* acting on an object. Even though at given place in a given gravitational field an object's weight turns out to be *proportional* to its mass, the *concepts* of mass and weight are *not* equivalent in physics.

system of units: a set of definitions that describe standard units for measuring quantities.

SI unit system: the internationally-accepted system of units for scientific measurements, based on what used to be called the metric system.

basic SI units: the SI units considered by the SI committee to be fundamental. These include the *second*, the *meter*, the *kilogram*, the **kelvin** (for temperature), the **ampere** (for electrical current), the **mole** (for the number of molecules), and the **candela** (for luminous intensity).

second: the SI unit of time, defined to be 9,192,631,770 oscillations of the radio waves emitted by a cesium-133 atom under specified circumstances.

meter: the SI unit of length, defined to be the distance that light travels in 1/299,792,458 of a standard second.

kilogram: the SI unit of mass, defined to be the mass of a certain platinum-iridium cylinder kept near Paris.

derived units: SI units that are defined in terms of combinations of basic units. These include the **newton**, the **joule**, the **watt**, the **pascal**, the **coulomb**, the **volt**, and the **ohm**. We will define these units later in the course.

unit operator: a ratio (equal to 1) of equivalent quantities expressed in different units. Unit operators are used to perform unit conversions.

pound: a non-SI unit of force commonly used in the United States. An object near the earth's surface whose mass is 1.0 kg weighs about 2.2 lbs.

conservation of momentum: a law of physics asserting that an interaction between two objects conserves their *total* momentum (that is, the sum of their individual momenta). One of our goals in this chapter (as well as chapter C4) is to refine our definition of *momentum* so that the law fits many situations as possible.

TWO-MINUTE PROBLEMS

C2T.1 A baseball player slides into third base. Why (according to the newtonian model) does the player eventually come to rest?
A. All moving objects naturally come to rest
B. Friction overcomes the player's force of motion
C. The force of the player's motion eventually wears out
D. Friction interactions change the player's motion
E. *B* and *C*.   T. *C* and *D*   F. other (specify)

C2T.2 An object moving at a constant speed must have a force acting on it to maintain its motion. (T or F).

C2T.3 A baseball player hits a line drive toward third base. What (if anything) keeps the ball moving after it leaves the bat (according to the newtonian model)?
A. No force is required to keep the ball moving
B. The force of the ball's inertia
C. The force of the ball's momentum
D. The force of the hit   E. Something else (specify)

C2T.4 A cart moving at speed v_0 collides with, and subsequently sticks to, an identical cart at rest. After the collision, the coupled carts are observed to move with a speed of $\frac{1}{2}v_0$ in the same direction that the originally moving cart was moving. This experiment is consistent with which of the following momentum models?
A. the "momentum = speed" model
B. the "momentum = mass times speed" model
C. the "momentum = arrow" model
D. *A* and *B*   E. *B* and *C*   T. all three   F. none

C2T.5 Two moving objects approach each other from opposite directions, collide, and stick together. After the collision, the objects are observed to be at rest. This experiment is consistent with which of the momentum models? (Use the answers in the previous problem.)

C2T.6 An object moving with speed v_0 due north hits an identical object moving with speed v_0 due west and they stick together. According to the momentum arrow model, in what direction will the coupled objects move afterwards?
A. north   C. northwest   E. other (specify)
B. west   D. southeast   F. the model doesn't apply
T. the objects will be at rest after the collision

HOMEWORK PROBLEMS

BASIC

C2B.1 If you say to a friend on the phone "I'll be over in half a kilosec," how many minutes will your friend wait?

C2B.2 Show that 1.00 m/s = 2.24 mi/h .

C2B.3 What is the speed of light in furlongs per fortnight? (You can find the speed of light on the inside front cover of the text. 1 furlong = 1/8 mi = length of a typical furrow in a medieval farm, and 1 fortnight = 14 days.)

C2B.4 A light-year is the distance that light travels in a year. Find this distance in both miles and meters. (The speed of light is $c = 3.00 \times 10^8$ m/s.)

C2B.5 Imagine that we perform the experiment described in Figure C2.4 to determine an unknown object's mass m. A reference object with a mass of 0.50 kg is given a speed of 1.00 m/s initially. The coupled objects after the collision are observed to have a speed of 0.25 m/s after the collision. What is the unknown object's mass m?

C2B.6 The density of water is very nearly 1000 kg/m³. Show that a cube of water that is 10 cm on a side has a mass of 1 kg, and that a cube of water 1 cm on a side has a mass of 1 g. (This was originally the international *definition* of the kilogram, enabling one to create a standard kilogram without having to go to France. The standard was redefined when it became clear that difficulty of measuring volumes of water precisely makes defining the unit of mass in terms of an actual specific object more reproducible.)

C2B.7 Compare the numerical value of the momentum of 20-kg anvil falling at 30 m/s with that of a 10-metric-ton railroad boxcar moving at 5 cm/s (1 metric ton = 1000 kg). (Be sure that you state your result with the correct units!)

SYNTHETIC

C2S.1 How big on a side would a cube of rock have to be to be more massive than you are? (*Hint:* Rock has a density of roughly three times that of water. See problem C2B.6.)

C2S.2 A cart with a mass m moving with an initial speed $v_0 = 1.00$ m/s hits a cart of mass $3m$ at rest. After the collision, the more massive cart is observed to move at a speed of $v_B = 0.50$ m/s in the same direction as the original motion of the other cart. According to the arrow model of momentum, what is the speed v_A and direction of motion of the lighter cart after the collision?

C2S.3 A cart with a mass m moving at an initial speed $v_0 = 1.00$ m/s hits a cart of unknown mass M at rest. After the collision, the first cart rebounds backwards (compared to

the original direction it was moving) with a speed $v_A = 0.60$ m/s, while the cart with unknown mass moves forward with a speed $v_B = 0.40$ m/s. According to the arrow model of momentum, what is the unknown mass M?

C2S.4 A cart with mass m moving at an initial speed of $v_A = 1.00$ m/s to the right hits a cart with mass $2m$ moving at a speed $v_B = 0.75$ m/s to the left. The two carts stick together after the collision. Use the arrow model of momentum to predict both the final speed v_f and the direction of motion (right or left) of the coupled carts.

C2S.5 A hockey puck with mass m sliding on frictionless ice at an initial speed of $v_A = 1.00$ m/s due north collides with an identical puck sliding with speed $v_B = 1.00$ m/s due west. Imagine that the pucks stick together after the collision. Use the arrow model and the pythagorean theorem to determine their joint speed v_f and their direction of motion (according to a compass) after the collision.

C2S.6 Imagine that a cart with mass m moving at a speed of v_0 collides with an identical cart at rest and they stick together. The actual experimental results in a case like this will be that the coupled carts will move after the collision at a speed of $\frac{1}{2}v_0$. Now, we could look at the final situation as either being two separate carts, each having mass m and moving at a speed of $\frac{1}{2}v_0$, or as a *single* object of mass $2m$ moving at that speed. Argue that if we assume that the numerical value of an object's momentum is proportional to its speed and that it must be conserved no matter which way we look at the final situation, then momentum must also be proportional to mass. (Therefore, momentum's proportionality to mass is really a *logical necessity* if we are to be able to treat a composite object as if it were a single object whose mass is the sum of the masses of its parts.)

RICH-CONTEXT

C2R.1 Estimate the total mass of the water in the earth's oceans. (*Hints:* About what fraction of the earth's surface is ocean? The greatest depths in the ocean are about 11 km: what might one estimate the average depth to be?)

C2R.2 Imagine that you have two carts, one with known mass m_0 and one with unknown mass m. Imagine that you put a spring between the carts and then push the carts together to compress the spring. When you then release the carts from rest, they will move away from each other with speeds you can measure. Apply the arrow model of momentum to this situation to come up with a *simpler* definition of mass than the one given in section C2.6. (I couldn't give this definition there because we hadn't yet developed an arrow model for momentum.)

ANSWERS TO EXERCISES

C2X.1 through **C2X.5** B, A, C, B, C respectively.
C2X.6 Both the ideas that "inertia" is a force and that a force is required to keep an object moving are non-newtonian, common-sense notions.
C2X.7 (a) A contact interaction between the player's foot and the ball gets the ball going. **(b)** No interaction is required to keep the ball moving. **(c)** Friction interactions acting between the ball and the air and ground slow the ball down.
C2X.8 In the collision shown in Figure C2.2, it doesn't matter whether the momentum is v_0 before and after the

collision or mv_0 before and after: it is still conserved.
C2X.9 Divide both sides of the equation on the left by $m_0 v_f$ and then subtract one from both sides.
C2X.10 The kilogram is a unit of *mass*, not weight.
C2X.11 In the collisions shown in Figures C2.2 and C2.3, all momentum arrows before and after the collisions happen to point in the same direction. In such a case, adding the arrows yields the same numerical result as simply adding the values of mv for each object, so our previous calculations showing that momentum is conserved in each case are still correct.

C3

VECTORS

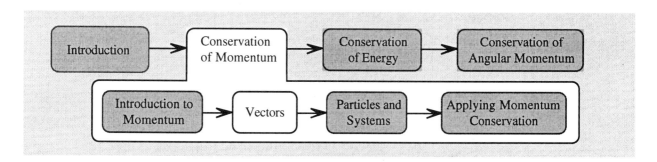

C3.1 OVERVIEW

In the last chapter, we saw that *momentum* is best described by an arrow-like quantity, that is, a quantity with both a direction (indicated by the arrow) and a magnitude (indicated by the arrow's length). We call such quantities *vectors.* In order to further develop the momentum-arrow model, we need to understand more about how to handle vector quantities. The purpose of this chapter is to give you an introduction to vector mathematics.

The tools and definitions developed in this chapter will not only provide a foundation for discussing the arrow model of momentum in its full, three-dimensional glory in chapter C5, but also for discussing vector quantities that we will encounter later in the course (*forces, velocities, accelerations, gravitational fields, electric* and *magnetic fields,* and *currents* are all examples of concepts that must be described by vector quantities).

Here is an overview of this chapter's sections.

C3.2 *DISPLACEMENT VECTORS* explores the character and properties of displacement vectors, the most fundamental kind of vector quantity.

C3.3 *REFERENCE FRAMES* discusses how we can define and establish a three-dimensional coordinate system or *reference frame* in space to help us quantify vector directions.

C3.4 *COMPONENTS* shows how we can use a reference frame to describe a displacement vector (magnitude *and* direction) entirely in terms of three signed numbers called *components.*

C3.5 *SYMBOLS, TERMS, AND CONVENTIONS* defines the symbols and technical terms that we will use when describing vectors in this text.

C3.6 *VECTORS IN ONE AND TWO DIMENSIONS* discusses how working with vectors becomes simpler if all vectors of interest in a given situation are confined to a line or a plane.

C3.7 *VECTOR OPERATIONS* describes how to add and subtract vectors and how to multiply a vector by a number.

C3.8 *VECTORS HAVE UNITS* discusses how we can define a vector's *units* and how these units flow through vector equations.

*** *MATH SKILLS: A REVIEW OF TRIGONOMETRY* provides a compact review of the trigonometric skills one commonly uses when working with vectors.

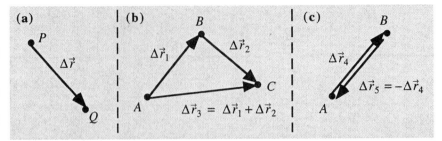

Figure C3.1: (a) We can draw the displacement vector representing the shift from point P to point Q as an arrow. **(b)** The definition of the sum of two displacement vectors. **(c)** Two vectors with equal magnitudes and opposite directions are like numbers with opposite signs.

C3.2 DISPLACEMENT VECTORS

As suggested in the previous chapter, a **vector** is a physical quantity involving a numerical value (called the vector's **magnitude**) and an associated **direction** in space. Many physical quantities and concepts, including *position, displacement, velocity, acceleration, force, momentum, angular momentum, torque,* and so on are most naturally described by vectors.

A displacement quantifies a *shift* in position

The most fundamental kind of vector is a *displacement vector*: the properties of all other vectors are defined by analogy to the properties of this vector. A **displacement vector** quantifies a shift in position from one point in space to another. We can completely specify such a shift by describing the *direction* of the shift and the *distance* from the first point to the second, so a displacement is indeed a vector quantity with both magnitude and direction. (In Latin, *vector* means "carrier": the displacement vector *carries* us from one point to the other.)

I will use the symbol $\Delta\vec{r}$ to represent displacement vectors in this text (for reasons that will become clearer in the next chapter). The little arrow over the symbol is meant to remind us that this symbol represents a vector quantity that has a direction as well as a magnitude. We can *visualize* a displacement vector as an *arrow* stretching from the first point to the second point (see Figure C3.1a): the length and direction of this arrow represent the magnitude and direction of the vector respectively.

The sum of displacements

We can learn some things about the properties of general vectors from the properties of displacement vectors without any further mathematical ado. For example, imagine that you walk from point A to point B (displacement $\Delta\vec{r}_1$ in Figure C3.1b), and then walk from point B to point C (displacement $\Delta\vec{r}_2$ in the same figure). Your *total* displacement from point A at this point is the displacement vector $\Delta\vec{r}_3$ that stretches from point A to point C. It makes sense, then, to think of $\Delta\vec{r}_3$ as being the *sum* of the displacements $\Delta\vec{r}_1$ and $\Delta\vec{r}_2$. We will define the sum of arbitrary vectors analogously in section C3.7.

Opposing displacements

Note that according to this definition the displacement from point A to point B (displacement $\Delta\vec{r}_4$ in Figure C3.1c) and the displacement from B back to A (displacement $\Delta\vec{r}_5$) sum to *no* displacement (since you end up where you started). This means that vectors with equal magnitudes pointing in opposite directions add to zero just like positive and negative numbers whose absolute values are the same add to zero: opposing vectors are like negatives of each other.

C3.3 REFERENCE FRAMES

A reference frame as a cubical lattice (jungle gym)

We could more easily work with vectors if we could express them entirely in terms of numbers (instead of having to deal with the vector's magnitude and direction separately). We can do this, but we first need to establish a **reference frame** (or **coordinate system**). I will formally define these terms shortly, but for now, let us imagine a reference frame as being a huge cubical lattice of meter sticks, like a playground jungle gym (see Figure C3.2a).

Origin and coordinate axes

Every reference frame must have an **origin** (an arbitrarily chosen lattice point that we will use as a base for determining the positions of other points). The three mutually perpendicular lines of connected meter sticks that intersect this origin point define what we will call the reference frame's **x, y** and **z**

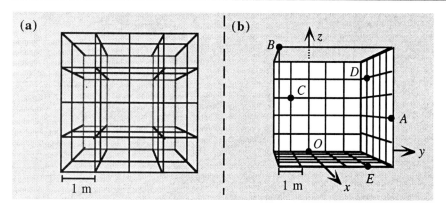

Figure C3.2: (a) A reference frame visualized as a cubical lattice of meter sticks (like a jungle gym). **(b)** A frame with axis directions and an origin specified. (For the sake of clarity, not all of the lattice has been drawn in.)

axes. The origin divides each axis into two parts, one of which we arbitrarily choose to be the *positive* side of the axis (the other then becomes the *negative* side). If we stand at the origin and point toward the positive side of the x axis, we are pointing in what we will call the **+x direction**; the **−x direction** is the opposite direction. The **±y** and **±z directions** are defined analogously. On a diagram of the reference frame, the positive directions are conventionally indicated by an arrow labeled with an x, y, *or* z (see Figure C3.2b).

Once we have defined the origin and axis directions, we can uniquely specify any point in the lattice by counting how many meters we have to travel along each of the lattice directions to go from the origin to the point in question. For example, to get to point A in Figure C3.2b from the origin, we have to travel 5.0 m in the $+x$ direction, 3.0 m in the $+y$ direction and 2.0 m in the $+z$ direction. These three numbers are called a point's **coordinates**; they are conventionally listed in brackets in the order [x coordinate, y coordinate, z coordinate]. The coordinates of point A are thus [+5.0 m, +3.0 m, +2.0 m].

If we have to travel in the negative direction along any axis direction to get from the origin to a point, we signify this by making the corresponding coordinate negative. For example, the coordinates of point B in Figure C3.2b are [+5.0 m, −2.0 m, +5.0 m], point C has coordinates [0 m, −1.0 m, +3.0 m], and so on. This scheme gives every point in space a *unique* set of coordinates.

We have considerable freedom in setting up reference frames. We can:

1. Attach a frame to *any* object that we please,
2. Choose which is the positive side of each axis,
3. Orient the frame any way that we like, and
4. Specify whatever origin is convenient.

We have this freedom because a reference frame is *not* part of the physical world but rather is a *mental construct* that *we* superimpose on physical space to help us quantify position.

In practice, in this text we will follow certain *conventions* that limit our choices but make things easier. (1) We will discuss the consequences of attaching reference frames to different kinds of objects (including moving objects) in Units *N* and *R*, but for now (unless explicitly stated otherwise), we will assume that all reference frames are attached to the surface of the earth. (2) No matter how we orient a reference frame, we will *always* choose the positive sides of the three axes so that if you point your (extended) right index finger in the direction of the $+x$ axis and your (bent) right second finger in the direction of the $+y$ axis, your extended right thumb will automatically point in the direction of the $+z$ axis: we will call such a reference frame a **right-handed reference frame**. (3) While other orientations are acceptable, we will say that a right-handed frame on the surface of the earth is in **standard orientation** if its $+x$, $+y$, and $+z$ directions point *east*, *north*, and *up* respectively. (4) There are *no* conventions constraining our choice of origin because it is advantageous to have the freedom to choose whatever origin is *most convenient* for solving a given problem.

Position coordinates

Things about reference frames that we can choose

Reference frame conventions (right-handed frames and standard orientation)

It is important to describe the choices that you make

Because you still have complete freedom to choose an origin, if you don't clearly *specify* your choice of origin when writing a problem solution, you are likely to confuse your reader. This goes *doubly* if you choose to violate any of the conventions discussed. For example, you are working a problem involving something moving along a line due northwest, you may find it easier if you orient your reference frame so that (say) the $+x$ direction points northwest. This is fine, but be sure to *describe* your non-standard choice in your solution.

It is important to be clear about these things because the coordinates of an object are *different* in frames having different origins and orientations. For example, a point might have position coordinates [3 m, 5 m, –2 m] in one frame, [3 m, 5 m, 3 m] in a frame with the same orientation but whose origin is lower by 5 m, and [5 m, –3 m, –2 m] in a frame with the same origin as the first but rotated 90° counterclockwise around the z axis. The point is that coordinates are *ambiguous* unless we clearly describe the frame's characteristics.

A real-life reference frame

Of course, physicists do not *really* use huge cubical lattices of meter sticks to quantify an object's position: this is meant as a metaphor to help you understand how a reference frame *works*. There are many ways to actually measure position coordinates. An interesting contemporary example of a real reference frame is the **Global Positioning System** (GPS). This system consists of a network of 21 satellites in circular orbits around the earth. Each satellite carries its own atomic clock and continually broadcasts a signal that identifies itself, describes its path, and states the time registered on its clock. Users of the system carry a device that detects these satellite signals, decodes them, and processes the information. By comparing the *arrival* time of signals from each satellite in view at a given time with that satellite's own report of when the signal was sent, a receiver anywhere on the earth can compute its own position to an accuracy of about 1 m in all three coordinates. Originally created for military applications, the GPS is now also used to locate airplanes, ships, small boats, and trucks. Geophysicists also use the GPS to monitor changes in the shape of the earth's crust that might indicate an impending earthquake or volcanic eruption.

A general definition of a *reference frame*

A more general definition of a **reference frame** thus might be "a cubical lattice *or its functional equivalent* superimposed on space in order to quantify positions." As long as we get the *same results* that we would get with a cubical lattice, it doesn't matter how we actually measure these positions.

Exercise C3X.1: List the coordinates of points D and E in Figure C3.2b.

Exercise C3X.2: The x, y, and z axes of a reference frame on the surface of the earth point *north*, *up*, and *west* respectively. Is the frame right-handed?

Exercise C3X.3: A point's position coordinates are [2 m, 2 m, –1 m] in a frame in standard orientation on the earth's surface. What are its coordinates in a frame whose origin is 2 m west of the first frame's origin and whose x, y, and z axes point south, up and west respectively? (*Hint:* Draw a picture!)

C3.4   COMPONENTS

The components of a displacement vector

Consider two points A and B whose coordinates in a given reference frame are [2 m, 3 m, 1 m] and [0 m, –2 m, 5 m] respectively. To shift position from point A to point B, we have to travel 2 m in the $-x$ direction, 5 m in the $-y$ direction, and 4 m in the $+z$ direction. The triplet of numbers [–2 m, –5 m, +4 m] *completely* describes how one can get to point B from point A in the given reference frame. (Note that each of these numbers is simply the difference between the corresponding coordinates of B and A). These numbers thus completely specify the displacement *vector* from point A to point B (see Figure C3.3).

Any displacement vector can be similarly described by such an ordered set of three numbers. We call the ordered triplet of numbers [Δx, Δy, Δz] that describe a

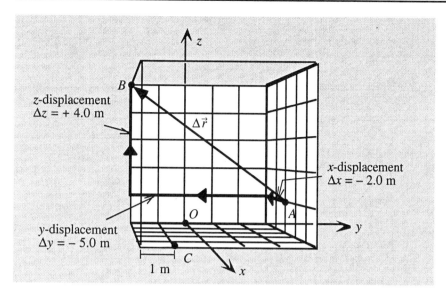

Figure C3.3: An illustration of how given the displacement vector between points *A* and *B* , we can determine its components, and how given the components we can reconstruct the vector.

displacement vector $\Delta \vec{r}$ the **components** of $\Delta \vec{r}$ (collectively) and the **x-displacement**, **y-displacement**, and **z-displacement** (individually).

Given the components of a displacement vector, we can determine the vector's *direction* by reconstructing the vector arrow (as shown in Figure C3.3). We can also compute its *magnitude* (the distance between the initial and final points of the shift) using the pythagorean theorem:

Finding the magnitude of the displacement vector

$$\text{(magnitude of } \Delta \vec{r}) = \sqrt{\Delta x^2 + \Delta y^2 + \Delta z^2} \qquad \text{(C3.1)}$$

Alternatively, if we are given the magnitude and direction of a displacement, we can draw its arrow with the appropriate length and direction in the reference frame grid and determine its components. Stating a displacement vector's components is thus *equivalent* to describing it in terms of its magnitude and direction: knowing the components, we can find its magnitude and direction and vice versa.

Exercise C3X.4: What is the magnitude of the vector $\Delta \vec{r}$ in Figure C3.3?

Exercise C3X.5: What are the components and magnitude of the displacement vector from point *A* to point *C* in Figure C3.3?

C3.5   SYMBOLS, TERMS, AND CONVENTIONS

Having discussed the properties of displacement vectors in some detail, we are now ready to discuss the features of more general vector quantities. In physics, a **vector** is *any* quantity that has a numerical *magnitude* and an associated *direction* in space. As discussed before, *many* quantities that we will encounter in this course are best described by vectors.

Basic definition of a vector

Even so, not all physical quantities are usefully described by vectors. We call any physical quantity that we can adequately describe with a single number and no associated direction a **scalar**. *Time, mass, energy, temperature,* and *electrical charge* are examples of scalar quantities in physics.

Scalar quantities

Since we handle scalar and vector quantities in very different ways mathematically, it is *essential* to keep these quantities distinct. The conventional notation for a *scalar* quantity is a simple italic letter: the symbols for time, mass, and energy (for example) are t, m, and E, respectively. On the other hand, in this text, any symbol with an arrow over it represents a *vector* quantity: the symbols for velocity, force, and momentum (for example) are $\vec{v}$, $\vec{F}$, and $\vec{p}$, respectively.

Distinct notation for vector and scalar quantities

(You should know that it is common in *printed* material to use boldface letters, like **v**, **F**, and **p**, to represent vectors. While this looks nice and clean in print, (1) it is not easy to reproduce in handwriting, and (2) evidence suggests that many beginners do not even *see* these boldface letters as being different, and thus confuse vectors with scalars: this adds unnecessarily to their difficulties with physics. I will *always* use the arrow notation in this text.)

Notation and short names for vector components

Like a displacement vector, *any* vector quantity can be represented by an ordered set of three signed numbers that we call **components**. If the symbol for a certain vector is $\vec{c}$, then its components are conventionally written c_x, c_y, and c_z. The vector $\vec{c}$ can be described by listing its components (either vertically or horizontally) as an ordered triplet enclosed in square brackets: $\vec{c} = [c_x, c_y, c_z]$. For example, the components of a force vector $\vec{F}$ are written $[F_x, F_y, F_z]$, the components of a momentum vector $\vec{p}$ are written $[p_x, p_y, p_z]$, and so on. (Note that the standard notation for displacement vectors violates this convention: the components of $\Delta\vec{r}$ are simply $[\Delta x, \Delta y, \Delta z]$, not $[\Delta r_x, \Delta r_y, \Delta r_z]$.)

Conventionally, we call the individual components of a given vector the *x*, *y*, and *z components* of (vector name). I will also call these components the *x*-(vector name), the *y*-(vector name), and the *z*-(vector name) respectively. For example, we can call the quantity p_x either "the *x* component of the object's momentum" (its formal name) or "the object's *x*-momentum" (for short). Using the short names will save us a lot of time and writing.

Definition and notation for the magnitude of a vector

Every vector quantity has a *magnitude* and a *direction*. In analogy to the magnitude of a displacement vector, the magnitude of *any* vector $\vec{c}$ is computed using the pythagorean theorem:

$$c \equiv \text{mag}(\vec{c}) \equiv \sqrt{c_x^2 + c_y^2 + c_z^2} \qquad (C3.2)$$

This definition implies that the magnitude of *any* vector can *never* be a negative number, any more than the distance between two points can be negative.

Equation C3.2 displays all three of the notations that we will use for the magnitude of a vector in this class. The *conventional* notation for the magnitude of a vector $\vec{c}$ is simply c, the same letter without the arrow. This notation can be problematic because while it is easy to write, it also makes it too easy to forget that c is connected to a vector quantity (particularly if the vector $\vec{c}$ is not mentioned anywhere nearby). Particularly for people unfamiliar with using vectors, both the connection and distinction between a vector and its magnitude are *very* important to keep in mind. Because of this, I will use the mag($\vec{c}$) notation often in unit C, and strongly urge you to do the same. This will help you make a habit of thinking correctly about the connection and distinction between vectors and their magnitudes. In subsequent units, I will use the longer notation only when there is a real possibility of ambiguity otherwise.

What components mean: How to recreate a vector arrow from components

A vector's components "represent" a vector by telling us how to reconstruct it, in analogy to how we reconstructed the displacement vector in Figure C3.3. To reconstruct an arrow on a diagram that represents an *arbitrary* vector $\vec{c}$, we would pick a starting point, move a distance on the diagram proportional to $|c_x|$ in the +*x* direction if c_x is positive or the –*x* direction if c_x is negative, and then repeat for the other two components to find the arrow's ending point. The resulting arrow in the diagram points in the same direction in space as $\vec{c}$ does and has a length proportional to the magnitude of $\vec{c}$, and thus visually and mathematically *represents* the vector $\vec{c}$ even if $\vec{c}$ is something like a force or momentum vector that is *not* a real displacement vector (but rather something more abstract). We will use such visual representations of vectors often in this text. Note that I will always label such arrow representations with the symbol for the vector (not the symbol for the magnitude, as you may have done before).

It is *crucial* that you understand that a vector component is *a simple signed number*, and not a vector itself. Using notation like $\vec{c}_x$, $\vec{c}_y$, and $\vec{c}_z$ for components is *very* misleading: it suggests that $\vec{c}_x$ (for example) is a vector instead of being an ordinary number. *Please avoid this kind of notation.* I suppose that the notation is tempting because in a certain sense, the sign of c_x, in conjunc-

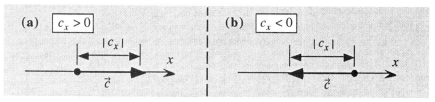

tion with its subscript, *does* implicitly specify a direction. However, mathematically, c_x is (and always will be treated in this text) as a simple signed number.

C3.6 VECTORS IN ONE AND TWO DIMENSIONS

In many practical circumstances, all vectors of interest lie either entirely along a certain *line* (as in the situations considered in the last chapter) or entirely in a certain *plane*. In these cases, the relationship between a vector's components and its magnitude and direction is simpler than it is in three dimensions.

Vectors in one dimension

If all vectors of interest in a given situation lie along a given *line*, we can generally orient our reference frame so that one axis coincides with this line. While we could choose to align *any* axis with the line of interest, we *conventionally* align the x axis with the line if the line is (at least mostly) horizontal and with the z axis if the line is (at least nearly) vertical.

If we choose to align the x axis with this line (for example), then the y and z components of any vector $\vec{c}$ are identically zero and the vector is *entirely* described by its x component c_x: the *sign* of c_x specifies the vector's direction, and its absolute value $|c_x|$ is equal to the vector's magnitude (see Figure C3.4). If we had chosen to align the z axis with the line, then it would be c_y and c_x that would be zero and c_z that would completely describe the vector.

It is more common for all vectors of interest to be confined to a certain two-dimensional plane. In such a case, we can generally orient our reference frame so that one axis is *perpendicular* to this plane. The component of any vector along this perpendicular axis is then identically zero, and all vectors are completely described by their *two* components in the plane of interest. (We conventionally choose the z axis to be the perpendicular axis if the plane of interest is essentially horizontal, and the y axis to be the perpendicular axis if the plane is vertical.)

Vectors in two dimensions

In this case, we can use simple trigonometry to translate back and forth between the components of a vector and its magnitude and direction. For the sake of argument, assume that we have oriented our frame so that the z axis is the perpendicular axis and thus all vectors lie in the xy plane. As illustrated in Figure C3.5, if we draw lines from the tip of the vector perpendicular to and intersecting the x and y axes, we form a pair of right triangles. The length of the hypotenuse of these triangles is the magnitude of the vector: the lengths of the legs of these triangles correspond to the *absolute values* of the vector's x and y components (absolute values because the *length* of a given leg is always a positive number, while the corresponding *component* may be positive or negative). The *sign* of a given component is indicated by whether the vector is aligned more closely with the positive or negative direction of the corresponding axis.

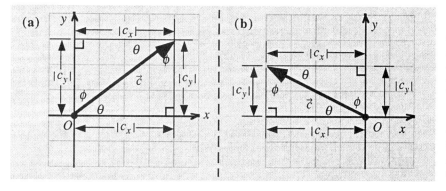

Figure C3.5: These drawings illustrate the relationship between the components of a two-dimensional vector and its magnitude and direction. If we draw perpendicular lines from the tip of the vector to the axes, we form two right triangles. The length of the *hypotenuse* of each is equal to the *magnitude* of the vector; the lengths of the *legs* of the triangle are equal to the *absolute values* of the vector's components.

Figure C3.5: (This is the same as Figure C3.5 on the previous page. It is repeated here so that references on this page will be easier to understand.)

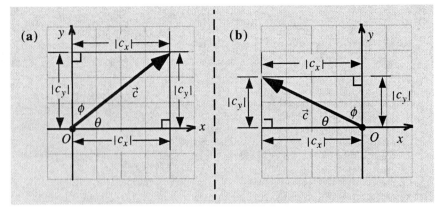

Converting magnitude and direction to components

Say we know the magnitude and direction of a vector $\vec{c}$ (where the direction is expressed in terms of either the angle θ that $\vec{c}$ makes with the x axis or the angle ϕ that it makes with the y axis). From basic trigonometry, the components of $\vec{c}$ have the absolute values (check Figure C3.5 to verify this):

$$|c_x| = \mathrm{mag}(\vec{c})\cos\theta = c\cos\theta \qquad\qquad \text{(C3.3a)}$$
$$|c_y| = \mathrm{mag}(\vec{c})\sin\theta = c\sin\theta \qquad\qquad \text{(C3.3b)}$$

or

$$|c_x| = \mathrm{mag}(\vec{c})\sin\phi = c\sin\phi \qquad\qquad \text{(C3.4a)}$$
$$|c_y| = \mathrm{mag}(\vec{c})\cos\phi = c\cos\phi \qquad\qquad \text{(C3.4b)}$$

(assuming that θ and ϕ are less than 90°). We can determine the *signs* of these components by *drawing a picture* of the vector according to the direction information given and seeing whether the vector is aligned more with the positive or negative direction along each axis. The components of the vector $\vec{c}$ shown in Figure C3.5a are both *positive*, but for the vector $\vec{c}$ shown in Figure C3.5b, c_x is negative and c_y is positive.

Converting components to magnitude and direction

On the other hand, if we know the components of $\vec{c}$, we can calculate its magnitude and direction as follows:

$$c \equiv \mathrm{mag}(\vec{c}) \equiv \sqrt{c_x^2 + c_y^2} \qquad\qquad \text{(C3.5)}$$

$$\theta = \tan^{-1}\left|\frac{c_y}{c_x}\right|, \qquad \phi = \tan^{-1}\left|\frac{c_x}{c_y}\right| \qquad\qquad \text{(C3.6)}$$

where $\tan^{-1}$ is the **inverse tangent** (sometimes called the **arctangent**) of the quantity that follows. Note that the angles generated by equation C3.6 are the angles to the *nearest* sides of the x and y axes respectively. We would report the direction of the vector in Figure C3.5a as being "37° counterclockwise from the $+x$ direction" or "53° clockwise from the $+y$ direction," and the direction of the vector in Figure C3.5b as being "22° clockwise from the $-x$ direction" or "68° counterclockwise from the $+y$ direction." Note again that you have to *draw a picture* of the vector to be able to state these directions correctly.

In a reference frame in standard orientation on the surface of the earth, the directions of these vectors could be described more concisely: the vector in Figure C3.5a might be described as being "37° north of east" or "53° east of north."

Exercise C3X.6: A displacement vector $\Delta\vec{r}_1$ has a magnitude of 5.0 m and is oriented 37° south of west in the horizontal plane. What are its components?

Exercise C3X.7: A displacement vector $\Delta\vec{r}_2$ has components $\Delta x_2 = 6.2$ m, and $\Delta y_2 = -1.5$ m. What is its magnitude and direction?

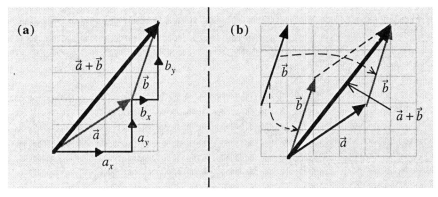

Figure **C3.6: (a)** I am representing vector components here by lines with direction indicators in the middle to depict the "walks" we must do to reconstruct the vector arrow. Note that the walk in the x direction required to reconstruct $\vec{a}+\vec{b}$ is the sum of the walks corresponding to a_x and b_x, as claimed by equation C3.7. **(b)** Vector arrows on a diagram are *movable*: vector $\vec{b}$ can be moved from its original position (shown in black) to either of the positions shown in gray (or anywhere else!). This diagram also illustrates the parallelogram method of constructing a vector sum.

C3.7 VECTOR OPERATIONS

The sum of two vectors

The **vector sum** of two vectors $\vec{a}$ and $\vec{b}$ produces a new vector $\vec{c}$ whose components are the sums of the corresponding components of $\vec{a}$ and $\vec{b}$. That is,

$$c_x = a_x + b_x \qquad (C3.7a)$$
$$c_y = a_y + b_y \qquad (C3.7b)$$
$$c_z = a_z + b_z \qquad (C3.7c)$$

We commonly write vectors by listing its components in a column enclosed by square brackets. Using this notation, equations C3.7 can be written:

$$\begin{bmatrix} c_x \\ c_y \\ c_z \end{bmatrix} = \begin{bmatrix} a_x \\ a_y \\ a_z \end{bmatrix} + \begin{bmatrix} b_x \\ b_y \\ b_z \end{bmatrix} \quad \text{where} \quad \begin{bmatrix} a_x \\ a_y \\ a_z \end{bmatrix} + \begin{bmatrix} b_x \\ b_y \\ b_z \end{bmatrix} \equiv \begin{bmatrix} a_x + b_x \\ a_y + b_y \\ a_z + b_z \end{bmatrix} \qquad (C3.8)$$

You should *always* remember that a column-vector equation like C3.8 is equivalent to three independent equations (one equation for each row) like C3.7.

Constructing the vector sum geometrically

Figure C3.6a shows (in two dimensions at least) that the vector sum of two displacement vectors defined this way is equivalent to the sum of displacements defined in section C3.2. Quite generally, we can construct the arrow $\vec{c}$ representing the vector sum of $\vec{a}$ and $\vec{b}$ from the arrows representing $\vec{a}$ and $\vec{b}$ by

1. placing the tail of $\vec{b}$ at the head of $\vec{a}$,
2. drawing $\vec{c}$ from the tail of $\vec{a}$ to the head of $\vec{b}$.

Note that vector arrows on a diagram are *movable*: since a vector expresses only a magnitude and direction (not a starting point), a vector arrow means the same thing no matter where it is placed. If the tail of $\vec{b}$ does not coincide with the head of $\vec{a}$ originally, we can simply move $\vec{b}$ so that it does (see Figure C3.6b).

Figure C3.6b also shows that we can also construct the sum by placing the vectors tail to tail and constructing a parallelogram whose sides are the two vectors. The vector sum stretches along the parallelogram's diagonal as shown.

The vector inverse

We can construct the **inverse** $-\vec{a}$ of a vector $\vec{a}$ by changing the sign of each of its components:

$$\text{if} \quad \vec{a} = \begin{bmatrix} a_x \\ a_y \\ a_z \end{bmatrix}, \quad \text{then} \quad -\vec{a} \equiv \begin{bmatrix} -a_x \\ -a_y \\ -a_z \end{bmatrix} \qquad (C3.9)$$

Note that the *magnitude* of $-\vec{a}$ will be the same as that of $\vec{a}$ (since we square the components when we compute the magnitude, their sign disappears). Geometrically, $-\vec{a}$ will be represented by an arrow whose length is the same as that for $\vec{a}$, but which points in the opposite direction (see Figures C3.7).

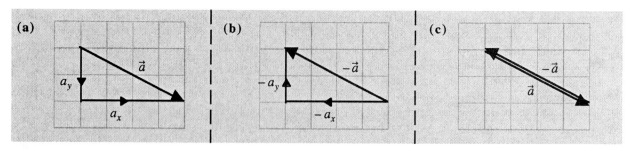

Figure C3.7: (a) and **(b)** A vector and its inverse have equal magnitudes and opposite directions (note that the "walks" required to reconstruct $-\vec{a}$ have the same lengths but opposite directions to the walks required to reconstruct $\vec{a}$). **(c)** The sum of a vector and its inverse is zero.

Vector subtraction

The vector sum of any vector and its inverse is the zero vector:

$$\vec{a} + (-\vec{a}) = \begin{bmatrix} a_x \\ a_y \\ a_z \end{bmatrix} + \begin{bmatrix} -a_x \\ -a_y \\ -a_z \end{bmatrix} \equiv \begin{bmatrix} a_x - a_x \\ a_y - a_y \\ a_z - a_z \end{bmatrix} = \begin{bmatrix} 0 \\ 0 \\ 0 \end{bmatrix} \tag{C3.10}$$

(see Figure C3.7c). Thus $-\vec{a}$ is to $\vec{a}$ what an ordinary number is to its negative.

The **vector difference** $\vec{b} - \vec{a}$ between two vectors $\vec{a}$ and $\vec{b}$ is defined (as you might expect) to be the vector sum of $\vec{b}$ and $-\vec{a}$ (see Figure C3.8a):

$$\vec{b} - \vec{a} \equiv \vec{b} + (-\vec{a}) = \begin{bmatrix} b_x \\ b_y \\ b_z \end{bmatrix} + \begin{bmatrix} -a_x \\ -a_y \\ -a_z \end{bmatrix} \equiv \begin{bmatrix} b_x - a_x \\ b_y - a_y \\ b_z - a_z \end{bmatrix} \tag{C3.11}$$

The difference $\vec{b} - \vec{a}$ can also be constructed by placing $\vec{a}$ and $\vec{b}$ tail-to-tail and drawing an arrow from the head of $\vec{a}$ to the head of $\vec{b}$. (This uses the fact that $\vec{a} + (\vec{b} - \vec{a}) = \vec{b}$: see Figure C3.8b.) This construction technique can be interpreted as describing how $\vec{a}$ would have to *change* to *become* $\vec{b}$. We will use this interpretation of the vector difference extensively in future chapters.

Multiplication by a scalar

When we **multiply** a vector $\vec{a}$ **by a scalar** q, we get a vector $q\vec{a}$ whose components are defined to be the components of $\vec{a}$ *each* multiplied by q:

$$q\vec{a} \equiv q \begin{bmatrix} a_x \\ a_y \\ a_z \end{bmatrix} \equiv \begin{bmatrix} qa_x \\ qa_y \\ qa_z \end{bmatrix} \tag{C3.12}$$

Note that the magnitude of $q\vec{a}$ is $|q|$ times the magnitude of $\vec{a}$:

$$\begin{aligned} \mathrm{mag}(q\vec{a}) &\equiv \sqrt{(qa_x)^2 + (qa_y)^2 + (qa_z)^2} \\ &= \sqrt{q^2(a_x{}^2 + a_y{}^2 + a_z{}^2)} = |q|\,\mathrm{mag}(\vec{a}) \end{aligned} \tag{C3.13}$$

The effect of multiplying a vector by q is thus to *stretch* that vector by the factor $|q|$, but since each component is stretched the same amount, $q\vec{a}$ points in the same direction as $\vec{a}$ (unless q is *negative*, in which case the vector's direction is flipped): see Figure C3.9.

Figure C3.8: (a) Subtracting a vector is defined to be the same as adding its inverse. **(b)** Alternatively you can imagine the difference as specifying how the subtracted vector $\vec{a}$ would have to *change* to become the other vector $\vec{b}$.

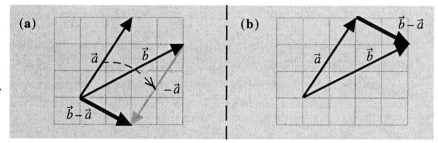

Dividing a vector $\vec{a}$ by a scalar q is the same as multiplying it by $1/q$:

Division by a scalar

$$\frac{\vec{a}}{q} \equiv \left(\frac{1}{q}\right)\vec{a} \qquad\qquad (C3.14)$$

Note that we have *not* defined what it means to multiply a vector by a vector, divide a scalar by a vector, or divide a vector by another vector: at present, neither $\vec{a}\vec{b}$, $q/\vec{a}$, nor $\vec{a}/\vec{b}$ make any sense. (Later we will define two *different* kinds of vector multiplication, but division by a vector *cannot* be defined.)

Operations not defined

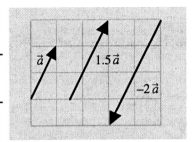

Exercise C3X.8: What are the components of the vector sum of the displacements [5 m, 4 m, 0 m] and [–1 m, –3m, 0 m]?

Exercise C3X.9: Sketch the two vectors in exercise C3X.8, and convince yourself that the geometrical definition of the vector sum yields the same result that you found in that exercise (Figure C3.10 provides a grid for your sketch).

Exercise C3X.10: Subtract the displacement vector [3 m, –5 m, 0 m] from the displacement [2 m, –2 m, 0 m]. Again, sketch the vectors and show that the method illustrated in Figure C3.8b yields an arrow whose components are the same as the ones you calculated directly.

Figure C3.9: Multiplying a vector by a positive scalar changes its length without changing its direction. Multiplying by a negative scalar flips the vector's direction in addition to stretching or shrinking it.

Exercise C3X.11: If we multiply the displacement vector [3 m, –1 m, 0 m] by –4, what do its components become? How does the magnitude of the new vector compare to that of the original vector? How do their directions compare?

C3.8 VECTORS HAVE UNITS

At the fundamental level, a vector is a quantity that has a numerical magnitude and a direction. While it doesn't make any sense to think of the *direction* of a vector as having units (the direction is simply an orientation in space), the numerical *magnitude* of a vector may have units associated with it. For example, a displacement vector's magnitude has units of meters, a momentum vector's magnitude has units of mass times speed (that is, kg·m/s), and so on.

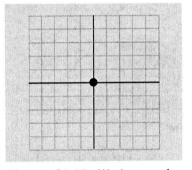

Figure C3.10: Workspace for exercises C3X.9 and C3X.10.

Units of a vector

The definition of the magnitude given by equation C3.2 makes it clear that each of the components of a vector must have the same units as the vector's magnitude (remember that we cannot add quantities that have different units!). So if a displacement's magnitude is measured in meters, *each component* of the displacement must also have units of meters. Therefore, we say that the vector as a *whole* has the same units as its magnitude.

Just as numbers with different units cannot be added, so vectors with different units cannot be added (this follows from the definition of vector addition given by equation C3.7). But just as we can multiply two numbers that have different units, so we can multiply a vector and a scalar having different units, and we treat the multiplied units exactly as if we had multiplied two numbers. For example, we will see in the next chapter that an object's velocity $\vec{v}$ is defined to be a tiny displacement $d\vec{r}$ divided by the tiny time dt that the object takes to travel that displacement: $\vec{v} \equiv d\vec{r}/dt$. Note that $d\vec{r}$ and dt have different units (meters and seconds, respectively), and so their ratio has units of m/s, the same as the units of speed (which turns out to be the *magnitude* of the velocity).

Rules for working with vector units

MATH SKILLS: A Review of Basic Trigonometry

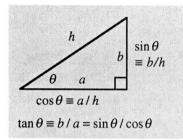

$$\sin\theta \equiv b/h$$
$$\cos\theta \equiv a/h$$
$$\tan\theta \equiv b/a = \sin\theta/\cos\theta$$

Figure C3.11: The most important things to remember about right triangles and trigonometric functions.

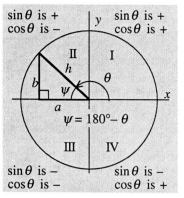

$\sin\theta$ is + $\cos\theta$ is − | $\sin\theta$ is + $\cos\theta$ is +

$\psi = 180° - \theta$

$\sin\theta$ is − $\cos\theta$ is − | $\sin\theta$ is − $\cos\theta$ is +

Figure C3.12: Signs of the trigonometric functions in the four quadrants of the circle.

The purpose of this section is to provide a brief review of trigonometric functions, which we will be using extensively in this course.

Figure C3.11 illustrates the most basic things that you should know about right triangles. The two acute angles in a right triangle add up to 90°. The sine of an angle is "opposite over hypotenuse" (b/h in the diagram), the cosine is "adjacent over hypotenuse" (a/h), and the tangent is "opposite over adjacent" (b/a). Note that since these trigonometric functions are defined in terms of the ratio of two lengths, they are always *unitless* quantities (the length units cancel out).

The trigonometric functions $\sin\theta$, $\cos\theta$, and $\tan\theta$ are actually defined for all angles from 0° to 360°. When defining these functions for angles θ greater than 90°, it is helpful to imagine an xy coordinate system, with the angle measured counterclockwise from the $+x$ axis. The xy plane is divided up into four **quadrants,** which are numbered counterclockwise from the x axis, as shown in Figure C3.12. To define the values of sine and cosine for general angles, we draw a hypotenuse at the angle θ and with length h, and then drop a line from the end of the hypotenuse to the x axis perpendicular to that axis to form a right triangle, as shown in Figure C3.12. The right triangle has an inner acute angle of $\psi = |180° - \theta|$. The functions are defined as before ($\sin\theta = b/h$, $\cos\theta = a/h$, and $\tan\theta = b/a$) except that a is considered negative if it is on the negative side of the x axis and b is considered negative if it is on the negative size of the y axis. This means that $\cos\theta$ is negative in the second quadrant (where $180° > \theta > 90°$) because a is negative), $\sin\theta$ is negative in the third and fourth quadrants (where $270° > \theta > 180°$) because b is negative, and so on.

Looking at Figures C3.11 and C3.12, you should be able to see that

$$\sin(90° - \theta) = \cos\theta \qquad \cos(90° - \theta) = \sin\theta \qquad \text{(C3.15a)}$$
$$\sin(180° - \theta) = \sin\theta \qquad \cos(180° - \theta) = -\cos\theta \qquad \text{(C3.15b)}$$

Negative angles are measured *clockwise* from the $+x$ direction, implying that

$$\sin(-\theta) = -\sin\theta \qquad \cos(-\theta) = \cos\theta \qquad \text{(C3.16)}$$

Scientific calculators make it easy to compute the sine, cosine, or tangent of any angle. It is also possible on most calculators to take the ratio defining the sine of an angle and compute the angle using an **inverse sine** or "arcsin" function (mathematically, $\sin^{-1}[b/h] = \theta$). Similarly, the **inverse cosine** takes a cosine and computes the angle, and **inverse tangent** takes a tangent and computes the angle. You should note that while the computation of a sine, cosine, or tangent from an angle is unambiguous, the inverse operation is not. For example, $\sin^{-1}(0.5) =$ either 30° or 150° (since both of these angles have the same sine). Your calculator will only give you the smaller of these angles: you may have to determine from context if the larger angle is more appropriate.

Here are some important mathematical identities regarding trigonometric functions that you might find useful:

$$\sin^2\theta + \cos^2\theta = 1 \qquad \text{(C3.17)}$$

$$\sin(\theta \pm \phi) = \sin\theta\cos\phi \pm \cos\theta\sin\phi \qquad \text{(C3.18a)}$$
$$\cos(\theta \pm \phi) = \cos\theta\cos\phi \mp \sin\theta\sin\phi \qquad \text{(C3.18b)}$$

$$\cos(0°) = \sin(90°) = 1, \qquad \cos(90°) = \sin(0°) = 0 \qquad \text{(C3.19a)}$$
$$\cos(30°) = \sin(60°) = \sqrt{3/4} = 0.866 \qquad \text{(C3.19b)}$$
$$\cos(45°) = \sin(45°) = \sqrt{1/2} = 0.707 \qquad \text{(C3.19c)}$$
$$\cos(60°) = \sin(30°) = 1/2 \qquad \text{(C3.19d)}$$

All of these equations are worth memorizing, but equations C3.16, C3.17 and C3.19 are especially important to have readily available.

I. DISPLACEMENT VECTORS
  A. A displacement $\Delta\vec{r}$ expresses a *shift in position* (its *direction* points toward the end point from the initial one; its *magnitude* is the distance)
  B. We can represent any displacement vector in a drawing using an arrow

II. REFERENCE FRAMES
  A. You can visualize a frame as a "jungle gym" lattice of meter sticks
    1. Any actual frame must be *functionally equivalent* to such a lattice
    2. The three mutually perpendicular lattice directions define three *axes*
  B. We can freely choose:
    1. The object to which frame is attached (usually the earth's surface)
    2. The orientation of frame in space (*standard orientation* is usual)
    3. Which side of each axis is positive (a *right-handed* choice is usual)
    4. Where the origin is located (no conventional constraints)
  C. A frame is *right-handed* if your extended right index finger, bent 2nd finger, and extended thumb point in the +x, y, z directions, respectively.
  D. *Standard orientation:* the positive x, y, z directions $\rightarrow$ east, north, up
  E. In an given frame, we describe a position by three *coordinates* [x,y,z]
    1. the *absolute value* of each specifies the distance to go along each axis direction from origin
    2. The *sign* of each distinguishes travel in + direction from – direction
  F. A displacement is described by 3 *components* (= coordinate differences)

III. SYMBOLS, TERMS, AND CONVENTIONS
  A. A *vector* is a physical quantity having both magnitude and direction
  B. It is distinct from a *scalar*, which is a simple number *without* direction
  C. Standard symbols for vectors and aspects of vectors:
    1. *Vector*: "arrow-over" notation ($\vec{c}$); contrast with *scalar* (m)
    2. *Components*: letters with x, y, z subscripts ($c_x, c_y,$ and c_z)
      a) The ordered triplet $[c_x, c_y, c_z]$ completely describes a vector
      b) Components are *scalars*: DON'T PUT ARROWS OVER!
    3. *Magnitude*: $c = \text{mag}(\vec{c}) = [c_x^2 + c_y^2 + c_z^2]^{1/2}$ (always ≥ 0!)
  D. *Any* vector can be represented on a diagram by an arrow

IV. VECTORS IN ONE AND TWO DIMENSIONS
  A. If all of the vectors of interest happen to lie along a given line
    1. We can orient our reference frame so one axis lies along that line
    2. A vector is then entirely described by its component along that axis
  B. If all of the vectors of interest happen to lie in a given plane
    1. We can orient our frame so that one axis is $\perp$ to the plane
    2. Then a vector is entirely described by the two components that lie *in* the plane. We can use trigonometry to convert these components to the vector's magnitude and direction and vice versa

V. VECTOR OPERATIONS
  A. To calculate the *sum* of two vectors
    1. Mathematically: Add corresponding components
    2. Geometrically: Place the arrows in a connected sequence, then draw an arrow from the start to the end (vectors are movable!).
  B. To calculate the *inverse* of a vector
    1. Mathematically: Negate the vector's components
    2. Geometrically: reverse the vector's direction
  C. To *subtract* a vector from another: negate the subtracted vector and then add to the other (*or* place the two vectors tail-to-tail and draw arrow from head of subtracted vector to head of other)
  D. To *multiply* a vector by scalar q
    1. Mathematically: Multiply each vector component by the scalar
    2. Geometrically: Multiply the vector's length by the factor |q| and reverse the vector's direction if q is negative
  E. Note that $\vec{a}\vec{b}$, $\vec{a}/\vec{b}$, and $q/\vec{a}$ are *not* defined

GLOSSARY

reference frame: an imaginary cubical lattice (or its functional equivalent) that we superimpose on space in order to quantify an object's position. Reference frames are also called **coordinate systems**.

origin: an arbitrarily-chosen point in a reference frame that we use as the reference position against which all other positions are compared.

x axis, y axis, z axis: names for the three mutually perpendicular lines that go through the origin and whose directions are defined by the lattice structure. We define one side of each of these lines (starting at the origin) to be the positive side and the other to be the negative side.

+x direction: If we stand at the origin and point along the x axis toward the side of the axis we have defined to be its positive side, we are pointing in the $+x$ direction. The **−x direction** is the opposite direction. The **±y direction** and **±z direction** are defined analogously.

right-handed reference frame: a frame whose $x, y,$ and z directions correspond to the directions indicated by a person's right index finger, middle finger, and thumb, respectively, when these fingers are held so that they are mutually perpendicular. Reference frames are conventionally constructed to be right-handed.

standard orientation: a frame on the surface of the earth is in standard orientation if its $x, y,$ and z directions point *east, north,* and *up,* respectively.

coordinates: An ordered set of numbers x, y, z that specify an object's position in a given reference frame by specifying the distance and direction (positive or negative) that one would have to travel along each axis direction to get from the frame's origin to the object.

Global Positioning System (GPS): a contemporary example of an actual reference frame. The system consists of a number of satellites orbiting the earth that constantly radiate signals detailing their position and the time that the signal was sent. By detecting signals from several satellites, a receiver on earth can calculate its own three-dimensional position to within several meters.

vector: any mathematical quantity having both a numerical magnitude and an associated direction. Any vector can be represented graphically by an *arrow* whose direction indicates the vector's direction and whose length is proportional to the vector's magnitude. The standard symbol for a vector in this text is any italic letter with a small arrow placed over it (for example, $\vec{c}, \vec{F}, \vec{p},$ etc.).

scalar: a quantity having *no* associated direction, meaning that it can be adequately represented by a *single* number. The standard symbol for a scalar is a simple italic letter (for example, $m, t, E,$ etc.)

components: a set of three signed numbers that provide an alternative and completely numerical representation of any vector. If a vector's symbol is $\vec{c}$, its components are written $c_x, c_y,$ and c_z, respectively, and the vector itself is described by the ordered triplet $[c_x, c_y, c_z]$.

magnitude: the numerical value associated with a vector. This quantity can be calculated from a vector's components in a given reference frame by squaring the components, adding them, and taking the square root (in a manner analogous to the pythagorean theorem). The magnitude of a vector $\vec{c}$ is either written mag($\vec{c}$) or simply c.

displacement vector: a vector indicating a shift in position. Its components specify the distance and direction that one would have to travel in the $x, y,$ and z directions to get from the initial position to the final position. (Equivalently, each component is simply the difference between the corresponding initial and final coordinates of the object.) The magnitude of a displacement vector indicates the straight-line distance between the positions.

x-, y-, z-displacement: short names for the $x, y,$ and z components of a displacement vector.

vector sum: The sum of two vectors is a vector whose components are the sum of the corresponding components of the vectors being summed. This is equivalent to placing those vectors so the head of one coincides with the tail of the other, and then drawing an arrow from the remaining tail to the remaining head. Alternatively, we can place the vectors tail to tail and construct a parallelogram whose sides correspond to the vectors being added. The sum vector is then the arrow that starts at the tails of the original vectors and goes along the diagonal of the parallelogram.

vector inverse: a vector's inverse is a vector whose magnitude is as the original vector but whose direction is opposite. The components of the inverse are found by negating the components of the original vector.

vector difference: A vector can be subtracted from another vector by inverting the vector to be subtracted and then adding. The resulting vector difference can also be constructed geometrically by placing the two vectors tail-to-tail, and then drawing an arrow from the head of the vector to be subtracted to the head of the other vector.

multiplication by a scalar: Multiplication of a vector and a scalar produces a vector whose components are simply the scalar value times the corresponding components of the original vector. This is equivalent to multiplying the vector's magnitude by the absolute value of the scalar, and flipping the vector's direction if the scalar is negative (otherwise, the direction is unchanged).

quadrants: If we orient our reference frame so that two of the three coordinate axes (say, the x and y axes) lie in a plane, these axes divide the plane into four quarters called *quadrants*. These quadrants are numbered I, II, III, and IV in the counterclockwise direction from the $+x$ direction.

inverse sine, inverse cosine, and **inverse tangent** (functions): trigonometric functions that convert the value of a sine, cosine, or tangent (respectively) of an angle to the angle.

TWO-MINUTE PROBLEMS

C3T.1 The magnitude and direction of a vector can be described without using a reference frame (T or F).

C3T.2 The *components* of a given displacement vector depend on one's choice of origin (T or F).

C3T.3 The x, y, and z directions of a reference frame point up, west, and north respectively. Such a coordinate system is right-handed (T or F).

C3T.4 A reference frame drawn on a sheet of paper has its y direction oriented towards the top of the sheet and its x direction toward its right edge. What direction must the z direction point if the frame is right-handed?
A. outward, perpendicular to the plane of the paper
B. inward, perpendicular to the plane of the paper
C. diagonally to the lower left, in the plane of the paper
D. diagonally to the lower right, in the plane of the paper
E. vertically downward in the plane of the paper
F. other (specify).

C3T.5 If an object is located 3.0 m north and 1.0 m west of the origin of a frame in standard orientation on the earth's surface, its coordinates in that frame are:
A. [3.0 m, 1.0 m, 0 m]   D. [–1.0 m, 3.0 m, 0 m]
B. [–3.0 m, –1.0 m, 0 m] E. [–1.0 m, 0 m, –3.0 m]
C. [1.0 m, 3.0 m, 0 m]   F. other (explain).

C3T.6 An object whose initial position coordinates are [1.5 m, 2.0 m, –4.2 m] in a frame in standard orientation is a short time later found at a position whose coordinates are [1.5 m, –3.0 m, –4.2 m]. What is the direction of this object's displacement during this time interval?
A. east   D. south
B. west   E. down
C. north   F. other (specify)

C3T.7 The components c_x, c_y, and c_z of a certain vector $\vec{c}$ are *all* negative numbers. The vector's magnitude c is then certainly negative as well (T or F).

C3T.8 The *only* way that a vector can have zero magnitude is for *all* its components to be zero (T or F).

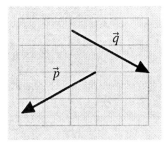

Figure C3.13: Vectors for problems C3T.9 through C3T.11.

C3T.9 Consider the two vectors shown in Figure C3.13. The sum of these vectors points most nearly
A. up.   B. down.   C. right.   D. left.

C3T.10 Consider the two vectors shown in Figure C3.13. The vector $\vec{q} - \vec{p}$ points most nearly
A. up.   B. down.   C. right.   D. left.

C3T.11 Consider the two vectors shown in Figure C3.13. To change $\vec{p}$ into $\vec{q}$ one would have to:
A. multiply by –1   D. add the vector $\vec{q} - \vec{p}$
B. multiply by 120°   E. add the vector $\vec{p} - \vec{q}$
C. add the vector $\vec{p} + \vec{q}$ F. none of the above.

C3T.12 mag($\vec{p} + \vec{q}$) = mag($\vec{p}$) + mag($\vec{q}$) (T or F).

C3T.13 mag($\vec{p} - \vec{q}$) ≥ | mag($\vec{p}$) – mag($\vec{q}$) | (T or F).

HOMEWORK PROBLEMS

BASIC SKILLS

C3B.1 A reference frame on the surface of the earth has an x axis that points upward and a y axis that points eastward. What direction should the z axis point to create a right-handed coordinate system? Explain using a picture.

C3B.2 Imagine that you walk 200 m south, 300 m up, and 60 m west in a reference frame in standard orientation on the earth's surface. Write your displacement as a column vector and compute its magnitude.

C3B.3 If you walk 85 m south and 25 m east from a certain starting position, what is the magnitude and direction of your displacement? (Specify the direction by specifying an angle relative to an appropriately chosen direction.)

C3B.4 A sailboat sails 25 km south and then 14 km west of Malibu. What is the magnitude and direction of its total displacement? (Specify the direction by specifying an angle relative to an appropriately chosen direction.)

C3B.5 Imagine that you walk 500 m in a direction 30° south of east. What are the components of your displacement in a reference frame in standard orientation on the earth's surface?

C3B.6 Imagine that during a certain interval of time, a jetliner flies a distance of 38 km along a straight line 35° west of north at a constant altitude of 10 km. What are the components of its displacement during this interval?

C3B.7 Compute the vector sum of the displacement vectors listed below. Determine the magnitude of this sum. (Please show your work.)

$$\vec{c} = \begin{bmatrix} 2\ m \\ -3\ m \\ 1\ m \end{bmatrix}, \quad \vec{q} = \begin{bmatrix} -4\ m \\ -1\ m \\ 3\ m \end{bmatrix} \qquad \text{(C3.20)}$$

C3B.8 Compute the components of the vector difference $\vec{q} - \vec{c}$ of the two vectors listed in problem CB3.7, and find the magnitude of this vector difference. (Please show your work.)

C3B.9 Compute the components of the vector given by $\vec{c} - 3\vec{q}$ for $\vec{c}$ and $\vec{q}$ as given in problem C3B.7.

C3B.10 Compute the components of the vector given by $\vec{c} + 2\vec{q}$ for $\vec{c}$ and $\vec{q}$ as given in problem C3B.7.

SYNTHETIC

C3S.1 An object is at position [2.0 m, 3.0 m, 5.0 m] in a certain reference frame in standard orientation on the earth's surface. The frame is rotated 180° around the x axis (so the z axis now points downward) and then the frame is moved 3.0 m to the east. (The object remains fixed relative to the earth in this process: only the frame's position and orientation is changed.) What are the object's coordinates now? Explain using a picture.

C3S.2 An object is at position [2.0 m, 3.0 m, –1.0 m] in a reference frame in standard orientation on the earth's surface. This reference frame is then lifted vertically 3.0 m and then is turned 90° around the x axis (so that the y axis now points vertically upward). (The object remains fixed relative to the earth in this process: only the frame's position and orientation is changed.) What are the object's coordinates now? Explain using a picture.

C3S.3 If a vector $\vec{p}$ is added to a vector $\vec{q}$, under what circumstances will mag($\vec{p} + \vec{q}$) = mag($\vec{p}$) + mag($\vec{q}$)? Under what circumstances will mag($\vec{p} + \vec{q}$) = 0? Can the value of mag($\vec{p} + \vec{q}$) ever be *greater* than mag($\vec{p}$) + mag($\vec{q}$)? Present a careful argument (preferably with diagrams) supporting each answer.

C3S.4 Can mag($\vec{p} - \vec{q}$) ever equal mag($\vec{p}$) + mag($\vec{q}$)? If so, specify the circumstances. If not, explain why not.

C3S.5 An object initially has a momentum of 15 kg·m/s due west. During a certain time interval, a force transfers 35 kg·m/s of eastward momentum to the object. What is the magnitude and direction of its total momentum? Justify your answer in terms of the component definition of vector addition. (*Hint*: You do not need to know anything about momentum to solve this problem except that momentum is a vector quantity with units of kg·m/s.)

C3S.6 An object initially has a momentum of 3 kg·m/s due west. After interacting with something else for a while, the object ends up with a momentum of 4 kg·m/s due south. What is the magnitude and direction of the momentum that the interaction has added to the object? Specify the direction as being roughly northwest, southeast, northeast or whatever is appropriate. (*Hint*: You do not need to know anything about momentum to solve this problem except that momentum is a vector quantity with units of kg·m/s.)

C3S.7 An object initially has a momentum of 5 kg·m/s due north. After interacting with something else for a while, the object ends up with a momentum of 12 kg·m/s east. What is the magnitude and direction of the momentum that the interaction has added the object? Specify the direction as being roughly northwest, southeast, northeast or whatever is appropriate. (*Hint*: You do not need to know anything about momentum to solve this problem except that momentum is a vector quantity with units of kg·m/s.)

C3S.8 A jetliner takes off from Los Angeles International Airport. After 5 minutes, the jet has an altitude of 5 km

above the level of the airport and is 25 km west and 10 km north of the airport. What is the magnitude and direction of its displacement vector during this time interval? Specify the direction by stating *two* angles: the angle of the displacement's direction west of north and the angle of the displacement's direction above the horizontal.

C3S.9 A boat leaves San Pedro and travels 35 km 15° west of south before its engine dies. You left San Pedro earlier in the morning and have traveled 42 km 23° south of west by the time the first boat's distress call reaches you. How far and in what direction is the first boat relative to you at that point?

RICH-CONTEXT

C3R.1 Is it possible to see the top of Mount Everest from a boat floating in the Bay of Bengal? Assume that the air is perfectly clear and that there are no other mountains, clouds, or buildings obstructing your line of sight. (*Hint*: What might possibly obstruct the view if there are no mountains, clouds, or buildings in the way? Use an atlas or map to estimate distances.)

C3R.2 Two teams of explorers leave a common point. The first team travels 5 km north across a plain, then follows a river 15° west of north for 7 km before making camp for the night. The second climbs a ridge, traveling basically due northeast for 6 km along a trail that climbs upward to an altitude of 2.5 km. This team then follows the ridge northward at approximately the same altitude for 4 km before setting up camp. Can the two teams communicate that night if their radios have a range of 5 km?

ADVANCED

C3A.1 Prove mathematically that for any two vectors $\vec{p}$ and $\vec{q}$ lying in the xy plane of a given reference frame

$$\mathrm{mag}^2(\vec{p} + \vec{q}) = \mathrm{mag}^2(\vec{p}) + 2\,\mathrm{mag}(\vec{p})\,\mathrm{mag}(\vec{q})\cos\theta$$
$$+\ \mathrm{mag}^2(\vec{q}) \qquad\qquad (C3.20)$$

where θ is the angle between the directions of $\vec{p}$ and $\vec{q}$.

C3A.2 Present a mathematical proof that uses *only* the definition of the magnitude of a vector, the component definition of vector addition, and basic algebra to show that (1) mag($\vec{p} + \vec{q}$) ≤ mag($\vec{p}$) + mag($\vec{q}$), and (2) the equality is only achieved when $\vec{p}$ is a positive multiple of $\vec{q}$.

ANSWERS TO EXERCISES

C3X.1 D: [1 m, 3 m, 4 m], E: [5 m, 2 m, 0 m].
C3X.2 No.
C3X.3 [–2 m, –1 m, –4 m].
C3X.4 6.7 m.
C3X.5 [3 m, –4 m, –1 m], 5.1 m.
C3X.6 [–4.0 m, –3.0 m, 0 m].
C3X.7 6.4 m, 13.6° clockwise from the x direction.
C3X.8 The sum is [4 m, 1 m, 0 m].
C3X.9 See Figure C3.14.
C3X.10 The difference is [–1 m, 3 m, 0 m]. See Figure C3.14.
C3X.11 [–12 m, +4 m, 0 m]. The magnitude is 4 times that of the original vector and the direction is *opposite* to that of the original vector.

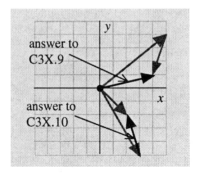

Figure C3.14.

C4

PARTICLES AND SYSTEMS

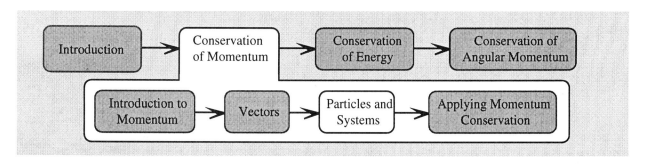

C4.1 OVERVIEW

In the last chapter, we studied how we could qualitatively describe vector quantities in three dimensions and use them in calculations. In this chapter, we will use this knowledge to define *momentum* more precisely. We will then use these definitions to discuss why we can treat the extended objects of our everyday existence as if they were point particles, an idea that lies at the heart of all modern theories of mechanics (including newtonian mechanics). The ideas presented in this chapter are therefore crucial background not only for our understanding of conservation of momentum (the topic of the next chapter) but all of units *C* and *N*. Here is a summary of the sections in this chapter.

C4.2 *POSITION, VELOCITY, AND MOMENTUM* defines the vectors that are at the heart of any discussion of motion in three dimensions.

C4.3 *INTERACTIONS TRANSFER MOMENTUM* describes how interactions effectively provide a conduit for particles to exchange momentum.

C4.4 *SYSTEMS OF PARTICLES* defines what we mean by a *system* of interacting particles and discusses how we can model extended objects by such systems.

C4.5 *A SYSTEM'S CENTER OF MASS* defines what we mean by the *center of mass* of a system of particles (and thus of an extended object).

C4.6 *HOW THE CENTER OF MASS MOVES* argues that the center of mass of any system moves as if it were a point particle responding to the system's external interactions. We will also see that the idea that interactions transfer momentum implies that the total momentum of an isolated system will be conserved.

C4.7 *APPLICATION: DISCOVERING PLANETS* illustrates how these ideas can be used to search for planets orbiting nearby stars.

**** *Math Skills: ILLEGAL VECTOR EQUATIONS* warns about mistakes in using vector algebra that seem to be easy to make and tells you how to recognize them.

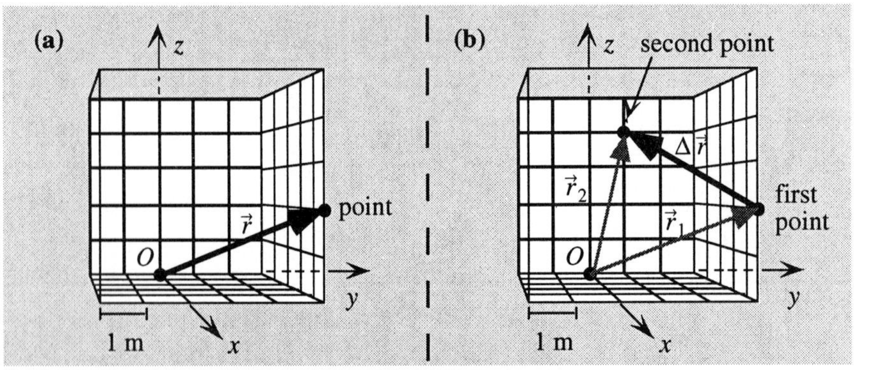

Figure C4.1: (a) The *position* vector of a point is its displacement from the origin. **(b)** The displacement vector between two points is the difference between their position vectors.

C4.2 POSITION, VELOCITY, AND MOMENTUM

Definition of the position vector of a point

In the last chapter, we saw that the position of a point in a given reference frame can be quantified by a set of three signed numbers $[x,y,z]$ that uniquely locate the point in the frame lattice. We can in fact represent the *position* of any point by a vector $\vec{r}$ with components $[x, y, z]$. As illustrated in Figure C4.1a, a **position vector** is a special case of a displacement vector: it is simply the displacement from the reference frame origin to the point in question. The magnitude of this vector is $r = \text{mag}(\vec{r}) = [x^2 + y^2 + z^2]^{1/2}$, which is simply the distance that the point is from the origin. (Note that the components of a position vector are conventionally written simply as $[x, y, z]$ instead of as $[r_x, r_y, r_z]$.)

Displacement as a difference of position vectors

As illustrated in Figure C4.1b, we can consider the **displacement vector** $\Delta\vec{r}$ between two arbitrary points to be the position vector $\vec{r}_2$ of the second point minus the position vector $\vec{r}_1$ of the first point:

$$\Delta\vec{r} \equiv \vec{r}_2 - \vec{r}_1 \quad \text{or} \quad \begin{bmatrix} \Delta x \\ \Delta y \\ \Delta z \end{bmatrix} \equiv \begin{bmatrix} x_2 \\ y_2 \\ z_2 \end{bmatrix} - \begin{bmatrix} x_1 \\ y_1 \\ z_1 \end{bmatrix} = \begin{bmatrix} x_2 - x_1 \\ y_2 - y_1 \\ z_2 - z_1 \end{bmatrix} \quad \text{(C4.1)}$$

As mentioned in chapter C2, we commonly use the symbol Δ to connote *difference* or *change in* some quantity (though this should not always be taken too literally). The symbol $\Delta\vec{r}$ for a displacement vector thus is meant to suggest a *change* in position.

What we mean by the term *particle*

A **particle** is an object of infinitesimal size and thus whose position is essentially a mathematical point in space. Ideal particles whose positions really are mathematical points probably don't really exist (though some subatomic particles, such as electrons, are pointlike down to the smallest distances physicists can measure). This concept is a useful abstraction, however, because the position of such a particle is mathematically well-defined.

The definition of *velocity*

A particle's **velocity** $\vec{v}$ at a given time is a vector quantity whose *magnitude* is the particle's speed v and whose *direction* is the particles's direction of motion at that instant of time. Note that the terms *velocity* and *speed* have different meanings in physics: velocity is a *vector* quantity characterizing both the rate and direction of motion, while speed is simply the *magnitude* of that vector.

We can quantitatively define a particle's velocity at a given instant of time t as follows. Let dt be the duration of a time interval containing t, and let dt be sufficiently short that neither the particle's speed nor its direction of motion changes appreciably during that time interval. Let $d\vec{r}$ be the particle's tiny displacement during this tiny interval (which is mathematically well-defined because its position is well-defined!). The particle's velocity at time t is then

$$\vec{v} \equiv \frac{d\vec{r}}{dt} \quad \text{or} \quad \begin{bmatrix} v_x \\ v_y \\ v_z \end{bmatrix} = \frac{1}{dt}\begin{bmatrix} dx \\ dy \\ dz \end{bmatrix} = \begin{bmatrix} dx/dt \\ dy/dt \\ dz/dt \end{bmatrix} \quad \text{(C4.2)}$$

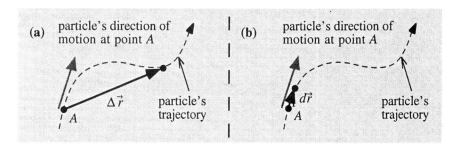

Figure **C4.2: (a)** A particle's displacement during a long time interval Δt beginning when it passes point A may only poorly reflect its direction of motion at point A. **(b)** The direction of the particle's displacement during a sufficiently short interval *dt does* accurately reflect the object's direction of motion at point A.

Note that since 1/*dt* is a positive scalar, the vector $\vec{v}$ ends up having the same direction as the short displacement $d\vec{r}$, which (as long as *dt* is sufficiently short) accurately reflects the direction that the object is moving (see Figure C4.2b).

Again, let me remind you that we use the symbols *dt* and $d\vec{r}$ to remind ourselves that *dt* must be *sufficiently short* so that the particle's speed and direction of motion are essentially constant during the interval. Figures C4.2 illustrates why this is important: the particle's displacement during an interval Δt that is too large does *not* accurately represent the particle's direction of motion.

The magnitude of a particle's velocity is

A particle's *speed* is the magnitude of its velocity

$$v \equiv \text{mag}(\vec{v}) \equiv \sqrt{v_x^2 + v_y^2 + v_z^2} = \sqrt{\left(\frac{dx}{dt}\right)^2 + \left(\frac{dy}{dt}\right)^2 + \left(\frac{dz}{dt}\right)^2}$$

$$= \frac{\sqrt{dx^2 + dy^2 + dz^2}}{dt} = \frac{dr}{dt} \qquad \text{(C4.3)}$$

where |*dr*| = mag($d\vec{r}$) is the distance the particle travels during the time interval *dt*. This coincides with the definition of *speed* given in chapter C2. We thus see that the velocity vector defined by equation C4.2 has a magnitude equal to the particle's *speed* and a direction equal to the particle's direction of motion.

A particle's **momentum** vector $\vec{p}$ at any given instant is defined to be the particle's velocity vector $\vec{v}$ multiplied by its scalar mass *m*:

Definition of *momentum*

$$\vec{p} \equiv m\vec{v} \quad \text{or} \quad \begin{bmatrix} p_x \\ p_y \\ p_z \end{bmatrix} \equiv \begin{bmatrix} mv_x \\ mv_y \\ mv_z \end{bmatrix} \qquad \text{(C4.4)}$$

The *magnitude* of a particle's momentum is therefore:

$$p \equiv \text{mag}(\vec{p}) \equiv \sqrt{p_x^2 + p_y^2 + p_z^2} = \sqrt{m^2(v_x^2 + v_y^2 + v_z^2)} = mv \qquad \text{(C4.5)}$$

or simply the particle's mass times its speed. Note also that because *m* is a *positive* scalar, a particle's momentum always has the same direction as its velocity vector, which (we saw earlier) points in the direction the particle is moving. We see, therefore, that this (newtonian) definition of momentum coincides with the arrow model of momentum discussed in chapter C2, which we found fit the available data as being something that was conserved in simple interactions.

Exercise   C4X.1: A particle moves with a constant speed around a circle. Is its velocity constant? Is its momentum constant?

Exercise   C4X.2: During a "sufficiently short" time interval of 0.25 s, a hypothetical particle with a mass of 2.0 kg moves a displacement of 4.0 m east, 1.0 m south, and 0.1 m downward relative to the earth's surface. What are the components of this particle's velocity and momentum at this time in a reference frame in standard orientation on the earth's surface? What is the particle's speed?

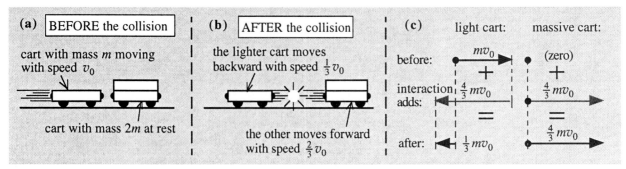

Figure C4.3: Parts **(a)** and **(b)** illustrate a collision between two carts that we studied in chapter C2. **(c)** Note that the collision interaction changes each cart's momentum by an amount whose magnitude is $\frac{4}{3}mv_0$ but in opposite directions.

Analysis of a simple collision

C4.3 INTERACTIONS TRANSFER MOMENTUM

We discussed in chapter C2 that an *interaction* between two objects is a physical relationship between them that allows them to affect each other's motion. In this section, we will construct a model that describes more precisely what happens during an interaction, a model that will be very helpful to us later.

Consider the collision between two carts shown in Figure C4.3. This is a collision interaction that we considered in chapter C2: we saw there that this collision conserves momentum as long as we treat momentum as a vector. But let's focus for the moment on what the collision interaction between the carts does to each cart individually. Clearly, the interaction changes the massive cart's momentum to be more rightward than it was before. The interaction also leaves the light cart with leftward momentum (it had rightward momentum before) so it must change that cart's momentum in the leftward direction. In fact Figure C4.3 shows that the interaction effectively takes each cart's original momentum and adds a vector whose magnitude is $\frac{4}{3}mv_0$ and whose direction is opposite to that added to the other cart. Thus we can think of this interaction as giving the carts opposing additional momentum vectors that have the same magnitude.

Exercise C4X.3: Imagine that a cart with mass m moving with speed v_0 collides with an identical cart at rest. After the collision, the carts stick together and move together at a speed of $\frac{1}{2}v_0$ in the same direction as the originally moving cart. Show (by drawing a picture analogous to Figure C4.3c) that we can also think of *this* collision as giving the carts opposing additional momenta with the same magnitudes and find that magnitude of that additional momentum.

An interaction *must* give its participants equal and opposite momenta to conserve momentum

When you think about it, an interaction *must* do this if it is to conserve momentum. By definition, an interaction affects the motion of the objects involved. If an interaction affects the motion of one object, then during some time interval it will change that object's initial momentum $\vec{p}_1$ by some $\Delta\vec{p}_1$. But if the total momentum of the interacting objects is conserved, then the initial momentum $\vec{p}_2$ of the *other* object must change during the same interval by some $\Delta\vec{p}_2$ that leaves the two objects' total momentum unchanged. This will only happen if $\Delta\vec{p}_1$ and $\Delta\vec{p}_2$ are vector inverses, so that they add up to *no* change:

$$(\vec{p}_1+\Delta\vec{p}_1)+(\vec{p}_2+\Delta\vec{p}_2) = \text{final } \vec{p}_{\text{TOT}} = \text{initial } \vec{p}_{\text{TOT}} = \vec{p}_1+\vec{p}_2$$

$$\text{if and only if} \quad \Delta\vec{p}_1+\Delta\vec{p}_2 = 0 \quad \Rightarrow \quad \Delta\vec{p}_1 = -\Delta\vec{p}_2 \tag{C4.6}$$

In fact, interactions *transfer* momentum

We can in fact think of the momentum change that the interaction gives each cart as being *transferred* from the other cart's momentum (making the idea that the interaction *conserves* momentum all that much more vivid). How does this work? Consider the lighter cart in Figure C4.3. In this interaction, it gains an amount of leftward momentum whose magnitude is $\frac{4}{3}mv_0$. If this has been really "transferred" from the massive cart, then adding $\frac{4}{3}mv_0$ of leftward momentum to the light cart must involve *subtracting* $\frac{4}{3}mv_0$ of leftward momentum from the massive cart. But since subtracting a vector is the same as adding its inverse, subtracting $\frac{4}{3}mv_0$ of leftward momentum is the same as *adding* $\frac{4}{3}mv_0$

of *rightward* momentum to that cart. This is exactly the amount and direction of momentum change that Figure C4.3c shows the interaction as giving that cart.

The situation is completely symmetric: we could just as easily think of the massive cart as gaining $\frac{4}{3}mv_0$ of *rightward* momentum that is subtracted from the lighter cart's momentum (which is the same as adding $\frac{4}{3}mv_0$ of *leftward* momentum). Physicists often speak of the two objects as "exchanging momentum" in a situation like this to emphasize the symmetry, but from the point of view of either *individual* cart, that cart is receiving a change in its momentum that comes at the expense of a change in the other cart's momentum.

An analogy might be helpful. Imagine that I use a credit card to pay a debt to you. From your perspective, this transaction transfers money from my credit card account to you. From my perspective, it transfers a *debt*, one that I owed you at first and I now owe my credit card account. Though we may be more used to thinking of such transactions as transferring money rather than debt, the *fiscal* consequences are the same whether we look at the transaction as transferring positive dollars to you or negative dollars to my account. Similarly, the *physical* consequences of the collision in Figure C4.3 are the same whether we think of the first cart as receiving a leftward momentum transfer from the other or the other as receiving rightward momentum transfer from the first.

When we use terms like "momentum transfer", we are really broadening the concept of "momentum" from the original definition $\vec{p} \equiv m\vec{v}$ given in the last section. The metaphor is now that "momentum" is like a substance or like money that can be moved around: at a given time a particle contains or holds a certain amount of momentum, but momentum is something that can also be *transferred* from particle to particle. In this model, $\vec{p} \equiv m\vec{v}$ describes the momentum *held by a particle* at a given time; the **momentum transfer** $d\vec{p}$ that an interaction delivers to a particle in a given time interval dt (for example, either gray arrow in Figure C4.3c) is a vector quantity having the same units as $\vec{p} \equiv m\vec{v}$, but that represents what that interaction contributes toward *changing* that particle's momentum, as the notation $d\vec{p}$ suggests (we will discuss the point of the bar through the d in the next chapter). The physical concepts of *momentum transfer* $d\vec{p}$, a *particle's momentum* $\vec{p} \equiv m\vec{v}$, and *momentum* in general roughly correspond to the fiscal concepts of *cash*, a *person's net worth*, and the general concept of *money*, respectively.

The word historically used for $d\vec{p}$ is **impulse**, a term that nicely expresses the idea that a momentum transfer changes an object's motion, but that does not adequately express the idea that the $d\vec{p}$ that one particle gets comes at the expense of another particle's momentum. While you should be aware that this historical term exists, we will use *momentum transfer* exclusively in this text.

We can therefore express the core idea of this section as follows:

> An interaction acting between two particles for a given time interval dt delivers a certain *momentum transfer* $d\vec{p}$ to one particle's momentum at the expense of the other particle's momentum. (We can think of *either* particle as "receiving" this momentum transfer: changing the recipient only changes the sign that we assign to $d\vec{p}$.)

As far as we know, this statement applies to *all* known physical interactions and is valid (with modest modifications) in all current physical theories. While this statement is basically equivalent to the law of conservation of momentum, it provides a better vantage point for examining a number of puzzles about mechanics and will be very helpful to us in the remainder of units *C* and *N*.

A monetary analogy for momentum transfer

The distinction between a *momentum transfer,* **a** *particle's momentum,* **and** *momentum* **in general**

Impulse **is the historical term roughly equivalent to** *momentum transfer*

The core idea of this section

Exercise C4X.4: A cart with mass m moving rightward at a speed of v_0 hits a second cart. Afterward, the first cart moves leftward with a speed of $\frac{1}{2}v_0$. What is the momentum transfer (magnitude and direction) that the second cart receives from this collision? Does it matter whether that cart was initially at rest?

C4.4 SYSTEMS OF PARTICLES

You may have noticed that I stated the general principle near the end of the last section in terms of interacting *particles*, not objects, even though the examples we considered involved macroscopic carts. This is because, technically, the definitions given in section C4.2 only allow us to talk about the momentum of *particles*. Yet we have seen that we can apply these ideas readily to at least rigid objects like carts. In the next few sections, we will see that *we can in fact treat interactions between macroscopic objects* (even *non*-rigid objects!) *as if they were interactions between particles*. This is a *crucial* idea that makes a simple physics of macroscopic objects possible, and which lies at the very heart of the newtonian model of mechanics. Let's see how this works.

Any extended object is a *system* of interacting elementary particles

A **system** in physics is any well-defined collection or set of interacting objects. An **extended object** is a material object with a well-defined boundary and a *nonzero* volume (making it *not* a particle). A basic assumption of newtonian mechanics is that we can treat *any* extended object as a system of interacting *particles*. This assumption is actually quite consistent with current views about the nature of matter. According to the contemporary theory known as the *standard model* (see chapter C1), every object in our daily experience is a system of interacting **atoms**, which involve **electrons** interacting with **nuclei**. Nuclei in turn are systems of interacting **protons** and **neutrons**, which are in turn systems of interacting **quarks**. According to the standard model, quarks and electrons are structureless **elementary particles**, and experiments do show that quarks and electrons are genuinely pointlike to the limits of our ability to measure. Therefore, the standard model asserts that every material object really *is* an immensely complicated interacting system of genuine particles.

Internal and external interactions

Any interaction involving at least one particle in such a system is either an **internal interaction** (if it acts between two particles that are *both* in the system) or an **external interaction** (if it acts between one particle *in* the system and one *outside* the system). This distinction is important because internal interactions mediate momentum transfers only between particles that are both *within* the system, so they *do not change* that system's total momentum. A system's total momentum is thus *only* affected by *external* interactions. It follows that if a system is *isolated* from such external interactions, its total momentum will then be conserved, no matter what is happening with the system internally.

C4.5   A SYSTEM'S CENTER OF MASS

Now, in the newtonian model of mechanics, a particle's position is sharply defined and unambiguous, and so its velocity and momentum are also sharply defined, as discussed in section C4.2. The basic issue that we have to face in attempting to describe the motion of extended objects is the problem of defining the position of such an object in a similarly crisp manner. The key needed to unlock this problem (as Newton himself found) is the concept of the *center of mass* of a system of particles.

The **center of mass** of *any* system of particles is a mathematical point whose position is defined as follows:

Definition of a system's center of mass (CM)

$$\vec{r}_{CM} \equiv \frac{1}{M}(m_1\vec{r}_1 + m_2\vec{r}_2 + \ldots + m_N\vec{r}_N) \tag{C4.7a}$$

where N is the total number of particles in the system and

$$M \equiv m_1 + m_2 + \ldots + m_N = \text{total mass of system} \tag{C4.7b}$$

Note that the position of a system's center of mass is essentially an average in which the position $\vec{r}_i$ of the ith particle in the system is weighted by its fraction m_i/M of the system's total mass. In column vector notation, this becomes:

$$\begin{bmatrix} x_{CM} \\ y_{CM} \\ z_{CM} \end{bmatrix} = \frac{1}{M}\left(m_1\begin{bmatrix} x_1 \\ y_1 \\ z_1 \end{bmatrix} + m_2\begin{bmatrix} x_2 \\ y_2 \\ z_2 \end{bmatrix} + \ldots + m_N\begin{bmatrix} x_N \\ y_N \\ z_N \end{bmatrix} \right) \qquad \text{(C4.8)}$$

which is equivalent to three separate component equations:

$$x_{CM} = \frac{1}{M}(m_1 x_1 + m_2 x_2 + \ldots + m_N x_N) \qquad \text{(C4.9a)}$$

$$y_{CM} = \frac{1}{M}(m_1 y_1 + m_2 y_2 + \ldots + m_N y_N) \qquad \text{(C4.9b)}$$

$$z_{CM} = \frac{1}{M}(m_1 z_1 + m_2 z_2 + \ldots + m_N z_N) \qquad \text{(C4.9c)}$$

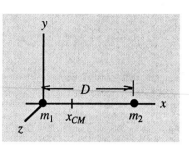

Figure C4.4: The center of mass of a system consisting of two point particles. The center of mass shown here would be accurate if $m_1 \approx 2m_2$.

Does this definition make sense? Imagine a system consisting of only *two* particles separated by some distance D. For the sake of simplicity, let us choose a reference frame in which both particles lie on the x axis (so that both have zero y and z coordinates) and where the first particle is located at the origin, meaning that $x_1 = 0$ and $x_2 = D$ (see Figure C4.4). Equation C4.8 then tells us that:

$$\begin{bmatrix} x_{CM} \\ y_{CM} \\ z_{CM} \end{bmatrix} = \frac{1}{M}\left(m_1\begin{bmatrix} 0 \\ 0 \\ 0 \end{bmatrix} + m_2\begin{bmatrix} D \\ 0 \\ 0 \end{bmatrix} \right) = \frac{1}{M}\begin{bmatrix} m_2 D \\ 0 \\ 0 \end{bmatrix} \qquad \text{(C4.10)}$$

meaning that in this particular case

$$x_{CM} = \frac{m_2 D}{M}, \qquad y_{CM} = z_{CM} = 0 \qquad \text{(C4.11)}$$

We see from this equation that the center of mass (1) *lies along the line connecting the two objects* (the x axis in this particular case), (2) has an x-position that lies *between* the two particles (the first part of equation C4.11 implies that $0 < x_{CM} < D$ because $0 < m_2/M < 1$), (3) is located exactly halfway between the two objects (at $x = \frac{1}{2}D$) when the two particles have the same mass, and (4) is located closer to the more massive particle if the two particles *don't* have the same mass (note that if $m_2 < m_1$, then $m_2/M < \frac{1}{2}$, implying that the center of mass is closer to m_1 than m_2). These features probably coincide with whatever intuitive sense you have about where the center of mass of a two-particle system ought to lie.

Exercise C4X.5: Imagine that particle A has a mass of 22 kg, and particle B has a mass of 2.0 kg. These particles are separated by a distance of 1.2 m. Where is the center of mass of this system relative to the position of particle A? (*Hint:* Choose your reference frame so that this system looks like that in Figure C4.4.)

We can (in principle) find the center of mass of any multiparticle system at a given time in a similar way by adding the weighted vector positions of each of its elementary particles at that time. In reality, however, this is impossible because of the outrageously huge number of elementary particles involved. A more practical (but approximate) method would be to break the object up into a more reasonable number of macroscopic hunks that are still small enough so that we can consider the particles in each to have essentially the same position. For example, when computing a galaxy's center of mass, we can to an excellent degree of approximation treat its stars as if they were point particles, rather than going all the way back to the galaxy's quarks and leptons (in a galaxy-sized reference frame, all of the particles in a given star *will* have the same position, unless we are keeping track of positions to better than one part in 10^{12}!).

A practical approach to calculating a system's center of mass

EXAMPLE C4.1

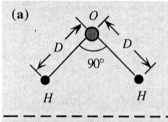

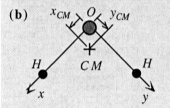

Figure C4.5: (a) A schematic diagram of a water molecule (the size of the atomic nuclei have been greatly exaggerated, and the electrons have been ignored). **(b)** One possible reference frame for analyzing this system.

Problem: A water molecule consists of one oxygen atom (O) and two hydrogen atoms (H) in roughly the configuration shown Figure C4.5a (actually, the angle between the arms is more like 107°, but taking it to be 90° makes the calculation simpler). The mass of the oxygen atom is very nearly 16 times that of the hydrogen atom, and the distance D between the hydrogen and oxygen nuclei is measured to be 0.096 nm (1 nm $= 10^{-9}$ m). Note that virtually all of the mass of any atom is concentrated in its nucleus, which is typically about 10^5 times smaller than the atom. Where is the center of mass of this system?

Solution Since virtually all of the mass of each atom is in its nucleus, and since these nuclei are so small that particles in the nucleus essentially all have the same position compared to the scale molecule as a whole, we will model the molecule as a system of *three* particles (corresponding to the three nuclei), rather than going back to the molecule's constituent quarks and electrons.

It is always helpful to choose a reference frame where as many quantities are zero as possible. Note that in the frame shown in Figure C4.5b, the z-positions of all of the nuclei are zero. In addition, the y-position of the hydrogen atom on the left is zero, the x-position of the hydrogen atom on the right is zero, and both the x and y-positions of the oxygen nucleus are zero. Let us define m to be the unknown mass of the hydrogen atom. Equation C4.8 then implies that:

$$\begin{bmatrix} x_{CM} \\ y_{CM} \\ z_{CM} \end{bmatrix} = \frac{1}{18m}\left(16m\begin{bmatrix} 0 \\ 0 \\ 0 \end{bmatrix} + m\begin{bmatrix} D \\ 0 \\ 0 \end{bmatrix} + m\begin{bmatrix} 0 \\ D \\ 0 \end{bmatrix}\right) = \begin{bmatrix} D/18 \\ D/18 \\ 0 \end{bmatrix} \qquad \text{(C4.12)}$$

This means that $x_{CM} = y_{CM} = D/18 = 0.0053$ nm $= 5.3$ pm in this reference frame, which means that it is a distance of roughly

$$\sqrt{x_{CM}^2 + y_{CM}^2 + z_{CM}^2} = \sqrt{\left(\frac{D}{18}\right)^2 + \left(\frac{D}{18}\right)^2 + 0^2} = \frac{D}{18}\sqrt{2} = 7.5 \text{ pm} \qquad \text{(C4.13)}$$

from the origin (that is, the oxygen nucleus). Since the position of the center of mass has equal x and y components, it is located directly *downward* from the oxygen nucleus in Figure C4.5b.

Important things to know about the center of mass

We will *not* spend time actually computing the centers of mass for strangely-shaped systems or extended objects in this text. It will be enough for our purposes to know that (1) a well-defined center of mass *does exist* for any extended object or system, as specified by equation C4.7, (2) the center of mass of a *symmetrical* object, such as a sphere, cube, or cylinder, is located at that object's geometrical center (as one might expect).

One can also prove that the following theorem follows from the definition of the center of mass of a system:

> We can calculate the position of the center of mass of any *set* of extended objects by treating each object as if it were a point particle with all of its mass concentrated at its *individual* center of mass.

(See problem C4A.1 for such a proof.) So, for example, the center of mass of two *spheres* with masses m_1 and m_2 whose centers are separated by a distance D is the same as that of two *point particles* with masses m_1 and m_2 separated by a distance D, no matter how large the spheres might be. This theorem makes it easy to find the center of mass of objects in a variety of practical situations.

Exercise C4X.6: In a binary star system (where two stars orbit each other), one star has three times the mass of the other. If the stars are 100 million km apart, how far is this system's center of mass from the larger star?

C4.6 HOW THE CENTER OF MASS MOVES

Why do we define the center of mass the way we do? It turns out that because of the principle that interactions mediate momentum transfers, a system's center of mass (as we have defined it) moves in an especially simple and predictable way in response to external interactions involving its particles.

Imagine that we look at the system at the beginning and end of a very short interval of time dt. Let the positions of its particles at the beginning of the interval be $\vec{r}_{1i}, \vec{r}_{2i}, \ldots, \vec{r}_{Ni}$ respectively, and let $\vec{r}_{1f}, \vec{r}_{2f}, \ldots, \vec{r}_{Nf}$ be the particles' positions at the end of the interval. The positions of the system's center of mass at the beginning and end of the interval are therefore:

A system's total momentum is equal to its mass times the velocity of its CM

$$\vec{r}_{CM,i} \equiv \frac{1}{M}(m_1\vec{r}_{1i} + m_2\vec{r}_{2i} + \ldots + m_N\vec{r}_{Ni}) \qquad \text{(C4.14a)}$$

$$\vec{r}_{CM,f} \equiv \frac{1}{M}(m_1\vec{r}_{1f} + m_2\vec{r}_{2f} + \ldots + m_N\vec{r}_{Nf}) \qquad \text{(C4.14b)}$$

The change in the position of the center of mass during this interval is thus:

$$d\vec{r}_{CM} \equiv \vec{r}_{CM,f} - \vec{r}_{CM,i}$$

$$= \frac{1}{M}(m_1\vec{r}_{1f} + m_2\vec{r}_{2f} + \ldots + m_N\vec{r}_{Nf}) - \frac{1}{M}(m_1\vec{r}_{1i} + m_2\vec{r}_{2i} + \ldots + m_N\vec{r}_{Ni})$$

$$= \frac{1}{M}(m_1[\vec{r}_{1f} - \vec{r}_{1i}] + m_2[\vec{r}_{2f} - \vec{r}_{2i}] + \ldots + m_N[\vec{r}_{Nf} - \vec{r}_{Ni}])$$

$$= \frac{1}{M}(m_1\,d\vec{r}_1 + m_2\,d\vec{r}_2 + \ldots + m_N\,d\vec{r}_N) \qquad \text{(C4.15)}$$

If we now multiply both sides by M and divide by dt, we get

$$M\frac{d\vec{r}_{CM}}{dt} = m_1\frac{d\vec{r}_1}{dt} + m_2\frac{d\vec{r}_2}{dt} + \ldots + m_N\frac{d\vec{r}_N}{dt} \qquad \text{(C4.16)}$$

But the definitions of velocity and momentum therefore imply that:

$$M\vec{v}_{CM} = m_1\vec{v}_1 + m_2\vec{v}_2 + \ldots + m_N\vec{v}_N = \vec{p}_1 + \vec{p}_2 + \ldots + \vec{p}_N \equiv \vec{p}_{TOT} \qquad \text{(C4.17)}$$

Now, look at what this equation says: it says that to find a system's total momentum, all that we need to do is multiply its total mass M by the velocity of its center of mass $\vec{v}_{CM}$, *exactly as if the system were a single particle located at its center of mass!* This is a direct consequence of the definition of the center of mass and the definitions of velocity and momentum.

Now, imagine that the system is *isolated*, so that interactions do not mediate momentum transfers into or out of the system. Internal interactions between particles in the system only shift momentum around *within* the system, so the system's total momentum is conserved. Equation C4.17 then implies that

The CM of an isolated system moves at a constant velocity

$$\vec{v}_{CM} = \text{constant (when the system is isolated)} \qquad \text{(C4.18)}$$

Since an extended object is a system, if an isolated object's center of mass is at rest it will remain at rest, and if it is moving, it will continue moving in the same direction at a constant speed. (This is a more precisely-stated version of Newton's first law of motion than the version given in section C2.4.)

What if the system is not isolated? Because *internal* interactions do *not* change a system's momentum, the net momentum transfer delivered to a system by any *external* interactions causes its momentum to change in exactly the same way that it would cause a *particle's* momentum to change. Equation C4.17 tells us that the system's total momentum is just $M\vec{v}_{CM}$, which is exactly the same as the momentum of a point particle of mass M moving along with the system's center of mass. So, since a system's momentum is calculated the same way that a particle's momentum is, and since its momentum changes in response to external momentum transfers just as a particle's momentum would,

A system's CM responds to external interactions exactly as a particle would

A system's center of mass moves in response to *external* momentum transfers exactly as if it were a particle of the same total mass responding to those momentum transfers, no matter how its parts interact internally.

Since an extended object is just a system of particles, this statement applies to all extended objects as well.

This is a powerful result that greatly simplifies physics!

This is a *very* important result! Imagine how difficult it would be to do physics (or even stay alive!) if the motion of an extended object depended on the detailed character of its internal interactions (which are so complicated we could not hope to understand them). It would be hard even to play catch in your back yard, for example, if the motion of a thrown ball depended on the details of how the atoms *inside* the ball happen to be interacting with each other.

The idea that we can totally *ignore* an extended object's internal interactions and model it as if it were a structureless particle is an idea, therefore, that makes it *much* easier to model the behavior of extended objects: it in fact makes a physics of extended objects practical. It is also so basic that we typically take it for granted. We have just seen, though, that this idea is a nonobvious consequence of the idea that *interactions mediate momentum transfers*. Because *that* principle in turn is valid in all accepted physical theories, the idea that we can model a system's response to external interactions by ignoring internal interactions and treating the system as if it were a particle is also valid in all current theories of physics (though "particle" is defined differently in quantum mechanics). This is one of the most important and useful principles in all of physics!

We will use the particle model of objects implicitly from now on

From now on, I will use this model implicitly whenever we deal with extended objects. Whenever I refer to an extended object's *position, velocity,* or *momentum* in what follows, what I am really talking about is the position, velocity or momentum of that object's *center of mass*. Whenever I talk about the interactions that the object participates in, I really mean the *external* interactions involving the object's particles.

Rigid objects

A **rigid** object is an object whose dimensions and shape do not change significantly, even in response to interactions. Many everyday objects are at least approximately rigid. Note if an object is rigid and is not rotating, any given point in the object has a fixed position relative to its center of mass. This means that as the object moves, its center of mass and the given point will undergo the same displacement in a given interval of time, which in turn means the two points have the same *velocity*. Thus if we want to determine the velocity of a cart's center of mass (for example), we can instead measure the velocity of *any* given point on the cart (its front edge, for example). You have probably done this intuitively in the past; now you know why this is the right thing to do.

Exercise C4X.7: Imagine a 60-kg person holding a 6-kg stone is at rest at the origin of certain reference frame in deep space. The person throws the stone in the $+x$ direction. If after 5 s, the stone has traveled 30 m from the origin in that frame, how many meters has the person moved in the $-x$ direction? (*Hint*: A system in "deep space" is isolated, by sheer distance, from external interactions.)

C4.7 APPLICATION: DISCOVERING PLANETS

Even with the best telescopes currently available, planets orbiting even the stars closest to the earth are too dim compared to their parent stars to be imaged directly (though this may be possible soon). Yet astronomers have recently discovered a number of planets orbiting such stars. How is this possible?

Consider an imaginary star system consisting of a single planet orbiting a single star. Assuming that this star system is far from other stars, external interactions involving the stars in system will have negligible influence. This means that its center of mass will move in an essentially straight line at a constant velocity through space. Now, the center of mass of a two-object system always lies between the objects along the line connecting them (and closer to the more massive object). Therefore, if at a given time the planet is some distance away from the center of mass in a certain direction, the star will at that time be displaced from the system's center of mass by a (smaller) distance in the opposite direction. Therefore when the planet orbits the star, the planet and the star really both go around the system's center of mass (like a pair of waltzing ballroom dancers) while the center of mass moves in a straight line (see Figure C4.6).

While we may not be able to see the planet directly, we *can* see the star, and if the star is close enough and its planet is massive enough, we just might be able to see that the star does not move in a straight line, but rather "wobbles" about it as shown in Figure C4.6. There are two ways that we might use to measure a star's wobbling motion due to the presence of a massive planet.

The easier method is to measure changes in the star's velocity by measuring the Doppler shift of the light that it radiates. You may know that the pitch of a car horn (say) appears higher if the car is approaching and lower if it is moving away. In a similar way, the frequency of light waves emitted by a star are somewhat higher than normal if the star is approaching us and slightly lower if the star is moving away. By carefully monitoring the frequencies of light waves emitted by the star, astronomers can look for the minute shifts in these frequencies that would result if the star is wobbling around the system's center of mass due to the presence of a planet. This method is particularly sensitive to planets that are close to the star, as such planets orbit faster than planets further out and thus cause larger changes in the star's velocity as well. Using this method, astronomers have discovered a number of planets circling nearby stars.

The harder method is to look for the telltale wobbling by actually measuring the position of the star frequently and very accurately over a long period of time. This method works best for planets that are far from the star, because the farther the planet is from the system's center of mass, the farther the star has to be from the center of mass as well (see equation C4.11). Planets far from a star tend to orbit slowly, though, and so it may require many years of careful observations to see the star wobble even once.

Improved technology has recently made it possible to locate a star in the sky much more accurately than ever before. Based on a detailed analysis of photographs from the 1930s onward (as well as measurements made since 1988 with better technology), astronomers at University of Pittsburgh announced in June of 1996 the tentative discovery of *two* roughly Jupiter-sized planets orbiting the nearby star Lalande 21185, one whose orbit is about 2.5 times the size of the earth's orbit (and lasts 8 years) and one whose orbit is 10 times the size of the earth's orbit and lasts 30 years. (More data needs to be collected over a period of many years to confirm this discovery.) As astronomical technology continues to improve, more planets will likely be discovered using this method.

This illustrates how the ideas discussed in this chapter, far from being stale and esoteric theoretical concepts divorced from the real world, can in fact provide a foundation for making exciting discoveries!

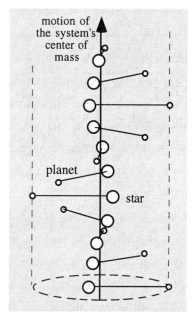

Figure C4.6: The motion of a star and planet through the sky. The large ball represents the star and the small ball the planet. The thick dashed line represents the path of the system's center of mass. One can see how the star "wobbles" around the system's center of mass as it interacts with the planet. (This wobble has been *greatly* exaggerated.)

Exercise C4X.8: The sun has a mass of 2×10^{30} kg, while Jupiter has a mass of about 1.9×10^{27} kg. If Jupiter is about 7.8×10^8 km from the sun, what is the approximate radius of the sun's wobble about the solar system's center of mass due to its interaction with Jupiter? (Ignore the rest of the planets.) Compare this to the radius of the sun, which is about 700,000 km.

MATH SKILLS: Illegal Vector Equations

Since so many important physical quantities are described by vectors, we will be doing a *lot* of mathematics with vectors from this chapter onward. Doing algebra with vector quantities is a lot like doing algebra with ordinary scalars *except* in a few important cases. Here is a list of things to keep in mind when doing vector algebra that will help you avoid making common mistakes.

(1) **Don't set a vector equal to a scalar**. A vector quantity has both a magnitude *and an associated direction*, while a scalar quantity has only a numerical value. Therefore, a vector is *never* equivalent to a scalar (even if their magnitudes are the same) any more than an apple is equivalent to an orange (even if they have the same size). So avoid writing equations like " $\vec{v}$ = 20 m/s" when what you *really* mean "mag($\vec{v}$) = 20 m/s" or perhaps " $\vec{v}$ = 20 m/s south." (The *only* exception to this rule is that " $\vec{c}$ = 0" is usually considered acceptable: this is conventionally taken to mean that *all* the components of $\vec{c}$ are zero.)

(2) **Vector magnitudes are *always* positive** (by definition!). For example, saying that $v = -32$ m/s is absurd: a particle's speed is the *magnitude* of its velocity vector and so *must* be positive. [It should be noted that such equations sometimes appear in textbooks when the author has not clearly distinguished vector magnitudes and components. Since components *can* be negative, what the author really means in such a case is something like $v_x = -32$ m/s,]

(3) **Division by a vector is *not defined*.** If you are given an equation like $\vec{v} = d\vec{r}/dt$ and are asked to find dt, you might be tempted to rearrange it in the usual way to get $dt = d\vec{r}/\vec{v}$. But the latter equation is meaningless, since division by a vector is not defined. Therefore, when you rearrange vector equations algebraically, be careful that you never execute a step that involves dividing both sides by a vector. [The *right* way to solve the vector equation $\vec{v} = d\vec{r}/dt$ for dt is take the magnitude of both sides to get mag($\vec{v}$) = mag($d\vec{r}$)/dt, and then rearrange these *scalar* values in the usual way to get mag($d\vec{r}$)/mag($\vec{v}$) = dt.]

(4) **Remember that mag($\vec{c}_1 + \vec{c}_2$) ≠ mag($\vec{c}_1$)+mag($\vec{c}_2$).** Figure C4.7 illustrates this. To take an even more extreme example, note that if $\vec{c}_1$ and $\vec{c}_2$ have equal magnitudes but opposite directions, mag($\vec{c}_1$)+mag($\vec{c}_2$) ≠ 0, but mag($\vec{c}_1 + \vec{c}_2$) = 0! Similarly, mag($\vec{c}_1 - \vec{c}_2$) ≠ mag($\vec{c}_1$) – mag($\vec{c}_2$). Therefore, whenever you take the magnitude of both sides of a vector equation, check carefully that you do not break up the magnitude of a vector sum (or difference) into the sum (or difference) of magnitudes. [It may help to note that we have to treat the *square root* of a sum or difference the same way, since $\sqrt{a \pm b} \neq \sqrt{a} \pm \sqrt{b}$. You are probably are used to this, though, so you might keep square roots in mind when you deal with vector magnitudes.]

(5) **Vector components are *not* vectors.** A vector's *x, y,* and *z* components are technically *scalars* (signed numbers), not vectors. Writing the components of a vector $\vec{c}$ as $\vec{c}_x$, $\vec{c}_y$, and $\vec{c}_z$ (which seems, for some reason, to be very tempting to beginners) is thus confusing, since it makes these components *look* like vector quantities when they are not. Always remember to write the components of $\vec{c}$ simply as c_x, c_y, and c_z.

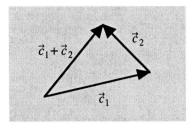

Figure C4.7: Note that the length of the arrow representing $\vec{c}_1 + \vec{c}_2$ is *not* the same as the sum of the lengths of the arrows representing $\vec{c}_1$ and $\vec{c}_2$ (it in fact is somewhat smaller).

Exercise C4X.9: Find the mistakes (if any) in each of the statements below.

(a) A 2.0-kg particle moving in the $-x$ direction at 10 m/s has momentum components $\vec{p}_x = -20$ kg·m/s and $\vec{p}_y = \vec{p}_z = 0$, so the magnitude of its momentum is $p = -20$ kg·m/s.

(b) A system consists of two particles, one moving northward with a momentum of $p_1 = 20$ kg·m/s and the other westward with a momentum of $p_2 = 10$ kg·m/s. The system's total momentum is thus $p_{TOT} = 30$ kg·m/s.

(c) If a particle moves with a velocity of $\vec{v} = 10$ m/s and has a momentum of $\vec{p} = 5$ kg·m/s, then its mass must be $m = \vec{p}/\vec{v} = 0.5$ kg.

I. POSITION, VELOCITY, AND MOMENTUM
  A. A point's *position* $\vec{r} \equiv$ the displacement from the origin to the point
    1. Its components are the point's coordinates $[x, y, z]$
    2. $\text{mag}(\vec{r}) \equiv r = [x^2 + y^2 + z^2]^{1/2}$
    3. The displacement from point 1 to point 2 is $\Delta\vec{r} = \vec{r}_2 - \vec{r}_1$
  B. A *particle* is a hypothetical object with no volume (so that its position
     at an instant of time is always a well-defined mathematical point)
  C. A particle's *velocity* vector at a given instant of time is $\vec{v} \equiv d\vec{r}/dt$
    1. dt is a tiny time interval embracing that instant (so tiny that the
       particle's velocity is essentially constant during dt)
    2. $d\vec{r}$ is the particle's tiny displacement during dt
    3. The components of $\vec{v}$ are $[v_x, v_y, v_z] = [dx/dt, dy/dt, dz/dt]$
    4. $\text{mag}(\vec{v}) \equiv v = |dr|/dt = speed$ [Note that speed $\neq$ velocity!!]
  D. A particle's *momentum* vector at a given instant is $\vec{p} \equiv m\vec{v}$
    1. $\text{mag}(\vec{p}) \equiv p = mv$ = mass times speed
    2. Its components are $[p_x, p_y, p_z] = [mv_x, mv_y, mv_z]$
    3. Its direction is the same as the particle's velocity at that instant

II. INTERACTIONS TRANSFER MOMENTUM
  A. CRUCIAL IDEA: Any interaction acting between two particles for a
     given interval dt mediates a *momentum transfer* from one to the other
    1. The momentum transfer vector $d\vec{p}$ an object gets is equal to the
       change in its momentum (if the interaction acts alone)
    2. This transfer does not change the sum of the particles' momentum
  B. "Transferring" here means adding the momentum transfer vector $d\vec{p}$ to
     the recipient's momentum and subtracting it from the giver's momentum
    1. Subtracting a vector is equivalent to adding its inverse, so this is
       equivalent to adding $d\vec{p}$ to one and $-d\vec{p}$ to the other
    2. It doesn't matter which particle we think is "gaining" the transfer
       and which is "losing" it (to switch, just change the sign of $d\vec{p}$)
  C. A *momentum transfer*, a *particle's momentum* and *momentum* in general
     are analogous to *cash*, a *person's net worth*, and *money* in general

III. SYSTEMS AND OBJECTS
  A. A *system* is any well-defined collection or set of particles or objects
  B. An *extended object* has a nonzero volume and a clear boundary: while it
     is thus *not* a particle, we can always model it as a *system* of particles
  C. Types of interactions involving a particle in a system:
    1. an *internal* interaction acts between two particles in the system (and
       thus does *not* change the system's total momentum)
    2. an *external* interaction acts between a particle inside the system and
       one outside (and *can* change the system's total momentum)

IV. A SYSTEM'S CENTER OF MASS (CM)
  A. A system's CM is a point whose position is the *weighted average* of
     the positions of the system's particles: if N is the number of particles,
     $\vec{r}_{CM} \equiv (1/M)(m_1\vec{r}_1 + m_2\vec{r}_2 + ... + m_N\vec{r}_N)$, M = system's total mass
  B. Implication: A system's total momentum = Mv_{CM}
  C. CRUCIAL IDEA: a system's (or object's) center of mass responds to *ex-
     ternal* momentum transfers just as a *particle* of mass M would
    1. So the CM of an *isolated* system moves at a constant velocity
    2. This allows us to model extended objects as if they were *particles*,
       completely ignoring internal interactions (a beautiful simplicity!)
  D. So from now on, "velocity of an object" means "velocity of its CM"
     (this is equal to the velocity of any well-defined point on a *rigid* object)
  E. We can calculate the CM of a system of *objects* by treating each object
     as if it were a particle located at its own CM

V. ILLEGAL VECTOR EQUATIONS (see the boldface headings in that section)

GLOSSARY

position $\vec{r}$ (of a point in a given reference frame): a vector equal to the displacement between the given frame's origin and the point. The components of $\vec{r}$ are the point's coordinates $[x, y, z]$ in that frame. The magnitude of $\vec{r}$ is the distance between the origin and the point. A displacement $\Delta\vec{r}$ *between* two points is the vector *difference* between the points' position vectors.

particle: an idealized object having mass but essentially zero volume, so that its position always corresponds to a well-defined mathematical point in space.

velocity $\vec{v}$ (of a particle at a given instant of time): a vector whose *magnitude* is the particle's speed and whose *direction* indicates the particle's direction of motion at the given instant. Mathematically, $\vec{v} \equiv d\vec{r}/dt$, where dt is a time interval around the given instant short enough so that the velocity is essentially constant during dt, and $d\vec{r}$ is the particle's displacement during dt. The components of this vector are $[v_x, v_y, v_z] = [dx/dt, dy/dt, dz/dt]$, where dx is the change in the particle's x coordinate during dt, etc.

momentum $\vec{p}$ **of a particle** at a given instant of time: a vector quantity whose *magnitude* is the particle's mass times its speed at the given instant, and whose *direction* is equal to the particle's direction of motion at that instant. Mathematically, $\vec{p} \equiv m\vec{v}$. The components of the momentum vector $\vec{p}$ are $[p_x, p_y, p_z] = [mv_x, mv_y, mv_z]$.

momentum transfer $d\vec{p}$ (or **impulse**): the amount by which an interaction (if it acts alone) changes a particle's momentum during a given time interval dt at the expense of the momentum of the other particle involved in the interaction. A *momentum transfer* is to a *particle's momentum* what *cash* is to a *person's net worth*.

system: any well-defined collection or set of interacting objects and/or particles.

extended object: a collection of matter having a nonzero volume and a well-defined boundary. The object need not be rigid (see below) as long as its boundary remains clear. Examples of extended bodies range from atoms to baseballs to planets to galaxies. An extended object can always be modeled as being a system of particles.

rigid (object): an extended object is rigid if its shape and dimensions do not change with time.

atoms, nuclei, protons, neutrons, electrons, and **quarks**: the building blocks of matter (according to the standard model). *Atoms* consist of *electrons* interacting with *nuclei*; nuclei are systems of interacting *protons* and *neutrons*; protons and neutrons in turn are systems of interacting *quarks*.

elementary particles: ultimate building blocks of matter that are structureless point particles (to the limits of our ability to measure). According to the standard model, electrons and quarks are elementary particles.

internal interaction: an interaction between two particles that are both *inside* a system of interest. The momentum transfers mediated by such interactions remain in the system and therefore do not change the system's total momentum.

external interaction: an interaction between two particles, one inside a system of interest and the other outside the system. The momentum transfers mediated by such interactions can affect the system's total momentum.

center of mass (of a system): a mathematical point representing the weighted average of the positions of all the particles in the system. Mathematically:

$$\vec{r}_{CM} \equiv \frac{1}{M}(m_1\vec{r}_1 + m_2\vec{r}_2 + ... + m_N\vec{r}_N) \qquad \text{(C4.7a)}$$

where $M = m_1 + m_2 + ... + m_N$ = total mass of the system.

TWO-MINUTE PROBLEMS

C4T.1 "The car rounded the corner at a constant velocity." Would this statement make sense to a physicist?
A. No, the word "velocity" is being used incorrectly
B. No, a car has to slow down to turn a corner
C. Could make sense or not, depending on the corner
D. Yes, this statement is acceptable

C4T.2 Which of the following things qualifies as being an "extended object"? For each object, answer T if it qualifies, F if it does not, and D if it is debatable.
(a) an electron   (e) the earth's atmosphere
(b) an atom   (f) the water in an ocean current
(c) a human being   (g) a cluster of galaxies
(d) a swarm of bees

C4T.3 Imagine that a 1.0-kg cart traveling rightward at 1.0 m/s hits a 3.0-kg cart at rest. Afterward, the smaller cart is observed to move leftward with a speed of 0.75 m/s. What momentum transfer did the collision give the smaller cart at the expense of the larger?
A. none; the larger cart was at rest and so had no $\vec{p}$ to give
B. none; the lighter cart gave a momentum transfer to the more massive cart, not the other way around
C. 0.75 kg·m/s leftward
D. 1.00 kg·m/s leftward
E. 1.75 kg·m/s leftward
F. other (specify)
T. Answers A and B are both correct.

C4T.4 A 8.0-kg bowling ball hits a 1.2-kg bowling pin. The momentum transfer that the contact interaction delivers to the pin has the same magnitude as the momentum transfer that it delivers to the ball (T or F).

C4T.5 Consider a system consisting of two particles, one with three times the mass of the other. If the distance between the particles is 1.0 m, the system's center of mass is what distance from the lighter object?
A. ≈ 1.0 m   C. 0.66 m   E. 0.25 m
B. 0.75 m   D. 0.33 m   F. other (specify)

C4T.6 In example C4.2, if we had modeled the atoms as solid spheres instead of point nuclei, we would have gotten the same result for the center of mass (T or F).

C4T.7 In a reference frame fixed on the sun, which do you think follows the straighter path?
A. the earth   B. the moon
C. the center of mass of the earth-moon system

C4T.8 Which of the following statements involving vectors are correct? Answer T if it is correct and F if it is not (be prepared to identify the error if you answer F).
(a) $\vec{p}_{TOT} = \vec{p}_1 + \vec{p}_2$ implies that $p_{TOT} = p_1 + p_2$.
(b) $\vec{p} = m\vec{v}$ implies that $\vec{p}/\vec{v} = m$.
(c) If $\vec{v} = [0, -5.0 \text{ m/s}, 0]$ then $\vec{v}_y = -5.0$ m/s.
(d) If $\vec{v} = [0, -5.0 \text{ m/s}, 0]$ then $v = +5.0$ m/s.
(e) If $\vec{v} = 5.0$ m/s and $m = 2.0$ kg, then $\vec{p} = 10$ kg·m/s.

HOMEWORK PROBLEMS

BASIC SKILLS

C4B.1 An object is observed in a certain reference frame to move from the position [2.2 m, –3.5 m, 1.6 m] to the position [–1.8 m, 1.3 m, –0.1 m] during a time interval of 0.65 s. What are the components of the object's velocity during this interval (assuming that the interval is sufficiently short so that the velocity is essentially constant)?

C4B.2 During a certain interval of time, an object whose velocity components in a certain frame are an essentially constant [1.5 m/s, –2.0 m/s, 0 m/s] moves a distance of 5.0 m. How long was the interval of time?

C4B.3 An object's momentum at a given time in a certain frame has components [2.4 kgm/s, –3.0 kgm/s, 0 kgm/s]. If its mass is 0.80 kg, what is its speed?

C4B.4 A 1.0-kg cart traveling at 1.0 m/s rightward hits a 4.0-kg cart at rest. After the collision, the lighter cart is observed to move to the left at 0.5 m/s. What momentum transfer did the interaction deliver to the massive cart (magnitude and direction)? What is that cart's velocity after the collision (magnitude and direction)?

C4B.5 Imagine that a 1.0-kg cart traveling at 1.0 m/s rightward collides with a cart at rest. If the collision interaction gives a momentum transfer of 1.5 kg·m/s of rightward to the cart originally at rest, what is the velocity of the originally moving cart *after* the collision?

C4B.6 The nuclei of the hydrogen and chlorine atoms in an HCl molecule are 0.13 nm apart. How far from the nucleus of the chlorine atom is the molecules center of mass? (The mass of the chlorine nucleus is roughly 35 time that of the hydrogen nucleus. Electron masses are negligible.)

C4B.7 Consider a system consisting of two point particles A and B. The particles are 25 cm apart, and the distance between particle A and the system's center of mass is 5 cm. What is the mass of particle B compared to the mass of A?

C4B.8 Two particles with a mass of 1.0 kg lie on along the x axis at x = ± 50 cm respectively. Two particles also lie on the y axis. One, with mass 1.0 kg, is at y = +40 cm, and the other, with mass 2.0 kg, is at y = –40 cm. Where is the center of mass of this system?

C4B.9 In a certain reference frame, a 0.20-kg point particle lies 22 cm due north of the origin, another 0.15-kg particle lies 38 cm due west of the origin, while a 0.40-kg particle lies at the origin. Locate the center of mass of this system in this reference frame.

C4B.10 Each of the equations or statements listed below is incorrect in some way. Describe the error in each case.
(a) Object A has a momentum of $\vec{p}$ = 2 kg·m/s.
(b) At the time in question, the object's x-velocity was $\vec{v}_x$ = –10 m/s.
(c) At the time, the object's velocity was 25 m/s.
(d) The displacement between points A and B is [3, 5, –1].
(e) Particle A's momentum is $\vec{p}_A$ = 2.0 kg·m/s westward while particle B's momentum is $\vec{p}_B$ = 2.0 kg·m/s eastward. The magnitude of the system's total momentum is therefore 4.0 kg·m/s.

SYNTHETIC

C4S.1 At a certain time, a car is 150 m due west of your house. If it is traveling with a constant velocity of 30 m/s

30° south of east, what is the magnitude and direction of its position relative to your house 5 seconds later?

C4S.2 An 2.0-kg object's momentum at a certain time is 10 kg·m/s 37° vertically upward from due west. What are the components of its velocity vector at this time (in a frame in standard orientation)?

C4S.3 Prove that in a two-particle system, the distance between the system's center of mass and each particle is inversely proportional to that particle's mass. That is, if d_A and d_B are the distances between the system's center of mass and particles A and B respectively, show that $d_A/d_B = m_B/m_A$ (note the order reversal!).

C4S.4 How far from the earth's geometrical center is the center of mass of the earth/moon system? Is this inside the earth? (The earth has a mass of 6.0×10^{24} kg and a radius of 6380 km. The moon has a mass of 7.4×10^{22} kg and orbits about 384,000 km from the earth. Note that the earth and moon are *not* particles!)

C4S.5 In a certain piece of modern sculpture, four iron spheres are connected in a line by lightweight rods. The separation between each sphere's geometric center and the next along the line is 42 cm. The spheres decrease in size along the line: their masses are 44 kg, 22 kg, 11 kg and 5.5 kg respectively, and their diameters are 22 cm, 17 cm, 14 cm, and 11 cm respectively. The artist wants to suspend this system of spheres by a single wire so that it rotates ponderously in the breeze above the viewers' heads. We will see in unit N that the appropriate place to attach the wire is at the system's center of mass. Where is this point (relative to the center of the most massive sphere)?

C4S.6 Two space walkers, one with a mass of 120 kg and the other with a mass of 85 kg, hold on to the ends of a lightweight cable 12 m long. The astronauts are originally at rest in deep space. How will its center of mass move? If the astronauts then start pulling themselves toward each other along the cable until they meet, roughly how far will the less-massive astronaut move? Does your answer depend on which astronaut is more active in the pulling process?

C4S.7 An asteroid is spotted moving directly toward the center of Starbase Alpha. The frightened residents fire a missile at the asteroid, which breaks it into two chunks, one with 2.4 times the mass of the other. The chunks both pass the starbase at the same time. If the lighter chunk passes 1800 m from one edge of the 2.2 km-wide starbase, will the other chunk hit or miss the starbase?

C4S.8 In a test of a new missile defense system, a missile is fired on a trajectory that would directly strike a certain bunker. A laser flash from the bunker ignites the missile's fuel, causing it to explode into two fragments, one with 1.8 times the mass of the other. If the fragments land at the same time 45 m apart, by how much does the larger fragment miss hitting the bunker? Ignore air friction. (*Hint:* The external gravitational interaction between the missile and the earth would have caused the missile's center of mass to reach the ground at the location of the bunker if the missile had not exploded.)

C4S.9 Imagine that a certain nearby star (whose brightness and other characteristics indicate that its mass is about 2×10^{30} kg) is observed to wobble back and forth a distance (from extreme to extreme) of about 3.2 million km with one cycle taking about 12 y. This period is consistent with the planet being about 800 million km from the star (we will see how to calculate this in unit *N*). What is the mass of the unseen planet? Does your answer depend on how the planet's (probably circular) orbit happens to be oriented with respect to our line of sight?

RICH-CONTEXT

C4R.1 You are the pilot of a jet plane traveling due north at 250 m/s. At a certain time, you see another plane at the same altitude at the 4 o'clock position relative to you and about 5 km away. Thirty seconds later, this plane is at the 3 o'clock position relative to you and 3 km away. Are you in danger of colliding with this plane? (*Hint:* Use a reference frame attached to your plane.)

C4R.2 A 56-kg canoeist sits at rest at the back end of a 23-kg canoe. The canoe is at rest in the still water of a lake with its front end about 0.50 m from the dock. The canoeist realizes that she has left the paddle on the dock, so she carefully works her way to the front of the 3.8-m canoe. Is she likely to be able to reach the dock from the front of the boat? (*Hint:* We can treat the system of the canoe and cano-ist as if it were isolated, for reasons we will discuss in the next chapter. How does this help?)

ADVANCED

C4A.1 Consider a system of N_o extended objects of arbitrary size and shape. Prove that the position of the center of mass of this object is given by

$$\vec{r}_{CM} = \frac{1}{M} \sum_{j=1}^{N_0} M_j \, \vec{r}_{CM,j} \qquad (C4.19)$$

where M_j is the mass of the j-th object and $\vec{r}_{CM,j}$ is the position of its center of mass. (*Hint:* Divide the sum for all *particles* in this system into groups of terms, one term for each object.)

C4A.2 The duration of a "sufficiently short" time interval depends on the accuracy you require. Imagine that an object travels at a constant speed once around a circle in time Δt. How big can dt be (as a fraction of Δt) if the magnitude of $\vec{v}$ in equation C4.2 is to be correct within 0.1%?

ANSWERS TO EXERCISES

C4X.1 No in both cases, because the particle's direction of motion is changing with time.

C4X.2 $\vec{v}$ = [16 m/s, –4.0 m/s, –0.4 m/s], v = 16.5 m/s, $\vec{p}$ = [32 kg·m/s, –8.0 kg·m/s, –0.80 kg·m/s]

C4X.3 The interaction gives the originally moving cart gains $\frac{1}{2}mv_0$ of backward momentum; the other cart gains the same amount of forward momentum.

C4X.4 The originally moving cart gained $\frac{3}{2}mv_0$ of leftward momentum, which is the same thing as saying that it *lost* $\frac{3}{2}mv_0$ of *rightward* momentum. Thus the other cart must have *gained* $\frac{3}{2}mv_0$ of rightward momentum, irrespective of how it was moving before the collision.

C4X.5 If we set up our reference frame so that the massive particle (particle *A*) is at the origin and particle *B* is a distance D = 1.2 m in the +*x* direction from the origin, then equation C4.11 tells us that the center of mass is 0.10 m = 10 cm from the origin (which is the position of particle *A*).

C4X.6 Let us choose our reference frame so that the more massive star (whose mass is $3m$) is at $x = 0$ and the lesser star (whose mass is m) is at $x = 100$ million km. Then the x-position of the system's center of mass is given by $x_{CM} =$ $(0+mx)/4m = x/4 = 25$ million km.

C4X.7 If the system consisting of the person and the rock is really isolated (by virtue of being in "deep space") and its center of mass is initially at rest in our chosen reference frame, then it will *remain* at rest no matter what the person does to the stone (since any interactions between the person and the stone are *internal* to the system). Let the person's mass be m_p = 60 kg and the stone's mass to be m_s =

6.0 kg. If we interpret d = 30 m to be the distance between the origin and the stone's *center of mass* after 5 s, then the distance D between the *person's* center of mass and the origin at this time can be found using the equation

$$\vec{r}_{CM} \equiv \begin{bmatrix} 0 \\ 0 \\ 0 \end{bmatrix} = \frac{1}{M} \left(m_s \begin{bmatrix} d \\ 0 \\ 0 \end{bmatrix} + m_p \begin{bmatrix} -D \\ 0 \\ 0 \end{bmatrix} \right) \qquad (C4.20)$$

The x component of this equation then tells us that

$$0 = \frac{1}{M}(m_s d - m_p D) \quad \Rightarrow \quad m_s d = m_p D \qquad (C4.21)$$

Solving this equation for D and plugging in the numbers, we find that the person has moved a distance D = 3.0 m in the –*x* direction from the origin.

C4X.8 The radius of the sun's wobble around its center of mass is the same as its distance from the center of mass. Plugging the numbers into equation C4.11, we get:

$$x_{CM} = \frac{1.9 \times 10^{27} \text{ kg}}{2.0 \times 10^{30} \text{ kg}} (7.8 \times 10^8 \text{ km}) = 740,000 \text{ km} \qquad (C4.22)$$

which is just a bit larger than the sun's radius.

C4X.9 (a) The momentum components are written incorrectly with arrows, and the magnitude of the momentum vector is quoted as being negative. (b) The magnitude of a sum of momentum vectors is not equal to the sum of the magnitudes. (c) Vectors are set equal to scalar values, and the final equality involves division by a vector.

APPLYING MOMENTUM CONSERVATION

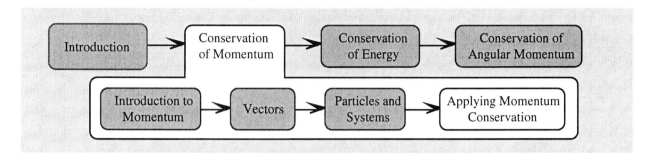

C5.1 OVERVIEW

In the last three chapters, we have developed a sense of what momentum is, learned how to deal with the fact that it is a vector, and discovered some very basic and important things about extended objects and how interactions work. In this chapter, we will bring all of these insights to bear on the task of applying the law of conservation of momentum to realistic situations in the world.

In addition to learning how to apply conservation of momentum, one of the main purposes of this chapter is to teach you something about how to solve complex physics problems. We will explore a generalized process or outline that will help you organize your thinking about such problems, a process that you will find useful in all units of this text (but especially in units C and N).

This chapter closes the subunit on conservation of momentum; in the next chapter we will take up the topic of conservation of energy. You will see, however, that the ideas we have developed in this unit represent a crucial background for understanding energy.

Here is a summary of the sections in this chapter.

C5.2 *INTERACTIONS WITH THE EARTH* opens with a puzzle: momentum does *not* seem to be conserved when something interacts with the earth. Solving this puzzle will help us deal more insightfully with situations involving interacting objects that have very different masses.

C5.3 *WHEN MULTIPLE INTERACTIONS ACT* looks at another puzzle: since conservation of momentum applies only to *isolated* systems, and the colliding carts we have considered before are *not* isolated, why does momentum conservation apply at all? Answering this question requires a further refinement of the momentum-transfer model of interactions.

C5.4 *WHAT COUNTS AS "ISOLATED"?* goes beyond this situation to argue that there are in fact three separate categories of situations where we can *model* a system as isolated even when it is not.

C5.5 *A FRAMEWORK FOR SOLVING PROBLEMS* presents a coherent approach to solving non-trivial physics problems, an approach that (when followed) helps get you started and then keeps you on track and paying attention to things that need attention. Examples illustrate the application of this problem-solving framework.

C5.6 *APPLICATIONS: PLANES AND ROCKETS* shows how conservation of momentum helps us understand how planes fly and how a rocket engine can change a spaceship's speed even in empty space (where there is nothing to push against).

C5.2   INTERACTIONS WITH THE EARTH

A puzzle: Does the earth's momentum change when interacting with you?

Here is a puzzle. Imagine that you get up on a table and then jump to the floor. As you fall, your gravitational interaction with the earth mediates a continuous momentum transfer that smoothly increases your downward momentum. When you hit the floor, your contact interaction with the ground brings you to a stop, so it must give you an upward momentum transfer that cancels the downward momentum you accumulated during your fall.

Your partner in both of these interactions is the earth itself. So as you fall, the model developed in the last chapter predicts that the earth must get an upward momentum transfer from the gravitational interaction that is equal in magnitude to the downward momentum transfer you get. When you hit the ground, the earth must get a downward momentum transfer from the contact interaction that is equal to the upward momentum transfer that you got. Otherwise the total momentum of the system consisting of you and the earth will not be conserved.

But this seems absurd! The earth is *obviously* at rest during both interactions, and therefore has zero momentum. But your momentum definitely changes with time, so the total momentum of this system is not conserved, and the law of conservation of momentum is false!? This is the puzzle.

Our model predicts that it does, but that the earth's motion is extremely small

But *is* it really obvious that the earth is at rest throughout this process? Imagine observing the earth from a reference frame floating in space (such as the frame defined by the Global Positioning System satellites at a given instant of time) in which the earth is at rest *before* you jump, but might in *principle* be able to measure the subsequent motion of the earth during your jump. How rapidly would our model predict that the earth should move in a situation like this?

Let's estimate that a person's mass is roughly 50 kg. Let's estimate that after falling a meter or so, a person is moving downward with a speed of roughly 10 mi/h ≈ 4 m/s (the exact numbers are not really relevant, as we will see). Thus the magnitude of the total momentum transfer that you have gotten from the gravitational interaction by the end of the fall is ≈ 200 kg·m/s, so the earth should get a momentum transfer of this magnitude from the interaction as well.

The earth has a mass of about 6×10^{24} kg. If the earth is originally at rest and then gains 200 kg·m/s of momentum, it (or more correctly, its center of mass) will be moving (just before you hit the ground) at a speed of very roughly

$$v_f \equiv \text{mag}(\vec{v}_f) = \frac{\text{mag}(\vec{p}_{\text{earth}})}{m_{\text{earth}}} = \frac{200 \text{ kg} \cdot \text{m/s}}{6 \times 10^{24} \text{ kg}} \approx 30 \times 10^{-24} \text{ m/s} \qquad \text{(C5.1)}$$

If the earth continued moving undisturbed at this rate for 10^{15} years or so (about 100,000 times the age of the universe), it would move about a meter, which is the approximate resolution of the GPS reference frame. In the approximately half-second that the interaction lasts, the earth moves about 10^{-23} m, which is about 100 million times smaller than an atomic nucleus.

In other words, the earth's motion in this circumstance is not just *hard* to detect, it is so impossibly small that we can hardly imagine *ever* being able to detect it. Therefore our model is not at all inconsistent with the observation that the earth seems to remain at rest: even though our model predicts that the earth's center of mass does *not* remain at rest, it also predicts that the motion will be so small as to be completely unobservable.

An analogy: the earth is to momentum like the ocean is to water

Here's an analogy. Imagine that you take a bucket of water from the ocean. Did you notice that the ocean's level falls a bit? No? Why not? You probably believe that the ocean's level really *does* fall a little bit: you intuitively know that if you take some water from the ocean, it does indeed have less water than it had before. But because the ocean is so immense, taking a bucket from it does not *measurably* affect its level. Similarly, the earth (because of its enormous mass) can provide (or absorb) momentum transfers without measurable effect.

The same kind of argument applies to situations where an object collides with a wall or barrier and either bounces off or is brought to rest. The object's

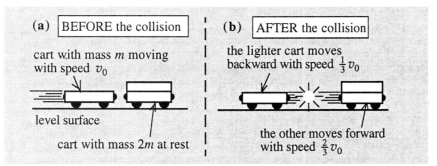

Figure C5.1: An example collision between two carts that does conserve momentum (This is an example that we have examined in both chapters C2 and C4.)

horizontal momentum clearly changes, so the earth must get a momentum transfer in the opposite direction, but its motion will not measurably change.

Our solution here actually points to a problem that we will examine more fully in unit N. In a reference frame that is *attached* to the earth, the earth is *always* at rest (by definition!). In *this* frame, your momentum changes in this interaction but the earth's momentum does not, so momentum is *not* conserved. Yet conservation of momentum is a basic law of physics! How can it *not* work?

The short answer is that some *reference frames* are better than others. As Newton himself first realized, the laws of newtonian mechanics work best when we use any reference frame that floats freely in space and is not rotating with respect to the distant stars: this is the standard to which we compare all other reference frames. In particular, when we want to apply newtonian mechanics to determine the earth's *response* to the interactions that involve it, we *must* use such a frame for the newtonian model to make sense.

A frame floating in space is the standard to which we compare other frames

However, we have just seen that even when we use such a frame, the change in the earth's motion due to normal, human-scale interactions is immeasurably small (because the earth's mass is so immense). Therefore, for all purposes *other* than calculating the earth's own response to an interaction, a frame fixed to the earth's center of mass is indistinguishable from a frame floating in space where the earth's center of mass is initially at rest (the distinction between these frames is completely immeasurable). We will, therefore, continue to use earth-based frames without worrying about this issue too much.

For most purposes, a frame attached to the earth is indistinguishable

---

Exercise C5X.1: A friend proposes the following doomsday scenario: what if China's leaders arrange for the entire population of China ($\approx 10^9$ people) to jump simultaneously from ladders to the ground. Won't this wreak global havoc as the earth shifts in response? Using a space-based frame where the earth is initially at rest, estimate the speed of the earth's center of mass just before the entire population of China hits the ground. Do you think that the motion of the earth's center of mass in this case is something to worry about?

C5.3 WHEN MULTIPLE INTERACTIONS ACT

Here is another puzzle. Consider a collision between two carts, as shown in Figure C5.1. We have seen that the total momentum of the two carts is conserved in such a collision. But we have also seen that the total momentum of a system is only conserved when it is *isolated* from external interactions. This is clearly not the case with the carts, each of which is involved in a gravitational interaction with the earth and a contact interaction with the surface on which they roll. Why are we justified in ignoring these external interactions?

A puzzle: How can a collision between carts conserve momentum when the carts are not isolated?

The ultimate justification is that ignoring these interactions *works*: experimentally we see that the carts' total momentum *is* conserved in spite of these interactions! But understanding *why* we can ignore these interactions will help us develop the model we are constructing of interactions and also broaden the range of situations where we can apply the law of conservation of momentum.

The situation here involves objects that participate in several interactions at once. During the collision, each cart participates in a contact interaction with the other cart, a gravitational interaction with the earth and a contact interaction with the level surface. In the last chapter, we saw that an object's change in momentum as it responds to an interaction is *equal* to the momentum transfer $d\vec{p}$ the interaction gives it. But what happens when several interactions act at once?

Multiple interactions operate *independently* on an object: their momentum transfers simply add

The *easiest* assumption to make is that the various interactions operate *independently* on the object during a tiny given interval of time dt (each giving the object the momentum transfer it would have delivered if acting alone) and that we find the interactions' total effect on the object's momentum during this interval by simply adding those momentum transfers (as vectors, of course):

$$d\vec{p} = d\vec{p}_1 + d\vec{p}_2 + d\vec{p}_3 + ... \qquad (C5.2)$$

where $d\vec{p}$ is the net change in the object's actual momentum during a given interval of time, $d\vec{p}_1$ is the momentum transferred to the object by interaction 1 during that interval, $d\vec{p}_2$ is that delivered by interaction 2, and so on. This is just an *assumption* whose ultimate justification is consistency with experimental results. The universe does not *have* to operate this way (multiple interactions could *in principle* reinforce each other in such a way that their net effect is greater than the sum of their parts). However, experimental results do in fact amply support the validity of this assumption.

Now the point of the bar through the delta in the notation for a momentum transfer $d\vec{p}_1$ may be clearer. When multiple interactions act on an object, no individual momentum transfer delivered during a given time interval dt is actually *equal* to the object's change in momentum $d\vec{p}$ during that interval: we have to *add* these momentum transfers to determine that change. The bar is there to remind us that any given momentum transfer $d\vec{p}$ contributes only *partially* the object's actual net momentum change $d\vec{p}$ when other interactions are involved.

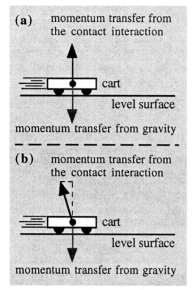

Figure C5.2: (a) When there is no friction, the momentum transfer delivered by a cart's interaction with a surface during a given interval dt is perpendicular to the surface and therefore can (if the surface is level) cancel the momentum transfer that gravity delivers during that time. **(b)** The presence of friction means that the momentum transfer from the contact interaction is not perfectly perpendicular, and so after adding the vertical one from gravity there is a small backward momentum transfer to the cart that reduces its forward momentum.

With this in mind, let us again consider the colliding carts in Figure C5.1. A gravitational interaction acting *alone* on a cart during a given time interval dt gives it a purely *downward* momentum transfer (to see this, drop the cart from rest and notice how its momentum changes from zero to something downward). But we observe that the momentum of a cart rolling by itself without friction on a level surface does not change. This means that if our model is true, the contact interaction between the cart and the surface *must* (during any given time interval dt) give the cart an *upward* momentum transfer equal in magnitude to that *downward* one it got from gravity during dt so the effects of these interactions cancel out. This is the only way our model can explain what we observe to be true! If the effects of these interactions cancel for each cart, then these external interactions do *not* change the total momentum of the system, and its total momentum will then be conserved by the internal collision interaction.

Of course, when there *is* friction, a rolling cart's momentum *does* change (because the cart slows down), so in such a case the effect of the object's contact interaction with the track must *not* be completely canceled by the effect of the gravitational interaction. Since gravity always delivers a *downward* momentum transfer to an object, its effects will only exactly cancel those of a contact interaction if the contact interact supplies a purely *upward* momentum transfer to the object. In the case of a level surface, this direction is perpendicular to the surface. In fact, a practical definition of *friction* and *frictionless* in this context is:

Practical definitions of *frictionless* and *friction*

A **frictionless** contact interaction between an object and a surface is one that during any given tiny time interval dt delivers a momentum transfer *exactly* perpendicular to the surface. Conversely, **friction** is the aspect of an interaction between an object and a surface that causes the momentum transfer it delivers to have a component in a direction *parallel* to the surface.

See Figure C5.2 for an illustration.

The way to test whether an object's contact interaction with a *level* surface is frictionless, then, is to do an experiment to see whether the object's velocity remains constant as it rolls or slides *by itself* along the surface: if it does, the interaction is frictionless by definition. (This probably coincides with what you would intuitively do if asked to check for friction!).

In summary, as long as each cart involved in collision shown in Figure C5.1 moves *frictionlessly* on a level surface, then the net effect of the external contact and gravitational interactions acting on that cart (and thus on the entire system) are *zero*, and the total momentum of the system is conserved as if external interactions did not exist. This justifies our ignoring such interactions earlier and solves the puzzle raised at the beginning of the section.

A test for friction

The effects of the external interactions acting on a frictionless cart *cancel*, so they can be ignored

---

Exercise C5X.2: A friend claims that a passive thing like a level surface *obviously* cannot deliver an active upward momentum transfer to an object, so the presence of a support must somehow shut down the gravitational interaction acting on the supported object. Flesh out an argument *against* this idea by considering two thought-experiments: **(a)** First imagine supporting the object by holding it in your hand above the floor. Does it *feel* like the gravitational interaction between the object and the earth is shut down when you hold it passively? What does this mean? **(b)** Consider supporting an object by hanging it from a spring. Can the passive spring really be giving the object an upward momentum transfer during any given interval of time? What do you think would happen to the hanging object if you *were* able to suddenly turn off the gravity in the room?

C5.4   WHAT COUNTS AS "ISOLATED"?

We saw in the last chapter that the total momentum of a system of particles and/or objects that is *isolated* from external interactions will be conserved (since internal interactions only transfer momentum around *within* the system). But in reality, *no* system is ever completely isolated from its surroundings. How then can we use the law of conservation of momentum at all?

The answer developed in the last section is that we can treat a system *as if* it were isolated in certain circumstances. In general, we can do this as long as the external interactions involving the system fail to change its total momentum *significantly* during the time interval of interest. There are three distinct types of situations where this happens.

There are three practical cases where we can apply momentum conservation

The first case is where the external interactions in question are *very weak*. External interactions by their nature execute momentum transfers into or out of a system, but during any given interval of time, a weak interaction (by definition) delivers less momentum transfer than one that is strong. Consider, for example, a situation where we have a system of objects in "deep space," which is very far away from any planets or stars that might interact with them gravitationally. The objects in our system still *do* interact gravitationally with these stars and planets, but since the strength of the gravitational interaction decreases with separation, the momentum transfer effected by these interactions in any given time interval will be small if the distances are very large.

First case: the system is *approximately isolated* (external effects are weak)

The way to test this is to take various objects, isolate them from each other, and then examine their motion to see whether they move with essentially constant velocities during a reasonably long time interval. If they do, then whatever external interactions are present must be weak. (We can at least *imagine* that objects in "deep space" really do behave this way.)

We say that any system involved in external interactions that are very weak is **approximately isolated**: its total momentum is then approximately conserved. The only "practical" realization of such a system is in fact one located in deep space. (In the end-of-chapter problems, therefore, "deep space" is essentially a code-word for "approximately isolated.")

Second case: the system is *functionally isolated* (external effects cancel)

A second kind of situation where we can model a system as being isolated is where significant external interactions *are* present, but during any given time interval, the momentum transfers they contribute essentially cancel, so that the system's total momentum remains constant in spite of the external interactions. In such a case, we say that the system is **functionally isolated**, meaning that it is not *really* isolated but since the external interactions cancel each other out, from a functional point of view the system behaves as if it *were* isolated.

This is exactly the kind of situation we explored at length in the last section. We found there that a system of objects moving frictionlessly on level surfaces qualifies as being functionally isolated, and that the way to *test* for functional isolation is to verify that each object *by itself* moves on the surface with a constant momentum. If there is significant friction (or if the surface is not level) at least one object will fail the test, and the system cannot be treated as isolated.

Third case: *collisions* (external effects do not have time to do much)

The third kind of situation is where significant external interactions *are* present and do *not* cancel, but the internal interaction is a *collision* of short duration and we limit ourselves to looking at the system's momentum *just before* and *just after* that collision. Technically, a **collision** in physics refers to *any* interaction between two objects of limited duration that mediates a much larger momentum transfer than other interactions involving the objects do during that time interval. (Note that this definition does *not* require that the objects actually touch during the collision!) The idea here is that if the duration of the collision is sufficiently short, external interactions simply will not have *time* to transfer much momentum to the system, so as long as we look at the system just before and just after the collision, its total momentum is approximately conserved.

Exercise C5X.3: Two billiard balls collide on a pool table. According to the definitions presented above, is the system consisting of the two balls *approximately*, *functionally*, or simply *not* isolated?

Exercise C5X.4: Two cars skidding on a road collide with each other. Can we apply conservation of momentum to this situation? If so, what justifies treating the cars as an isolated system?

C5.5 A FRAMEWORK FOR SOLVING PROBLEMS

In general, solving a physics problem successfully involves taking a realistic situation and constructing a simplified model that captures its essence (often by deliberately suppressing complicating details) and can be connected easily to the larger and more abstract models of physics that we have developed in the text. This is *not* an easy thing: doing it well requires practice.

Experienced physics problem-solvers find one approach uniquely effective

However, I *can* give you a head start. Studies show that experienced physics problem-solvers (unlike novices) usually solve complex physics problems using general framework that is fairly independent of either the person or the problem, a pattern they have found by experience to be effective at generating correct solutions. What I plan to do is teach you this framework. You may find it strange or awkward at first (like the correct way of holding a violin bow seems awkward at first) but it really *works* (trust me!), and increasing your familiarity with it will give you more power and flexibility down the line.

This effective problem-solving framework has four important parts

This successful approach is founded on constructing *three representations* of the problem situation that tap into three different ways that the brain processes information: (1) a **pictorial representation**, (2) a **conceptual representation**, and (3) a **mathematical representation**. Fully developing each of these representations is usually equivalent to solving the problem. Experts (knowing how easy it is to make errors) also do an (4) **evaluation** of the result, where they step back from the answer and check it in various ways to see if it makes sense. Let's look at each of these four steps in more detail.

Physicists almost always begin *any* problem solution by *drawing a picture* of the situation. Drawing a good picture provides you with a great opportunity to do at least four very important things. (1) It makes you translate the verbal statement of the problem into something that you can *visualize*. Not only is the brain usually much better at processing relationships between things presented visually instead of verbally, but the very act of translation often makes the situation clearer in your mind. (2) It forces you to define your reference frame and present your choice visually for the reader. (In a complex problem, "the reader" may be *you* reviewing the decisions you have made.) (3) It provides an opportunity to define mathematical symbols for quantities of interest by using those symbols to label objects, distances, arrows, and so on. Defining symbols as part of the picture this way also saves you *time* by making their meaning clear to a reader (in an accessible, visual way) with only a minimal amount of verbal explanation. (4) The process of defining symbols usually highlights which quantities you know and which you don't. I recommend listing values of known quantities and indicating unknown quantities as a basic part of the picture.

First part: a *pictorial representation* of the situation of interest

The *conceptual representation* is the part of a solution where you make (and record) basic decisions about how to construct your particular model of the situation and how to connect it to the abstract physical models in the text. Here is where you wrestle with questions like: What kind of problem is this? What basic abstract models and/or principles apply? What simplifications and/or approximations do I have to make to construct a usable model of the situation? The particular questions you need to address will depend somewhat on the problem, but the main idea is to write *verbal* responses to questions of this type. This is useful not only because it makes your thinking clear to your reader (who may be grading you on the quality of that thinking!) but also because the very act of writing responses in complete English sentences to questions like these almost *forces* you to make your thinking about these issues coherent and logical, which helps you avoid making conceptual errors.

Second part: a *conceptual representation*

Once you have clarified the basic features of your model and its connections to the abstract physics models, selecting the basic mathematical equations that describe the behavior of your model of the situation is not usually hard. Your tasks in the *mathematical representation* part of a solution are to: (1) write down these basic equations using the symbols defined in your pictorial representation, (2) to solve these equations *symbolically* for any unknown symbols, and then (3) to plug in known values and calculate a numerical answer (if required), *keeping very careful track of each quantity's units* during the calculation.

Third part: a *mathematical representation*

The last two items here are very important! Novices tend to make things difficult for themselves by plugging in numbers *way* too early. Experts solve the equations *symbolically* (inserting only zeros or simple unitless integers or integer ratios) for three very practical reasons: (1) you are *much* less likely to make errors when doing symbolic algebra, (2) using symbols exclusively makes it much easier to *read* your work, and thus makes it easier for either you or someone else to *find* errors if you do make them, and (3) it *saves time*, because writing multi-digit numbers with their required units usually take about five to ten times the effort of writing a symbol (compare, for example, writing 2.28×10^6 m/s to writing v_0).

The final step is *evaluation*. There are many ways that you can check that a numerical result makes sense, but here are three general ways that are almost always useful. (1) First and foremost, *check the units* of your answer. If you have kept track of units (as I have urged above) when you finally start plugging in numbers, then you should be left at the end with units appropriate to your final answer (m/s for a speed, for example). This provides a very useful and essentially independent check on your algebra: if you made an algebraic error earlier, it often shows up as a unit problem. My experience is that the value of being sensitive to units becomes more and more obvious with experience. (2) It is also usually valuable to *check the sign* of your result, for similar reasons. For example, if a

Fourth part: *evaluating* the result

speed comes out negative, something *must* be wrong! (3) Finally, it is useful to *check a result's magnitude*. Ask yourself whether the magnitude seems reasonable. (Does a car end up traveling faster than the speed of light? Is a cart's mass larger than the mass of the sun?) Correct results also *tend* to be of the same order of magnitude as known values of the same kind of quantity in the problem.

The *model* is the answer

In spite of the importance of evaluating a result for correctness, I want to make it clear that the number that you get at the end is emphatically NOT what I think of as being the "answer" to a physics problem at this level: the *model you build* of a situation (which is described by the first three parts of your solution) is the answer. The main goal of this text (and thus of the problems) is to help you learn to model physical situations correctly, thoughtfully, and with real insight. Therefore, arriving at the wrong answer (because of some silly mistake) after thinking carefully and constructing a good model shows you to be further toward realizing this goal than somehow pulling the right numerical result from a wrongheaded model. Take this as your mantra: *the model is the answer*.

While expert problem-solvers usually go through the framework in roughly the order I have given, you may find that as you construct your model, you will jump back and forth between various parts (particularly the pictorial representation and the conceptual representation parts) to add things you have forgotten and make everything consistent. This is normal and appropriate.

Now, I have described the framework in very general terms that apply to almost *any* kind of physics problem that involves making a prediction about a hypothetical situation. Let's see how we can use this framework in problems that specifically involve applying the law of conservation of momentum.

Applying the framework to conservation of momentum problems

Conservation of momentum problems almost always involve comparing a system's total momentum *before* some internal interaction to that *after* the interaction. In such problems, your *pictorial representation* should therefore include *two* sketches: one showing the system's initial state and one showing the system's final state. The quantities of interest are the momenta of the objects involved, which are calculated from their masses and velocities, so it is important that you label these quantities on the diagram.

Here are the questions that you need to address in the *conceptual representation*: (1) What exactly is the *system* in this situation? (Circling the system in your initial and final pictures can help answer this.) (2) What external and internal interactions do objects in this system participate in? (3) How do we know that we can apply conservation of momentum to this situation (that is, is this really a conservation-of-momentum problem)? Is this system *approximately* or *functionally* isolated, or are we talking about a *collision* process? (4) Are there any approximations or assumptions we have to make to solve the problem? Answering these questions requires you to construct your model of the system and link it to the abstract physics model describing conservation of momentum.

Once you have established that this is a conservation-of-momentum problem, the basic equation that you will start with is the law of conservation of momentum, which states that the system's initial total momentum is equal to its final total momentum:

$$\vec{p}_{1i} + \vec{p}_{2i} + \vec{p}_{3i} + ... = \vec{p}_{1f} + \vec{p}_{2f} + \vec{p}_{3f} + ... \tag{C5.3}$$

where the subscripts 1, 2, 3, ... refer to the objects in the system and the *i* and *f* subscripts mean *initial* and *final*, respectively. Completing the mathematical representation then means plugging in the symbols for masses and velocities that you defined in your picture (using $\vec{p} \equiv m\vec{v}$), expressing the vector equation in component form, and solving for any unknown quantities.

On the next two pages, you will find example solutions to conservation-of-momentum problems accompanied by an outline of the solution framework I have just described. The circled numbers link features of the solution to items in the framework.

EXAMPLE C5.1 (Captain, We've Got a Problem in Engineering...)

OUTLINE OF THE FRAMEWORK

1. Pictorial Representation

a. Draw a picture of the situation that includes:

① (1) sketches of the system in its initial and final states

② (2) reference frame axes

③ (3) labels defining symbols for relevant quantities (in this case, the objects' masses and velocities)

b. List values for all known quanti-
④ ties and specify which quantities are unknown.

2. Conceptual Representation

The general task is to construct a conceptual model of the situation and link it to an abstract physics model or principle. In conservation-of-momentum problems, we do the following:

⑤ a. Identify the *system* involved (by circling it on the sketches)

b. Decide if conservation of momentum applies to this system: is it

 (1) *approximately* isolated, because external interactions are weak?

 (2) *functionally* isolated, because external interactions cancel out?

 (3) involved in a *collision* of short duration so that we can ignore external interactions?

⑥ (Be sure to support your conclusion with a short argument.)

c. Do we have to make any approxi-
⑦ mations or assumptions to solve the problem? (If so, describe.)

3. Mathematical Representation

a. Apply the mathematical equation
⑧ that appropriately describes the situation (equation C5.3 here)

⑨ b. Solve for unknowns symbolically

⑩ c. Plug in numbers and units and calculate the result and its units.

4. Evaluation

Check that the answer makes sense:

⑪ a. Does it have the correct units?

⑫ b. Does it have the right sign?

⑬ c. Does it seem reasonable?

Problem: A 10,000-kg spaceship in deep space travels at 40 km/s toward the Andromeda galaxy. Its engines suddenly explode, blowing the ship apart into two hunks. The front (8,000-kg) hunk continues moving toward Andromeda at 60 km/s. What is the velocity (magnitude and direction) of the other hunk?

Solution: Let's orient our reference frame so that "toward Andromeda" is the $+x$ direction. We'll assume for the sake of the picture that the back hunk moves *away* from Andromeda after the collision (though we don't really *know* this yet, since $\vec{v}_B$ is what we are trying to find).

BEFORE: ①

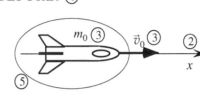

KNOWN: ④

$m_0 = 10{,}000$ kg,

$m_A = 8{,}000$ kg

$m_B = m_0 - m_A = 2{,}000$ kg

$$\vec{v}_0 = \begin{bmatrix} v_{0x} \\ v_{0y} \\ v_{0z} \end{bmatrix} = \begin{bmatrix} +40 \text{ m/s} \\ 0 \\ 0 \end{bmatrix}$$

AFTER: ①

$$\vec{v}_A = \begin{bmatrix} v_{Ax} \\ v_{Ay} \\ v_{Az} \end{bmatrix} = \begin{bmatrix} +60 \text{ m/s} \\ 0 \\ 0 \end{bmatrix}$$

UNKNOWN: ④

$$\vec{v}_B = \begin{bmatrix} v_{Bx} \\ v_{By} \\ v_{Bz} \end{bmatrix} = \begin{bmatrix} ? \\ ? \\ ? \end{bmatrix}$$

The system in this case is the spaceship (or its fragments), ⑤ as shown circled in the diagrams. The explosion probably has a very short duration, so we *could* consider this a *collision* and ignore external interactions, but the fact that this happens in "deep space" means that external interactions are weak anyway and the system is *approximately isolated*. We can thus apply momentum conservation without making any further approximations. So equation C5.2 tells us that:

⑧ $$\vec{p}_{1i} + \vec{p}_{2i} + \vec{p}_{3i} + \ldots = \vec{p}_{1f} + \vec{p}_{2f} + \vec{p}_{3f} + \ldots$$

which here means $m\vec{v}_0 = m_A\vec{v}_A + m_B\vec{v}_B$; or in component form:

$$m_0\begin{bmatrix} v_{0x} \\ 0 \\ 0 \end{bmatrix} = m_A\begin{bmatrix} v_{Ax} \\ 0 \\ 0 \end{bmatrix} + m_B\begin{bmatrix} v_{Bx} \\ v_{By} \\ v_{Bz} \end{bmatrix}$$

The last two rows of this equation tell us that $v_{By} = v_{Bz} = 0$, so the back hunk *does* move in along the x axis as we guessed in the picture. Extracting the top row of this equation and solving for v_{Bx}, we get:

$$m_0 v_{0x} = m_A v_{Ax} + m_B v_{Bx} \quad \Rightarrow \quad v_{Bx} = \frac{m_0 v_{0x} - m_A v_{Ax}}{m_B} \quad ⑨$$

⑩
$$v_{Bx} = \frac{(10{,}000 \text{ kg})(+40 \text{ km/s}) - (8000 \text{ kg})(+60 \text{ km/s})}{2000 \text{ kg}} = -40 \text{ km/s}$$

The answer has the right units, ⑪ and its magnitude seems reasonable (comparable to other speeds in the problem). ⑬ The sign seems OK, too, showing that our original guess that the back hunk might move *away* from Andromeda (in the $-x$ direction) was correct. ⑫

EXAMPLE C5.2
(Stoplight? What Stoplight?)

OUTLINE OF THE FRAMEWORK

1. Pictorial Representation

  a. Draw a picture of the situation that includes:

  ① (1) sketches of the system in its initial and final states

  ② (2) reference frame axes

  (3) labels defining symbols for relevant quantities (in this ③ case, the objects' masses and velocities)

  b. List values for all known quanti- ④ ties and specify which quantities are unknown.

2. Conceptual Representation

The general task is to construct a conceptual model of the situation and link it to an abstract physics model or principle. In conservation-of-momentum problems, we do the following:

  ⑤ a. Identify the *system* involved (by circling it on the sketches)

  b. Decide if conservation of momentum applies to this system: is it

  (1) *approximately* isolated, because external interactions are weak? ⑥

  (2) *functionally* isolated, because external interactions cancel out?

  (3) involved in a *collision* of short duration so that we can ignore external interactions?

  ⑥ (Be sure to support your conclusion with a short argument.)

  c. Do we have to make any approximations or assumptions to solve ⑦ the problem? (If so, describe.)

3. Mathematical Representation

  a. Apply the mathematical equation ⑧ that appropriately describes the situation (equation C5.3 here)

  ⑨ b. Solve for unknowns symbolically

  ⑩ c. Plug in numbers and units and calculate the result and its units.

4. Evaluation

  Check that the answer makes sense:

  ⑪ a. Does it have the correct units?

  ⑫ b. Does it have the right sign?

  ⑬ c. Does it seem reasonable?

Problem: A 1000-kg car traveling west at 20 m/s collides with an 800-kg car traveling north at 16 m/s. The collision locks the cars together. What is the velocity of the two-car unit just after the collision?

Solution: Let's set up our reference frame in standard orientation. Just looking at the initial momentum arrow here suggests that the cars' final total momentum *has* to be toward the northwest, as shown.

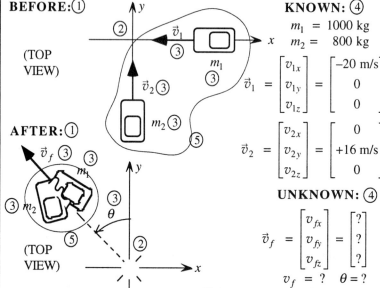

BEFORE: ① (TOP VIEW)

AFTER: ① (TOP VIEW)

KNOWN: ④

$$m_1 = 1000 \text{ kg}$$
$$m_2 = 800 \text{ kg}$$

$$\vec{v}_1 = \begin{bmatrix} v_{1x} \\ v_{1y} \\ v_{1z} \end{bmatrix} = \begin{bmatrix} -20 \text{ m/s} \\ 0 \\ 0 \end{bmatrix}$$

$$\vec{v}_2 = \begin{bmatrix} v_{2x} \\ v_{2y} \\ v_{2z} \end{bmatrix} = \begin{bmatrix} 0 \\ +16 \text{ m/s} \\ 0 \end{bmatrix}$$

UNKNOWN: ④

$$\vec{v}_f = \begin{bmatrix} v_{fx} \\ v_{fy} \\ v_{fz} \end{bmatrix} = \begin{bmatrix} ? \\ ? \\ ? \end{bmatrix}$$

$$v_f = ? \quad \theta = ?$$

The system in this case is two cars, ⑤which I have circled in the diagrams. Friction between the cars' tires and the road will likely be significant here, so the system will not be functionally isolated. But we do have a collision, so as long as we recognize that the final velocity we ⑥ find applies only *just after* the collision, we can apply momentum conservation without making further approximations. Equation C5.2 tells ⑦ us that $\vec{p}_{1i} + \vec{p}_{2i} + \vec{p}_{3i} + \ldots = \vec{p}_{1f} + \vec{p}_{2f} + \vec{p}_{3f} + \ldots,$ ⑧ which in component form in this case reads:

$$m_1 \begin{bmatrix} v_{1x} \\ 0 \\ 0 \end{bmatrix} + m_2 \begin{bmatrix} 0 \\ v_{2y} \\ 0 \end{bmatrix} = (m_1 + m_2) \begin{bmatrix} v_{fx} \\ v_{fy} \\ v_{fz} \end{bmatrix}$$

The last row of this equation tells us that $v_{fz} = 0$, so the cars do not move vertically (as we might have guessed). The top two rows of this equation read $m_1 v_{1x} = (m_1 + m_2) v_{fx}$ and $m_2 v_{2y} = (m_1 + m_2) v_{fy}$, respectively. Solving these two equations for v_{fx} and v_{fy}, we get:

⑨
$$v_{fx} = \frac{m_1 v_{1x}}{m_1 + m_2} = \frac{(1000 \text{ kg})(-20 \text{ m/s})}{1800 \text{ kg}} = -11 \text{ m/s} \quad ⑩$$

⑨
$$v_{fy} = \frac{m_2 v_{2y}}{m_1 + m_2} = \frac{(800 \text{ kg})(+16 \text{ m/s})}{1800 \text{ kg}} = +7.1 \text{ m/s} \quad ⑩$$
⑪

(These units are correct for velocity components.) Since v_{fx} is negative but v_{fy} is positive, $\vec{v}_f$ points northwest as expected, ⑫ specifically

$$\theta = \tan^{-1} \left| \frac{v_{fx}}{v_{fy}} \right| = \tan^{-1} \left| \frac{-11 \text{ m/s}}{+7.1 \text{ m/s}} \right| = \tan^{-1}(1.55) = 57°$$

west of north. The magnitude of $\vec{v}_f$ is

$$v_f \equiv \text{mag}(\vec{v}_f) = \sqrt{v_{fx}^2 + v_{fy}^2 + 0} = \sqrt{(11 \text{ m/s})^2 + (7.1 \text{ m/s})} = 13 \text{ m/s}$$

which is positive ⑫ and comparable in magnitude to $\vec{v}_1$ and $\vec{v}_2$. ⑬

These examples illustrate what I mean by "creating a model" of a situation. The first two parts of the problem-solving framework especially require you to *simplify* the physical situation by representing it in a schematic diagram and making appropriate approximations. Both of these activities require you to pare away the inherent but fundamentally irrelevant complexities* (note, for example, that in *both* problems I ignored the possibility that small fragments might carry away some of the system's momentum). In the second and third parts of the framework require you to link your simplified model of the situation to the abstract models of physics in the text (in this chapter, the model that describes conservation of momentum). This is also an important part of constructing your model. In short, what I consider to be your model of a situation is your development of the first three parts of the problem-solving framework: it is *this* that (from my perspective) is the answer to a problem.

What I mean by "building a model" of a situation

Fleshing out your model in the required detail does entail some written English (the mathematical representation is only one *part* of the solution, after all!). If you are writing a solution only for yourself, you will probably write less English than I have in the examples. But the amount of English in the examples is only a tad more than the *minimum* appropriate for a solution written to be read by someone else (especially if that solution is to be graded). In such circumstances, I urge you to emulate the style of the example solutions.

Other advice (write English, avoid early numbers)

Finally, note in the examples that I have not hesitated to plug in *zeros* early on in the mathematical representation section, but I have not plugged in any *other* numbers until I absolutely need them. Relatively simple problems like these do not really show just how worthwhile this is, but it is good to get into the habit, because you will encounter more complicated problems soon enough, and if you put in numbers too soon in a complicated problem, you will get lost.

C5.6 AIRPLANES AND ROCKETS

What keeps an airplane from falling? Many textbooks that address this question appeal to *Bernoulli's principle*, which describes how the pressure of a fluid (such as air) varies with flow speed. But we can answer this question even more directly using the concept of conservation of momentum.

Conservation of momentum keeps a plane in the air

Perhaps you can see that the *shape* of a typical airplane wing redirects the airflow above the wing somewhat *downward* in the end, since as the air moves over the wing, the air must follow the downward slope of the wing's rear upper surface (see Figure C5.3a). If, during a given time interval, the interaction between the wing and air gives the air a downward momentum transfer at the expense of the wing, this effectively gives the wing an upward momentum transfer to conserve momentum. *This* provides the required lift. (During level flight, the upward momentum-transfer the plane gains from the air during a given dt exactly replaces the downward momentum transferred to the plane by gravity during dt.)

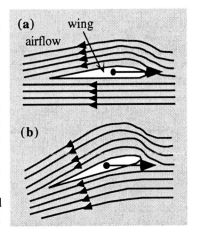

This effect is greatly enhanced if the wing is tipped somewhat upwards (this is called increasing the wing's "angle of attack": see Figure C5.3b), partly because then even some of the air flowing *under* the wing is redirected downward too. The wing flaps that pilots of commercial jets extend during takeoff and landing also are designed to do this. While both of these options more firmly direct air downward, they also increase the friction between the air and the wing, and so are only used during takeoff and landing (when having more lift at low air speeds is more important than fuel economy).

This explanation depends on the deeply fundamental principle that interactions conserve momentum. It may comfort you to know that your airplane is being supported by one of the most basic principles in all of physics!

Figure C5.3: (a) A diagram of the airflow around a cross-section of a typical airplane wing, as viewed by someone at the end of the wing. Note how the air flowing over the top of the wing is deflected downward. **(b)** The same wing at a higher "angle of attack."

---

*A possibly apocryphal example of the extremes to which physicists go to eliminate complicating details is the professor who wanted to do an example problem that involved estimating the heat lost by a horse during a given time interval. The professor began the solution by saying "Consider a spherical horse…".

Rockets also employ conservation of momentum

Conservation of momentum also explains how a rocket can increase its momentum even in space (where there is nothing to "push" against). All rockets operate by pushing propellant backward at as high a velocity as possible. In order to do this, the rocket engine has to transfer backward momentum to the propellant. The momentum of the remainder of the rocket must then increase in the forward direction by the same amount to conserve momentum (see Figure C5.4).

In a standard liquid-fuel rocket, the body of the rocket consists of tanks holding two substances that react energetically when combined (for example, liquid hydrogen and liquid oxygen). These substances are brought into contact in the rocket engine nozzle and ignited. The resulting chemical reaction increases the temperature of the exhaust gases dramatically, which makes these gases expand rapidly. Since they have no place to go except backward out of the nozzle, they are propelled rearward with a large speed (commonly $\approx$ 2 to 3 km/s).

A natural quantity for describing rocket performance is the *momentum transferred per unit mass* of the propellant used. The greater this quantity is, the less propellant the rocket has to carry to achieve the same change in momentum, and the less propellant the rocket has to carry, the smaller the momentum change it needs to achievea given final velocity. So increasing the momentum transferred per mass of a rocket's propellant *doubly* contributes to its performance.

A rocket engine's performance depends on the propellant's exhaust speed

How might we improve this quantity? Consider a liquid-fuel rocket engine that ejects propellant with an exhaust speed of 2000 m/s. To do this, the engine must transfer 2000 kg·m/s of backward momentum to each kilogram of fuel, so this is also the magnitude of the forward momentum transfer the rocket gets from that kilogram of fuel. The momentum transfer per unit mass is therefore (2000 kg·m/s)/kg = 2000 m/s, which is the exhaust speed! Thus the crucial thing determining a rocket's performance is the magnitude of its *exhaust speed*.

How can we increase the exhaust speed? In a chemical rocket, this can be done by increasing the temperature at which the fuel is burned. But temperatures cannot be made too high or the engine nozzle will melt. The exhaust speed of the best available chemical rockets is about 4.5 km/s.

Ion engines are sometimes used in deep space probes where keeping propellant mass small is especially important. Ion rockets use electrical fields to accelerate charged atoms to *very* high velocities. For example, the ion engine used by NASA's Deep Space 1 probe (which will visit the asteroid McAuliffe in 1999 and comet West-Kohoutek-Ikemura in 2000) ejects xenon propellant at speed of 31.5 km/s. The *rate* (in kg/s) at which it ejects that propellant is very small, so it exerts a small thrust (0.02 lbs), but it exerts that thrust *very* efficiently.

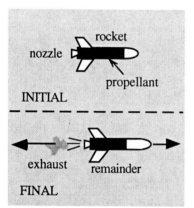

Figure C5.4: A rocket works by pushing propellant backward as rapidly as possible. Since momentum has to be conserved, the rocket's forward momentum increases as it transfers backward momentum to the propellant.

The best possible rocket engine would use matter and antimatter, which when combined, annihilate each other to create pure energy in the form of gamma rays, which can (at least in principle) be directed rearward. As we will see in Unit *R*, the gamma rays produced by the annihilation of equal amounts of matter and antimatter of total mass m would carry away momentum equal in magnitude to mc, where c is the speed of light. This means that the momentum transferred per unit mass would also be c = 300,000 km/s. Since the speed of light is the highest exhaust velocity possible, such an engine would deliver the highest possible performance. (Matter/antimatter engines are still hypothetical at present.)

Specific impulse

For historical reasons, a rocket engine's performance is often stated in terms of its **specific impulse**, which is the momentum transferred per unit *weight* of propellant instead of mass (the propellant's weight is measured at the earth's surface). The units of specific impulse turn out to be simply *seconds,** and has a numerical value equal to roughly 0.1 times the propellant's exhaust velocity in m/s. For example, a chemical rocket engine that gives its propellant an exhaust speed of 4.5 km/s = 4500 m/s has a specific impulse of about 450 s.

---

*Weight is measured in units of force, which we will see in chapter C8 is the momentum transferred by an interaction per second. Therefore *momentum transferred per unit weight* has units of momentum/(momentum/second) = second.

I. INTERACTIONS WITH THE EARTH   **SUMMARY**
   A. A puzzle: Objects interacting with the earth seem to gain or lose momen-
      tum without apparently affecting the earth's momentum
   B. The answer: the earth's momentum *does* change according to our model
      1. One could (in principle) measure this in a frame floating in space
      2. But the earth's response is *very* tiny because of the earth's huge mass
   C. The earth's momentum is to most $d\vec{p}$ s like an ocean is to a bucket

II. WHEN MULTIPLE INTERACTIONS ACT
   A. A puzzle: Why is momentum conserved in a collision between carts when
      the carts are clearly *not* an isolated system?
   B. The key is to understand what happens when multiple interactions act:
      1. Each interaction transfers momentum independently of the others
      2. The net change $d\vec{p}$ in an object's momentum during an interval dt is
         the sum of the momentum transfers during dt: $d\vec{p} = d\vec{p}_1 + d\vec{p}_2 + ...$
         (The bar in the d reminds us that the $d\vec{p}$ from an interaction is gener-
         ally only one *contribution* to the object's change in momentum $d\vec{p}$.)
   C. A practical definition of *friction*: that aspect of an interaction between an
      object and a surface that (during a time interval dt) delivers a $d\vec{p}$ to the ob-
      ject that has a component *parallel* to that surface.
   D. The puzzle's answer: the vertical momentum transfers from the external
      gravitational and contact interactions *cancel* for a frictionless cart on a lev-
      el surface, so the system's momentum is unchanged by these interactions

III. WHAT COUNTS AS "ISOLATED"?
   A. Conservation of momentum technically applies only to isolated systems
   B. There are three cases where we can apply this law to a non-isolated system
      1. If external interactions are weak, the system is *approximately* isolated
      2. If external interactions cancel, the system is *functionally* isolated
      3. If the internal interaction is short and strong (a *collision*) and we focus
         on the system's momentum *just before* and *just after* the interaction,
         external interactions don't have *time* to deliver a significant $d\vec{p}$

IV. A FRAMEWORK FOR SOLVING PROBLEMS
   A. Experienced folk tend to use a common framework when writing solutions
   B. The framework involves four important parts:
      1. A *pictorial representation* of the situation, where the problem-solver
         a) draws a simplified diagram of the situation
         b) establishes the reference frame needed to solve the problem
         c) defines symbols for important quantities by labeling the diagram
         d) lists known and unknown quantities
      2. A *conceptual representation*, where the problem-solver
         a) defines the "system" involved in the situation
         b) finds the abstract physical models that illumine the situation
         c) discusses any approximations and/or assumptions that are needed
      3. A *mathematical representation*, where the problem-solver
         a) takes the basic equation supplied by abstract physics models
         b) expresses it in terms of the symbols defined earlier
         c) solves it algebraically for unknown quantities
         d) plugs in numbers (with units) and calculates results (with units)
      4. An *evaluation* of the result, where the problem-solver at least
         a) checks that the result's *units* are correct
         b) checks that the result's *sign* makes sense
         c) checks that the result's *magnitude* is plausible
   C. The examples illustrate its use in conservation of momentum problems
   D. "Constructing a model of a situation" = working the first three parts fully
   E. The *model* is the answer to a physics problem (not the final number!)

V. AIRPLANES AND ROCKETS: both work by conserving momentum

GLOSSARY

friction (in the context of an object interacting with a surface): that aspect of the interaction between an object and a surface which causes the interaction to deliver (during a given interval dt) a momentum transfer $d\vec{p}$ that is not purely perpendicular to the surface. If the interaction delivers (during dt) a $d\vec{p}$ that is always exactly perpendicular to the surface, the interaction is **frictionless**.

approximately isolated: a system is approximately isolated if its external interactions are very weak, so that its total momentum is approximately conserved.

functionally isolated: a system is functionally isolated if the effects of its significant external interactions cancel, so that its total momentum is conserved anyway.

collision: a relatively brief but powerful internal interaction between objects in a system. (Note that objects do not have to actually touch to collide according to this definition.) If we look at the system's total momentum *just before* and *just after* such a collision, we will find it to be approximately conserved because external interactions just don't have enough *time* to transfer much momentum.

pictorial representation: the part of the problem-solving framework introduced in this chapter where you:

(1) draw a picture, (2) define your reference frame, (3) define symbols, and (4) list knowns and unknowns.

conceptual representation: the part of the problem-solving framework where you (1) define your system, (2) construct links between the model of your situation and the larger abstract models, and (3) describe approximations and/or assumptions you need to make.

mathematical representation: the part of the problem-solving framework where you (1) select an appropriate starting equation (like the law of conservation of momentum) from an abstract physics model, (2) express it in terms of the symbols you defined earlier, (3) solve symbolically for unknown quantities, and (4) plug in numbers (with units) to calculate those unknown quantities.

evaluation: the part of the problem-solving framework where you check your result's (1) units, (2) sign, and (3) magnitude, to see that they make sense.

specific impulse: a measure of rocket-engine performance, defined to be the momentum transfer delivered to the rocket per unit weight of propellant. Its numerical value (in its standard units of seconds) is equal to about 0.1 times the exhaust speed expressed in meters per second.

TWO-MINUTE PROBLEMS

C5T.1 A 0.5-kg cart moving at a speed of 1.0 m/s in the $+x$ direction along a level track runs into a 1.0-kg cart initially at rest. Someone claims to have determined that after the collision, the massive cart moves in the $+x$ direction at 0.6 m/s and the other moves in the $-x$ direction at 0.2 m/s. This claim is consistent with the law of conservation of momentum (T or F). Be prepared to explain your response. (Assume that the carts have nearly frictionless wheels.)

C5T.2 A 1.0-kg cart moving at a speed of 1.0 m/s in the $+x$ direction along a level track runs into a 0.5-kg cart initially at rest. After the collision, the lighter cart moves in the $+x$ direction at 1.5 m/s and the massive cart with a speed 0.25 m/s. Assume that the carts have nearly frictionless wheels. In what direction does the massive cart move?
A. the $+x$ direction   B. the $-x$ direction
C. neither direction makes the supplied information consistent with conservation of momentum.
D. this system is not isolated, so it is impossible to say

C5T.3 Hockey puck A slides due north on a level plane of essentially frictionless ice. It then collides with puck B, which was initially at rest. Just after the collision, puck A is observed to move due west. If this is so, in what (approximate) direction must puck B move just after the collision?
A. northeast   C. southeast
B. northwest   D. southwest
E. this system is not isolated, so it is impossible to say
F. some other direction (specify)
T. the answer depends on the pucks' masses

C5T.4 Two football players run into each other at midfield. We might be able to realistically apply conservation of momentum to this situation because
A. the players are an approximately isolated system
B. the players are a functionally isolated system
C. we can treat the interaction as a collision
D. (conservation of momentum does *not* apply here)

C5T.5 Two magnetic hockey pucks sliding on a flat plane of frictionless ice attract each other, changing each other's direction of motion as they pass. We can realistically apply conservation of momentum to this situation because
A. the pucks are an approximately isolated system
B. the pucks are a functionally isolated system
C. we can treat the interaction as a collision
D. (conservation of momentum does not apply here)

C5T.6 Two stars in deep space pass near to each other, gravitationally changing each other's direction of motion as they pass. We might be able to realistically apply conservation of momentum to this situation because:
A. the stars are an approximately isolated system
B. the stars are a functionally isolated system
C. we can treat the interaction as a collision
D. (conservation of momentum does not apply here)

The remaining two-minute problems all imagine a situation where two hockey pucks are sliding on a flat, horizontal plane of frictionless ice. One puck has twice the mass of the other. They approach each other as described in each problem, collide, and then *stick together*.

C5T.7 Initially, the light puck is moving east at 3 m/s while the heavy puck is moving west at 2 m/s. The final velocity of the joined pucks is:
A. eastward   D. impossible to determine
B. westward   E. some other direction (explain)
C. zero

C5T.8 Initially, the light puck is moving west at 4 m/s while the other puck is moving south at 2 m/s. The final velocity of the joined pucks is
A. northeast   D. southwest
B. northwest   E. zero
C. southeast   F. some other direction (explain)

C5T.9 Originally the light puck was moving south, and the final speed of the joined pucks is zero. The original velocity of the heavy puck *must* have been northward (T or F).

HOMEWORK PROBLEMS

BASIC SKILLS

C5B.1 A 0.3-kg cart rolling on essentially frictionless wheels at an initial speed of 1.0 m/s in the +x direction collides with a 0.6-kg cart initially at rest. After the collision, the more massive cart is observed to move in the +x direction with a speed of 0.55 m/s. What is the velocity (magnitude and direction) of the lighter cart?

C5B.2 A cart rolling on essentially frictionless wheels at an initial speed of 1.0 m/s in the +x direction collides with an identical cart initially at rest. After the collision, the front cart is observed to move in the +x direction with a speed of 0.85 m/s. What is the velocity (magnitude and direction) of the other cart?

C5B.3 A person firing a rifle feels it recoil against his or her shoulder. Explain why.

C5B.4 Imagine a cannon that is free to roll on wheels. Initially, both the cannon and cannonball are at rest. When the cannonball is fired, though, the momentum transferred to the cannonball comes at the expense of the cannon, so the cannonball and cannon end up with momenta having equal magnitudes but opposite directions. If this is so, why does the cannonball fly away at a large speed while the cannon recoils only very modestly? Explain your response.

C5B.5 Two identical hockey pucks slide on a flat, frictionless plane of ice. Originally, one is sliding westward at a speed of 3 m/s, while the other is sliding eastward at a speed of 1 m/s. The pucks collide and stick together. What is their joint velocity (magnitude and direction) after the collision?

C5B.6 Two hockey pucks, one with mass m and one with mass $3m$, slide on a flat, frictionless plane of ice. Originally, the lighter puck is sliding westward at a speed of 2 m/s, while the other is sliding eastward at a speed of 1 m/s. The pucks collide and stick together. What is their joint velocity (magnitude and direction) after the collision?

C5B.7 Two hockey pucks, one with mass m and one with mass $3m$, slide on a flat, frictionless plane of ice. Originally, the lighter puck is sliding eastward at a speed of 2 m/s, while the other is sliding northward at a speed of 2 m/s. The pucks collide and stick together. What is their joint velocity (magnitude and direction) after the collision? [*Hint:* Draw a picture.]

C5B.8 Two hockey pucks, one with mass m and one with mass $3m$, slide on a flat, frictionless plane of ice. Originally, the lighter puck is sliding westward at a speed of 6 m/s, while the more massive puck is sliding southward at a speed of 2 m/s. The pucks collide and stick together. What is their joint velocity (magnitude and direction) after the collision? [*Hint:* Draw a picture.]

SYNTHETIC

C5S.1 In a certain time Δt during an interaction, a certain momentum transfer is given one object at the expense of the other. Prove that the magnitude of the change in velocity of each is inversely proportional to its mass.

C5S.2 A 110-kg football player running at 3 m/s collides head on with a 55-kg referee by accident. This collision transfers momentum to the referee at the expense of the player's momentum. Irrespective of how *large* the momentum transfer is, how will the magnitude of the change in the referee's velocity during the collision compare with that of the player? Explain carefully.

C5S.3 Imagine that someone places you at rest on a flat, utterly frictionless surface. You cannot walk to the edge of the surface, because your shoes will not grip it. Is there another way to use those shoes and the law of conservation of momentum to get off the surface? Explain your solution.

C5S.4 Imagine that a rocket is launched from an asteroid in deep space and fires its engines until the speed of the rocket relative to the asteroid is equal to the speed of the rocket's exhaust. The exhaust ejected by the engine is now at *rest* with respect to the asteroid. If the engines continue to fire, will the rocket's speed with respect to the asteroid still increase? (If it does, note that the exhaust will now move in the same direction as the rocket relative to the asteroid.) Explain whether or not the rocket can still go faster from the point of view of an observer on the asteroid.

C5S.5 Two hockey pucks, one with mass m and one with mass $2m$, slide on a flat, frictionless plane of ice. Originally, the lighter puck is sliding in a direction 30° west of south at a speed of 3 m/s while the more massive puck is sliding in a direction 60° north of east at 1.5 m/s. The pucks collide and stick together. What is their joint velocity (magnitude and direction) after the collision?*

C5S.6 Two identical hockey pucks slide on a flat, frictionless plane of ice. Originally, one is sliding in a direction 60° south of west at a speed of 2 m/s, while the other is sliding in a direction 30° west of north at a speed of 2 m/s. The pucks collide and stick together. What is their joint velocity (magnitude and direction) after the collision?*

C5S.7 Two people slide on a frictionless, flat, horizontal plane of ice. Person A (whose mass is 54 kg) is sliding due east at a speed of 2.5 m/s. Person B (whose mass is 68 kg) is sliding due south at a speed of 1.8 m/s. These people collide and hold on to each other. What are the magnitude and direction of their joint velocity after the collision?*

C5S.8 In the All-Alaska Ice Floe Softball finals, the right fielder for the Nome IceSox (who is floating on a small chunk of ice in still water) makes an outstanding catch of a line drive. If the combined mass of the fielder and the ice is 540 kg, and it was traveling due north at 0.15 m/s (due to the fielder's frenzied paddling) before the catch, and the ball has a mass of 0.25 kg and is traveling at 32 m/s due east when caught, what is the final heading of the fielder just after the ball is caught?*

C5S.9 A pontoon boat (weight 1200 lbs) sits at rest on a still lake near a dock. Your friend Dana, whose weight is 160 lbs, runs off the end of the dock at a speed of 15 mi/hr and jumps onto the deck of the boat. Dana doesn't know anything about physics and so is surprised that the boat ends up moving away from the dock. How fast is it moving after Dana lands?*

---

*Please make sure that your solution for these starred problems follows (and includes all of the elements in) the problem-solving framework as it appears in the outlines shown on the left side of Examples C5.1 and C5.2.

C5S.10 During the filming of a certain movie scene, the director wants a small car (mass 750 kg) traveling due east at 35 m/s to collide with a small truck (mass 3200 kg) traveling due north. The director also wants the collision to be arranged so that just afterwards, the interlocked vehicles travel straight towards the camera (which is placed at a safe distance, of course). If the line between the camera and the collision makes an angle of 29° with respect to north, with what speed should the trucker drive?*

RICH-CONTEXT

C5R.1 A small asteroid of mass 2.6×10^9 kg is discovered traveling at a speed of 18 km/s on a direct heading for Starbase Alpha, which is in deep space well outside the solar system. Lacking weapons of sufficient power to destroy the asteroid, the frightened starbase inhabitants decide to deflect it by hitting it with a remote controlled spaceship. The spaceship has an empty mass of 25,000 kg and a top speed of 85 km/s when its fuel is exhausted. The asteroid has to be deflected so that by the time it reaches the starbase, its center is 1800 m away from its original path. What is the minimum time before the asteroid's projected impact that the spaceship must reach the asteroid? Explain carefully (lives are at stake here!).*

C5R.2 An astronaut repairing a communications satellite in deep space floats at rest with respect to the astronaut's spaceship but at a distance of 22 m away from its open airlock door. The astronaut is not tethered to the ship, but instead uses a jet pack to maneuver around the satellite. The jet pack suddenly fails. The astronaut needs to get back to

the ship, but does not want to push on the communications satellite, for fear of changing its position. The astronaut has in hand the satellite's failed circuit board, which has a mass of about 0.15 kg. How can the astronaut use it to get back to the ship? Estimate the time (within about a factor of two or so) that it will take to get back to the shuttle if the astronaut uses this method.*

---

*Please make sure that your solution for these starred problems follows (and includes all of the elements in) the problem-solving framework as it appears in the outlines shown on the left side of Examples C5.1 and C5.2.

ADVANCED

C5A.1 Consider a rocket in deep space whose empty mass is 5200 kg that can carry 52,000 kg of propellant. If the rocket engine can eject 1300 kg/s of propellant from its nozzle at a a speed of 3300 m/s relative to the rocket, and if the rocket starts at rest, what is its final speed? This problem is difficult because the ship's mass changes constantly as the propellant is ejected. Either solve the problem *mathematically* using calculus, taking the constantly decreasing mass of the rocket into account, or *numerically* using a calculator or a computer program. If you do the latter, pretend that each second the rocket ejects a 1300-kg "chunk" of propellant, and use conservation of momentum to compute the final speed of the rocket (including the remaining propellant) You will have to repeat this calculation for each second that the engines fire.

ANSWERS TO EXERCISES

C5X.1 Let's estimate that the average mass of a person in China is 50 kg, and that they get on sufficiently tall ladders so that everybody hits the ground traveling at about 10 m/s (roughly 22 mi/h). So the total momentum transferred to the earth by 10^9 people doing this is $\approx 5 \times 10^{11}$ kg·m/s, which will cause the earth's center of mass to move at a final speed (just before they all hit the ground) of about

$$\text{mag}(\vec{v}) = \frac{\text{mag}(\vec{p}_{\text{earth}})}{m_{\text{earth}}} = \frac{5 \times 10^{11} \text{ kg} \cdot \text{m/s}}{6 \times 10^{24} \text{ kg}} \approx 10^{-13} \frac{\text{m}}{\text{s}} \quad \text{(C5.4)}$$

At this speed, the earth's center of mass would take about 20 minutes to cover the diameter of an atom. While the seismic waves radiated by this event might be interesting, the motion of the earth's center of mass is insignificant.

C5X.2 (a) If your friend's model is correct, the object you hold should be shielded from gravity's effects while it is in your hand. But if you hold an object in your hand, it still *feels* like gravity is still working on it, and you definitely still have to push upward on the object to hold it at rest. What you feel is better explained by the model in the text, which asserts that (during any given time interval) gravity still transfers downward momentum to the object and you (through the contact interaction between the object and your hand) have to supply upward momentum to cancel this (which is why you have to push). **(b)** If you hang an object from a spring, the spring will stretch until it is able to hold the object at rest. Now, perhaps you can imagine that if we were to turn gravity off, the spring would relax, launching

the object vertically upward. This is exactly what our model would predict. When the object is at rest, our model asserts that (during any given interval of time) gravity still transfers downward momentum to the object but the spring transfers upward momentum that cancels it. If gravity were suddenly removed, the spring would continue to deliver a (now uncanceled) upward momentum transfer that would give the object a net upward momentum. This would be harder for the model proposed by your friend to explain.

C5X.3 Depending on the level of approximation you are willing to tolerate, the balls can be either *functionally isolated* or *not isolated*. The downward momentum transfer each ball gets from gravity during any given time interval would exactly canceled by an upward momentum transfer from ball's contact interaction with the table if the balls roll frictionlessly, but with billiard balls there is some friction that leads to imperfect cancellation of these momentum transfers. The cancellation is fairly good, though, because the momentum of a ball usually doesn't change much as it rolls.

C5X.4 In this case, the frictional part of the interaction between the cars' tires and the road are pretty significant, so the system is not isolated. Even so, we *can* usefully apply conservation of momentum to the collision if we focus on the cars' momenta *just before* and *just after* the collision: the duration of the collision is so short that the net momentum transferred to the system due to the imperfect cancellation of external momentum transfers will be small.

C6

INTRODUCTION TO ENERGY

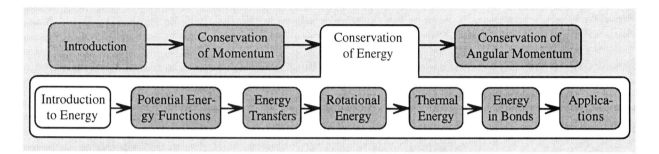

C6.1 OVERVIEW

In the past four chapters, we have studied the law of conservation of momentum, its implications, and its applications. In the process, we have laid a foundation upon which we will build much of the rest of units *C* and *N*. In this chapter we will begin a seven-chapter subunit on conservation of energy, which is one of the richest and most illuminating ideas in all of physics.

This particular chapter lays the foundations for all of the chapters in this subunit by defining the two most basic forms of energy: *potential energy* and *kinetic energy*. Here is a summary of this chapter's sections:

C6.2 *THE IDEA OF CONSERVATION OF ENERGY* looks at the behavior of falling objects for clues about how we might qualitatively define potential energy and kinetic energy.

C6.3 *DEFINING ENERGY* argues that the potential energy of an object's gravitational interaction with the earth (when it is near the surface of the earth) must increase *linearly* with the object's height, and then uses this as a basis for finding the quantitative definition of kinetic energy.

C6.4 *INTERACTIONS AND ENERGY* presents an abstract model of how energy is stored and transferred, and looks at the basic differences between the concepts of energy and momentum.

C6.5 *MEASURING POTENTIAL ENERGIES* explores how we can use the principle of conservation of energy to measure the potential energy associated with an interaction. We will see that we can really only measure potential energy *differences*, which means that we have some flexibility in *choosing* an interaction's potential energy.

C6.6 *NEGATIVE ENERGY?* shows that this flexibility implies that we can choose an interaction's potential energy to be *negative* if we want, and discusses what negative energy means.

C6.7 *A FRAMEWORK FOR ENERGY PROBLEMS* presents a version of the problem-solving framework introduced in the last chapter especially adapted for solving physics problems involving conservation of energy. An example illustrates how we can use the framework.

C6.2 THE IDEA OF CONSERVATION OF ENERGY

The law of conservation of energy is one of the richest and most productive ideas in all of physics. It is also in a certain sense more subtle than conservation of momentum: while Newton himself understood that interactions conserve momentum, it was not until the middle decades of the 1800s that the physics community realized fully that conservation of energy was also universally true. Our quest to understand the full meaning of this idea will take us on a journey into new realms of physics and greatly broaden our understanding of the physics of everyday phenomena.

Our goal in this section: a simple qualitative sense of what energy is

Even the greatest journey begins with small steps, though. We will begin by examining an everyday situation that simply and clearly illustrates how the idea of conservation of energy might work. Consider a book sitting on a shelf high above the floor. We know that if we nudge this book off the shelf, it will fall, moving faster and faster as it approaches the ground. We *could* examine this situation in terms of the models we have developed previously; that is, in terms of how the gravitational interaction between the book and the earth steadily feeds the book downward momentum that steadily increases its downward speed as it falls. But let's step back and and look at this situation from a new perspective.

A qualitative definition of *kinetic energy*

Imagine that a moving object, in addition to having momentum in the direction of its motion, also has an *energy* associated with its motion that we will call its **kinetic energy**. We will only define this quantity very qualitatively at this point by suggesting that a moving object's kinetic energy has something to do with how much "damage" the object would do when it hits a barrier (for example, how big a noise a book makes when it hits the floor or how big a splash it makes when it falls into the tub). A few simple experiments with this qualitative definition in mind should convince you that:

1. An object's kinetic energy increases as its *speed* increases. (Evidence: the noise a book makes when it hits the floor increases as the book's speed just before it hits increases.)

2. An object's kinetic energy increases as its *mass* increases. (Evidence: a large book hitting the floor makes a bigger noise than a small book when they are traveling at the same speed.)

(These observations might prompt you to think that kinetic energy is the same as momentum, but let's not jump to conclusions!)

A qualitative definition of *potential energy*

Now, while the book is sitting on the shelf, it has no kinetic energy, but a little nudge will cause it to fall, and the fall gives the book a certain amount of kinetic energy by the time it hits the floor. Indeed, a few simple experiments should convince you that the higher the shelf from which the book falls, the greater the bang the book makes when it hits the floor, and thus the greater the kinetic energy the book has when it hits the floor. We might say, therefore, that there is a certain **potential energy** associated with the book's separation from the earth that can be *converted* to kinetic energy if the book is allowed to fall. Moreover, the potential energy associated with the book's separation from the earth increases as that separation gets larger (that is, as the shelf gets higher).

If this energy is just converted (rather than being created or destroyed), then as the book falls, the potential energy associated with its separation from the earth *decreases* (as the book gets closer to the earth) and the book's kinetic energy *increases* (as the book speeds up during its fall) in such a way that **total energy** E (defined to be the sum of the potential and kinetic energies) will be *conserved*. (The basic idea here is illustrated in Figure C6.1.)

C6.3 DEFINING ENERGY

Let us see if we can *define* the concepts of potential and kinetic energy to make a law of conservation of energy true for a falling object like a book. Doing

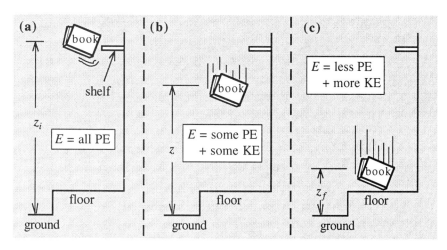

Figure C6.1: Conservation of energy as a book falls from a shelf. PE stands for "potential energy" and KE for "kinetic energy." *E* is the total energy, whose value remains constant (that is, it is conserved) during the entire process. Note also that we are measuring the book's vertical coordinate *z* from the earth's surface (marked "ground"), which is not necessarily the same as the floor on which the book lands.

this will not *prove* that the law has any validity or utility when applied to *other* situations, of course, but we will find that nature is kind: the law of conservation of energy, using the definitions we determine by argument and experiment here, *does* happen to be useful for describing many other situations as well.

In this section, we will develop some *plausible* definitions for potential energy and kinetic energy in this context, definitions that are the simplest consistent with the results of some simple qualitative experiments. Other definitions of these quantities might be possible: the ultimate test of *any* definition is whether or not it works. We will see that our definitions *do* work in the sense that they make the model of conservation of energy consistent with experimental results.

Working toward quantitative definitions of kinetic and potential energy

It will help if we define a few symbols and discuss a few basics. Let $V(z)$ be the potential energy associated with the separation between an object and the earth when the object has a vertical position coordinate (z-position) of z in a given frame. The potential energy that is released and converted to kinetic energy when an object falls is the *difference* $V(z_i) - V(z_f)$ between the potential energy when the object is at z_i and that when the object is at z_f. How big a bang a book makes when it hits the floor at z_f after falling from rest at z_i depends on its kinetic energy just before it hits the ground, which in turn depends on the potential energy $V(z_i) - V(z_f)$ that was converted to kinetic energy as it falls.

Now let's see what some simple book-dropping experiments can tell us about the form of the function $V(z)$. We know that the released potential energy $V(z_i) - V(z_f)$ must increase with increasing drop distance $z_i - z_f$, because the bang a book makes when it hits increases as the drop distance increases. If we drop books of different *masses* through the *same* vertical distance $z_i - z_f$, we find that the more massive books make bigger bangs, implying that the released potential energy $V(z_i) - V(z_f)$ increases with increasing mass. Finally, we can at least imagine that $V(z_i) - V(z_f)$ depends on the strength of the gravitational field near the earth's surface: if we could somehow turn up gravity's strength, you can imagine that a book dropped through a given distance would be slammed against the floor harder than it would be under normal conditions.

What simple experiments can tell us about potential energy

With these things in mind, we will *define* the gravitational potential energy released when an object of mass m falls from vertical position z_i to vertical position z_f (at least while it is relatively close to the earth's surface) to be

$$V(z_i) - V(z_f) = mg(z_i - z_f) \qquad \text{(C6.1)}$$

The gravitational potential energy of an object interacting with the earth

where g is a constant describing the **gravitational field strength** whose empirical value we will find shortly. Note that this definition satisfies the experimental evidence that we have gathered so far. It implies that the potential energy released during a fall *does* increase as the drop distance increases, as the mass of the falling object increases, and also as the gravitational field strength increases. Equation C6.1 is the *simplest* definition consistent with these observations.

A test of this definition

In fact, this definition makes a specific *prediction* that we can check: it implies that the potential energy released when a book falls depends *only* on $z_i - z_f$ (the vertical distance fallen), but *not* otherwise on the values of z_i or z_f. Imagine doing an experiment where we drop a book from rest through a *fixed* distance $z_i - z_f$. If we vary z_i and z_f by doing this experiment on various floors of a tall building while keeping $z_i - z_f$, our definition implies that the potential energy released (and thus the bang produced) be the *same*, independent of z_f. If you try this, you will see that dropping a book through a given distance *does* indeed produce the same effect whether you are on the ground floor or the top floor. This suggests that we are on the right track.

Exercise C6X.1: We *might* have defined the potential energy released to be something like $V(z_i) - V(z_f) = mg(z_i^2 - z_f^2)$: this also increases as the drop distance increases. Show, however, that this is *not* consistent with the observation just discussed. (*Hint:* Factor $z_i^2 - z_f^2$ into binomials.)

Exercise C6X.2: We *might* have defined the potential energy released to be something like $V(z_i) - V(z_f) = m^2g(z_i - z_f)$: this also increases as the mass of the falling object increases. Show, however, that if this were true, the total potential energy released by two identical books dropped side by side but separately through a given distance $z_i - z_f$ is *not* the same as that released when the two books are bound together into a single object and dropped though the same distance. (It seems absurd that tying the books together should make a difference in the potential energy released, so this definition should be rejected.)

A plausible definition of kinetic energy

Now let's look at an object's kinetic energy. In section C2, I asserted that an object's kinetic energy should get larger as the object's *mass* increases and as its *speed* increases. It also makes sense that the kinetic energy associated with an object's motion should be zero when the object is at *rest*. There is really nothing other than mass and speed that the kinetic energy plausibly ought to depend on. With these things in mind, we will *define* the kinetic energy of an object with mass m traveling at a speed v to be

$$K \equiv \tfrac{1}{2} m v^n \tag{C6.2}$$

where n is an exponent that remains to be determined, and the factor of $\tfrac{1}{2}$ is conventional (its presence here makes certain *other* equations simpler). Again, this definition is not the only one consistent with our qualitative ideas about kinetic energy, but it is nearly the simplest.

The only unknown quantities in these definitions are the gravitational field strength constant g and the exponent n in the kinetic energy. We can determine both of these constants with a simple quantitative experiment.

How to test these definitions (*and* determine *g* and the exponent *n*)

Imagine that we set up a device that registers the speed of an object moving vertically through it. We then hold a ball (which is a bit easier to use in this context than a book) at a vertical position z_i above this device, release it, and allow it to freely fall until it goes through the device at vertical position z_f (see Figure C6.2a). If the total energy E involved in this situation (which we define to be the gravitational potential energy V plus the ball's kinetic energy K) is really *conserved* in this process, the *initial* value E_i of the total energy (when the ball is released) must be the same as its final value E_f (when the ball passes through the device that registers its speed). Therefore:

$$K_i + V(z_i) \equiv E_i \equiv E_f \equiv K_f + V(z_f) \tag{C6.3}$$

where K_i and K_f are the ball's initial and final kinetic energies. If we drop the ball from rest, its initial kinetic energy K_i will be zero. Solving equation C6.3 for K_f, and using $K \equiv \tfrac{1}{2} m v^n$ and $V(z_i) - V(z_f) = mg(z_i - z_f)$, we find that

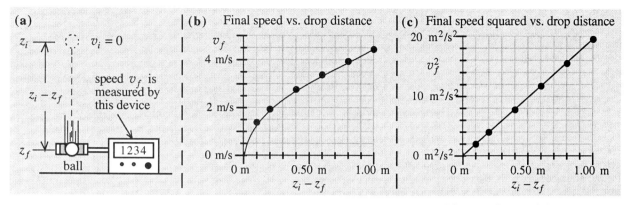

Figure C6.2: (a) An experiment to determine how an object's kinetic energy depends on speed. A ball is dropped from rest through a measured distance and then its final speed is measured. (b) A graph of the results. Note that drop distance is proportional to the final kinetic energy, so this is essentially a graph of final kinetic energy versus final speed. (c) A graph of drop distance (and thus final kinetic energy) versus speed squared.

$$K_f = V(z_i) - V(z_f) \quad \Rightarrow \quad \tfrac{1}{2}mv_f^n = mg(z_i - z_f) \tag{C6.4}$$

Multiplying both sides of equation C6.4 by $2/m$, we find that if conservation of energy is to work in this context *and* our definitions are correct, we must have

$$v_f^n = 2g(z_i - z_f) \tag{C6.5}$$

for some value of n. So, when we plot the appropriate power of v_f versus the drop distance $z_i - z_f$, we *should* get a straight line with slope $2g$.

The results of such an experiment are shown in Figure C6.2b. Note that the graph of v_f versus $z_i - z_f$ is *not* a straight line, so $n \neq 1$. On the other hand, Figure C6.2c shows that a graph of v_f^2 versus $z_i - z_f$ *is* a straight line within our measurement uncertainties. This strongly suggests that our final definition of the kinetic energy of an object of mass m moving at a speed v should be

$$K \equiv \tfrac{1}{2}mv^2 \tag{C6.6}$$

The final definition of kinetic energy

We can also use our results to determine the value of the gravitational field strength constant g. According to the graph in Figure C6.2c, the slope of the straight line has a value of 19.6 m/s². Therefore, the results of this experiment shows that g appearing in equation C6.1 has an empirical value of 9.8 m/s².

Exercise C6X.3: Verify that the slope of the line in the graph shown in Figure C6.2c has an approximate value of 19.6 m/s².

We see now that we have definitions of potential and kinetic energy that make sense and are consistent with experiment (at least for an object falling from rest). But there is one last question we ought to ask before we become complacent: is energy a scalar or a vector? So far, we have treated both potential energy and kinetic energy as *scalars*. But we have so far only considered simple situations where an object is falling vertically downward from rest. Is it possible that other situations will display aspects that will require us to pay attention to the direction of motion in an object's kinetic energy, for example?

Imagine that instead of dropping the ball from rest in the experiment shown in Figure C6.2a, we give it an upward initial velocity, and then measure the ball's final speed as it falls through the device. Then we repeat the experiment, giving it an initial *downward* velocity of the same magnitude. If the kinetic energy does *not* depend on direction, then the ball's initial kinetic energy K_i is the same in both cases, and conservation of energy implies that

An experiment showing that energy is a *scalar*

$$K_i + V(z_i) = K_f + V(z_f) \quad \Rightarrow \quad K_f = K_i + V(z_i) - V(z_f) \tag{C6.7}$$

which, since $V(z_i) - V(z_f)$ is the same in both experiments, implies that the final kinetic energy (and thus final speed) should be the *same* whether we throw the ball initially upward or downward. On the other hand, if the initial kinetic energy somehow depends on the direction of motion, then we would expect the ball to have different final kinetic energies (and thus speeds) at the bottom.

Experimental results show that the final kinetic energy *is* the same whether we throw the ball initially upward or downward. Therefore, direction of motion does appear to be irrelevant, and energy really does seem to be a *scalar*. This is an important *difference* between energy and momentum!

C6.4 INTERACTIONS AND ENERGY

My goal in the last section was to help develop your intuitive sense of what energy is by showing you how the definitions of potential and kinetic energy emerge fairly naturally from basic qualitative ideas, simple experiments, and the principle of conservation of energy itself. In this section, we will step back and take a more comprehensive (and abstract) look at the way physicists currently look at the model of conservation of energy.

The fundamental elements of reality are *particles* and *interactions*

The fundamental elements of physical reality (according to the current theory that physicists call the *standard model*) are *particles* and *interactions*. All four of the known **fundamental interactions** between elementary particles are *long-range* interactions in the sense that they operate between particles separated by some distance. (At the level of elementary particles, there is no such thing as a contact interaction, since two particles that occupy essentially zero volume can never really bump into each other!) We have already discussed the *gravitational* and *electromagnetic* interactions: the other two "long-range" interactions are the *weak* and *strong* interactions. The reason these are not so familiar is that their effective range is so short (roughly 10^{-15} m) that while they have significant effects *within* individual atomic nuclei (which are about this size), they rarely affect anything else. We will, therefore, pretty much ignore the existence of these interactions until we discuss nuclear structure in unit Q.

We can think of *any* of the four types of interactions between two particles as being like a bridge that carries momentum transfers between them: this is the model that leads to conservation of momentum. But we can also think of an interaction between two particles as being something that contains *potential energy*, a quantity that depends only on the type of interaction and the *separation* of the two particles. Any change in the separation of two interacting particles leads to a *transfer* of energy from the interaction's potential energy to the particles' kinetic energies or vice versa: the total *energy* involved in the interaction, which is defined to be

The total energy involved in an interaction between two particles

$$E = K_1 + K_2 + V(r) \qquad (C6.8)$$

(where K_1 and K_2 are the kinetic energies of the two particles and r is their separation) is conserved. All four fundamental interactions behave this way.

What happens if we have a system that involves more than two interacting particles? As one might guess, the total energy of the system is the simple sum of the particles' kinetic energies plus the potential energies of all internal interactions involving those particles:

The total energy of a multi-particle system

$$E = K_1 + K_2 + K_3 + \ldots + V(r_{12}) + V(r_{13}) + V(r_{23}) + \ldots \qquad (C6.9)$$

where r_{12} is the separation between particles 1 and 2 and so on. (If more than one *type* of interaction operates between a given pair of particles, we have to include one potential energy term for each type of interaction between each pair.) Since internal interactions only involve transfers between the kinetic and potential energies that appear in this sum, the system's total energy is not affected by such internal interactions. But the definition of a system's energy excludes potential energies involved in any *external* interactions, which can transfer energy into or out of the kinetic energies of particles in the system, and therefore change a system's total energy. The upshot is that the total energy of a system will be conserved *if* it is isolated.

Exercise C6X.4: What if we were to define the energy of a system to *include* the potential energy of external interactions? Explain why this doesn't help.

Note that a particle's kinetic energy $K \equiv \frac{1}{2}mv^2$, an interaction's potential energy V, and thus a system's total energy E are *scalar* quantities that ignore everything about the *directions* of any motions or separations involved.

At the *fundamental* level, then, there are only two types of energy: (1) the interaction's potential energy, and (2) the kinetic energies of the participating particles. The total energy involved in a given interaction is also *always* conserved. When we start dealing with *macroscopic* objects, though, things become more complex. While we can generally treat long-range (that is, gravitational and electromagnetic) interactions between extended objects as if they were interactions between particles located at the objects' respective centers of mass, *contact* interactions (which are very important at the macroscopic level) are more complicated. Contact interactions between two macroscopic objects are *really* electromagnetic interactions between the atoms on the two surfaces in contact. Therefore, these interactions actually *do* conserve energy, but some of this energy is generally hidden from the macroscopic observer, since it appears in the form of microscopic motions and/or separations of those atoms. This means that (except in certain special circumstances) we *cannot* define a meaningful potential energy function for a contact interaction, though sometimes we can *ignore* such interactions (as we will see in chapter C8). Changes in the motions and/or separations of atoms at the microscopic level may absorb or release energy that appears to the macroscopic observer to be going or coming from nowhere. We will learn how to deal with such hidden forms of energy in chapters C10 and C11.

Equation C6.8 tells us that the total energy of an interacting pair of objects includes a kinetic energy term for *each* of the objects. We can see that this is important if we consider the behavior of two identical carts that repel each other magnetically. If we press them together against the effect of repulsion, hold them at rest, and then release them, they will fly apart, converting magnetic potential energy to kinetic energy in *both* carts. (Indeed, the interaction *must* deliver momentum transfers to the carts that are equal in magnitude but opposite in direction to conserve momentum!) There is no logical reason to include the kinetic energy of one cart but not the other when calculating the system's total energy.

But if this is so, don't we have to include the kinetic energy of the earth in our consideration of falling objects in the previous section, since the falling object *is* interacting with the earth? The answer is that the earth's response to the interaction is so tiny (because it is so massive) that its kinetic energy essentially does not change and can be ignored. We will *prove* this in chapter C8.

Complexities arise at the macroscopic level, giving rise to "hidden" energy

We cannot generally define a potential energy for a contact interaction

A system's conserved energy includes the kinetic energies of all its objects

...except we can usually ignore the *earth's* kinetic energy

Exercise C6X.5: Because of this issue, people sometimes speak carelessly of the potential energy "of the book" when it is at a certain height. Why is it better to think of the *interaction* as "owning" the potential energy, do you think?

Finally, note that since kinetic energy is defined to be $K \equiv \frac{1}{2}mv^2$, and since we cannot add terms unless they have the same units, kinetic energy and potential energy (and thus total energy) must have the same SI units of $kg \cdot (m/s)^2 = kg \cdot m^2/s^2$. Since energy is such an important concept, it has its own special SI unit called the **joule**, which is defined to be:

$$1\,J \equiv 1\,\text{joule} \equiv 1\,kg \cdot m^2/s^2 \qquad (C6.10)$$

The SI unit of energy

The unit is named for James Joule, one of the physicists who helped develop the modern concept of conservation of energy.

C6.5 MEASURING POTENTIAL ENERGIES

How to measure the change in an interaction's potential energy

Consider an interaction between two otherwise isolated particles. If the total energy E of this isolated system is to be conserved, then

$$K_{1i} + K_{2i} + V(r_i) = E = K_{1f} + K_{2f} + V(r_f) \qquad (C6.11)$$

where the subscripts i and f distinguish quantities measured at some initial and some final time, respectively. If we don't know anything about the interaction's potential energy function $V(r)$, we can learn something about it by setting up the particles with a certain separation r_i and then allowing the system to evolve by itself until we reach a new separation r_f. Equation C6.10 then implies that

$$V(r_i) - V(r_f) = K_{1f} + K_{2f} - K_{1i} - K_{2i} \qquad (C6.12)$$

telling us that we can determine the change in the interaction's potential energy by measuring the particles' initial and final kinetic energies. Since we know how to measure a particle's mass and its speed, if we accept $K \equiv \frac{1}{2} m v^2$ as being *the* definition of kinetic energy, this means that performing such an experiment completely *determines* the value of $V(r_i) - V(r_f)$. If this value turns out to be independent of the particular initial velocities we choose (while keeping r_i and r_f fixed) at all separations, then the interaction's potential energy is *well-defined* and consistent with the idea of conservation of energy (all fundamental interactions have such well-defined potential energies).

But this only measures a *change* in potential energy, not its "true" value!

However, this experiment only determines the *difference* $V(r_i) - V(r_f)$. Conservation of energy thus allows us to *compare* the value of V at two different particle separations, but does not provide a way to determine *uniquely* the value of $V(r)$ at any specific separation. In fact, there is *no known way* to determine the "true" value of *any* interaction's potential energy at a given separation.

For example, if we *start* with the idea that $K \equiv \frac{1}{2} m v^2$ (and ignore the kinetic energy of the earth) the ball-dropping experiment shown in Figure C6.2a shows clearly that *difference* between the potential energies of the gravitational interaction when the ball is at vertical positions z_i and z_f, respectively, is

$$V(z_i) - V(z_f) = mg(z_i - z_f) \qquad (C6.13)$$

(Note that different vertical positions z_i and z_f correspond to different separations r_i and r_f between the ball and the earth's center of mass.) This only defines the gravitational potential energy when the ball is at a position z to within an unknown constant, since the function

$$V(z) = mgz + C \qquad (C6.14)$$

satisfies equation C6.13 no matter what the constant C is.

The only way to determine $V(r)$ uniquely is to choose a *reference separation*

The only way that we can completely determine the value of V at a given separation is to choose (arbitrarily!) a **reference separation** and *define* the interaction's potential energy to be zero at that separation. Then equation C6.12 allows us to determine uniquely the potential energy at any other separation.

Exercise C6X.6: Explain how equation C6.12 and setting $V = 0$ at one separation allows us to find $V(r)$ at any other separation.

We can take the opportunity to choose a *convenient* reference separation

At first glance, having to choose a reference separation seems like a *problem*: there is no way to determine uniquely the "actual" value of an interaction's potential energy V at any given separation. But it is better to look at this situation as an *opportunity*: we can choose a *convenient* reference separation!

For example, imagine that we set up a coordinate system in standard orientation on the earth's surface. We can use our freedom to define a reference separation to set $V = 0$ when an object interacting gravitationally with the earth is at

$z = 0$ in our frame. This is convenient because (1) we don't have to even *think* about the actual separation between the object and the earth's center of mass, and (2) the potential energy function for the interaction becomes simply

$$V(z) = mgz \quad \text{(if } V = 0 \text{ at } z = 0) \qquad \text{(C6.15)}$$

(This choice amounts to setting the constant C appearing in equation C6.14 to zero, since $z = 0$ implies $V = 0$ in that equation only if $C = 0$.) We could have just as easily chosen V to be zero at $z = +22$ m or $z = -47$ m. It also doesn't matter whether our origin is at the top of a mountain or the bottom of the sea (even though $z = 0$ corresponds to very different separations between the object and the earth's center in such cases). Since the predictions that the law of conservation of energy makes in each case depend only on the *difference* between V_i and V_f, all choices of reference separation are physically equivalent.

Choosing a reference separation is equivalent to specifying the constant in equation C6.14

Exercise C6X.7: Show that if we add the same constant term C to the potential energy terms in equation C6.11, equation C6.12 is not affected, meaning that *adding such a constant has no physically observable consequences*. (Defining a reference separation is the same as choosing the constant's value.)

Exercise C6X.8: Imagine that we define the reference separation for potential energy of a 3-kg object's gravitational interaction with the earth to be when that object is at $z = +10$ m. What is the interaction's potential energy when the object is at $z = 0$? When it is at $z = +20$ m? What would be the value of the constant appearing in equation C6.14 in this case?

C6.6 NEGATIVE ENERGY?

Our freedom to choose the reference separation where $V = 0$ means that we can choose an object's potential energy to be *negative*. For example, if we set up a standard coordinate system on the surface of the earth and choose the reference separation for an object interacting gravitationally with the earth to be when the object is at $z = 0$ (on the surface of the earth), then if the object is anywhere *below* the surface of the earth (say, in a pit or well) its gravitational potential energy will be *negative* (since $V(z) = mgz$ and $z < 0$). To be specific, if a 3-kg object is placed 5.0 m below the ground, the interaction's potential energy is $mgz = (3.0 \text{ kg})(9.8 \text{ m/s}^2)(-5.0 \text{ m}) = -147 \text{ kg} \cdot \text{m}^2/\text{s}^2 = -147$ J.

What does it mean for a system to have a negative potential energy? The negative sign here has nothing to do with *direction* (as it does when we are considering vectors): energy is a *scalar* and thus has no direction. If an interaction's potential energy is negative at a given separation, this simply means its value at that separation is *smaller* than it would be at the reference separation, that's all! So when we say that the interaction potential energy is -147 J when our 3-kg object is 5 m below the ground, we are really saying only that this energy is in this case 147 J smaller than it would be when the object is at ground level.

How to interpret negative potential energies

Perhaps you can see that our freedom to choose the reference separation means that we can *choose* to make the system's potential energy at any given separation either positive or negative. Neither the sign nor the value of a potential energy has any direct physical meaning: what is physically important is the *difference* between potential energy values at different separations.

Exercise C6X.9: If we define the reference separation for a 3-kg object interacting gravitationally with the earth to be when the object is at $z = +20$ m, what is the interaction's potential energy V when it is at $z = -5$ m? What is V when it is at $z = 0$? What is the *difference* between these potential energy values? Is this *difference* the same as when we used $z = 0$ as the reference separation?

How to interpret negative total energies

By choosing the reference separation a certain way, we might even make our system's *total* energy negative. For example, if we have a 3-kg object gravitationally interacting with the earth at rest at $z = -5$ m and our reference separation is when the object is at $z = 0$, the *total* energy E of the system involving the earth and the object is $E = K_1 + K_2 + V = 0 + 0 - 147\,\text{J} = -147\,\text{J}$. This negative total energy should be interpreted as meaning simply that the system's total energy in this situation is 147 J smaller than it would be if the earth and object were at rest at the reference separation. Negative potential or total energies should not be a source of alarm (though a negative kinetic energy *is* impossible).

We can *never* determine the absolute total energy in a system!

This emphasizes, though, that because there is no known way to determine the absolute amount of *potential* energy involved in an interaction, there is no way to determine the absolute amount of total *energy* in a system. The total energy in a system is conserved, but its actual *value* depends on choices we make.

C6.7 A FRAMEWORK FOR ENERGY PROBLEMS

We can adapt the problem-solving framework discussed in the last chapter to conservation of energy problems by making a few minor changes of emphasis.

Object *positions* are important in energy problems

In conservation of energy problems, we are most interested in the masses, velocities, and *positions* of interacting objects, as these are the quantities that will help us determine kinetic and potential energies. Therefore, you need to be sure to define symbols for these quantities in the *Pictorial representation* part. (If one of the interacting objects is the earth, as it often is, then you can ignore the earth's mass and speed because we will consider the earth's kinetic energy to be *zero* for most interactions, for reasons we will discuss in chapter C8.)

Systems still have to be isolated...

In the *Conceptual representation* part, you have *two* important tasks to accomplish instead of one. The first is to define the system and determine whether it is isolated (as as you did in the last chapter). We will see in chapter C8 that systems that are *functionally isolated* or involve *collisions* (defined just as we did in the last chapter) can still be treated as if they were isolated. In many cases, though, the system will be an object interacting with the earth: you can consider such a system to be *approximately* isolated, since it floats in space.*

You must also categorize each internal interaction

The second major task is to examine each internal interaction in the system to make sure that you can handle it by either (1) keeping track of its potential energy, or (2) ignoring it. The next few chapters will help you learn to sort interactions into these categories. The basic approach to conservation of energy discussed in this chapter applies only if the system can be treated as isolated AND its interactions fit into these categories. (In chapters C9 and C10, we will adjust this part somewhat to add new categories.)

Be sure to describe your reference separation!

If we *can* describe an interaction using a potential energy function, then we must define the reference separation where $V \equiv 0$. Since this choice is arbitrary, your readers will not know what choice you have made unless you tell them (and this will also remind you that you do have to make this choice!).

The core equation describing conservation of an isolated system's energy

In the *Mathematical representation* part, you should start with the basic equation that describes conservation of energy

$$K_{1i} + K_{2i} + ... + V(r_{12,i}) + ... = K_{1f} + K_{2f} + ... + V(r_{12,f}) + ... \qquad (C6.16)$$

(adding kinetic energy terms or potential energy terms as needed) instead of the law of conservation of momentum. (Again, when hidden energies are involved we will use a somewhat different starting point.)

Except for these adjustments, you should essentially follow the framework as described in the last chapter. Example C6.1 illustrates how to use the adapted framework to solve a specific conservation of energy problem.

---

*While we really *can* consider a system involving an object interacting with the earth to be *approximately isolated*, saying that this is because the system "floats in space" is an over-simplification. We will discuss the subtleties involved in this situation in chapter N11 of unit *N*.

EXAMPLE C6.1

OUTLINE OF THE FRAMEWORK

1. Pictorial Representation

  a. Draw a picture of the situation that includes:

    ① (1) sketches of the system in its initial and final states

    ② (2) reference frame axes

    ③ (3) labels defining symbols for relevant quantities (in this case, objects' masses, velocities, and separations)

  b. List values for all known quantities and specify which quantities are unknown. ④

2. Conceptual Representation

The general task is to construct a conceptual model of the situation and link it to an abstract physics model or principle. In conservation-of-energy problems, we do the following:

  ⑤ a. Identify the *system* involved. (If it involves the earth, we can ignore the earth's kinetic energy)

  ⑥ b. Determine whether it is *approximately* isolated, *functionally* isolated, or involved in a *collision* (as defined in chapter C5). Support your conclusions briefly.

  ⑦ c. Identify the interactions between objects in the system and for each interaction, determine whether we can handle it by

    (1) keeping track of its potential energy (if so, define the reference separation)

    (2) ignoring it (because it is very weak or for another reason)

    Be sure to support your conclusions with a brief argument.

  ⑧ d. Do we have to make any approximations or assumptions to solve the problem? (If so, describe.)

3. Mathematical Representation

  ⑨ a. Apply the mathematical equation that appropriately describes the situation (equation C6.16 here)

  ⑩ b. Solve for unknowns symbolically

  ⑪ c. Plug in numbers and units and calculate the result and its units.

4. Evaluation

Check that the answer makes sense:

  ⑫ a. Does it have the correct units?

  ⑬ b. Does it have the right sign?

  ⑭ c. Does it seem reasonable?

Problem: Imagine that you accidently drop a penny from the observation deck of the Empire State Building (height ≈ 1200 ft = 370 m). Ignoring air friction, what will be the penny's approximate speed when it hits the ground? Why would you guess that throwing things off the observation deck is forbidden?

Solution: We will use a reference frame in standard orientation on the earth's surface, with $z = 0$ corresponding to street level.

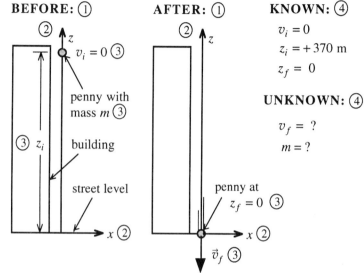

The system involved here is the earth and the penny,⑤ which we take to be *approximately isolated* because the system as a whole is floating in space.⑥ If we ignore air friction,⑧ the only interaction between the earth and the penny as the latter falls is a *gravitational* interaction, ⑦ which we *can* describe using a potential energy function: that function is simply $V(z) = mgz$ if we take $z = 0$ to be the reference separation where $V = 0$. Therefore, we *can* apply conservation of energy in this case, which (according to equation C6.16) requires that

$$⑨ \quad K_{i,\text{penny}} + K_{i,\text{earth}} + V(z_i) = K_{f,\text{penny}} + K_{f,\text{earth}} + V(z_f)$$

We can ignore the kinetic energy of the earth,⑤ so in this particular case, this equation reads (since $v_i = 0$ and $V(z_f) = mgz_f = 0$):

$$0 + 0 + mgz_i = \tfrac{1}{2}mv_f^2 + 0 + 0$$
$$\Rightarrow \quad v_f^2 = 2gz_i \quad \Rightarrow \quad v_f = \sqrt{2gz_i} \quad ⑩$$

(Note that the penny's unknown mass m cancels out of the problem: this is nice!) Plugging in numbers, we find that

$$⑪ \quad v_f = \sqrt{2(9.8 \text{ m/s}^2)(370 \text{ m})} = \sqrt{7250 \text{ m}^2/\text{s}^2} = 85 \text{ m/s}$$
$$= 85 \text{ m/s}\left(\frac{2.24 \text{ mi/h}}{1 \text{ m/s}}\right) = 190 \text{ mi/h}!$$

This answer does have the right units,⑫ and is positive (as a speed should be).⑬ The final speed is pretty large, but doesn't seem unbelievable.⑭ It is pretty clear, though, that throwing things off the observation deck is forbidden because even something as small as a penny traveling this fast could have potentially fatal consequences if anyone were to be hit by it.

SUMMARY

I. THE IDEA OF ENERGY CONSERVATION
  A. An example experiment: a book falls from a high shelf
  B. Imagine that we define two forms of energy in this situation:
    1. A kinetic energy associated with the book's motion
    2. A potential energy associated with its separation from the earth
    3. Might the sum of these energies be conserved as the book falls?

II. DEFINING ENERGY (What can we figure out from simple experiments?)
  A. A trial definition for gravitational potential energy $V(z)$
    1. Simple qualitative experiments show that the potential energy released as an object falls increases with the object's mass m, the drop distance $z_i - z_f$, and the gravitational field strength g.
    2. So perhaps $V(z_i) - V(z_f) = mg(z_i - z_f)$?
  B. A trial definition for kinetic energy
    1. Simple qualitative experiments show that an object's kinetic energy increases with its mass and its speed
    2. So perhaps $K = \frac{1}{2}mv^n$? (The $\frac{1}{2}$ makes other equations simpler.)
  C. A simple quantitative experiment shows that these definitions work if $n = 2$ ($\Rightarrow K = \frac{1}{2}mv^2$) and $g = 9.8$ m/s^2 near the earth's surface
  D. Another simple experiment suggests that energy must be a *scalar*

III. INTERACTIONS AND ENERGY (The big picture!)
  A. The fundamental elements of reality are *particles* and *interactions*
    1. Particles have a *kinetic energy* $K = \frac{1}{2}mv^2$
    2. Fundamental interactions have a well-defined *potential energy* $V(r)$ that depends only on the particles' separation r
    3. An interaction transfers energy between these two forms
  B. When we have a system of more than two particles
    1. The system's total energy is the sum of the particles' kinetic energies and a potential energy term for *each internal* interactions
    2. This total energy is conserved if the system is isolated
  C. At the macroscopic level
    1. Long-range interactions behave just like particle interactions
    2. Complications involving *contact* interactions
      a) These interactions *do* conserve energy at the microscopic level
      b) But some energy may be hidden in microscopic forms, making energy seem to appear or disappear to a macroscopic observer
      c) As a result, we cannot define a $V(r)$ for contact interactions
    3. We will deal with such complications in chapters C10 and C11
  D. If a system involves the earth, we can ignore the earth's kinetic energy
  E. The SI unit of energy is the *joule*: $1 \text{ J} \equiv 1 \text{ kg} \cdot \text{m}^2/\text{s}^2$

IV. MEASURING POTENTIAL ENERGIES
  A. Conservation of energy only allows us to find potential energy *changes*
    1. Thus $V(r)$ at a given separation is defined only up to a constant
    2. Only potential energy differences have physical meaning
  B. We can determine the value of $V(r)$ at a given separation r only by choosing an arbitrary *reference separation* r_0 where $V(r_0) \equiv 0$
    1. $V(r)$ at any other r is defined to be the change in V from $V(r_0)$
    2. This essentially fixes the arbitrary constant in the value of $V(r)$
  C. We can choose whatever reference separation is convenient

V. NEGATIVE ENERGY?
  A. We can choose a reference separation so that $V(r) < 0$ for some r
    1. This simply means that the $V(r)$ is smaller than it is at r_0
    2. It has nothing to do with *direction* (energy is a *scalar*!)
  B. Total energies can be negative, too!

VI. A FRAMEWORK FOR ENERGY PROBLEMS
  (See example C6.1 for a complete summary)

GLOSSARY

kinetic energy K: the energy an object has by virtue of its motion. The kinetic energy of an object with mass m moving at a speed v is defined to be $K \equiv \frac{1}{2}mv^2$.

potential energy V: the energy involved in an interaction between two objects. All fundamental interactions have well-defined potential energy functions that depend *only* on the separation between the two interacting particles. At the macroscopic level, all long-range interactions between macroscopic objects have well-defined potential energy functions, but contact interactions (which involve complex microscopic processes) may not.

total energy (E): the numerical sum of the kinetic energies of all particles in the system plus the potential energies of all of their internal interactions.

joule: the standard SI unit of energy: $1 \text{ J} \equiv 1 \text{ kg·m}^2/\text{s}^2$.

fundamental interaction: one of the four known interactions that act between elementary particles. [The four interactions are the gravitational, electromagnetic, the weak (nuclear), and the strong (nuclear) interactions.]

gravitational field strength g: a constant appearing in the formula for the gravitational potential energy involved in the interaction between an object and the earth that expressis the strength of the earth's gravitational field near its surface. Its measured value is 9.80 m/s^2.

reference separation: the separation between two objects participating in a long-range interaction where the potential energy of that interaction is *defined* to be zero.

TWO-MINUTE PROBLEMS

C6T.1 Which has the larger kinetic energy, a 50-kg person running at a speed of 2 m/s, or a 5-g nickel falling at a speed of 200 m/s?
A. The running person   B. The falling nickel
C. Both have the same kinetic energy.

C6T.2 How does the kinetic energy K_{fast} of a car traveling at 50 mi/h compare with the kinetic energy K_{slow} of an identical car traveling at 25 mi/h? (The consequences of a collision are in rough proportion to the energy involved!)
A. Both cars are identical, so $K_{fast} = K_{slow}$.
B. $K_{fast} \approx 1.5\, K_{slow}$.   D. $K_{fast} \approx 4\, K_{slow}$.
C. $K_{fast} \approx 2\, K_{slow}$.   E. other (explain).

C6T.3 A person throws three identical rocks off a cliff of height h with exactly the same speed v_0 each time (see the drawing below). Rock A is thrown almost vertically upward, rock B is thrown horizontally, and rock C is thrown almost vertically downward. Which rock hits the ground with the greatest *speed*? (Ignore air friction.)

A. Rock A
B. Rock B
C. Rock C
D. All rocks hit with the same speed
E. other (specify)

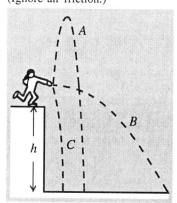

C6T.4 Imagine that we know from experiments that when the object moves from point A to point B, the potential energy of its gravitational interaction with the earth *increases* by 24 J, and that when the object moves from point B to point C, the potential energy of its system *decreases* by 18 J. If we define the system's reference separation to be when the object is at point C, what is the value of the system's potential energy when the object is at point A?
A. +6 J   C. –52 J   E. zero
B. –6 J   D. +52 J   F. other (specify)

C6T.5 In a coordinate system where the z axis is vertical, we choose the gravitational potential energy of a 4-kg rock interacting with the earth to be zero when $z = -5$ m. The formula for the potential energy as a function of z is thus $V(z) = mgz + C$. What is the (approximate) value of C?
A. –50 J   C. –200 J   E. zero
B. +50 J   D. +200 J   F. other (specify)

C6T.6 There is no way to *experimentally* determine the actual value of a system's total energy (T or F).

C6T.7 Consider a rock interacting gravitationally with the earth. Imagine that we define the interaction's potential energy to be zero if the rock were at ground level. A person standing at the bottom of a well throws the rock vertically upward from 20 m below ground level. The rock makes it all the way up to 1 m below ground level before falling back into the well. The total energy of the rock-earth system is
A. negative   B. zero
C. positive (in this particular case)
D. positive because energy is *always* positive
E. The answer depends on the rock's mass
F. The answer depends on the rock's initial speed
T. answer depends on something else (specify)

HOMEWORK PROBLEMS

BASIC SKILLS

C6B.1 A car is traveling north at 30 mi/h. A truck having four times the mass of the car is traveling at 60 mi/h west. How many times greater is the truck's kinetic energy compared to the car's? Explain your reasoning.

C6B.2 A typical arrow might have a mass of 100 g and move at a speed of about 100 m/s. How does its kinetic energy compare to that of person weighing 110 lbs running at a speed of 8.8 mi/h?

C6B.3 Consider an object interacting gravitationally with the earth. If we move the object from vertical position A to vertical position B, we find that the system's gravitational potential energy *increases* by 10 J. If we move it from vertical position B to vertical position C, the system's potential energy *decreases* by 5 J. If we take the system's reference separation to be when the object is at position B, what is the system's potential energy when the object is at each of the three points?

C6B.4 Consider a 5-kg object interacting gravitationally with the earth. Imagine that we set up a standard reference frame with the z axis pointing vertically upward. If the interaction's potential energy when the object is at $z = 5$ m is -50 J, what is the approximate z-position of the object when it is at its reference separation from the earth?

C6B.5 Consider a 0.25-kg ball interacting gravitationally with the earth. Imagine that we set up a reference frame in standard orientation on the earth's surface and define ground level to be the reference separation and set $z = 0$ there. Imagine that a person throws the ball upward into the air and that as the ball leaves the person's grasp 2.0 m above the ground, it has a speed of 12 m/s. What is the *system* involved here and what is its total energy at this time?

C6B.6 Consider a 0.20-kg ball interacting gravitationally with the earth. Imagine that we set up a reference frame in standard orientation on the earth's surface and define ground level to be the reference separation and set $z = 0$ there. Imagine that a person at the bottom of a well throws the ball upward and that as the ball leaves the person's grasp 8.0 m below the ground, it has a speed of 6 m/s. What is the system's total energy at this time?

SYNTHETIC

C6S.1 A 1000-kg car travels down a road at 25 m/s (55 mi/hr). What is its kinetic energy? Now imagine that the car's speed increases to 35 m/s (77 mi/h), which is 40% faster. Is the kinetic energy 40% larger or not? (Note that the severity of a crash is roughly proportional to the kinetic energy that participants bring to it.)

C6S.2 Imagine that if you drop an object from a certain height, its final speed is 20 m/s when it reaches the ground. If you throw the object vertically downward from the same height with an initial speed of 20 m/s, will its final speed be 40 m/s? Carefully explain why or why not.

C6S.3 A 2.0-kg coconut (initially at rest) falls from the top of a coconut tree 15 m high. What is the coconut's kinetic energy when it hits the ground? What is its speed?*

C6S.4 If a person wanting to dive from a seaside cliff does not feel safe hitting the water faster than 20 m/s (44 mi/hr) what is the maximum height from which they should dive?*

C6S.5 Imagine that you are standing at the top of a cliff 45 m high overlooking the ocean and you throw a rock straight downward at a speed of 15 m/s. What is the rock's speed when it hits the water?*

C6S.6 Imagine that you are throwing a tennis ball at a Frisbee™ lodged in a tree 15 m above the ground. If you want the ball's speed to be at least 5 m/s when it hits the Frisbee™, what should its speed be as it leaves your hand? Does your answer depend on the angle that the ball's velocity makes with the horizontal when it leaves your hand?*

> *Please follow the problem-solving framework discussed in section C6.7 in your solution for any starred problem.

RICH-CONTEXT

C6R.1 You are designing a safety net for use by firefighters that can safely catch a person jumping from the top of a 30-story building. What will be the person's approximate speed when hitting the net? How much kinetic energy will the net have to convert safely to other forms? (Make appropriate estimates.)

C6R.2 In July of 1994, about 20 fragments of comet Shoemaker-Levy struck the planet Jupiter, each traveling at a final speed of roughly 60 km/s. These impacts were closely studied because they promised to be the most cataclysmic processes ever witnessed. No one knew exactly *how* cataclysmic, though, because the fragments' sizes (and thus masses) were too small to measure. One estimate of the total energy released by fragment G's impact was 4×10^{22} J (equivalent to the detonation of roughly 100 million typical atomic bombs). Use *this* to estimate fragment G's size, first assuming first that it was solid rock and then that it was solid ice, which have densities of about 3000 kg/m^3 and 920 kg/m^3, respectively. Don't worry about being excessively precise. (This illustrates how even a little knowledge about kinetic energy can help answer questions about objects that can barely be *seen* by the best telescopes!)

ANSWERS TO EXERCISES

C6X.1 Factoring the expression, we find that

$$mg(z_i^2 - z_f^2) = mg(z_i - z_f)(z_i + z_f) \qquad \text{(C6.17)}$$

Note that for a given drop distance $z_i - z_f$, this expression increases as $z_i + z_f$ increases, meaning that the potential energy released as an object falls a given distance would be greater if we did the experiment at the top of building than at the bottom, contrary to what we observe.

C6X.2 The potential energy released by two separate books would be $2[m^2g(z_i - z_f)]$, while the potential energy released when they are tied together into one object of mass $2m$ would be $(2m)^2 g(z_i - z_f) = 4[m^2g(z_i - z_f)]$.

C6X.3 The line goes essentially through the graph's origin, so using the origin and the last point, we find that

$$\text{slope} = \frac{\text{rise}}{\text{run}} = \frac{19.6 \text{ m}^2/\text{s}^2 - 0}{1.0 \text{ m} - 0} = 19.6 \text{ m/s}^2 \quad \text{(C6.18)}$$

C6X.4 As the separation between the interacting particles change, the potential energy of an external interaction will be converted to or from kinetic energy in *both* particles, the one outside as well as the one inside the system. Therefore even if we include the energies of the external interactions in the system's total energy, these interactions

can transfer energy into or out of the system.

C6X.5 The language works well enough when one interacting object is the earth, but becomes absurd when you consider two objects (like the repelling magnetic carts) that have almost equal masses. Which cart in that case would you want to say "has" the potential energy? The interaction language also emphasizes the fact that there would *be* no potential energy without the interaction!

C6X.6 Set up the system so the particles initially have the reference separation, so $V(r_i) = 0$ by definition. Let the system evolve to any separation r_f you desire, and then calculate the unique value of $V(r_f)$ using equation C6.12.

C6X.7 Note that $[V(r_i) + C] - [V(r_f) + C] = V(r_i) - V(r_f)$, so adding a constant C to the potential energy does not affect the *difference* that appears in equation C6.12.

C6X.8 $V(z) = -294$ J at $z = 0$, $V(z) = +294$ J at $z = 20$ m. In general, $V(z) = mgz + C$, where $C = -294$ J.

C6X.9 Since the object at $z_1 = -5$ m is 25 m below the reference separation z_0, $V(z_1) - V(z_0) = mg(z_1 - z_0)$ and $V(z_0) = 0$ mean that $V(z_1) = (3 \text{ kg})(9.8 \text{ m/s}^2)(-25 \text{ m}) = -735$ J. Similarly, at $z_2 = 0$, $V(z_2) = -588$ J. However, the system's potential energy at $z_2 = 0$ is *still* 147 J larger than at $z_1 = -5$ m.

C7

POTENTIAL ENERGY FUNCTIONS

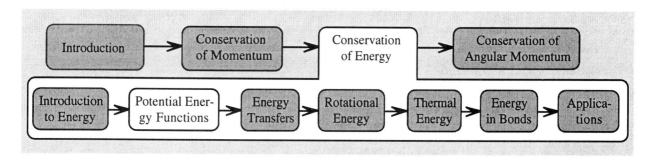

C7.1 OVERVIEW

In the last chapter, we introduced the concept of conservation of energy and explored kinetic and potential energy in the straightforward context of an object interacting gravitationally with the earth near the earth's surface. But this is only one of many ways that two objects can interact. In this chapter, we will discuss the potential energies involved for three other cases, two fundamental long-range interactions (the gravitational and electromagnetic interactions) and a contact interaction that we can treat as if it were a long-range interaction. This will both broaden the range of situations to which we can apply conservation of energy and deepen our understanding of the concept potential energy.

Here is an overview of the sections in this chapter.

C7.2 *THE ELECTROMAGNETIC INTERACTION* discusses the potential energy function for the electromagnetic interaction between two charged particles.

C7.3 *THE GRAVITATIONAL INTERACTION* describes the potential energy function for the gravitational interaction between two particles and compares it to the electromagnetic interaction.

C7.4 *GRAVITATION NEAR THE EARTH* explores the link between the general formula for the gravitational interaction presented in the last section with the empirical formula presented in the last chapter.

C7.5 *THE POTENTIAL ENERGY OF A SPRING* explores the potential energy function for a pair of objects connected by a spring. This potential energy function provides a useful approximate model for many kinds of more complicated interactions.

C7.6 *SOME EXAMPLES* illustrates how we can use conservation of energy and the ideas in this chapter to solve various kinds of problems.

*** *PHYSICS SKILLS: SIGNIFICANT DIGITS* discusses a convention for expressing the inevitable uncertainties in physical quantities.

*** *PHYSICS SKILLS: FORMULAS* offers suggestions for how to think about and remember the various formulas that appear in this text.

C7.2   THE ELECTROMAGNETIC INTERACTION

The electromagnetic inter-action acts between *charged* particles

We begin our study of the potential energies associated with interactions by looking at the two long-range fundamental interactions, the *electromagnetic* and *gravitational* interactions. Of these two, the electromagnetic interaction is by far the one that is most crucial for objects that are much smaller than planets.

The electromagnetic interaction acts between any two particles that have electrical **charge**. You probably know from previous experience that there are exactly *two* kinds of electric charge, which are called *positive* and *negative*. The historical definition of positive and negative charge end up implying that protons have positive charge and electrons have negative charge.

The SI unit of charge is the **coulomb**, where (for historical reasons) 1 C is equivalent to the charge of about 6.242×10^{18} protons. Positive and negative charges are represented by positive and negative numbers, respectively.

As long as two particles with charges q_1 and q_2 are not moving at relativistic speeds, the potential energy of their electromagnetic interaction depends on their separation r approximately as follows:

The formula for electro-static potential energy

$$V(r) = +k\frac{q_1 q_2}{r} \qquad \left(\begin{array}{l} \text{reference separation:} \\ V(r) \equiv 0 \ \text{when } r = \infty \end{array} \right) \qquad \text{(C7.1)}$$

This formula is an excellent approximation when the particles' speeds are much less than the speed of light, but is only *exact* when the particles are at rest, so this formula is called the **electrostatic** potential energy function. Note that in order to determine uniquely the value of $V(r)$ at a given r, we have to choose a reference separation: the conventional choice for interacting point particles is to take $V(r)$ to be zero at $r = \infty$, which leads to the formula above.

The Coulomb constant

The **Coulomb constant** k expresses how strongly the potential energy of the interaction depends on the magnitude of the charges involved (at a given separation): it thus characterizes the strength of the interaction. The *value* of k (which is also sometimes written $1/4\pi\varepsilon_0$ for historical reasons) depends on the units that one uses to express charge: if charge is expressed in Coulombs, k is

$$k = 8.99 \times 10^9 \ \frac{\text{J} \cdot \text{m}}{\text{C}^2} \qquad \text{(C7.2)}$$

If $V(r)$ *decreases* as r increases, the interaction is repulsive

Figure C7.1a and C7.1b show graphs of equation C7.1 when $q_1 q_2 > 0$ (the particles' charges have *like* signs) and when $q_1 q_2 < 0$ (the particles' charges have *opposite* signs), respectively. Note that if the particles' charges have *like* signs, the potential energy of their interaction *decreases* as their separation gets larger. If the particles are isolated, their total energy should remain constant: this means that as their separation increases and potential energy decreases, their kinetic energy should increase. This means that the particles will speed up as they move away from each other. This is characteristic of a repulsive interaction; therefore, we say that *like charges repel*.

If $V(r)$ *increases* as r increases, the interaction is attractive

On the other hand, if the particles' charges are opposite, their potential energy (though it is always negative) *increases* as the particles' separation increases. This means that the kinetic energy of an isolated pair of such particles will increase as they *approach* each other. This is characteristic of an attractive interaction: therefore, *opposite charges attract*.

These arguments show that we can understand much about the qualitative nature of an interaction by looking at a graph of $V(r)$. We will discuss this further in chapter C11.

Exercise C7X.1: If two protons are separated by 10^{-12} m, what is the potential energy of their electrostatic interaction? (The charge of a proton is $+e$, where e is the elementary charge whose value appears on the inside front cover.)

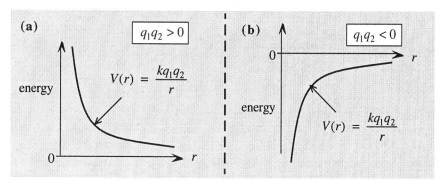

Figure C7.1: (a) A graph of the electrostatic potential energy function $V(r)$ as a function of separation r for a pair of particles whose charges have *like* signs. **(b)** A graph of $V(r)$ as a function of r for a pair of particles whose charges have *opposite* signs.

Note: Since we often plot total energies and kinetic energies on graphs along with potential energies, the vertical axis in a graph of $V(r)$ is conventionally labeled simply "energy."

The reason that charges are described as being "positive" and "negative" is because the *physical* behavior of charge when combined is analogous to the *mathematical* behavior of positive and negative numbers when combined. For example, a hydrogen atom is a combination of a proton (whose charge is +1 in proton units) and an electron (whose charge is −1 in proton units). When viewed from a distance, the hydrogen atom behaves as if it were uncharged: the combination of the proton charge and the electron charge in close proximity is physically equivalent to *zero* charge. Analogously, if we add the numbers (+1 and −1) representing the proton and electron charges we get the number 0.

Why are charges "positive" and "negative"?

An atom behaves as if it were electrically neutral only if its interaction partner is so far away that the atom seems to be a point particle. A charged particle placed close to a hydrogen atom *can* interact with it electromagnetically since the particle (depending on its placement at a given time) may be significantly closer to either the proton or the electron, and as a result, the effects of a particle's interaction with the proton may *not* exactly cancel its the effects of interaction with the electron.

Neutral atoms *can* interact electromagnetically

Indeed, when two hydrogen atoms are brought close together, such unbalanced interactions happen to have the effect of changing the shape of the electron orbitals in the atoms so that there is a net electrostatic attraction that binds the atoms together: this is a chemical bond. All of chemistry is a detailed exploration of how atoms interact as a result of the imperfect cancellation of the electromagnetic interactions between atoms that are brought close together. Such unbalanced interactions also give rise to contact interactions, as discussed in section C6.4.

When the two interacting charged particles also move with respect to each other, they interact *magnetically* as well as electrostatically. The magnetic part of an interaction between two charged particles does not affect their kinetic energy, and so we can ignore it in the electromagnetic potential energy. When other interactions are involved, magnetic effects can (indirectly) have energy implications. It turns out, for example, that the north and south magnetic poles of two interacting bar magnets behave *qualitatively* like positive and negative charges and we can treat such interactions between poles of such magnets *as if* they had potential energies with same inverse-r dependence as for point charges. But we won't worry about magnetism much until we explore it in depth in Unit *E*.

C7.3   THE GRAVITATIONAL INTERACTION

It is ironic that the gravitational interaction, which is *by far* the weakest of the four fundamental interactions, is nonetheless the most obvious of the four in daily life, and more than any other shapes objects that are larger than asteroids. This is because the gravitational interaction acts between any pair of objects having mass, and *there is no such thing as negative mass*. Therefore, the gravitational effects of particles in an object tend to add instead of canceling out (as electromagnetic effects tend to do). Even an interaction that is extraordinarily weak between two elementary particles can become dominant when a huge number of particles all pull together.

Gravitation is observable because there is no such thing as negative mass!

The formula for gravitational potential energy

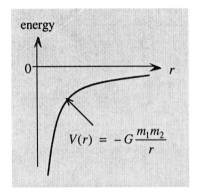

Figure C7.2: A graph of the gravitational potential energy $V(r)$ between a pair of particles with nonzero mass.

The potential energy of the gravitational interaction between two point particles with masses m_1 and m_2 separated by a distance r is given by

$$V(r) = -G\frac{m_1 m_2}{r} \qquad \begin{pmatrix} \text{reference separation:} \\ V(r) \equiv 0 \ \ \text{when } r = \infty \end{pmatrix} \qquad \text{(C7.3)}$$

as long as neither particle is moving at a speed close to the speed of light. As in the case of the electromagnetic potential function, we conventionally choose the reference separation for the gravitational potential energy function to be $r = \infty$, as shown. Indeed, note that this function has *the same form* as the electromagnetic potential energy function given by equation C7.1, except that the masses m_1 and m_2 here play the role that the charges q_1 and q_2 did there, the constant G here replaces k there, and the sign of the gravitational potential energy is *always* negative. The negative sign is necessary so that the gravitational potential energy *increases* with increasing separation, which is a necessary characteristic of an *attractive* interaction, as we've seen. A graph of this potential energy function is shown in Figure C7.2.

The **gravitational constant** G expresses how strongly the potential energy of a gravitational interaction depends on the magnitude of the masses involved (at a given separation): it thus characterizes the strength of the interaction. In SI units, this constant has the measured value

$$G = 6.67 \times 10^{-11} \ \frac{\text{J} \cdot \text{m}}{\text{kg}^2} \qquad \text{(C7.4)}$$

Equation C7.3 (like the electromagnetic potential energy formula) strictly applies only to an interaction between *particles*. To find the total potential energy between two extended objects A and B (for either kind of interaction), we treat the extended objects as collections of microscopic particles (which is what they are), find the interaction potential energy for each possible *pair* of particles (such that one particle is in A and the other is in B) and then simply *add* these interparticle potential energies.

Spherical objects can be treated as point particles

While the principle is simple, actually *doing* such a sum for a given pair of extended objects would be *very* tedious. In the case of gravitating objects, this is rarely necessary. An important characteristic of *both* the gravitational and electrostatic interactions is that when a *spherical* object (or charge distribution) interacts with another object, *the potential energy of interaction turns out to be the same as what you would calculate for a particle with the same mass (or charge) located at the sphere's center* (assuming the other object is *outside* the sphere). You can prove this theorem fairly easily if you are handy with integrals (see problem C7A.1): otherwise, you can accept this on faith for now.

Since most objects having significant mass in the universe are very nearly spherical, this theorem means we can apply equation C7.3 directly to such objects, treating them as point particles. Any *non*spherical extended object (like a person) interacting with a planetary body will likely be so tiny compared to the planetary body that it can be approximated as a point mass. So in virtually every common situation, we can use equation C7.3 without complication.

Exercise C7X.2: What is the gravitational potential energy of a system of two 10-kg lead balls, separated (center to center) by 2 m?

C7.4 GRAVITATION NEAR THE EARTH

Reconciling the two gravitational $V(r)$ formulas

The only puzzle is that the potential energy formula $V(r) = -Gm_1 m_2 / r$ stated in the last section looks *nothing* like the potential energy formula $V(z) = mgz$ that we found empirically described gravitational interactions between the earth and objects near its surface (see section C6.3). The first equation tells us that the gravitational potential energy is *negative*, and that it *decreases* in magnitude as $1/r$ as the separation between the objects increases. The other says that the gravitational potential energy is *positive* (for $z > 0$) and *increases* linearly as the separation z between the earth and the object increases. Yet equation C7.3 is *supposed* to apply to an object interacting with the earth! How can it when it seems to be so different?

Part of the difference between these equations has to do with different choices of *reference separation*. In equation C7.3, the reference separation where $V(r) \equiv 0$ is chosen to be $r = \infty$, whereas in the empirical formula, the reference separation is defined to be when the object is at $z = 0$ in whatever coordinate system we are using. If the coordinate system is placed on the surface of the earth, then the actual separation between the earth and the object when $z = 0$ is the radius of the earth r_e (since we have to treat the earth as if its mass were concentrated at its *center*, which is a distance r_e below its surface). We can redefine equation C7.3 so that its reference separation is *also* at the earth's surface by adding an appropriate constant term to the potential energy:

First step: choose a common reference separation

$$V(r) = -G\frac{m_1 m_2}{r} + G\frac{m_1 m_2}{r_e} \qquad (\text{now } V(r) \equiv 0 \text{ when } r = r_e) \qquad (C7.5)$$

where r_e is the radius of the earth. (Can you see that this potential energy will indeed be zero when $r = r_e$?)

I will now show you that equation C7.5 reduces to $V(z) = mgz$ for an object near the earth. Let us define M to be the mass of the earth, and m to be the mass of the object interacting with the earth. Note that when an object is at position z, its distance from the earth's center is $r = z + r_e$. If you plug these things into equation C7.5 and rearrange things a bit, you can express the general gravitational potential energy formula for $V(r)$ as a function of z as follows:

$V(r) = mgz$ **is an approximation valid near the earth**

$$V(z) = m\frac{GM}{r_e}\left[1 - \frac{1}{1 + (z/r_e)}\right] \qquad (C7.6)$$

Exercise C7X.3: Verify equation C7.6.

By putting the two terms in the square brackets over a common denominator and doing a bit of algebra, you can show that

$$V(z) = m\left[\frac{GM}{r_e^2}\frac{1}{1 + (z/r_e)}\right]z \qquad (C7.7)$$

Exercise C7X.4: Verify equation C7.7.

Now, notice that if the object is close to the earth's surface, then $z \ll r_e$ and the quantity in brackets in equation C7.7 will be *almost* equal to GM/r_e^2. The numerical value of GM/r_e^2 is 9.80 m/s^2, which is the empirical value of g. So

$$V(z) \approx m\left[\frac{GM}{r_e^2}\right]z = mgz \qquad (\text{as long as } z \ll r_e) \qquad (C7.8)$$

Exercise C7X.5: Show by direct calculation that GM/r_e^2 has the same value and units as g. (See the inside front cover for the earth's mass and radius.)

So the empirical formula $V(z) = mgz$ represents an *approximation* to the true gravitational potential energy of an object's interaction with the earth, an

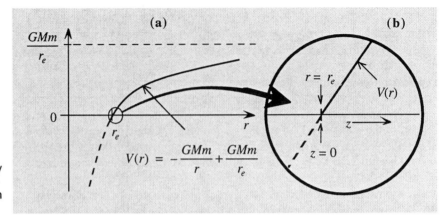

Figure C7.3: Any sufficiently tiny part of the graph of the gravitational potential energy function $V(r)$ will look like a straight line.

approximation that is excellent as long as the object is always close to the earth's surface. Figure C7.3 illustrates what this axpproximation means. Figure C7.3a shows the actual potential energy for the interaction between an object and the earth as a function of the separation between that object and the earth's center. (Note that I have reset the reference point so that $V = 0$ at the earth's surface, as in equation C7.5.) But a sufficiently short segment of any curve will look like a straight line, as illustrated in Figure C7.3b. This means that for sufficiently small displacements from the earth's surface, the potential energy function increases almost linearly as z increases: mg is simply the constant of proportionality for this linear increase.

Whenever you do a problem involving an object interacting gravitationally with the earth, you should first look at whether the separation r between the earth and the object is ever likely to be significantly different than the earth's radius r_e. If so, you should use the general gravitational potential energy formula given by equation C7.3. If not, feel free to use the approximation $V(z) = mgz$.

Exercise C7X.6: Imagine that a 3.0-kg object falls to the ground from an airplane flying at an altitude of 20.0 km. According to the formula $V(z) = mgz$, the gravitational potential energy released as the object falls is $\Delta V = mg\,\Delta z = (3.0\text{ kg})(9.80\text{ m/s}^2)(-20{,}000\text{ m}) = -588{,}000$ J. What is ΔV according to the exact formula given by equation C7.3? (*Hint*: $GM = 3.99 \times 10^{14}$ J·m/kg for the earth. Keep track of at least four or five digits in your calculations.)

C7.5 THE POTENTIAL ENERGY OF A SPRING

Consider now two objects connected by a lightweight spring. The interaction between the objects mediated by the spring is attractive if the spring is stretched beyond its natural length and repulsive if the spring is compressed to be shorter than its natural length.

This interaction would have to be classified as a *contact* interaction according to the scheme described in chapter C2: it arises because each object is in contact with the spring. As the string is stretched or compressed, the separations between its atoms change microscopically, which leads to energy being transferred to or from the microscopic potential energies of the interactions between atoms. In spite of the complexity of these interactions, it so happens that the potential energy of these interactions can be almost exactly described by a simple function of the separation between the objects, *as if* the objects were participating in a long-range interaction like the gravitational or electrostatic interaction! The potential energy function for an interaction mediated by an **ideal spring** is

Formula for potential energy of an ideal spring

$$V(r) = \tfrac{1}{2}k_s(r - r_0)^2 \qquad \left(\begin{array}{l}\text{reference separation:}\\ V(r) \equiv 0 \text{ when } r = r_0\end{array}\right) \qquad (C7.9)$$

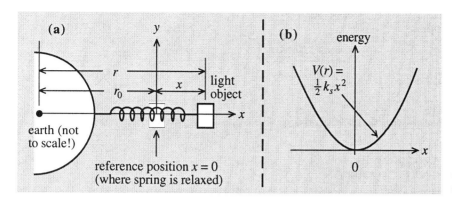

Figure C7.4: **(a)** A lightweight object connected to the earth by a spring. We can define the origin of our reference frame so that the object is at $x = 0$ when the spring is relaxed. **(b)** The potential energy function for the spring in this situation is a parabola.

where r is the separation between the objects, r_0 is their separation when the spring is completely relaxed, and k_s is a **spring constant** that characterizes the stiffness of the spring (the larger k_s is, the more energy has to be transferred to potential energy to stretch or compress the spring a given amount). The reference separation for this potential energy function is *conventionally* defined to be the separation of the objects when the spring is completely relaxed. (The conventional factor of $\frac{1}{2}$ in this equation makes certain other equations simpler.)

This potential energy function, while idealized, generally describes the potential energy stored in a realistic spring quite well, particularly if the spring is not stretched or compressed very far from its natural length. If the spring also has a very small mass compared to the two objects that it connects, then we can ignore the small kinetic energy of the moving parts of the spring compared to the kinetic energies of the connected objects, and the system behaves very nearly *as if* the two objects were participating in a long-range interaction with the potential energy function given in equation C7.9.

In many realistic situations, a low-mass object is connected by a spring to a very massive object (such as the earth). In such a case (as we will see in the next chapter) we can consider the massive object to be at rest and have essentially zero kinetic energy. If the low-mass object moves along a straight line parallel to the spring, we can define our reference frame so that one axis (say the x axis) lies along this line, and we can define the frame's origin so that the low-mass object is at $x = 0$ when the spring is relaxed (that is, when the separation between the two objects is $r = r_0$). Then, when the position of the low-mass object is some $x \neq 0$, the separation of the two objects will be $r = r_0 + x$, implying that $x = r - r_0$ (see Figure C7.4a). Plugging this into equation C7.9, we get

$$V(x) = \tfrac{1}{2}k_s x^2 \quad \left(\begin{array}{l} \text{reference separation:} \\ V(x) \equiv 0 \ \text{at} \ x = 0 \end{array} \right) \qquad \text{(C7.10)}$$

A simplified version of the spring formula

This is the form of the spring potential energy function that we will most commonly use. Note that a graph of this $V(x)$ is a *parabola* (see Figure C7.4b). Because the interaction's potential energy *increases* if the low-mass object moves away from $x = 0$, the object's kinetic energy must *decrease* as it does this (since the system's total energy is fixed). If the low-mass object slows down as it moves away from $x = 0$, the spring interaction is *attracting* it towards $x = 0$.

Understanding the spring interaction is important in physics not because objects connected by springs are all that common, but because this situation serves as a useful *model* for more complicated situations. For example, imagine that the complicated electromagnetic interaction between two atoms has the potential energy function as shown in Figure C7.5a, which has a local minimum when the atoms are separated by $r = r_0$. If we redefine the origin of our reference frame so that $x = 0$ corresponds to $r = r_0$, and the reference separation where $V \equiv 0$ to be $x = 0$ (Figure C7.5b), then the potential energy curve for values of x near to zero looks a *lot* like a parabola and can be approximated by $V(x) = \tfrac{1}{2}k_s x^2$ with

The spring interaction is a useful *model*

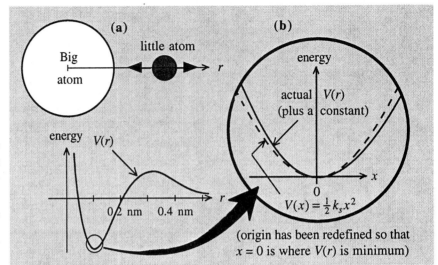

Figure C7.5: (a) A hypothetical potential energy function for the complicated electromagnetic interaction between two atoms. **(b)** If we add an appropriate constant to the potential energy, and redefine $x = 0$ to coincide with the bottom of the local minimum circled, then for values of x close to the new $x = 0$, $V(x) = \frac{1}{2}k_s x^2$.

an appropriately-chosen value of k_s. Thus when $x \approx 0$ ($r \approx r_0$) these two atoms will behave as if they were connected by a massless spring.

Similarly, if the potential energy function for *any* complex interaction between two objects has a local minimum at some separation r_0, then the potential energy for separations near r_0 can *almost always* be approximated by a parabola. Therefore, the potential energy function $V(r) = \frac{1}{2}k_s(r - r_0)^2$ is a good model for almost any situation where the interaction between two objects tends to push them toward a specific separation (and deviations from this separation r_0 are relatively small). Examples include the interactions between atoms in a molecule, between the earth and a ball rolling in a bowl, and between the earth and a pendulum bob. (Indeed, the fact that the microscopic interactions between atoms in spring steel are accurately described by this kind of potential energy function is why a spring itself behaves this way!)

Exercise C7X.7: Explain why k_s must have SI units of J/m^2.

Exercise C7X.8: A typical spring might have a k_s whose value is roughly 100 J/m^2. If such a spring has a relaxed length of 5.0 cm and is stretched to a length of 8.0 cm, what is the potential energy stored in the spring?

C7.6 SOME EXAMPLES

The remainder of this chapter is devoted to some examples that illustrate applications of these potential energy formulas and further illustrate the use of the problem-solving framework in conservation of energy problems.

Note especially example C7.2, which introduces the idea of an **escape speed**. One of the most interesting implications of the gravitational potential energy formula is that if a rocket has a sufficiently high speed near a planet, it can coast away from that planet *indefinitely* without using its engines (even though the planet is always pulling it back!). Example C7.2 shows how one can use conservation of energy to compute rather easily what this speed needs to be.

EXAMPLE C7.1

OUTLINE OF THE FRAMEWORK

1. Pictorial Representation

  a. Draw a picture of the situation that includes:

    ① (1) sketches of the system in its initial and final states

    ② (2) reference frame axes

    ③ (3) labels defining symbols for relevant quantities (in this case, objects' masses, velocities, and separations)

  b. List values for all known quantities and specify which quantities are unknown.
  ④

2. Conceptual Representation

The general task is to construct a conceptual model of the situation and link it to an abstract physics model or principle. In conservation-of-energy problems, we do the following:

  ⑤ a. Identify the *system* involved. (If it involves the earth, we can ignore the earth's kinetic energy)

  ⑥ b. Determine whether it is *approximately* isolated, *functionally* isolated, or involved in a *collision* (as defined in chapter C5). Support your conclusions briefly.

  ⑦ c. Identify the interactions between objects in the system and for each interaction, determine whether we can handle it by

    (1) keeping track of its potential energy (if so, define the reference separation)

    (2) ignoring it (because it is very weak or for another reason)

    Be sure to support your conclusions with a brief argument.

  ⑧ d. Do we have to make any approximations or assumptions to solve the problem? (If so, describe.)

3. Mathematical Representation

  ⑨ a. Apply the mathematical equation that appropriately describes the situation (equation C6.16 here)

  ⑩ b. Solve for unknowns symbolically

  ⑪ c. Plug in numbers and units and calculate the result and its units.

4. Evaluation

  Check that the answer makes sense:
  ⑫ a. Does it have the correct units?
  ⑬ b. Does it have the right sign?
  ⑭ c. Does it seem reasonable?

Problem: The nucleus of a deuterium atom consists of a single positively-charged proton bound to a single uncharged neutron of about the same mass. If one can get two such nuclei close enough together so that they essentially touch (that is, so their separation is less than about 1.5 fm = 1.5×10^{-15} m), the strong interaction takes over and the nuclei fuse, releasing energy. However, since the nuclei have the same charge, they electrostatically repel each other. Imagine that we fire two deuterium nuclei directly toward each other with equal initial speeds v_i. How large would v_i have to be for the nuclei to fuse? Express your answer as a fraction of the speed of light c.

Solution: Let us orient our frame so that the x axis coincides with the direction of motion of the nuclei. We will *assume* that the initial separation of the nuclei is large enough that we can approximate it by infinity. The separation between the nuclei will be smallest when as much of their initial kinetic energy as possible has been converted to electrostatic potential energy. Since the initial *velocities* of the nuclei add up to zero, the system's total momentum is zero also, so the kinetic energy of both nuclei could both go to *zero* without violating conservation of momentum. So, our initial and final sketches look like:

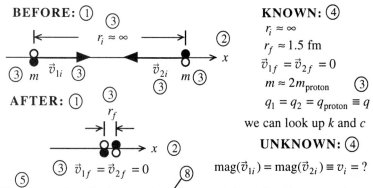

KNOWN: ④
$$r_i \approx \infty$$
$$r_f \approx 1.5 \text{ fm}$$
$$\vec{v}_{1f} = \vec{v}_{2f} = 0$$
$$m \approx 2m_{\text{proton}} \quad ③$$
$$q_1 = q_2 = q_{\text{proton}} \equiv q$$

we can look up k and c

UNKNOWN: ④
$$\text{mag}(\vec{v}_{1i}) = \text{mag}(\vec{v}_{2i}) \equiv v_i = ?$$

The system here is the two deuterium nuclei. While this system is not really isolated, we will *assume* that external electromagnetic and gravitational interactions are weak compared to their electromagnetic interaction with each other (otherwise, we can't apply conservation of energy!). The nuclei also interact gravitationally, but this is *far* weaker than the electromagnetic interaction, and we will ignore it. The potential energy function for the electromagnetic interaction is $V(r) = kq_1q_2 / r$ (using the conventional reference separation where $V(r) = 0$ at $r = \infty$). Conservation of energy then tells us that

$$⑨ \qquad K_{1i} + K_{2i} + V(r_i) = K_{1f} + K_{2f} + V(r_f)$$

Since $V(r_i) \approx V(\infty) = 0$, $\text{mag}(\vec{v}_{1i}) = \text{mag}(\vec{v}_{2i}) \equiv v_i$, the final speeds of the nuclei are zero, and $q_1 = q_2 = q_{\text{proton}} \equiv q$ this becomes

$$\tfrac{1}{2}mv_i^2 + \tfrac{1}{2}mv_i^2 + 0 = 0 + 0 + \frac{kq_1q_2}{r_f} \;\Rightarrow\; v_i^2 = \frac{kq^2}{mr_f}, \text{ so} \quad ⑩$$

$$\frac{v_i}{c} = \frac{q}{c}\sqrt{\frac{k}{mr_f}} = \frac{1.60\times10^{-19}\,\cancel{C}}{3.0\times10^8 \text{ m/s}}\sqrt{\frac{8.99\times10^9 \text{ J}\cdot\cancel{\text{m}}/\cancel{C}^2}{2(1.67\times10^{-27}\text{ kg})(1.5\times10^{-15}\,\cancel{\text{m}})}}$$

$$= \frac{0.023}{\cancel{\text{m/s}}}\sqrt{\frac{\cancel{\text{J}}}{\cancel{\text{kg}}}\left(\frac{1\,\cancel{\text{kg}}\cdot\text{m}^2/\text{s}^2}{1\,\cancel{\text{J}}}\right)} = 0.023 \quad ⑪$$
$$\qquad\qquad ⑫ \qquad\qquad ⑬$$

This ratio is unitless and positive (as the ratio of speeds should be!) and less than 1, meaning that $v_i < c$ ($v_i > c$ would be suspicious). ⑭

EXAMPLE C7.2

OUTLINE OF THE FRAMEWORK

1. Pictorial Representation

a. Draw a picture of the situation that includes:

① (1) sketches of the system in its initial and final states

② (2) reference frame axes

③ (3) labels defining symbols for relevant quantities (in this case, objects' masses, velocities, and separations)

④ b. List values for all known quantities and specify which quantities are unknown.

2. Conceptual Representation

The general task is to construct a conceptual model of the situation and link it to an abstract physics model or principle. In conservation-of-energy problems, we do the following:

⑤ a. Identify the *system* involved. (If it involves the earth, we can ignore the earth's kinetic energy)

⑥ b. Determine whether it is *approximately* isolated, *functionally* isolated, or involved in a *collision* (as defined in chapter C5). Support your conclusions briefly.

⑦ c. Identify the interactions between objects in the system and for each interaction, determine whether we can handle it by

(1) keeping track of its potential energy (if so, define the reference separation)

(2) ignoring it (because it is very weak or for another reason)

Be sure to support your conclusions with a brief argument.

⑧ d. Do we have to make any approximations or assumptions to solve the problem? (If so, describe.)

3. Mathematical Representation

⑨ a. Apply the mathematical equation that appropriately describes the situation (equation C6.16 here)

⑩ b. Solve for unknowns symbolically

⑪ c. Plug in numbers and units and calculate the result and its units.

4. Evaluation

Check that the answer makes sense:
⑫ a. Does it have the correct units?
⑬ b. Does it have the right sign?
⑭ c. Does it seem reasonable?

Problem: Imagine that we launch a rocket away from the surface of the earth. Assuming that its engines fire only very briefly at the beginning of its flight, what is the *minimum* initial speed v_i that the rocket must have when its engines shut down if it is able to coast away from the earth forever? (We call this speed the earth's **escape speed**.)

Solution: We will assume that the rocket is still near the earth's surface when the engines shut off, so that $r_i \approx r_e$ = the earth's radius. "Coasting away forever" means that $v_f \equiv \mathrm{mag}(\vec{v}_f) > 0$, no matter how far from the earth the rocket gets. We'll set up a reference frame on the surface of the earth with its z axis upward and its origin at the earth's center (but we really don't need it in this problem).

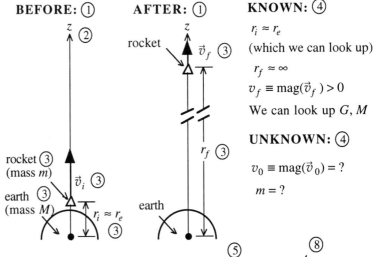

BEFORE: ①   **AFTER:** ①   **KNOWN:** ④

$r_i \approx r_e$
(which we can look up)

$r_f \approx \infty$

$v_f \equiv \mathrm{mag}(\vec{v}_f) > 0$

We can look up G, M

UNKNOWN: ④

$v_0 \equiv \mathrm{mag}(\vec{v}_0) = ?$

$m = ?$

The system here is the rocket and the earth, which we will take to be ⑤ ⑧ *approximately* isolated. Since the earth is so massive compared to the rocket, we will ignore its kinetic energy. If we assume the rocket is ⑥ outside the earth's atmosphere, then the gravitational interaction is the only internal interaction in this system. Since the separation of the ⑦ rocket from the earth will eventually get large compared to r_e, we will use the potential energy formula $V(r) = -GMm/r$, which assumes that the reference separation is $r = \infty$. Conservation of energy (ignoring the earth's kinetic energy) then tells us that

$$⑨ \quad K_i + V(r_i) = K_f + V(r_f) \quad \Rightarrow \quad \tfrac{1}{2}mv_i^2 - \frac{GMm}{r_i} = \tfrac{1}{2}mv_f^2 - \frac{GMm}{r_f}$$

Since v_f^2 must be greater than zero, and $GMm/r_f \approx 0$ as r goes to infinity, we must have

$$\tfrac{1}{2}mv_i^2 - \frac{GMm}{r_i} > 0 \quad \Rightarrow \quad v_i^2 > \frac{2GM}{r_i} \approx \frac{2GM}{r_e} \quad \overset{⑩}{\Rightarrow} \quad v_i > \sqrt{\frac{2GM}{r_e}}$$

$$\Rightarrow v_i > \sqrt{\frac{2(6.67\times10^{-11}\ \cancel{\text{N}}\cdot\text{m}/\cancel{\text{kg}}^2)(5.98\times10^{24}\ \cancel{\text{kg}})}{(6{,}380{,}000\ \cancel{\text{m}})}\left(\frac{1\ \cancel{\text{kg}}\cdot\text{m}^2/\text{s}^2}{1\ \cancel{\text{N}}}\right)}$$
⑪

$$\Rightarrow v_i > 11{,}200\ \text{m/s} = 11.2\ \text{km/s}$$
⑬ ⑫

So the *minimum* speed required to escape is about 11.2 km: this is the earth's escape speed. This result's sign and units are appropriate for a speed. The magnitude does not seem outrageous; I seem to remember something about deep space probe speeds being tens of km/s. ⑭ (Note that the unknown rocket mass cancels out: this was nice!)

EXAMPLE C7.3

OUTLINE OF THE FRAMEWORK

1. Pictorial Representation

a. Draw a picture of the situation that includes:

① (1) sketches of the system in its initial and final states

② (2) reference frame axes

(3) labels defining symbols for ③ relevant quantities (in this case, objects' masses, velocities, and separations)

b. List values for all known quantities and specify which quantities are unknown. ④

2. Conceptual Representation

The general task is to construct a conceptual model of the situation and link it to an abstract physics model or principle. In conservation-of-energy problems, we do the following:

⑤ a. Identify the *system* involved. (If it involves the earth, we can ignore the earth's kinetic energy)

⑥ b. Determine whether it is *approximately* isolated, *functionally* isolated, or involved in a *collision* (as defined in chapter C5). Support your conclusions briefly.

⑦ c. Identify the interactions between objects in the system and for each interaction, determine whether we can handle it by

(1) keeping track of its potential energy (if so, define the reference separation)

(2) ignoring it (because it is very weak or for another reason)

Be sure to support your conclusions with a brief argument.

⑧ d. Do we have to make any approximations or assumptions to solve the problem? (If so, describe.)

3. Mathematical Representation

⑨ a. Apply the mathematical equation that appropriately describes the situation (equation C6.16 here)

⑩ b. Solve for unknowns symbolically

⑪ c. Plug in numbers and units and calculate the result and its units.

4. Evaluation

Check that the answer makes sense:
⑫ a. Does it have the correct units?
⑬ b. Does it have the right sign?
⑭ c. Does it seem reasonable?

Problem: A friend of yours sits on a coiled spring that has been compressed to a length 55 cm shorter than its normal length and then held at that length. What is this spring's spring constant k_s if, when the spring is suddenly released, your friend flies into the air 2.0 m above his or her initial position?

Solution: We will use a reference frame in standard orientation on the earth's surface, with $z = 0$ corresponding to the original position of the friend's center of mass when the spring is compressed (this turns out to be easiest). The separation between the center of masses of the earth and my friend is r_i initially and r_0 when the spring is relaxed. Let's define h to be the the distance that the spring is compressed ($h = r_0 - r_i$). Also note that my friend's velocity will be zero at the peak in his or her trajectory after the spring is released.

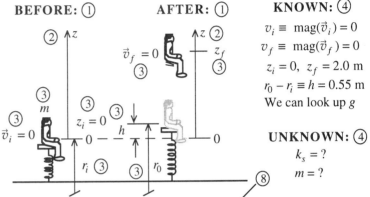

BEFORE: ①   **AFTER:** ①   **KNOWN:** ④

$v_i \equiv \mathrm{mag}(\vec{v}_i) = 0$
$v_f \equiv \mathrm{mag}(\vec{v}_f) = 0$
$z_i = 0, \ z_f = 2.0 \ \mathrm{m}$
$r_0 - r_i \equiv h = 0.55 \ \mathrm{m}$
We can look up g

UNKNOWN: ④
$k_s = ?$
$m = ?$

⑤ The system in this case is the person and the earth, which we will take
⑥ to be approximately isolated. If we ignore air friction, then two interactions act between the earth and my friend, a *gravitational interaction*, which we will handle using the approximate potential energy function $V_g(z) = mgz$ ($V_g \equiv 0$ at $z = 0$), and (initially at least) a *spring interac-*
⑦ *tion*, which we can handle using the potential energy function $V_s(z) = \frac{1}{2} k_s (r - r_0)^2$ ($V_s \equiv 0$ at $r = r_0$: note that we need not use the same reference separation for both interactions!). Note that after my friend leaves the seat, the spring is relaxed, and so there is zero final potential energy involved in this interaction. We will assume that both the spring and
⑧ the seat have very small masses compared to the person (and thus ignore these unknown masses). Conservation of energy then tells us that

$$⑨ \quad K_i + V_s(r_i) + V_g(z_i) = K_f + V_s(r_0) + V_g(z_f)$$

where we are ignoring the earth's kinetic energy, as usual. The friend's initial and final velocities (and thus K_i and K_f) are zero, $V_g(z_i) = 0$ because $z_i = 0$, and $V_s(r_0) = 0$ by definition of the reference separation. Therefore, this equation becomes:

$$0 + \tfrac{1}{2} k_s (r_i - r_0)^2 + 0 = 0 + 0 + mgz_f \ \Rightarrow \ k_s = \frac{2mgz_f}{(r_i - r_0)^2} = \frac{2mgz_f}{h^2} \quad ⑩$$

We know everything in this last expression except for m which it looks like we will actually need. Let's assume my friend has a mass of 55 kg, which is fairly typical for human beings. Then

$$k_s = \frac{2(55 \ \mathrm{kg})(9.8 \ \mathrm{m/s^2})(2.0 \ \mathrm{m})}{(0.55 \ \mathrm{m})^2} \left(\frac{1 \ \mathrm{J}}{1 \ \mathrm{kg \cdot m^2/s^2}} \right) = 7100 \ \mathrm{J/m^2} \quad ⑪$$

⑫ The units are right, and a positive sign is appropriate. ⑬ Normal lab springs have $k_s \approx 100 \ \mathrm{J/m^2}$, but it makes sense that a spring that can throw a person 2.0 m in the air will have to be unusually strong! ⑭

PHYSICS SKILLS: Significant Digits

Unlike purely mathematical problems, physics problems involve quantities like times, masses, distances, speeds, etc. that would have to be *measured* in real life, and thus would be somewhat uncertain (as all measured quantities are). This means the *answers* to such physics problems are uncertain as well. For example, if an object covers 100 m (± 1 m) in 30 s (±1 s), then its speed could be anywhere from a maximum value of (101 m)/29 s = 3.5 m/s to a minimum value of (99 m)/31 s = 3.2 m/s. In such a context it would be *absurd* to say that its speed is 3.333333333 m/s (which is what your calculator says): such an answer would suggest that you know the speed to 9 decimal places when in fact even the digit in the *first* decimal place is uncertain in this situation.

Conventions for dealing with significant figures

When doing an experiment or writing a formal journal article, you would want to keep track of all uncertainties very carefully, but spending such effort on a homework problem solution is overkill. Even so, it is still important to recognize and communicate that quantities (and results) often have *some* uncertainty.

Let's deal with this problem by agreeing to abide by the following conventions. First of all, unless otherwise stated, let's *assume* in this course that the rightmost stated digit for any measurable quantity is uncertain (except in the case of integers over 100, where we will consider the last *nonzero* digit to be uncertain). Thus we will consider a stated value of 2.000 to be uncertain in the thousandth's place, a value of 80 to be uncertain in the one's place, a value of 0.20 to be uncertain in the hundredth's place, 23,000 to be uncertain in the thousands place, and so on. The digits from the leftmost nonzero digit to the uncertain digit (inclusive) are called the quantity's **significant digits**. Thus, 2.000 has four significant digits, 0.20 has two significant digits and so on.

A rule for determining the number of significant digits in a calculated result

Second, we will assume that any *calculated* quantity has the same number of significant digits as whatever factor going into the calculation has the *least* number of significant digits. In *most* cases, this simple rule reasonably approximates the results of a more careful uncertainty analysis.

In problems in this text, I will *generally* state quantities to two significant digits. Therefore, you should generally state *results* to two significant digits unless you have specific reasons (which you should state) to do otherwise. If you want to keep track of *intermediate* results to three or maybe four significant digits, this is fine. But *whatever* you do, don't slavishly copy a long calculator result without considering the uncertainties involved: doing this shows for the world to see that you are not *thinking* about what you write.

PHYSICS SKILLS: Formulas

In a certain sense, this chapter is about three *formulas* (the formulas for the potential energy involved in electrostatic, gravitational, and spring interactions). These three formulas are fundamental and useful enough that you will probably save some time in the long run if you *memorize* them now.

But a formula in physics is more than just a mathematical equation. *Every* formula consists of *at least* the following:

Parts of a formula

1.   A mathematical equation,
2.   Definitions for each symbol in the equation, and
3.   A statement specifying the conditions under which the equation applies.

(Note how the chapter summary on the facing page lists exactly this information for each of our three formulas.) When you memorize or summarize a formula, you should make sure that you capture *all* parts of the formula, *especially* the last (applying a formula in inappropriate circumstances is a *very* common error).

Ways of telling whether a formula is important

A basic question to ask about any formula is "Is this *important*?" Important formulas usually either define basic physical quantities (like kinetic energy) or describe fundamental models (like the law conservation of momentum). Formulas of lesser importance have narrower ranges of applicability (and about 90% of the equations in this text are just stepping stones in an argument). Here is a useful rule: if a formula appears in a chapter summary, it is probably important!

I. THE ELECTROMAGNETIC INTERACTION

A. The potential energy of this interaction is given by $V(r) = + kq_1q_2/r$ (this *assumes* that the reference separation where $V(r) \equiv 0$ is $r = \infty$)
   1. q_1 and q_2 are the two particles' *charges*, expressed in *coulombs*
   2. r is the separation between the particles
   3. $k = 8.99 \times 10^9$ J·m/C^2 characterizes the EM interaction's strength
   4. This formula only applies to *particles* whose speeds are $\ll c$
B. The formula implies that like-signed charges repel and opposites attract: (generally, if $V(r)$ *decreases* with increasing r, the interaction is repulsive; if it *increases*, the interaction is attractive)
C. The concept of *positive* and *negative* charges is metaphorical
   1. The behavior of charges when combined is *analogous* to the behavior of positive and negative numbers when added
   2. A collection of charged particles can therefore be uncharged!
D. Electrically neutral objects *can* interact electromagnetically if they are constructed from electrically charged particles and
   1. They are close enough so the particles' interactions do not cancel
   2. OR at least one of the objects involves *moving* charges
E. The latter case gives rise to the *magnetic* part of the EM interaction
   1. This magnetic part does not affect a *particle's* kinetic energy so we cannot (and do not need to) describe it with a potential energy $V(r)$
   2. We won't worry much about magnetism until unit *E*.

II. THE GRAVITATIONAL INTERACTION

A. The weakest of all the fundamental interactions dominates astronomy: (since mass is never negative, gravitational effects add, and do not cancel)
B. The potential energy of this interaction is given by $V(r) = - Gm_1m_2/r$ (this *assumes* that the reference separation where $V(r) \equiv 0$ is $r = \infty$)
   1. m_1 and m_2 are the masses of the particles, expressed in kilograms
   2. r is the separation between the particles
   3. $G = 6.67 \times 10^{-11}$ J·m/kg^2 characterizes the interaction's strength
   4. This formula only applies to *particles* whose speeds are $\ll c$
C. Since $V(r)$ grows with increasing r, gravity is always *attractive*
D. To find the total $V(r)$ for interacting extended objects:
   1. We treat each object as a collection of particles
   2. We then add the potential energies for the interaction between all possible particle pairs that involve one particle from each object
E. An important theorem for both gravitational and EM interactions: a spherical object interacts as if it were concentrated at its center of mass
F. $V(z) = mgz$ is a good *approximation* to $V(r) = -Gm_1m_2/r$ if:
   1. The reference separation of the latter is readjusted to be $z = 0$, and
   2. The value of $|z| \ll$ the radius of the earth

III. THE SPRING INTERACTION

A. This is a contact interaction that behaves like a fundamental interaction
B. The potential energy of this interaction is $V(r) = \frac{1}{2}k_s(r - r_0)^2$ (this assumes that the reference separation where $V(r) \equiv 0$ is $r = r_0$)
   1. r is the separation between the interacting objects
   2. r_0 is their separation when the spring is relaxed
   3. k_s is a constant that specifies the spring's stiffness
   4. Applies *pretty* accurately to two objects connected by a light spring
C. A more common version of the formula, $V(x) = \frac{1}{2}k_sx^2$, applies if:
   1. One of the two objects is very massive (for example, the earth)
   2. The other moves along a line we take to be the x axis
   3. We define $x = 0$ to be the light object's center of mass when $r = r_0$
D. $V(x) = \frac{1}{2}k_sx^2$ is important because it is a good approximation to the $V(r)$ of almost *any* complicated interaction near a local minimum.

GLOSSARY

charge: a property possessed by a particle or object that enables it to participate in an electromagnetic interaction.

coulomb: the SI unit of charge, approximately equivalent to the charge of 6.242×10^{18} protons.

electrostatic: pertaining to the part of the electromagnetic interaction that would operate between two charged particles if they were at rest (that is, the velocity-*independent* part of the electromagnetic interaction).

Coulomb constant k: a fundamental physical constant that expresses the potential energy involved in the electrostatic interaction between two particles with unit charge separated by unit distance. If charge is measured in coulombs and distance in meters, then $k = 8.99 \times 10^9$ J·m/C^2.

gravitational constant G: a fundamental physical constant that expresses the potential energy involved in the gravitational interaction between two particles with

unit mass separated by unit distance. If mass is measured in kg and distance in meters, then $G = 6.67 \times 10^{-11}$ J·m/kg^2.

ideal spring: an idealized massless spring whose potential energy is exactly proportional to the square of the distance by which it is compressed or expanded. This is a good approximation to the behavior of realistic springs.

spring constant k_s: a constant that expresses the potential energy involved in a spring interaction when the spring is extended or compressed by a unit length. This constant essentially expresses how *stiff* the spring is.

escape speed: the speed an object would have to have at a given point to be able to escape entirely the gravitational field of another object.

significant digits: the digits in an uncertain and/or measured number from the leftmost non-zero digit through the first digit whose value is uncertain.

TWO-MINUTE PROBLEMS

C7T.1 The electrostatic potential energy between the proton and electron in a normal hydrogen atom (with the conventional choice of reference separation) is:
A. negative   C. positive
B. zero   D. could be any of the above

C7T.2 Water molecules weakly attract each other (this is why water molecules coalesce into a liquid and then a solid at decreasing temperatures). What do you think is the interaction responsible for this attraction?
A. Incompletely canceled strong interactions between the molecule's quarks
B. Incompletely canceled electromagnetic interactions between the molecule's charged parts
C. The weak interaction
D. The gravitational interaction

C7T.3 The general gravitational potential energy formula $V(r) = -Gm_1m_2/r$ is always negative for $r > 0$, but the empirical formula $V(r) = mgz$ is always positive for $z > 0$. Why are the signs in these expressions different?
A. The empirical formula is wrong
B. The equations refer to different kinds of interactions
C. The first equation does not apply to objects that are not point particles
D. The equations assume different reference separations
E. other (specify)

C7T.4 The graph below shows the potential energy function of a certain interaction. This interaction is
A. always attractive
B. always repulsive
C. attractive for small x, repulsive for large x
D. repulsive for small x, attractive for large x
E. not enough info for a meaningful answer

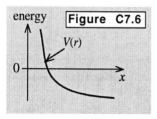

Figure C7.6

C7T.5 Assuming that $z = 0$ at the earth's surface, at roughly what value of z is the potential energy equation $V(r) = mgz$ (with $g = 9.80$ m/s) wrong by about 1%?
A. $z = 1$ km   C. $z = 60$ km
B. $z = 15$ km   D. $z = 250$ km
E. The equation is never in error: it is exact

C7T.6 On a planet with twice the mass and twice the diameter of the earth, the value of g at its surface would be what factor times g at the surface of the earth?
A. 2 times larger   D. 2 times smaller
B. 4 times larger   E. 4 times smaller
C. 8 times larger   F. 8 times smaller
                         T. other (specify)

C7T.7 When an atom in a crystal is moved 0.02 nm to the right or left, its potential energy of interaction with the crystal increases by 4×10^{-18} J. If the spring potential energy function is a model for the potential energy of this interaction, what is the effective value of k_s?
A. 10^{-14} J/m^2 C. 10,000 J/m^2 E. other (specify)
B. 2×10^{-14} J/m^2 D. 20,000 J/m^2

C7T.8 The potential energy function for a spring is shown in the graph below. What is the approximate spring constant for this spring?
A. 0.05 J/m^2 C. 50 J/m^2 E. 200 J/m^2
B. 5 J/m^2 D. 100 J/m^2 F. other (specify)

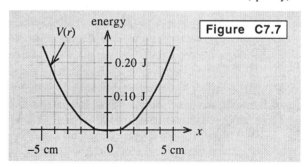

Figure C7.7

HOMEWORK PROBLEMS

BASIC SKILLS

C7B.1 The two protons in a helium nucleus are separated by about 1.2 fm. What is the *approximate* potential energy of their electromagnetic interaction? (Assume that we can treat the protons as point particles, even though their size is comparable to their separation here.)

C7B.2 Imagine that two small objects are given equal charges of about $+1.0 \times 10^{-5}$ C and then are placed 25 cm apart. What is the potential energy involved in their electrostatic interaction?

C7B.3 Two spheres with a radius of 0.10 m and a mass of 25 kg are floating in deep space. Their gravitational attraction keeps them in contact. If we go in and manually separate these spheres to a large distance, by how much will the potential energy of these spheres increase?

C7B.4 Imagine that an object of mass $m = 0.10$ kg falls to the ground from a jet flying at an altitude of 35 km. What is its change in gravitational potential energy according to the formula $V(z) = mgz$? What is its change in potential energy according to the formula $V(r) = -GMm/r$?

C7B.5 A spring with a spring constant $k_s = 60$ J/m^2 has a relaxed length of 6.0 cm. If the spring is compressed to half its length, what is the change in its potential energy?

C7B.6 If it takes 50 J of energy to compress a spring so that it is 2.0 cm shorter than its equilibrium length, what is the spring's spring constant k_s?

C7B.7 The gravitational and contact interactions acting on a boat floating in a lake make it behave *as if* its vertical position were maintained by a spring connected to the lake bottom. If you have to put 100 J of energy into these interactions to push the boat 3 cm deeper into the water, what is the effective spring constant of this imaginary spring?

C7B.8 A mass hanging vertically from the end of a long string behaves when it is moved from side to side as if it were connected to its center position (directly below the point of suspension) by a weak spring with zero relaxed length. If the object has a mass of 0.10 kg and it takes 0.010 J of energy to move it 10 cm away from the central position, what is the effective spring constant k_s of the imaginary spring connecting it to the center point?

SYNTHETIC

C7S.1 Jump vertically as high as you can from the ground. Use conservation of energy to estimate your speed just as you leave the ground.*

C7S.2 Imagine that two identical steel spheres, each having a mass of 1.0 kg, are placed a certain distance apart. They are given an equal charge q such that when the separation between the objects changes, the change in the gravitational potential energy between the objects is exactly balanced by an opposite change in the electrostatic potential energy between the objects. What is q?

C7S.3 If aliens were to drop an asteroid of mass 10^{14} kg from about the radius of the Moon's orbit (384,000 km), how much kinetic energy would it have (to convert to other forms of energy) when it hit the earth? Compare with the energy released by a very large nuclear bomb ($\approx 10^{16}$ J).*

C7S.4 A rocket is fired vertically from the surface of the earth. Its engines fire only briefly, and then the rocket continues to coast upwards. What must the rocket's initial speed be if its speed is to be not less than 5.0 km/s when it is very far from the earth?*

C7S.5 You are trying to design a "rail gun" to launch canisters with masses ranging from 200 kg to 1200 kg from the surface of the moon so that they'd still have a speed of at least 500 m/s very far from the moon. What initial speed do you want the rail gun to give to each canister as it leaves the moon's surface? (The moon's radius is 1740 km and its mass is 7.36×10^{22} kg.)*

C7S.6 Imagine that a bullet is shot vertically into the air with an initial speed of 9800 m/s. If we ignore air friction, how high will it go? Can we use the empirical gravitational potential energy formula here? Justify your response.*

C7S.7 Imagine that you fire a proton at the nucleus of a gold atom (which contains 79 protons and 118 neutrons). What does the proton's initial speed have to be if it is to penetrate the gold nucleus (whose radius is about 6 fm)? Express your answer as a fraction of the speed of light. (One way to measure nuclear radii is to find the speed that such a proton must have to be absorbed.)*

C7S.8 A 550-g glider sliding on a frictionless air track with a speed of 0.80 m/s hits a spring bumper at the end of the air track. It compresses the spring bumper a maximum distance of 1.0 cm before rebounding. What is the spring constant of the spring?*.

C7S.9 You are trying to design a spring gun that is able to launch a 7.0-g marble to a vertical height of 22 m (measured from the starting position of the marble). The specifications for the gun state that when it is loaded, the spring will be compressed 8.0 cm from its relaxed length. (When the gun is fired, the ball is released when the spring reaches its relaxed length.) What should the spring's k_s be?*

C7S.10 A 2.0-kg block is dropped from a height of 48 cm above a plate supported by a spring. If the spring has a spring constant of $k_s = 1600$ J/m^2, what is the maximum distance that the spring will be compressed? (*Hints:* There is no potential energy associated with the spring interaction until the block hits the plate. Remember that the system's gravitational potential energy continues to decrease as the spring is compressed!)*

> *Please write your solution to a starred problem using the problem-solving framework discussed in section C6.7 (and illustrated in examples C7.1 through C7.3).

RICH-CONTEXT

C7R.1 A pogo stick is constructed of a long metal cylinder with two footrests at the bottom and a handle at the top. A spring-loaded pipe with a rubber "foot" fits into the bottom of the main cylinder, so that the spring resists the pipe being pushed into the cylinder. A child can use the pogo stick to bounce around by grabbing the handle and placing both feet on the footrests and then bouncing up and down on the spring-loaded foot. Imagine that you are asked to design a pogo stick that will allow a typical 10-year-old to bounce high enough so that the fully extended "foot" is about 50 cm above the ground, but no higher. What might be a reasonable range of possible values for the spring constant k of the spring you should use in your pogo stick? What constraints limit the value of k_s at either end?

C7R.2 Imagine that you are prospecting for rare metals on a spherical asteroid composed mostly of iron (density $\approx$ 7800 kg/m^3) and whose radius is 4.5 km. You've left your spaceship in a circular orbit 400 m above the asteroid's surface and gone down to the surface using a jet pack. However, one of your exploratory explosions knocks you back against a rock, ruining your jet pack. (This is why you have a back up jet pack, which is, unfortunately, "back up" in the spaceship.) Is it possible for you to simply jump high enough in this situation to get back to the spaceship? (See Problem C7S.1.)

ADVANCED

C7A.1 The gravitational potential energy of a sphere interacting with a point object is exactly as if the mass of the sphere's mass were concentrated at the sphere's center. We can prove this very useful theorem as follows. First of all, consider a very thin spherical *shell* of mass M and radius a. Let R be the distance between the shell's center and the external point object (mass m). To find the total potential energy of the shell's interaction with the point object, we have to sum the potential energies of each particle in the shell interacting with the point object. Consider the thin strip of shell shown in Figure C7.8. If $d\theta$ is small, all particles in this strip are essentially the same distance r from the external point mass. The length of the strip is $2\pi a \sin\theta$ and its width is $a\, d\theta$, so its area is $2\pi a^2 \sin\theta\, d\theta$. Since the total mass M of the shell is spread evenly over the whole area $4\pi a^2$ of the shell, the total mass m_s in this strip is to M as its area is to the shell's total area, implying that the mass of particles in the strip is:

$$m_s = \frac{2\pi a^2 \sin\theta\, d\theta}{4\pi a^2} M = \frac{M}{2} \sin\theta\, d\theta \qquad (C7.11)$$

The bit of the gravitational potential energy associated with this strip interacting with the point particle is thus

$$dV = \frac{-Gm_s m}{r} = \frac{-GMm \sin\theta\, d\theta}{2r} \qquad (C7.12)$$

To find the total potential energy of all particles in the shell interacting with the point particle, we simply have to sum equation C7.12 for all such strips, which amounts to integrating this expression over all θ. Now, r can be expressed in terms of θ using the pythagorean theorem:

$$r^2 = a^2 \sin^2\theta + (R - a\cos\theta)^2$$
$$= a^2 - 2Ra\cos\theta + R^2 \qquad (C7.13)$$

Verify this last expression, plug it into equation C7.12 and integrate from $\theta = 0$ to $\theta = \pi$. (I suggest a change of variables: define $u = \cos\theta$.) You should find that the total value of V for the interaction between the point and the shell is $V = -GMm/R$, which is what it would be if the shell's mass M were concentrated at its center. (Since a sphere can be constructed from a nested series of such shells, this proves the result for a sphere as well.)

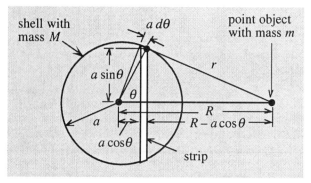

Figure C7.8: Computing the gravitational potential energy of a thin shell interacting with a point.

C7A.2 If you know about Taylor series expansions, you can easily see *why* the spring potential energy function is a good approximation to almost any potential energy function $V(r)$ near a local minimum. Consider an *arbitrary* potential energy function $V(r)$ that has a local minimum at separation r_0. Write out a Taylor series expansion of $V(r)$ around the point r_0. Define $x \equiv r - r_0$ and let's assume that x is small (so that we are *close* to the minimum). Argue that we can make the first term in the expansion go away by using our freedom to choose a reference separation to choose r_0 as the reference separation. Argue that at a local minimum, the second term is automatically zero. Argue that the fourth and succeeding terms will be small compared to the third term if x is small, and so can be ignored. Under these conditions, then, the entire function $V(r)$ is well approximated by the third term in the Taylor series expansion. Then argue that the third term essentially has the form $V(x) = \frac{1}{2} k_s x^2$, and explain how k_s is linked to the second derivative of $V(r)$ with respect to r evaluated at r_0. Since this works as long as the second derivative of $V(r)$ is defined and not zero, perhaps you can see just how general a model $V(x) = \frac{1}{2} k_s x^2$ might be!

ANSWERS TO EXERCISES

C7X.1 about 2.3×10^{-16} J.

C7X.2 about 3.3 nJ.

C7X.3 Here are some of the missing steps:

$$V(r) = -G\frac{Mm}{r} + G\frac{Mm}{r_e} = \frac{GMm}{r_e}\left[-\frac{r_e}{r} + 1\right]$$

$$= \frac{GMm}{r_e}\left[-\frac{r_e}{r_e + z} + 1\right] = \frac{GMm}{r_e}\left[-\frac{1}{1 + z/r_e} + 1\right] \qquad (C7.14)$$

C7X.4 Here are some of the missing steps:

$$V(z) = m\frac{GM}{r_e}\left[\frac{1 + (z/r_e)}{1 + (z/r_e)} - \frac{1}{1 + (z/r_e)}\right]$$

$$= m\frac{GM}{r_e}\left[\frac{1 + (z/r_e) - 1}{1 + (z/r_e)}\right] = m\frac{GM}{r_e}\left[\frac{z/r_e}{1 + (z/r_e)}\right] \qquad (C7.15)$$

C7X.5 This is just a matter of plugging in the numbers (but be sure to convert the earth's radius to *meters*).

C7X.6 –586,000 J. (Not much different!)

C7X.7 $V(x) = \frac{1}{2} k_s x^2$, so $2V(x)/x^2 = k_s$. Since V has units of J, and x has units of m, k_s must have units of J/m^2.

C7X.8 0.045 J.

C8

ENERGY TRANSFERS

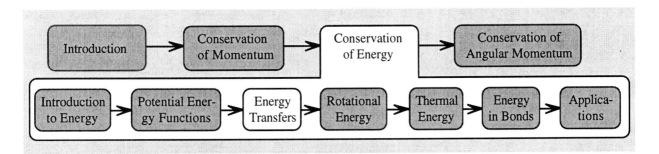

C8.1 OVERVIEW

In the last chapter, we learned how to write potential energy functions for two important long-range interactions (the gravitational and electromagnetic interactions) and an interaction that behaves much *like* a long-range interaction (the spring interaction). But *contact* interactions are *very* important in many situations of interest. This chapter and chapter C10 will discuss how to bring contact interactions under the umbrella of the conservation of energy model.

In this chapter, we begin with a look at the details of how an interaction executes a transfer of energy from potential to kinetic energy and vice versa. Understanding this will help us see why we can ignore the earth's kinetic energy in interactions between a small object and the earth, and why we can also ignore certain kinds of contact interactions. This chapter also introduces the concepts of *force* and the *dot product* of vectors, concepts that will be very useful to us as we go on. Here is a summary of this chapter's sections.

C8.2 *MOMENTUM AND KINETIC ENERGY* explores how an object's kinetic energy is related to its momentum, and discusses how the momentum transferred to an object by an interaction affects that object's kinetic energy.

C8.3 *THE DOT PRODUCT* introduces a mathematical tool that helps us compactly and powerfully express the relationship between the momentum transfer delivered and a change in kinetic energy.

C8.4 *A MODEL FOR ENERGY TRANSFER* uses the ideas explored in the previous sections to construct a comprehensive model of how and when interactions transfer energy.

C8.5 *THE EARTH'S KINETIC ENERGY* uses the ideas presented in section C8.4 to explain why we can ignore the earth's kinetic energy in an interaction between an object and the earth.

C8.6 *CONTACT INTERACTIONS* uses the ideas presented in section C8.4 to determine when we can and cannot ignore a contact interaction, and why a functionally isolated system counts as being isolated from the point of view of conservation of kinetic energy.

C8.7 *MOMENTUM, FORCE, AND ENERGY* argues that it makes sense to define the *force* an interaction exerts on an object to be the *rate* at which the interaction delivers momentum, using the gravitational force as a basic example.

Figure C8.1: (a) An interaction *can* transfer momentum to a particle without changing the magnitude of its momentum and thus its kinetic energy. **(b)** What happens when we add an arbitrary bit of momentum $d\vec{p}$ to a particle's momentum

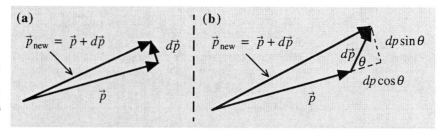

C8.2   MOMENTUM AND KINETIC ENERGY

The most fundamental characteristic of an interaction between two objects is that it affects their motion by mediating momentum transfers between them. In chapter C6, we saw that an interaction can also mediate energy transfers from the interaction's potential energy to the kinetic energies of the interacting objects (or vice versa). In this section, we will explore how these ideas are connected.

The relationship between a particle's momentum and its kinetic energy

An object's kinetic energy is definitely related to its momentum. The newtonian definitions of momentum and kinetic energy tell us that:

$$\vec{p} \equiv m\vec{v} \quad \text{and} \quad K = \tfrac{1}{2}mv^2 = \tfrac{1}{2}m[\text{mag}(\vec{v})]^2 \tag{C8.1}$$

If you take the magnitude of both sides of the definition of momentum, divide both sides by m, and plug the result into the definition of kinetic energy, you get

$$K = \frac{p^2}{2m}, \quad \text{where} \quad p \equiv \text{mag}(\vec{p}) \tag{C8.2}$$

Exercise C8X.1: Verify equation C8.2.

This shows that if an interaction changes an object's momentum, it will generally also change its kinetic energy.

Momentum transfers do not necessarily lead to changes in kinetic energy

The interesting thing is that even though an interaction acting by *itself* on an object *must* change its momentum (because by its very nature it mediates a momentum transfer from the other object) it need *not* change its kinetic energy! Imagine that during a tiny time interval dt, the interaction delivers a momentum transfer $d\vec{p}$ to the object. If the interaction is the *only* one acting on the object, this will cause the object's momentum to change by $d\vec{p} = d\vec{p}$. If the direction of $d\vec{p}$ is such that adding it to the object's initial momentum $\vec{p}$ changes the *direction* of $\vec{p}$ but not its magnitude (as illustrated in Figure C8.1a), then the interaction does *not* change the object's kinetic energy. Thus, the degree to which the interaction changes an object's kinetic energy generally depends on the relative directions of $\vec{p}$ and $d\vec{p}$.

We can quantify this relationship as follows. Figure C8.1b shows what happens when we add an arbitrary momentum change $d\vec{p}$ to an object's initial momentum $\vec{p}$. The **law of cosines** in this case tells us that the magnitude of the object's new momentum $\vec{p}_{\text{new}}$ is given by

$$p_{\text{new}}^2 \equiv [\text{mag}(\vec{p} + d\vec{p})]^2 = p^2 + 2p\,dp\cos\theta + dp^2 \tag{C8.3}$$

where $p \equiv \text{mag}(\vec{p})$, $dp \equiv \text{mag}(d\vec{p})$, and θ is the angle between the directions of $d\vec{p}$ and $\vec{p}$. You can easily prove that this is right: note on Figure C8.1b that p_{new} is the hypotenuse of a right triangle whose legs have lengths $p + dp\cos\theta$ and $dp\sin\theta$. Equation C8.3 then follows directly from the pythagorean theorem and the trigonometric identity $\cos^2\theta + \sin^2\theta = 1$.

Exercise C8X.2: Verify equation C8.3.

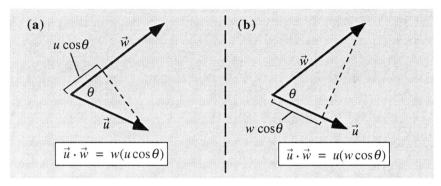

Figure C8.2: Alternative interpretations of the dot product. The **projection** of one vector on another is found by placing the tails of the two vectors together, dropping a perpendicular from the first vector's head to the second vector to form a right triangle, and and then measuring the length of the leg along the second vector. The projection is considered to be negative if $\theta > 90°$. In this case, simple trigonometry implies that **(a)** the projection of $\vec{u}$ on $\vec{w}$ is $u\cos\theta$ and **(b)** the projection of $\vec{w}$ on $\vec{u}$ is $w\cos\theta$.

The change dK that this $d\vec{p}$ produces in the particle's kinetic energy is

$$dK = K_{\text{new}} - K = \frac{p_{\text{new}}^2}{2m} - \frac{p^2}{2m} = \frac{2p\,dp\,\cos\theta + dp^2}{2m} \qquad \text{(C8.4)}$$

If the time interval dt is sufficiently short so that dp is very small compared to p then dp^2 will be negligible compared to $2p\,dp\,\cos\theta$, meaning that

$$dK \approx \frac{p}{m}\,dp\,\cos\theta = v\,dp\,\cos\theta \quad \text{(when } dp \ll p\text{)} \qquad \text{(C8.5)}$$

A tiny momentum transfer's effect on an object's kinetic energy

where v is the particle's speed when the momentum transfer is delivered.

Exercise C8X.3: Argue that equation C8.5 means that an object's kinetic energy *increases* if its velocity and the change in momentum point in the same direction, and *decreases* if they are opposite. Does this make sense?

C8.3   THE DOT PRODUCT

We can express the relationship described in equation C9.6 more compactly in terms of the *dot product* between $d\vec{p}$ and $\vec{v}$. The **dot product** $\vec{u}\cdot\vec{w}$ of any two vectors $\vec{u}$ and $\vec{w}$ is defined to be the *scalar* quantity

Definition of the dot product of two vectors

$$\vec{u}\cdot\vec{w} = uw\cos\theta \qquad \text{(C8.6)}$$

where $u \equiv \text{mag}(\vec{u})$, $w \equiv \text{mag}(\vec{w})$, and θ is the angle between the directions of $\vec{u}$ and $\vec{w}$. Figure C8.2 shows that we can interpret this product as being either u times the *projection* of $\vec{w}$ on $\vec{u}$ or w times the projection of $\vec{u}$ on $\vec{w}$.

From this definition, one can prove that the dot product has the following mathematical properties:

Mathematical properties of the dot product

$\vec{u}\cdot\vec{w} = \vec{w}\cdot\vec{u}$	(the dot product is *commutative*)	(C8.7a)
$\vec{u}\cdot(\vec{w}+\vec{c}) = \vec{u}\cdot\vec{w} + \vec{u}\cdot\vec{c}$	(the dot product is *distributive*)	(C8.7b)
$\vec{u}\cdot(q\vec{w}) = q(\vec{u}\cdot\vec{w})$	(the dot product is *linear*)	(C8.7c)
$\vec{u}\cdot\vec{u} = u^2$		(C8.7d)
$\vec{u}\cdot\vec{w} = 0 \quad \Leftrightarrow \quad \vec{u} \perp \vec{w}$		(C8.7e)

All of these properties are easy to prove from the definition of the dot product except for the distributive property, whose proof is discussed in problem C8S.1. The basic point of these properties is that the dot product of two vectors behaves algebraically pretty much like the ordinary product of two numbers.

Exercise C8X.4: Prove the property C8.7d follows from equation C8.6.

Exercise C8X.5: Prove the property C8.7e follows from equation C8.6 (be sure to prove this for both directions of the double arrow!).

The dot product in terms of vector components

One important consequence of these properties is that we can calculate the dot product of two vectors from their components as follows:

$$\vec{u} \cdot \vec{w} = u_x w_x + u_y w_y + u_z w_z \qquad \text{(C8.8)}$$

Problem C8A.1 shows how to prove that this is equivalent to equation C8.6.

The dot product seems made to order for equation C8.5, which can be rewritten very compactly in terms of a dot product between $d\vec{p}$ and $\vec{v}$:

A tiny momentum transfer's effect on an object's kinetic energy

$$dK = \vec{v} \cdot d\vec{p} \quad \text{(when } dp << p\text{)} \qquad \text{(C8.9)}$$

Let me remind you again that this dK can be positive (if the angle between the $d\vec{p}$ and $\vec{v}$ is less than 90°) or negative (if the angle between $d\vec{p}$ and $\vec{v}$ is greater than 90°). If dK is positive, the object's kinetic energy increases as a result of the momentum transfer; if dK is negative, the object's kinetic energy decreases as a result of this momentum transfer.

Exercise C8X.6: Imagine that during a certain tiny time interval dt, an object whose velocity is $\vec{v} = [-4.0 \text{ m/s}, +2.0 \text{ m/s}, 0 \text{ m/s}]$ is involved in an interaction that changes its momentum by $d\vec{p} = [0.020 \text{ kg·m/s}, -0.010 \text{ kg·m/s}, 0 \text{ kg·m/s}]$. Compute the change dK in the object's energy using equation C8.8 and verify that it has the right units for an energy change.

Exercise C8X.7: Argue that the two vectors in the previous exercise point in *opposite* directions. Then use equation C8.5 to compute dK and show that you get the same result as in the previous exercise.

C8.4 A MODEL FOR ENERGY TRANSFER

Now we are in a position to extend equation C8.9 to the case where an object participates in more than one interaction at a time. In such a circumstance, the *total* change $d\vec{p}$ in the object's momentum during a tiny time interval dt will be the vector sum of the momentum transfers $d\vec{p}_1, d\vec{p}_2, \ldots$ delivered during dt by the various interactions acting on the object:

$$d\vec{p} = d\vec{p}_1 + d\vec{p}_2 + \ldots \qquad \text{(C8.10)}$$

Under these circumstances, equation C8.9 reads

$$dK = \vec{v} \cdot d\vec{p} = \vec{v} \cdot (d\vec{p}_1 + d\vec{p}_2 + \ldots) = \vec{v} \cdot d\vec{p}_1 + \vec{v} \cdot d\vec{p}_2 + \ldots \qquad \text{(C8.11)}$$

where in the last step, I have used the distributive property of the dot product. Therefore, we can say that the energy transferred to an object's kinetic energy by any *one* interaction when it delivers a tiny momentum transfer $d\vec{p}$ is

The contribution each interaction makes to a change in kinetic energy

$$dK \equiv \vec{v} \cdot d\vec{p} \qquad \text{(C8.12)}$$

and that the total change in the object's kinetic energy during an interval dt is the simple sum of the energy transferred by all interactions during dt:

$$dK = dK_1 + dK_2 + \ldots \qquad \text{(C8.13}$$

We see that $dK \equiv \vec{v} \cdot d\vec{p}$ plays the same role for energy that $d\vec{p}$ does for momentum: just as the momentum $d\vec{p}$ transferred by an interaction is generally only a *part* of the object's actual total change in momentum $d\vec{p}$, so the energy dK transferred by an interaction to an object's kinetic energy is only a *part* of its total change in kinetic energy dK if several interactions act at once. Just as we had to give $d\vec{p}$ a special name (*momentum transfer*) to distinguish it from *momentum of an object* defined as $\vec{p} \equiv m\vec{v}$ (which is the momentum *held* by that object), so we should give dK a special name to distinguish it from from *kinetic energy of an object* defined as $K \equiv \frac{1}{2}mv^2$ (which is the energy *held* by the object). *Both* are analogous (as I first stated in chapter C4) to the distinction between *cash* and a *person's net worth*: you can change a person's net worth by transferring cash to or from that person, but net worth is something a *person* holds and has no meaning apart from a person.

We will call dK an **energy transfer**; this emphasizes both its similarity to the concept of momentum transfer and the fact that this energy comes from somewhere else. When the energy transfer dK an interaction delivers to an object is positive, the particle's kinetic energy *increases* (and the interaction's potential energy decreases by the same amount) and when it is negative, the particle's kinetic energy decreases (and the interaction's potential energy increases).

**The definition of an
*energy transfer***

I should note that the historical word in physics for (roughly) this concept is **work**, and dK is written in many books as dW. However, there is a similar but distinct idea in thermal physics that has the same name, and there has been much discussion in recent years about the difficulties that students have separating between a variety of related ideas that are all called "work" in physics. So, while I would like you to *know* that dK is historically called *work*, in this text, I will reserve the term *work* for the concept in thermal physics, and always use *energy transfer* for the concept $dK \equiv \vec{v} \cdot d\vec{p}$.*

So here, in broad strokes, is our model of energy transfer. During a tiny time interval dt, the various interactions acting on an object by their very nature deliver to the object momentum transfers $d\vec{p}_1, d\vec{p}_2, \ldots$, the vector sum of which yield the total change $d\vec{p}$ in the object's momentum. At the same time, those various interactions deliver energy transfers $dK_1, dK_2, \ldots$ to the object (where each energy transfer is given by the equation $dK = \vec{v} \cdot d\vec{p}$). The ordinary (scalar) sum of these energy transfers yields the total change dK in the object's kinetic energy. An object's kinetic energy K is like the balance in a bank account into which the interactions acting on that object make their individual deposits or withdrawals $dK_1, dK_2, \ldots$.

**A summary of our model of
energy transfer**

The momentum transfer $d\vec{p}$ delivered by an interaction to the object comes at the expense of the momentum of whatever object is at the other end of the interaction. At the fundamental level, by contrast, the energy transfer dK delivered by an interaction comes from (if dK is positive) or goes to (if dK is negative) the interaction's *potential* energy, *not* the energy of the other object involved.

At the macroscopic level, it may not be clear that energy transfers really do always involve energy transfers from kinetic to potential or vice versa, since the potential and/or kinetic energies being transferred might manifest themselves as microscopic separations between atoms or motions of atoms, and thus be hidden from the eye of a macroscopic observer. At the macroscopic level, then, a nonzero dK will always signal an energy transfer to the object's kinetic energy from *somewhere* (or vice versa), the "somewhere" being either macroscopically obvious potential energy or some hidden form of energy via microscopic forms of potential energy. We will discuss hidden energies in chapters C10 and C11.

C8.5 THE EARTH'S KINETIC ENERGY

The relation $dK \equiv \vec{v} \cdot d\vec{p}$ makes it quite clear why we can ignore the earth's kinetic energy when it interacts with a normal object. Consider, for the sake of argument, an object interacting gravitationally with the earth. As discussed in section C5.2, when we want to talk about the earth's motion, we *must* use a reference frame floating in space, and it is easiest to use such a frame where

---

*When applied to extended objects, the specific concept that I am calling *energy transfer* has been called *center-of-mass work* (also *pseudowork*), since the velocity in equation C8.12 is really the velocity of an extended object's center of mass.

the earth is initially at rest. During a short time interval dt as the object falls, the interaction gives the object and the earth the following energy transfers:

$$dK_{obj} = \vec{v}_{obj} \cdot d\vec{p} \quad \text{and} \quad dK_{earth} = \vec{v}_{earth} \cdot (-d\vec{p}) \qquad \text{(C8.14)}$$

In the floating frame, the kinetic energy the earth gets in a normal interaction is negligible

where I have defined $d\vec{p}$ to be the momentum transfer the interaction gives the *object* (the earth thus gets an momentum transfer of $-d\vec{p}$). However, we know from section C5.2 that the earth's speed $v_{earth} \equiv \text{mag}(\vec{v}_{earth})$ at any time during the interaction (as observed in our floating frame) is *much* smaller than the object's speed $v_{obj} \equiv \text{mag}(\vec{v}_{obj})$ at that time (by about a factor of 10^{23}!). On the other hand, $\text{mag}(d\vec{p}) = \text{mag}(-d\vec{p})$. Since the dot product depends on the product of these magnitudes, the energy transfer the earth gets from this interaction is thus clearly *completely negligible* compared to what the object gets, and the earth's kinetic energy will always remain essentially *zero*. The same kind of argument applies whenever we have a light object interacting with a very massive object that is initially essentially at rest.

(Note that while the *momentum transfers* delivered by an interaction to each object *must* be equal in magnitude (since the momentum transferred to one object comes at the expense of the other), there is no reason why the *energy transfers* delivered by that interaction must be equal: the energy transferred to each object comes at the expense of the interaction's potential energy, not the other object.)

In fact, there is a real difference between how we might use conservation of momentum or conservation of energy to think about an object interacting with the earth. When an object interacts with the earth, we know from our model that the earth gets the *same* magnitude of momentum transfer that the object gets, but we cannot really *apply* momentum conservation in such a case because the response of the earth cannot be measured (we just shrug and write off what looks like a momentum transfer from nowhere). On the other hand, we can see here that we *can* apply conservation of energy to interactions between an object and the earth, since earth essentially gets *no* energy in the interaction, and it looks like energy is conserved even if we *ignore* the earth!

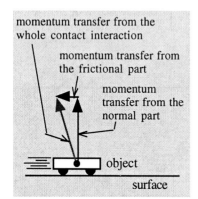

momentum transfer from the whole contact interaction

momentum transfer from the frictional part

momentum transfer from the normal part

object

surface

Figure C8.3: We can usefully divide up the contact interaction between an object and a surface into two parts, a *normal* part that during a given time interval dt gives the object a momentum transfer perpendicular to the surface, and a *frictional* part that gives it a momentum transfer parallel to the surface.

Dividing a contact interaction into *normal* and *frictional* parts

We can *ignore* the normal part of the contact interaction when an object slides on a surface

C8.6 CONTACT INTERACTIONS

In section C5.3, we talked about how we could describe an arbitrary contact interaction between an object and a surface as being frictionless if and only if the momentum transfer it delivers to the object during a given dt is perpendicular to the surface. In fact we can usefully divide the contact interaction between an object and a surface into two parts that we can treat as if they were separate interactions: (1) a **normal** part that during any given time interval dt gives the object a momentum transfer $d\vec{p}$ that is *perpendicular* to the surface, and (2) a **frictional** part that gives it a momentum transfer *parallel* to the surface. This is illustrated in Figure C8.3. ("Normal" is being used here in the sense of "perpendicular," not in the sense of "conventional or customary.")

If the object always moves *parallel* to the surface in question, then the relation $dK \equiv \vec{v} \cdot d\vec{p}$ means that the *normal* (perpendicular) part of such a contact interaction *does not affect the object's kinetic energy* (because $\vec{v}$ and $d\vec{p}$ are perpendicular, their dot product is zero). This means that the normal part of a contact interaction does *not* mediate an energy transfer of any kind either to or from potential energy (either macroscopic or microscopic), and we can *completely ignore* this part of the interaction when applying conservation of energy.

So, if an object slides frictionlessly down a wire or a track, or if it rolls without friction along an undulating road, we can see that while the contact interaction does have a significant part to play in influencing the object's motion, it does not affect the object's kinetic energy in any way. This opens up a whole range of possibilities for applications of the law of conservation of energy. Example C8.1 illustrates one such possibility.

EXAMPLE C8.1

OUTLINE OF THE FRAMEWORK

1. Pictorial Representation

a. Draw a picture of the situation that includes:

① (1) sketches of the system in its initial and final states

② (2) reference frame axes

③ (3) labels defining symbols for relevant quantities (in this case, objects' masses, velocities, and separations)

b. List values for all known quantities and specify which quantities
④ are unknown.

2. Conceptual Representation

The general task is to construct a conceptual model of the situation and link it to an abstract physics model or principle. In conservation-of-energy problems, we do the following:

⑤ a. Identify the *system* involved. (If it involves the earth, we can ignore the earth's kinetic energy)

⑥ b. Determine whether it is *approximately* isolated, *functionally* isolated, or involved in a *collision* (as defined in chapter C5). Support your conclusions briefly.

⑦ c. Identify the interactions between objects in the system and for each interaction, determine whether we can handle it by

(1) keeping track of its potential energy (if so, define the reference separation)

(2) ignoring it (because it is very weak or for another reason)

Be sure to support your conclusions with a brief argument.

⑧ d. Do we have to make any approximations or assumptions to solve the problem? (If so, describe.)

3. Mathematical Representation

⑨ a. Apply the mathematical equation that appropriately describes the situation (equation C6.16 here)

⑩ b. Solve for unknowns symbolically

⑪ c. Plug in numbers and units and calculate the result and its units.

4. Evaluation

Check that the answer makes sense:
⑫ a. Does it have the correct units?
⑬ b. Does it have the right sign?
⑭ c. Does it seem reasonable?

Problem: A roller-coaster car with effectively frictionless wheels rolls over a crest in the track at a speed of 3.0 m/s, then rolls down the track to a point that is 50 m east and 22 m lower than the crest. What is the car's speed at that point?

Solution: I have set up a reference frame in standard orientation on the earth's surface and defined the origins so that the car's z coordinate at its final position is $z_f = 0$ and so its x coordinate at its initial position is $x_i = 0$. The initial and final sketches therefore look like this:

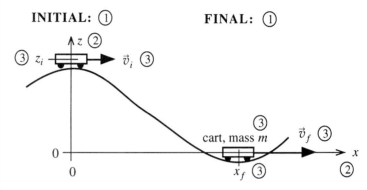

INITIAL: ①   **FINAL:** ①

KNOWN: ④

$z_i = +22$ m $x_i = 0$ m $v_i \equiv \text{mag}(\vec{v}_i) = 3.0$ m/s

$z_f = 0$ m $x_f = +50$ m   (we can look up g)

UNKNOWN: ④

$v_f \equiv \text{mag}(\vec{v}_f) = ?$

$m = ?$

⑤ The system here is the car and the earth, which we can model as being
⑥ approximately isolated. The car participates in *two* interactions with the earth: a gravitational interaction and a contact interaction (the latter is actually with the track, but since the track is rigidly connected to the earth, we will consider it part of the earth). We can handle the gravita-
⑦ tional interaction by describing it using the approximate potential energy function $V(z) = mgz$ (which assumes that the reference separation where $V \equiv 0$ is $z = 0$). We can ignore the contact interaction, because normal part of the interaction does not mediate any energy transfers and we are told that the interaction is frictionless. We will also assume that air friction is not significant. So, ignoring the earth's kinetic energy,
⑧ conservation of energy tells us that:

$$K_i + V(z_i) = K_f + V(z_f) \quad \Rightarrow \quad \tfrac{1}{2}mv_i^2 + mgz_i = \tfrac{1}{2}mv_f^2 + 0$$
⑨

since $z_f = 0$. Dividing through by $\tfrac{1}{2}m$, we get:

$$v_i^2 + 2gz_i = v_f^2 \quad \Rightarrow \quad v_f = \sqrt{v_i^2 + 2gz_i} \quad ⑩$$

(Note that the car's unknown mass cancels out, which is nice!) Plugging in the numbers, we get:

$$v_f = \sqrt{(3.0 \text{ m/s})^2 + 2(9.8 \text{ m/s}^2)(22 \text{ m})} = 21 \text{ m/s} \quad ⑪$$

⑬   ⑫

The positive sign and units are right for a speed (both terms under the radical have units of m^2/s^2. The magnitude is about 45 mi/h, which is plausible. (Note that the x-displacement is irrelevant here.) ⑭

On the other hand, the frictional part of a contact interaction clearly *does* affect an object's kinetic energy. For example, if we launch a book along a level tabletop, friction slows the book down quite noticably, indicating that the frictional part of the interaction continually drains energy from the book. There is no obvious potential energy that is increasing here, so where is the kinetic energy going? We will discuss this mystery in chapter C10.

The definitions of *lift* and *drag* for a wing (we can ignore the lift part)

One can see why this distinction between the normal part and the frictional part of a contact interaction is useful: the normal part does *not* affect an object's kinetic energy but the friction part *does*. Indeed, physicists and engineers make a similar useful distinction between parts of the contact interaction between the air and the wing of an airplane: they call the part that (during any given tiny interval dt) delivers a momentum transfer that is perpendicular to the plane's motion **lift** (this part does *not* affect an airplane's kinetic energy), and the part that delivers a momentum transfer that is opposite to the plane's motion **drag** (this part drains an airplane's kinetic energy). In conservation of energy problems, we can completely ignore the *lift* part of this interaction.

We can also ignore an object's contact interaction with an inextensible string

Knowing that $dK \equiv \vec{v} \cdot d\vec{p}$ opens up other possible situations where we can apply conservation of energy. For example, imagine an object swinging at the end of an inextensible string. A string can only deliver a momentum transfer whose direction is *parallel* to its length (this is why the string has to be vertical when supporting the object is at rest: only then can it supply upward momentum transfers needed to cancel downward momentum transfers from gravity). But if the string is inextensible, then the velocity of the object at the end of the string can never have a component *parallel* to the string (if the object had any component of velocity parallel to the string, the string would have to stretch or shrink). Therefore, $\vec{v}$ and $d\vec{p}$ must be perpendicular for such an object, meaning that $dK \equiv \vec{v} \cdot d\vec{p} = 0$. Therefore, the contact interaction exerted by an inextensible string on an object attached to it can be ignored when considering conservation of energy.

Why conservation of energy applies to systems that are *functionally isolated* or involved in *collisions*

Finally, consider a system consisting of two objects moving frictionlessly on a level surface. In chapter C5, we classified this system as being *functionally isolated* (even though it is not really isolated from external interactions) because during any given interval dt the upward momentum transferred to either object by the normal part of its contact interaction with the surface cancels the vertically downward momentum transferred by gravity. This meant that there was zero net momentum transfer into the system from these external interactions, meaning that the system's total momentum is be conserved.

In conservation of energy problems, such a system is still *functionally isolated*, but for a somewhat different reason. In this case it isn't so much that the effects of the gravitational and contact interactions *cancel*, it is that the velocity of objects in such a system are always horizontal while the momentum transfers delivered by the interacions are vertical. Thus the energy transfer mediated by either of these external interactions is zero, implying that the system's total energy is conserved.

In the case of collisions, we discussed how (as long as we focused on the momenta just before and just after the collision) there would not be enough time during the collision for momentum transfers due to external interactions to accumulate and significantly affect conservation of momentum. But if these external momentum transfers into the system are not significant, then $dK \equiv \vec{v} \cdot d\vec{p}$ implies that the external energy transfers won't be very significant either, so we can also usefully apply conservation of energy to collisions (as long as we look at the system's energy just before and just after the collision)..

In summary, we see that knowing that $dK \equiv \vec{v} \cdot d\vec{p}$ opens up a wide variety of new practical applications of the law of conservation of energy, applications that we might not otherwise suspect would qualify. In particular, we now know when we are able to ignore certain kinds of contact interactions, which certainly broadens our ability to deal with such a common type of interaction.

Exercise C8X.8: Argue that one of the implications of the ideas discussed in this section is that the final speed of an object sliding from rest down a frictionless incline will be the *same* as it would be if it were dropped from rest through the same vertical distance. (This is something we could experimentally check!)

C8.7 MOMENTUM, FORCE, AND ENERGY

In chapter C2, we defined *force* informally as being the "push or pull" an interaction exerts on an object. We are now in a position to benefit from a more formal definition of this crucial concept.

We have seen that the most basic feature of an interaction is that it allows interacting objects to influence each other's motion by mediating a *momentum transfer* to one interaction partner at the expense of the other. At a more qualitative level, though, we often think of the interaction as exerting on each interaction partner a *force* (push or pull) that influences its motion. How might we bridge the gap between our formal momentum-transfer model of interactions and this intuitive idea of force?

Imagine that you and I sit facing each other on two carts at rest that are free to roll frictionlessly on a level surface. Imagine that you and I then push on each others' hands: our contact interaction will deliver equal and opposite momentum transfers to us that will cause us to move away from each other. Note that the *direction* of the momentum transfer I get from the interaction is the same as the direction that you push on me, and vice versa. Also, if we push *harder* on each other, the magnitude of the momentum transfer that the contact interaction delivers to each of us during a given time interval dt becomes greater.

Therefore, we see that our intuitive ideas about the direction and strength of a "push" coincide with the more formal ideas of the direction of the momentum transfer an interaction delivers and how much momentum it transfers per unit time. Therefore, we will formally *define* the **force** that a given interaction exerts on an object to be a vector quantity equal to *the rate at which that interaction transfers momentum to the object*:

Building an intuitive link between the ideas of force and momentum transfer

$$\vec{F} \equiv \frac{d\vec{p}}{dt} \qquad (C8.15)$$

The formal definition of force

where $d\vec{p}$ is the momentum transfer the interaction delivers to the object during the tiny time interval dt. In this case, "tiny" means that dt is short enough so that neither the magnitude nor direction of the interaction's "push" changes measurably during the interval. This definition is consistent with our qualitative idea about a force being a push or pull, but it also gives the concept of force a precise and quantitative meaning, linking it to something we can measure.

Since force is defined as the ratio of a quantity with units of momentum to something with units of time, the units of force are (kg·m/s)/s = kg·m/s². The (derived) SI unit for force is the **newton**, where

The units of force

$$1\,\text{N} \equiv 1\,\text{kg} \cdot \text{m/s}^2 \qquad (C8.16)$$

A newton is the magnitude of the force an interaction exerts if during 1 s it transfers enough momentum to get a 1-kg object initially at rest moving with a speed of 1 m/s. A *pound* of force is equivalent to 4.45 N.

We can use this definition to rewrite $dK \equiv \vec{v} \cdot d\vec{p}$ as follows:

$$dK \equiv \vec{v} \cdot d\vec{p} = \frac{d\vec{r}}{dt} \cdot d\vec{p} = d\vec{r} \cdot \frac{d\vec{p}}{dt} = d\vec{r} \cdot \vec{F} = \vec{F} \cdot d\vec{r} \qquad (C8.17)$$

How force is connected to energy transfers

(where the last step follows because the dot product is commutative). In words, this says that the energy transferred to an object by an interaction during a very short time interval dt is equal to the dot product of two vectors: (1) the force $\vec{F}$

How force is connected to momentum transfers

How to determine the gravitational force from its potential energy function

that the interaction exerts on the object and (2) the tiny displacement of the object's center of mass $d\vec{r}$ during that interval. An analogous formula for momentum transfer follows directly from equation C8.15:

$$d\vec{p} = \vec{F}\,dt \qquad (C8.18)$$

The pair of formulas $d\vec{p} = \vec{F}\,dt$ and $dK = \vec{F}\cdot d\vec{r}$ thus link the concept of force to the concepts of momentum transfer and energy transfer.

We can use $dK = \vec{F}\cdot d\vec{r}$ to determine the force that the gravitational interaction exerts on an object (that is, the object's *weight*). If an object with mass m moves a tiny displacement $d\vec{r}$ in any direction near the earth's surface, its potential energy changes by

$$dV = mg\,dz \qquad (C8.19)$$

since only the z component of the displacement $d\vec{r}$ has any effect on the object's separation from the earth's center (assuming a reference frame in standard orientation). As the object moves a certain displacement $d\vec{r}$, the energy transfer that it gets from the interaction is $dK = \vec{F}\cdot d\vec{r}$. If we use the component definition of the dot product (equation C8.8) and $d\vec{r} = [dx, dy, dz]$, we can rewrite this equation as follows:

$$dK = F_x dx + F_y dy + F_z dz \qquad (C8.20)$$

Whatever gravitational energy transfer it gets comes at the *expense* of gravitational potential energy, so we have

$$F_x dx + F_y dy + F_z dz = dK = -dV = -mg\,dz \qquad (C8.21)$$

Now, this equation has to be true no matter *what* the horizontal displacement components dx and dy might be, since displacements in these directions do not affect the object's separation from the earth. The only way that this equation can be automatically independent of dx and dy is if F_x and F_y are both identically *zero*, implying that the gravitational force is entirely vertical (something that doesn't come as a great shock to you, I expect). So the equation boils down to $F_z dz = -mg\,dz$, implying that:

$$F_z = -mg \qquad (C8.22)$$

meaning that the gravitational force is vertically *downward* (since its z component is negative) and its magnitude has the constant value mg, where g is a constant we found in chapter C6 to have the value 9.80 m/s^2 (at least near the earth's surface).

Again, this result may not be surprising: you may have even seen this formula before. You can also feel for yourself that the force that gravity exerts on an object is always downward and that a given object seems to experience the same magnitude of force, no matter how far away from the floor you hold it (within reason). In this context, this result simply gives us even more confidence that the definition of force given by equation C8.15 makes sense.

Exercise C8X.9: From your weight in pounds, calculate your weight in newtons and your mass in kilograms.

Exercise C8X.10: Imagine that you and I sit facing each other on two carts at rest that are free to roll on a level, frictionless surface. Imagine this time, instead of pushing on each others' hands, you push directly on my cart while I sit passively. Does the contact interaction still exert forces having equal magnitudes on both of our carts? Defend your reasoning.

I. MOMENTUM AND KINETIC ENERGY
  A. Momentum and kinetic energy are related: $K = p^2 / 2m$ $[\, p \equiv \text{mag}(\vec{p}) \,]$
    1. This means when $\vec{p}$ changes, K often changes too
    2. But not necessarily [if p doesn't change, K doesn't either]
  B. Generally, $dK = v\, dp \cos\theta$ [as long as $dp \equiv \text{mag}(d\vec{p}) << p$]
  C. This can be expressed nicely using a *dot product*
    1. $\vec{u} \cdot \vec{w} \equiv uw \cos\theta$ (where θ is the angle between $\vec{u}$ and $\vec{w}$)
      a) Note that the dot product of two vectors is a *scalar*
      b) $\vec{u} \cdot \vec{w} = $ (length of $\vec{u}$) $\times$ (projection of $\vec{w}$ on $\vec{u}$) or vice versa
    2. In terms of vector components: $\vec{u} \cdot \vec{w} = u_x w_x + u_y w_y + u_z w_z$
    3. Properties of the dot product:
      a) Commutative property: $\vec{u} \cdot \vec{w} = \vec{w} \cdot \vec{u}$
      b) Distributive property: $\vec{u} \cdot (\vec{w} + \vec{c}) = \vec{u} \cdot \vec{w} + \vec{u} \cdot \vec{c}$
      c) Linearity: $\vec{u} \cdot (q\vec{w}) = q(\vec{u} \cdot \vec{w})$
      d) $\vec{u} \cdot \vec{u} = u^2$
      e) $\vec{u} \cdot \vec{w} = 0$ $\Leftrightarrow$ $\vec{u} \perp \vec{w}$
    4. So $dK = \vec{v} \cdot d\vec{p}$

II. ENERGY TRANSFER
  A. When many interactions act at the same time on an object
    1. The energy contribution that one interaction makes is $dK = \vec{v} \cdot d\vec{p}$
    2. The net change in the object's K is the sum $dK = dK_1 + dK_2 + \ldots$
  B. We call dK the *energy transfer* to an object from an interation
    1. This is to energy what a momentum transfer $d\vec{p}$ is to momentum
    2. If $dK > 0$, the object's K increases; if $dK < 0$, K decreases
    3. This energy transfer comes from the interaction's *potential energy*
      a) It does *not* come from the other object (as in the case of $d\vec{p}$)!
      b) If the potential energy is due to microscopic interactions, it
          may *appear* that the energy comes from some hidden energy

III. IMPLICATIONS OF $dK = \vec{v} \cdot d\vec{p}$
  A. The earth gets almost no kinetic energy in an ordinary interaction
    1. $d\vec{p}$ has the same magnitude for the earth and the interacting object
    2. But the earth's $\vec{v}$ is *much* smaller (in the floating frame where the
        earth is initially at rest)
    3. So we can treat the earth essentially as if it always has $K = 0$
  B. Contact interactions where an object slides on a surface
    1. We can ignore the normal part of the interaction
      a) This part delivers a $d\vec{p}$ that is perpendicular to the object's $\vec{v}$
      b) Therefore $dK = \vec{v} \cdot d\vec{p} = 0$
    2. The frictional part *does* affect the object's kinetic energy
  C. Similarly, for contact interactions between air and a wing
    1. We can ignore the lift part (that delivers a $d\vec{p} \perp \vec{v}_{\text{wing}}$)
    2. The drag part does transfer energy away from the wing
  D. When an object swings at the end of an inextensible string, we can ig-
      nore the contact interaction with the string (the string always delivers
      $d\vec{p}$ parallel to itself, but the object's $\vec{v}$ is always perpendicular to this)
  E. When a system is *functionally isolated* or involved in a *collision*, we
      can treat it as isolated as far as conservation of energy is concerned

IV. FORCE, MOMENTUM AND ENERGY
  A. The force exerted by an interaction is defined to be the *rate* at which
      that interaction transfers momentum to the object: $\vec{F} \equiv d\vec{p} / dt$
    1. This coincides with our intuitive sense of force as a push or pull
    2. The SI unit of force is the *newton*: $1\ \text{N} = 1\ \text{kg} \cdot \text{m/s}^2$
  B. Equations relating force to momentum and energy transfers:
    1. $d\vec{p} = \vec{F}\, dt$ (dt is tiny enough so $\vec{F} \approx$ constant during dt)
    2. $dK = \vec{F} \cdot d\vec{r}$ ($d\vec{r}$ is a tiny displacement of the object's CM)
  C. Implication of the latter: the force of gravity is mg downward

GLOSSARY

law of cosines: the mathematical law that asserts that if the legs of a triangle have lengths a, b, and c, then

$$a^2 = b^2 + 2ab\cos\theta + c^2$$

where θ is the *outside* angle between legs b and c, as shown in Figure C8.1. (If you want θ to be the angle between b and c *inside* the triangle, then make the cosine term negative.)

dot product (of two vectors): a product of two vectors that yields a *scalar* value defined as follows:

$$\vec{u} \cdot \vec{w} = uw\cos\theta = u_x w_x + u_y w_y + u_z w_z$$

The dot product behaves algebraically pretty much like the ordinary product of two numbers.

projection (of a vector $\vec{u}$ on a vector $\vec{w}$): $u\cos\theta$, where θ is the angle between $\vec{u}$ and $\vec{w}$. (See Figure C8.2a.)

energy transfer dK: the amount $dK = \vec{v} \cdot d\vec{p}$ that an interaction would change an object's kinetic energy during a given time dt if it were to act alone. A nonzero dK signals an energy *transfer* (from potential energy, ultimately, though it may *appear* to come from hidden energy). dK is

historically called **work** and written dW, but we are reserving that word and symbol for an idea in thermal physics.

normal and **frictional** (parts of a contact interaction involving a surface): the parts of the contact interaction that give the objects momentum transfers that are perpendicular to and parallel to the surface, respectively. ("Normal" here is being used in the sense of "perpendicular.")

lift and **drag**: the parts of the contact interaction between the air and a wing that deliver momentum transfers perpendicular to and opposite to the wing's motion, respectively. These are analogous to the *normal* and *frictional* parts of a contact interaction between an object and a surface.

force $\vec{F}$: the force that an interaction exerts on an object is a vector quantity formally defined in this chapter to be the *rate* at which the interaction transfers momentum to that object: $\vec{F} \equiv d\vec{p}/dt$. The parallel equations $d\vec{p} = \vec{F}\,dt$ and $dK = \vec{F} \cdot d\vec{r}$ describe how the force the interaction exerts on the object is related to the momentum transfer and energy transfer that the interaction delivers to the object.

newton: the SI unit of force: $1 \text{ N} \equiv 1 \text{ kg}\cdot\text{m/s}^2$. 1 lb of force ≈ 4.45 N

TWO-MINUTE PROBLEMS

C8T.1 Two hockey pucks are initially at rest on a horizontal plane of frictionless ice. Puck A has twice the mass of puck B. Imagine that we apply the same constant force to each puck for the same interval of time dt. How do the puck's kinetic energies compare at the end of this interval?
A. $K_A = 4K_B$ D. $K_B = 2K_A$
B. $K_A = 2K_B$ E. $K_B = 4K_A$
C. $K_A = K_B$ F. other (specify)

C8T.2 Two hockey pucks are initially at rest on a horizontal plane of frictionless ice. Puck A has twice the mass of puck B. Imagine that we apply the same constant force to each puck until each puck crosses a finish line 1 m from its starting point. How do the puck's kinetic energies compare when each crosses this finish line?
A. $K_A = 4K_B$ D. $K_B = 2K_A$
B. $K_A = 2K_B$ E. $K_B = 4K_A$
C. $K_A = K_B$ F. other (specify)

C8T.3 A crate is being lifted vertically upward at a constant speed. Which interaction delivers a *negative* energy transfer to the crate as it rises? (Ignore friction.)
A. the crate's contact interaction with the cable lifting it
B. the crate's gravitational interaction with the earth
C. other (specify)
D. *neither*: the crate's kinetic energy is constant!

C8T.4 Imagine that we suspend an object from the ceiling by a string and then set it swinging back and forth. Which of the following is/are responsible for significant changes in the object's kinetic energy as it swings?
A. the object's gravitational interaction with the earth
B. the object's contact interaction with the string
C. the centrifugal interaction pulling the object outward
D. A and B only   F. none of the above
E. all of the above   T. other (specify)

C8T.5 When an object slides down a frictionless incline, the contact interaction between the object and the incline does not transform any energy to or from the object's kinetic energy (T or F). This means that it also does not transfer any momentum to the object (T or F).

C8T.6 Imagine that a very heavy ball is suspended by a chain. Imagine that I pull the ball away from its equilibrium position, hold it against my nose (with the chain taut) and release the ball from rest. The ball swings away from me, and then back toward me. I can be confident that it will not smash my nose (as long as I don't move). (T or F).

C8T.7 A bead slides from rest down a frictionless wire in the earth's gravitational field. The diagram below shows a set of possible shapes that the wire might have. At the bottom of which will the bead have the highest speed? (If the final speed is the same for all shapes, answer F.)

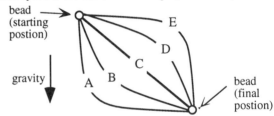

C8T.8 In the situation described in the previous problem, along the wire of which shape will the bead take the *shortest time* to get from the top to the bottom? (If the time is the same for all shapes, answer F.)

C8T.9 A skier starts from rest, slides down a frictionless slope, and slides off a ski jump angled upward at 45° with respect to the vertical. How does the skier's height h at the peak of the jump compare to his or her original height H?

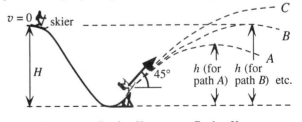

A. $h < H$ B. $h = H$ C. $h > H$
D. not enough information provided to tell

HOMEWORK PROBLEMS

BASIC SKILLS

C8B.1 During a certain time interval, object moving at 12 m/s receives an momentum transfer of 200 kg·m/s opposite to its motion from a friction interaction. What energy transfer does this interaction deliver to the object? Does this increase to or reduce the object's kinetic energy? Please explain.

C8B.2 An object is sliding at 2 m/s down an incline that makes an angle of 30° with respect to the horizontal. If the gravitational interaction delivers to the object 10 kg·m/s of downward momentum every second, what energy transfer does it deliver to the object every second?

C8B.3 Prove property C8.7c of the dot product. (*Hint:* see equation C3.13).

C8B.4 What is the dot product of the two displacement vectors $\vec{u} = [2\text{ m}, -1\text{ m}, 3\text{ m}]$ and $\vec{w} = [5\text{ m}, 2\text{ m}, -2\text{ m}]$. What is the angle between these vectors?

C8B.5 Two displacement vectors $\vec{u} = [3\text{ m}, -5\text{ m}, 2\text{ m}]$ and $\vec{w} = [-4\text{ m}, -2\text{ m}, ?]$ are perpendicular. What is the value of w_z?

C8B.6 A car whose weight is 20,000 N (mass ≈ 2000 kg) is traveling at a constant speed of 25 m/s up an incline that makes an angle of 4° with respect to the horizontal. What energy transfer does the gravitational interaction deliver to the car every second? Does this particular interaction transform energy *to* or *from* the car's kinetic energy? Explain.

C8B.7 A car rolls 300 m down a straight incline that makes a constant angle of 8° with the horizontal. Equation C8.17 only applies if the time interval during which the displacement takes place is "tiny" in a certain sense described just below equation C8.15. Is the time that it takes the car to roll this distance "tiny" in this case for us to use equation C8.17 to compute the energy transformed by the gravitational interaction as the car rolls this distance? Does it matter whether the car rolls at a constant speed or not? Please explain your answers carefully.

C8B.8 Show that if $g = 9.80\text{ m/s}^2$ (as we found empirically in chapter C6) then F_z in equation C8.22 has units of newtons (correct SI units for a force). Argue also that an object's weight in newtons is a bit less than 10 times its mass in kilograms.

SYNTHETIC

C8S.1 We can prove that the dot product is distributive as follows. Let $\vec{a} \equiv \vec{w} + \vec{c}$. We can think of the dot product $\vec{u} \cdot \vec{a}$ as being u times the projection of $\vec{a}$ on $\vec{u}$. This projection, as well as the projections of $\vec{w}$ and $\vec{c}$ on $\vec{u}$ are shown in Figure C8.4. Use this figure to prove that $\vec{u} \cdot (\vec{w} + \vec{c}) = \vec{u} \cdot \vec{w} + \vec{u} \cdot \vec{c}$. (The vectors $\vec{w}$ and $\vec{c}$ are shown lying in the same plane as $\vec{a}$ and $\vec{u}$, but the same basic argument applies even if they do not. Think about it!)

C8S.2 Why not simply define the product of two vectors to be the product of their magnitudes: $\vec{u}\vec{w} \equiv uw$? Prove that this product does *not* satisfy the distributive property. (A product that does not satisfy the distributive property is much less useful than one that does.)

C8S.3 Here is one way to prove the component expression for the dot product (in two dimensions at least). Figure

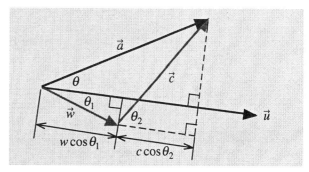

Figure C8.4: Proving the distributive property of the dot product.

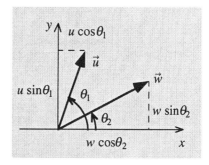

Figure C8.5: One way to prove that the component equation for the dot product is correct.

C8.5 shows two arbitrary vectors $\vec{u}$ and $\vec{w}$ in the xy plane. The x components of $\vec{u}$ and $\vec{w}$ are $u_x = u\cos\theta_1$ and $w_x = w\cos\theta_2$, respectively, while the y components of these vectors are $u_y = u\sin\theta_1$ and $w_y = w\sin\theta_2$ respectively. Use this information and the trigonometric identity

$$\cos(\theta_1 - \theta_2) = \cos\theta_1 \cos\theta_2 + \sin\theta_1 \sin\theta_2 \qquad (C8.23)$$

to show that equation C8.8 is consistent with equation C8.6 (at least for vectors in the xy plane).

C8S.4 Tarzan stands on a branch 3.0 m above the ground, holding onto a vine. He steps off the branch and swings downward on the vine. If his feet are about 1.0 m above the ground at the swing's lowest point, what is his speed there?*

C8S.5 You are investigating an accident where a 1500-kg car that was parked without its emergency brake on rolled down a hill with a slope of 8° a distance of 150 m (measured along the road) and hit a parked van. How fast was the car moving when it hit the van, assuming little friction?*

C8S.6 A bicyclist climbs a hill 32 m tall and then coasts down the other side without pedaling. If the cyclist's speed was 2.2 m/s at the top, what is it at the bottom (if there were no friction).*

*Please write your solution to a starred problem using the problem-solving framework discussed in section C6.7.

C8S.7 A bicyclist coasts without pedaling down an incline that makes an angle of 3° with the horizontal at a steady speed of 13 m/s. If the mass of the cyclist and the bike combined is 68 kg , estimate the force of friction that must be acting on the bicyclist. Explain your method. (*Hint*: Think about what happens during a time interval of one second.)

C8S.8 Imagine an object attached to something massive by a spring. The object is free to move along the x axis, If we choose $x = 0$ to be the object's position when the spring is relaxed, the potential energy function for the spring is $V(x) = \frac{1}{2}k_s x$, as we discussed in the last chapter. Imagine now that we move the object slightly from position x to position $x + dx$. Show that

$$dV \equiv V(x+dx) - V(x) \approx k_s x\, dx \qquad (C8.24)$$

when dx is small. Then use this to find the x component of the force that the spring exerts on the object at x.

RICH-CONTEXT

C8R.1 A pilot makes a crash landing on the top of a mesa that stands 250 m above the surrounding plain (a mesa is a hill with very steep sides and a flat top). The pilot fixes the plane and wants to take off again, but the only reasonably smooth road that could be used for a runway is not long enough: the pilot estimates that the maximum speed the plane is likely to reach before going off the edge of the mesa is about 45 mi/h, but the plane needs an airspeed of about 120 mi/h before the wing's lift becomes significantly larger than the plane's weight. Noting that the side of the mesa is essentially a vertical cliff, the pilot thinks that by deliberately driving the plane off the edge at 45 mi/h and diving downward as well as forward, the pilot might cause the plane to pick up enough air speed to pull out of the dive before hitting the ground. What would you advise the pilot to do: try it, or hope for rescue (and risk dying of exposure and dehydration)? Do not ignore either the lift or drag interactions between the plane and the air, but do remember that the plane also has a propellor.

C8R.2 You are investigating a mishap on a mountain railroad. On the night of June 15, one railroad car was left

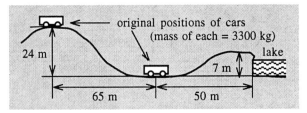

Figure C8.6: The situation for problem C8R.2.

parked at the top of a hill above another car of the same mass. In the morning, both cars are found coupled together in a lake, as shown in Figure C8.6. (The tracks go right up to the lake to facilitate loading boats with ore.) The supervisor claims that the engineer must have not set the brake on the upper car, and during the night, it rolled down, hit, and coupled with the lower car, and its momentum carried both into the lake. The engineer disputes this, saying that someone must have released the brake and then *pushed* the upper car. Can you use physics to resolve this dispute? (*Hint:* Momentum is conserved in the collision.)

ADVANCED

C8A.1 Here is a way to prove the component equation for the dot product (equation C8.8) from equation C8.6. Imagine that $\vec{e}_x, \vec{e}_y,$ and $\vec{e}_z$ are three vectors, each having length equal to 1, that point in the x, y, and z directions respectively. Convince yourself that an arbitrary vector $\vec{u}$ can be written $\vec{u} = u_x \vec{e}_x + u_y \vec{e}_y + u_z \vec{e}_z$. Take the dot product of two vectors written this form and show that equation C8.8 follows from this and the five properties of the dot product listed as equations C8.7. Since we can prove these properties from equation C8.6, this shows that C8.8 also follows from equation C8.6.

ANSWERS TO EXERCISES

C8X.1 Taking the magnitude of $\vec{p} = m\vec{v}$ yields $p = mv$ or $v = p/m$. This means that

$$K = \tfrac{1}{2}mv^2 = \tfrac{1}{2}m\left(\frac{p}{m}\right)^2 = \frac{p^2}{2m} \qquad (C8.25)$$

C8X.2 According to the pythagorean theorem

$$
\begin{aligned}
p_{new}^2 &= (p + dp\cos\theta)^2 + (dp\sin\theta)^2 \\
&= p^2 + 2p\,dp\cos\theta + dp^2\cos^2\theta + dp^2\sin^2\theta \\
&= p^2 + 2p\,dp\cos\theta + dp^2 \qquad (C8.26)
\end{aligned}
$$

since $\cos^2\theta + \sin^2\theta = 1$.

C8X.3 If $d\vec{p}$ and $\vec{v}$ point in the same direction, then the angle θ between them is 0° and $\cos\theta = +1$, so dK is positive, meaning that the kinetic energy K is increasing. If $d\vec{p}$ and $\vec{v}$ point in opposite directions, then the angle θ between them is 180° and $\cos\theta = -1$, so dK is negative, meaning that K decreases. This makes sense: a momentum transfer delivered in the direction of motion should cause the object to speed up (giving it a greater kinetic energy), while one in the reverse direction will slow it down.

C8X.4 The angle between a vector and itself is zero, so $\vec{u} \cdot \vec{u} = u^2 \cos 0 = u^2(1) = u^2$.

C8X.5 If $\vec{u} \cdot \vec{w} = 0$ but $u \neq 0$ and $w \neq 0$, then $\cos\theta$ must be zero, implying that θ must be ±90°: thus the vectors are perpendicular. If the vectors are perpendicular, then the angle between the vectors is ±90°, so $\cos\theta = 0$, implying that $\vec{u} \cdot \vec{w} = uw\cos(\pm 90°) = uw(0) = 0$.

C8X.6 According to equation C8.8:

$$
\begin{aligned}
dK &= \vec{v} \cdot d\vec{p} = v_x\,dp_x + v_y\,dp_y + v_z\,dp_z \qquad (C8.27) \\
&= (-4.0\ \text{m/s})(0.020\ \text{kg·m/s}) + (+2.0\ \text{m/s})(-0.010\ \text{kg·m/s}) + 0 \\
&= (-0.080 - 0.020 + 0)\ \text{kg·m}^2/\text{s}^2 = -0.10\ \text{kg·m}^2/\text{s}^2
\end{aligned}
$$

$\text{kg·m}^2/\text{s}^2 = \text{J}$ are the correct units for energy!

C8X.7 Note that $d\vec{p} = (-0.05\ \text{kg})\vec{v}$ in this particular case. Since multiplying a vector by a negative scalar flips its direction, this tells us that $d\vec{p}$ is parallel to a vector that is the opposite of $\vec{v}$, and so itself must be opposite to $\vec{v}$. (Alternatively, a sketch of the vectors would show them to point in opposite directions.) So, the angle between them is 180°, and $\cos(180°) = -1$, so $dK = -v\,dp$. You can use the pythagorean theorem to show that $v^2 = 20\ \text{m}^2/\text{s}^2$ and $(dp)^2 = 0.00050\ \text{kg}^2\text{m}^2/\text{s}^2$, so

$$dK = -(\sqrt{20}\ \text{m/s})(\sqrt{0.00050}\ \text{kg·m/s}) = -0.10\ \text{J} \qquad (C8.28)$$

C8X.8 The frictionless contact interaction does not do anything to the sliding object's kinetic energy, so kinetic energy the object gets will have to come from gravitational potential energy, which would be no different if it fell the same vertical distance.

C8X.9 A person whose weight is 140 lbs would weigh 620 N and have a mass of about 64 kg.

C8X.10 The contact interaction (to conserve momentum) *must* during any given interval dt deliver $d\vec{p}$s to each object that are equal in magnitude and opposite in direction, so the forces exerted must have equal magnitudes.

C9

ROTATIONAL ENERGY

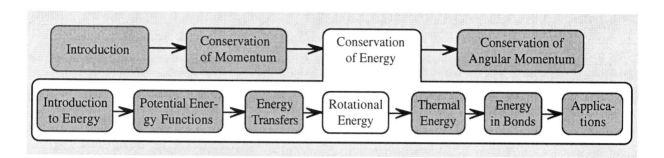

C9.1 OVERVIEW

In the last two chapters, we have been steadily broadening the range of interactions to which we can apply energy concepts. We now know how to write potential energy functions for gravitational, electromagnetic, and spring-like interactions, and we have seen that we can completely ignore the normal (perpendicular) part of a contact interaction when applying conservation of energy.

In this chapter and the next, we continue this process by looking at how we can handle the *frictional* part of a contact interaction. In this chapter, we examine the common case where such a contact interaction causes an object to roll without slipping. This leads us to a more general study of rotational kinetic energy, which serves as a nice bridge between our study of the most tangible forms of energy (potential and kinetic) and our study of hidden forms of energy in the next two chapters. The concepts of rotational motion introduced here are also essential background for understanding angular momentum in chapter C13.

Here is an overview of the sections in this chapter.

C9.2 *INTRODUCTION TO ROTATIONAL ENERGY* compares objects sliding without friction and rolling without slipping down a given incline to illustrate why keeping track of rotational energy is essential.

C9.3 *MEASURING ANGLES* looks at how we can quantify angles and handle various angular units such as degrees, radians, and revolutions.

C9.4 *ANGULAR VELOCITY* describes how we can quantify the rate of rotation of an extended object.

C9.5 *THE MOMENT OF INERTIA* shows that we can calculate an object's rotational kinetic energy from its angular velocity and a quantity that physicists call the object's *moment of inertia*.

C9.6 *CALCULATING MOMENTS OF INERTIA* illustrates how we can calculate moments of inertia for various kinds of extended objects.

C9.7 *TRANSLATION AND ROTATION* proves that an extended object's total kinetic energy is the sum of its rotational kinetic energy and the kinetic energy associated with its center of mass.

C9.8 *ROLLING WITHOUT SLIPPING* illustrates how we can apply these ideas to situations where an object rolls without slipping.

*** *MATH SKILLS: SUMMATION NOTATION* discusses the notation used in this chapter used to describe sums.

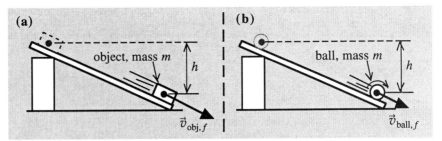

Figure C9.1: (a) An object of mass m slides from rest down a frictionless inclined track, going down a vertical distance h. **(b)** A ball with mass m rolls from rest without slipping along a similar incline, going the *same* vertical distance h as in part (a). Its final speed is smaller than the sliding object's final speed is.

C9.2 INTRODUCTION TO ROTATIONAL ENERGY

A puzzle concerning the behavior of a rolling object

Here is a puzzle. Figure C9.1a shows an object sliding without friction down a straight inclined track. Figure C9.1b shows a ball with the same mass rolling without slipping down a straight track inclined at the same angle. Assume that both objects start from rest and move through the same vertical and horizontal distances. Since we can ignore the normal part of the contact interaction with the track in both cases, and since both objects have the same mass and move through the same vertical distance, they both have converted the same amount of gravitational potential energy to kinetic energy in this process. Therefore, they must have the same kinetic energy at the end, right? Unfortunately, when we actually do this experiment, we find that the rolling ball is moving significantly more slowly than the sliding object when it reaches the end of the track! How can this be? If the change in the ball's potential energy has not all been transferred to kinetic energy of its motion, where has the rest gone?

On closer examination, we can see that there is a difference between these two situations: the ball is *rotating* around its center of mass when it reaches the end of the track, but the sliding object is *not*. This rotation cause the ball's constituent particles to move *around* the ball's center of mass as well as along with it. Perhaps there is a kinetic energy associated with this rotational motion in addition to the kinetic energy of its forward motion.

Could taking account of rotational kinetic energy solve the puzzle?

If this is true, then it could resolve the puzzle. While the gravitational interaction converts the same amount of potential energy to kinetic energy in each case, maybe the energy released goes entirely to the kinetic energy of the sliding object's center-of-mass motion but only *partly* to the kinetic energy of the rolling ball's center-of-mass motion, the rest going to the kinetic energy associated with its rotational motion. This would explain why the ball's center of mass is not moving as rapidly as that of the sliding object at the end of the track.

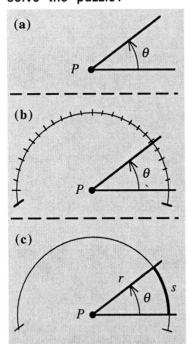

To make sure that this qualitative proposal does indeed solve the puzzle, we need to know how to calculate the extra kinetic energy involved with rolling, and then see whether including this energy accounts for the entire observed difference in speed. The main purpose of this chapter is therefore to teach you how to calculate the kinetic energy associated with an extended object's rotational motion.

C9.3 MEASURING ANGLES

In order to do this, we first need to know how we can quantify an object's rate of rotation. The first step toward doing *that* is to think more deeply about how we quantify the *angle* through which an object has rotated.

When two line segments intersect at a point, they define an angle θ (see Figure C9.2a). How can we quantify this angle? One method is to superimpose on the line segments a circle whose center coincides with the point where the line segments intersect. If we then divide the circle's circumference up into an arbitrary number of equally-sized parts, we can then quantify the angle by counting the number of such parts that are enclosed (or *subtended*) by the two line segments (see Figure C9.2b). This is exactly what we do when we measure an angle using a protractor: the protractor defines a circle whose center we align with the point where the lines intersect. The circumference of this circle is conventionally

Figure C9.2: (a) Two line segments that intersect at some point P define an angle θ. **(b)** To quantify θ, we can superimpose a circle centered at P, divide the its circumference into an arbitrary number of equally-spaced units, and find out how many units the angle spans. **(c)** A more natural approach is to define θ to be the arclength s subtended divided by the circle's radius r: $\theta \equiv s/r$.

divided up into 360 equal parts, called *degrees*, and reading the angle in degrees amounts to counting up how many of these circumference-parts fit between the two line segments. Why 360 parts and not 100, or 1000, or 47? This choice is simply conventional. The numerical value of an angle measured this way thus depends on making some kind of artificial choice of angular unit.

But there is another way of quantifying the angle that in a very real sense is much more natural. Consider Figure C9.2c. Let *r* be the radius of the arbitrary circle that we superimpose on the angle, and let *s* be arclength along that circle's circumference that is bracketed by the angle. We can *define* the magnitude of the angle θ this way:

The natural definition of angle

$$|\theta| \equiv \frac{s}{r} \tag{C9.1}$$

(The sign of θ, as stated in chapter C3, specifies whether the angle is counter-clockwise or clockwise.) This particular ratio is independent of the particular *circle* that we use because, just as the circle's total circumference varies in direct proportion to its radius *r*, so the arclength *s* subtended by the angle θ (which represents a fixed fraction of a circle) varies in direct proportion to *r*, meaning that *s/r* remains fixed for a given angle as we vary *r*. The numerical value of this ratio is also independent of the *units* we use to express both *s* and *r*. Therefore, the angle defined this way is relatively free of "artificial ingredients."

Moreover, this definition proves to be very *convenient* both mathematically and (as we will see shortly) physically. It is mathematically convenient because it yields a *unitless* number (the ratio of two lengths is unitless). This is important because mathematical functions like sin θ, e^x, and so on are technically defined to convert a unitless number to another unitless number, so it is important when dealing with trigonometric functions specifically that θ be unitless.

According to equation C9.1, the angle corresponding to an entire circle has a value of $s/r = 2\pi r/r = 2\pi$ (since the circumference of an entire circle is $s = 2\pi r$). Since a right angle corresponds to a quarter of a circle, its numerical value is $2\pi/4 = \pi/2$. Similarly, the angle corresponding to 45° (an eighth of a circle) is $\pi/4$, that corresponding to 30° is $\pi/6$, and so on.

It is conventional to say that when we define an angle this way, we are expressing it "in radians," as if the radian were a unit of angle like the meter is a unit of distance. However, θ as defined by equation C9.1 is strictly *unitless*. There is actually a continuing debate as to whether the **radian** (and by extension, the **degree**, the **revolution**, and other measures of angle) should really be thought of as being "units" of angle or not. In practice, I think that it is best to think of the radian as being a *special kind* of unit whose definition according to equation C9.1 is 1 rad = 1 m/m = 1. Since we can always multiply an equation by 1 without changing its meaning, we can (when calculating units) either supply or delete the radian unit at will (this is what makes it different from most units). It is useful to *supply* this special unit in two cases: when

Rules for handling angular "units" (which are rather peculiar)

1. we want to make it clear that a given quantity is or involves an angle, or
2. we need to recalculate an angular quantity that has been first given in degrees or revolutions. In this case, we treat the radian, degree, and/or revolution, *as if* they were ordinary units. For example:

$$1 = 1 \text{ rad} = 1 \,\cancel{\text{rad}}\left(\frac{\text{rev}}{2\pi\,\cancel{\text{rad}}}\right) = 0.159 \,\cancel{\text{rev}}\left(\frac{360°}{1\,\cancel{\text{rev}}}\right) = 57.3° \tag{C9.2}$$

In all *other* situations, we will avoid displaying the radian unit.

So from now on, we will *assume* that angles are defined as specified by equation C9.1. We will also *assume* that angles specified in units other than radians get converted to radians *before* they they are used in calculations. Your calculator does this automatically when you calculate sin(15°), for example, but in other cases, you should do the conversion *explicitly*.

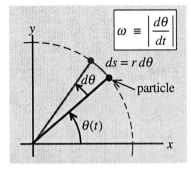

Figure C9.3: How to define the *angular speed* of a particle moving along a circular path.

A particle's *rotational speed* in a rotating object

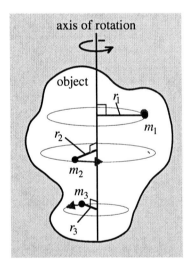

Figure C9.4: Particles (m_1, m_2, and m_3) in rigid rotating object follow circular paths perpendicular to the axis of rotation.

C9.4 ANGULAR VELOCITY

Consider a point particle in circular motion around the origin of a reference frame in the *xy* plane of that frame (see Figure C9.3). At every instant of time, the radius vector connecting the origin to the particle makes a certain angle $\theta(t)$ with the coordinate system's *x* axis. The **angular speed** ω of the particle at an instant is defined to be the rate at which this angle changes at that instant:

$$\omega \equiv \left| \frac{d\theta}{dt} \right| \qquad (C9.3)$$

where dt is an interval of time centered on the instant in question that is sufficiently short so that the rotation speed does not change much during the interval, and $d\theta$ is the particle's change in angle during this interval. The absolute values ensure that we are talking about the *magnitude* of the change in the angle $d\theta$, no matter whether θ is increasing with time (so that $d\theta$ is positive) or decreasing with time (so that $d\theta$ is negative).

The quantity ω is a case where it is helpful to supply the unit of radians to make it clear that ω expresses the rate-of-change of an *angle*. Thus, we often specify ω as being in rad/s (rather than the equivalent but opaque units of s^{-1}).

According to equation C9.1, the arclength ds in Figure C9.3 is related to the tiny angle $d\theta$ that the particle travels through in the time dt as follows:

$$|d\theta| \equiv \frac{ds}{r} \qquad \Rightarrow \qquad ds = r|d\theta| \qquad (C9.4)$$

Since the particle's *ordinary* speed due to its circular motion is the distance it covers in a tiny interval dt divided by dt, equations C9.3 and C9.4 imply that

$$v = \text{mag}(\vec{v}) = \frac{ds}{dt} = \frac{r|d\theta|}{dt} = r\omega \qquad (C9.5)$$

Note that this is *not* the same quantity as angular speed ω: this is the ratio of the *distance* the particle covers (not the angle) to the time interval. When the particle is part of a rotating object we will call this quantity the particle's **rotational speed**. In this case, we want the units to express that v is an ordinary speed, so we *drop* the radians in the units of ω, so that the units of $r\omega$ become simply $\text{m} \cdot \text{s}^{-1} = \text{m/s}$, the ordinary units of speed. Even so, it is *very* important to note that both equations C9.4 and C9.5, we are *assuming* the definition of angle given by equation C9.1. This means that it is *essential* that ω be expressed "in radians" to make the numbers come out correctly.

Now consider a rigid, extended object rotating around a certain axis (Figure C9.4). We can treat *any* extended object as a set of particles. If the object is really rigid, each particle in the object will follow a circular path in a plane perpendicular to the axis of rotation. Since all particles in a rigid object rotate together, every particle will rotate through the *same* angle in its plane during a given interval dt and thus will have the *same* angular speed ω. We define a rigid object's angular speed of rotation ω to be the common angular speed of its particles.

In linear motion, a particle's *speed* is the magnitude of its *velocity*: the particle's velocity vector not only specifies the rate at which the particle moves but its direction of motion. In an analogous manner, a rotating object's *angular speed* is the magnitude of its **angular velocity** $\vec{\omega}$, a vector that specifies not only the *rate* at which the object rotates but also its *direction* of rotation.

But how can we define a rotating object's "direction of rotation"? As the object rotates, the velocities of its various particles point in a variety of different directions and so do not help us fix a unique "direction of rotation" for the object. But if you think about it, there *is* an unambiguous line in space associated with any rotation: the *axis* of the rotation! We therefore *define* the direction of the angular velocity vector $\vec{\omega}$ to be parallel to the axis of rotation.

This does not yet completely specify the direction of $\vec{\omega}$, since there are two possible directions that are both parallel to the axis of rotation. This issue can only be resolved by making an arbitrary choice: the direction of $\vec{\omega}$ is defined *by convention* to be the direction indicated by your right thumb if you wrap the fingers of your right hand around the axis in the direction that the particles in the object are moving as they rotate (see Figure C9.5).

Let me again emphasize that if the magnitude of an object's angular velocity $\vec{\omega}$ is originally specified in rev/s or deg/s, it *must* be converted to rad/s for the equations that we have been developing to be meaningful. For example if the object is rotating at a rate of 10 turns per second, then ω is given by

$$10 \ \frac{\text{rev}}{\text{s}} \ = \ 10 \ \frac{\text{rev}}{\text{s}} \left(\frac{2\pi \ \text{rad}}{1 \ \text{rev}} \right) \ = \ 62.8 \frac{\text{rad}}{\text{s}} \ = \ 62.8 \ \text{s}^{-1} \ = \ \omega \qquad \text{(C9.6)}$$

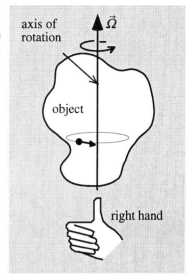

A rotating object's *angular velocity* vector $\vec{\omega}$ has a magnitude of $\omega = |d\theta/dt|$ and a direction as shown in Figure C9.5

Exercise C9X.1: Does the earth's angular velocity vector point away from the north pole or away from the south pole?

Figure C9.5: Right-hand rule for determining the direction of an object's angular velocity $\vec{\omega}$.

C9.5 THE MOMENT OF INERTIA

Consider a rigid object whose center of mass is at rest, but which is rotating with a certain angular velocity $\vec{\omega}$. Even though the object as a whole is at rest, its rotation means that most of its particles are actually moving. Since the particles in the object have mass and they are moving, they have kinetic energy. *An object's **rotational kinetic energy** is simply the total kinetic energy its particles have as a result of its rotation.*

How might we link this to $\vec{\omega}$? The speed at which any specific particle in the object moves as a result of this rotation is $v = r\omega$, where r is the distance that particular particle is from the axis of rotation. Let us number the particles in an object from 1 to N, let the mass of the ith particle be m_i, its speed due to rotation be v_i, and its distance from the axis of rotation be r_i. The total kinetic energy of the particles in a rotating but otherwise motionless rigid object is thus

$$K^{\text{rot}} \ = \ \sum_{i=1}^{N} \tfrac{1}{2} m_i v_i^2 \ = \ \tfrac{1}{2} \sum_{i=1}^{N} m_i (r_i \omega)^2 \ = \ \tfrac{1}{2} \left[\sum_{i=1}^{N} m_i r_i^2 \right] \omega^2 \qquad \text{(C9.7)}$$

where the angular speed ω can be pulled out of the sum because it is the same for all particles in the object. Note that the "rot" superscript on K^{rot} is not an exponent but simply means "rotational." (See the **Math Skills** section on *Summation Notation* if you are unfamiliar with the other notation used here.)

The sum in square brackets is called the object's **moment of inertia** I for rotation around that axis

$$I \ \equiv \ \sum_{i=1}^{N} m_i r_i^2 \ \equiv \ \text{moment of inertia} \qquad \text{(C9.8)}$$

Definition of an object's moment of inertia

Note that I depends on the object's *mass*, its *shape* (specifically, the distances that each particle in the object is from the axis of rotation), and *the axis of rotation* (since the distances r_i will change if the axis changes).

But whatever I happens to be for a given object and rotation axis, the formula for an object's rotational kinetic energy looks quite a bit like the formula for the kinetic energy associated with the movement of its center of mass:

$$K^{\text{rot}} \ = \ \tfrac{1}{2} I \omega^2 \quad \text{(compare with } K \ = \ \tfrac{1}{2} m v^2 \text{)} \qquad \text{(C9.9)}$$

Formula for an object's rotational kinetic energy

In the rotational kinetic energy formula, the moment of inertia I and the angular speed ω play the same roles respectively that the mass m and speed v do in the usual kinetic energy formula. You can think of the moment of inertia I, therefore, as being like an "effective rotational mass" for the object.

C9.6 CALCULATING MOMENTS OF INERTIA

How can we calculate the value of I for a given object? The actual number of elementary particles in any extended object is so large as to make the *literal* application of equation C9.9 impractical. But what we *can* do is group the particles in an object into a reasonable number of pieces that all have *approximately* the same distance from the axis of rotation and then sum over the pieces. The examples that follow illustrate this process.

EXAMPLE C9.1:
Calculating *I* for a Hoop

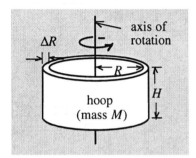

Figure C9.6: A thin hoop rotating around an axis through its center and parallel to its sides.

Problem: Imagine a thin cylindrical hoop of mass M, radius R, height H, and thickness $\Delta R \ll R$. What is its moment of inertia for rotations around an axis going through its center of mass and parallel to its sides (see Figure C9.6)?

Solution The moment of inertia is fairly easy to calculate in this case. As long as the hoop's thickness ΔR is very small compared to its radius R, *all* particles in the hoop are approximately the same distance R from the axis of rotation. This means that we can pull the factor of R^2 out of the sum that defines the moment of inertia as follows:

$$I \equiv \sum_{i=1}^{N} m_i r_i^2 \approx \sum_{i=1}^{N} m_i R^2 = R^2 \sum_{i=1}^{N} m_i = MR^2 \qquad (C9.10)$$

since the sum of the masses m_i of all particles in the hoop is simply M.

(In this case, we can accurately treat the entire hoop as a *single* "piece" because all particles in the hoop are equally distant from the axis.)

EXAMPLE C9.2:
Calculating *I* for a Rod

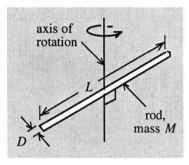

Figure C9.7: A thin rod rotating around an axis perpendicular to the rod.

Problem: Imagine a thin rod with mass M, length L, and diameter $D \ll L$. What is this rod's moment of inertia for rotations around an axis perpendicular to the rod and going through its center (see Figure C9.7)?

Solution The trick here is to divide the rod into a countable number of pieces (each embracing a set of particles that are approximately the same distance from the axis of rotation), as if the rod were comprised of a countable number of fairly massive particles instead of a huge number of elementary particles.

So let us divide the rod into n equal pieces, each with length $\Delta L = L/n$, and let us number the pieces using an index $j = 1$ to n. The mass of the particles in each piece compared to the total mass of the rod is

$$\frac{m_j}{M} = \frac{\Delta L}{L} \quad \Rightarrow \quad m_j = M\frac{\Delta L}{L} \qquad (C9.11)$$

(Computing m_j/M like this turns out to be very helpful in these kinds of problems.) The moment of inertia of the rod is thus approximately

$$I \approx \sum_{j=1}^{n} m_j r_j^2 = \sum_{j=1}^{n} \frac{M\Delta L}{L} r_j^2 = M\frac{\Delta L}{L} \sum_{j=1}^{n} r_j^2 \qquad (C9.12)$$

A helpful trick

where r_j is the distance from the axis of rotation to the center of the jth piece. It turns out to be very helpful to multiply the outside of the sum by L^2 and divide each term on the inside by L^2 to compensate, as follows:

$$I \approx ML^2 \left[\frac{\Delta L}{L} \sum_{j=1}^{n} \left(\frac{r_j}{L}\right)^2 \right] \qquad (C9.13)$$

Note that the quantity inside the brackets is unitless, since it involves ratios of lengths. So this sum will be a simple numerical factor that multiplies the ML^2 in the front. Our job is to compute the value of this numerical factor.

The more finely we divide the rod (that is, the greater the value of n), the more work we have to do to compute the sum but the more accurate the result will be. Let's take $n = 10$. The values of r_j / L will then be (working from one end of the rod to the other) 0.45, 0.35, 0.25, 0.15, 0.05, 0.05, 0.15, 0.25, 0.35, and 0.45 for $j = 1$ to 10 respectively (see Figure C9.8). The value of $\Delta L/L = 0.1$. The sum that we have to evaluate is thus

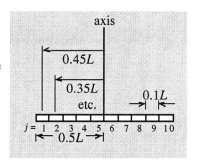

Figure C9.8: Dividing the rod into 10 equal pieces.

$$\frac{\Delta L}{L}\sum_{j=1}^{n}\left(\frac{r_j}{L}\right)^2 = (0.1)\cdot\left(0.45^2 + 0.35^2 + 0.25^2 + 0.15^2 + 0.05^2\right.$$
$$\left. + 0.05^2 + 0.15^2 + 0.25^2 + 0.35^2 + 0.45^2\right) = 0.0825 \quad \text{(C9.14)}$$

Exercise C9X.4: Verify the value of the sum, and that $0.0825 = 1/12.1$.

So $I = 0.0825\,ML^2 = \frac{1}{12.1}ML^2$. Now, we would get a better approximation if we had chosen $n = 20$ or 100 or even larger. It turns out in this case that if you were to try larger and larger values of n, the sum in equation C9.14 gets closer and closer to 1/12 (see problem C9B.7). Thus the theoretical value of the rod's moment of inertia is $I = \frac{1}{12}ML^2$. Even so, it is amazing how close we can get (within 1%) by dividing the rod into just 10 pieces!

**EXAMPLE C9.3:
Calculating I for a Disk**

Problem: Imagine a uniform solid disk with mass M, radius R, and height h. What is this disk's moment of inertia for rotations around an axis perpendicular to the disk and going through its center (see Figure C9.9)?

Solution In this case, we imagine dividing the disk into n thin hoops with equal radial thickness $\Delta r \ll R$, one of which is shown shaded in Figure C9.9: note that all of the particles in such a hoop are approximately the same distance r from the axis of rotation. The volume of each hoop is the hoop's circumference $2\pi r$ times its radial thickness Δr times its height h. The mass of the jth hoop is to the whole disk what its volume is to the volume of the whole disk:

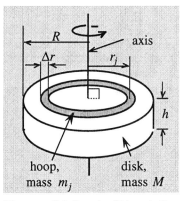

$$\frac{m_j}{M} = \frac{(\text{volume})_j}{\text{total volume}} = \frac{2\pi r_j \Delta r h}{\pi R^2 h} = \frac{2r_j \Delta r}{R^2} \quad \text{(C9.15)}$$

The moment of inertia of the disk can thus be written

$$I \approx \sum_{j=1}^{n} m_j r_j^2 = \sum_{j=1}^{n}\left(\frac{M 2 r_j \Delta r}{R^2}\right)r_j^2 = MR^2\left[\frac{2\Delta r}{R}\sum_{j=1}^{n}\left(\frac{r_j}{R}\right)^3\right] \quad \text{(C9.16)}$$

Figure C9.9: A disk rotating around an axis perpendicular to its face and going through its center.

where in the last step I have pulled constant factors out of the sum and have again used the trick of multiplying the outside of the sum by R^2 and dividing the terms inside of the sum by R^2 to get a sum of unitless numbers. If we divide the disk into 10 hoops with equal radial thickness Δr, then $\Delta r/R = 0.10$ and $r_j / R = 0.05, 0.15, \ldots, 0.95$. The unitless quantity in the square brackets turns out to have a value of 0.4975, so

$$I = 0.4975\,MR^2 \approx \frac{1}{2}MR^2 \quad \text{(C9.17)}$$

As n becomes larger, the sum gets even closer to $\frac{1}{2}$ (see Problem C9B.8).

Exercise C9X.5: Verify that the quantity in square brackets in equation C9.16 is equal to 0.4975.

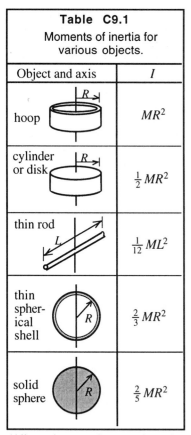

Table C9.1

Moments of inertia for various objects.

Object and axis	I
hoop	MR^2
cylinder or disk	$\frac{1}{2}MR^2$
thin rod	$\frac{1}{12}ML^2$
thin spherical shell	$\frac{2}{3}MR^2$
solid sphere	$\frac{2}{5}MR^2$

(All rotation axes here go through the object's center of mass.)

An object's total kinetic energy is the simple sum of its translational and rotational kinetic energies

First step: finding the velocity of each particle

Second step: finding the kinetic energy of each particle

I am much more interested that you get out of these examples an *intuitive* understanding of the process of calculating I for an object than I am in you memorizing the particular results that we found. For easy future reference, I have listed moments of inertia for various simple objects in Table C9.1.

If you are familiar with the methods of integral calculus, you can evaluate the sums involved exactly and more easily using integrals. This is not required at this point in the course, but if you are interested, look at problem C9A.3.

Since the moment of inertia of any object is simply a sum of $m_i r_i^2$ over all the particles in an object, it follows that if we can divide a complicated object up into pieces with various moments of inertia $I_1, I_2, \ldots$, the object's total moment of inertia is $I = I_1 + I_2 + \ldots$ (as long as each moment of inertia is evaluated for rotations around the same axis), because the moment of inertia of each piece is simply a portion of the sum of $m_i r_i^2$ for that object. For example, we can evaluate the moment of inertia of a sphere by dividing it into *disks* of equal thickness and summing the moments of inertia of these disks (see Problem C9A.1).

Exercise C9X.6: Consider an object consisting of two point particles each with mass m, connected by a rod of length L and mass m. What is the moment of inertia around an axis going through the center and perpendicular to the rod?

C9.7 TRANSLATION AND ROTATION

Now we are in a position to answer the question raised in section C9.2: What is the total kinetic energy of an object that is both moving *and* rotating (such as a rolling object)? It turns out that the answer is surprisingly simple. If $\vec{v}_{CM}$ is the velocity of the object's center of mass, then the total kinetic energy of an object of mass M that is rotating *and* moving is

$$K = K^{cm} + K^{rot} = \tfrac{1}{2}Mv_{CM}^2 + \tfrac{1}{2}I\omega^2 \qquad (C9.18)$$

The object's total kinetic energy is thus the simple sum of the **translational kinetic energy** of its center of mass (computed as if it were a particle of mass M) and its rotational kinetic energy (computed as if it were not moving).

This is a nice result, but it is by no means obvious. Consider an extended object that is both moving and rotating. The velocities of its particles point in all kinds of different directions and are constantly changing in complicated ways. It is not at all clear that things should always work out as nicely as equation C9.18 claims. How might we show this? We will prove this in *four steps*.

The first step is to determine how the motions of the particles in an object are related to its translational and rotational motions. Let $\vec{v}_{CM}$ be the velocity of the object's center of mass, $\vec{v}_i$ be the velocity of the ith particle in the object, and $\vec{u}_i$ be the part of that particle's velocity that is due to its rotational motion *around* the object's center of mass (I am using $\vec{u}$ instead of $\vec{v}$ to keep the notation simpler). Figure C9.10 shows that the velocity of the ith particle is just the vector sum of its rotational velocity $\vec{u}_i$ and the velocity of the center of mass:

$$\vec{v}_i = \vec{v}_{CM} + \vec{u}_i \qquad (C9.19)$$

The next step is to compute the kinetic energy of a single particle in the object. The dot product of any vector $\vec{w}$ with itself is $\vec{w} \cdot \vec{w} = w^2 \cos\theta = w^2$, since the angle θ between a vector and itself is zero. This means that the kinetic energy of the ith particle in our object can be written

$$K_i \equiv \tfrac{1}{2}m_i v_i^2 = \tfrac{1}{2}m_i(\vec{v}_i \cdot \vec{v}_i) \qquad (C9.20)$$

We also know that the dot product satisfies the distributive property of multiplication, so that $(\vec{A} + \vec{B}) \cdot (\vec{C} + \vec{D}) = \vec{A} \cdot \vec{C} + \vec{B} \cdot \vec{C} + \vec{A} \cdot \vec{D} + \vec{B} \cdot \vec{D}$, just as if we

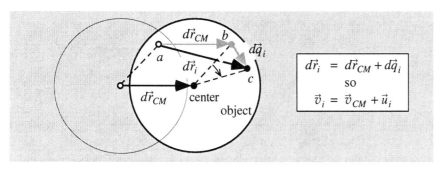

Figure C9.10: Assume that during a tiny time interval dt, the object's center of mass moves the displacement $d\vec{r}_{CM}$. The particle originally at point *a* would move the same displacement to point *b* during this interval, but the object's rotation carries it an additional displacement $d\vec{q}_i$ from *b* to *c*. The object's total displacement is thus $d\vec{r}_i = d\vec{r}_{CM} + d\vec{q}_i$. Dividing both sides of the equation by dt yields equation C9.19.

were multiplying two ordinary binomials. Using this, the commutative property of the dot product ($\vec{A} \cdot \vec{B} = \vec{B} \cdot \vec{A}$), and equation C9.19, you can show that

$$K_i = \tfrac{1}{2} m_i v_{CM}^2 + m_i \vec{v}_{CM} \cdot \vec{u}_i + \tfrac{1}{2} m_i u_i^2 \qquad (C9.21)$$

Exercise C9X.7: Verify equation C9.21.

Now, the *first* term on the right in equation C9.22 is the *i*th particle's kinetic energy due to the motion of the object's center of mass, and the *third* term is its kinetic energy due to the object's rotational motion around its center of mass. So if we sum equation C9.21 over all particles in the object, we get:

$$K = K^{\text{cm}} + \sum_{i=1}^{N} m_i \vec{v}_{CM} \cdot \vec{u}_i + K^{\text{rot}} \qquad (C9.22)$$

where K^{cm} and K^{rot} are the *total* kinetic energies (that is, the kinetic energies summed over all particles) associated with the motion of the object's center of mass and its rotation around the center of mass, respectively. If we can show that the sum in the middle is zero, we will have equation C9.18.

Since the quantity $\vec{v}_{CM}$ is common to all terms in that middle sum, we can factor it out in front of the sum as follows

$$\sum_{i=1}^{N} m_i \vec{v}_{CM} \cdot \vec{u}_i = \vec{v}_{CM} \cdot \left(\sum_{i=1}^{N} m_i \vec{u}_i \right) \qquad (C9.23)$$

Now, using equation C9.19, we can write the term in parentheses as

$$\sum_{i=1}^{N} m_i \vec{u}_i = \sum_{i=1}^{N} m_i (\vec{v}_i - \vec{v}_{CM}) = \sum_{i=1}^{N} m_i \vec{v}_i - \sum_{i=1}^{N} m_i \vec{v}_{CM} \qquad (C9.24)$$

The first sum on the right in equation C9.24 is the object's total momentum, which (according to equation C4.17) is equal to the object's mass M times the velocity of the center of mass $\vec{v}_{CM}$. Since $\vec{v}_{CM}$ is common to all terms in the second sum, this term is $(m_1 + m_2 + ...)\vec{v}_{CM} = M\vec{v}_{CM}$ also. So:

$$\sum_{i=1}^{N} m_i \vec{v}_i = M\vec{v}_{CM} - M\vec{v}_{CM} = 0 \qquad (C9.25)$$

Therefore, the term in parentheses in equation C9.23 is zero, implying that the middle term in equation C9.22 is zero. So, C9.22 *is* equivalent to C9.18.

Equation C9.18 is a powerful equation with many useful applications. While it is not at all obvious that it should be true, the proof just given shows that it is a logical consequence of the definitions of velocity, kinetic energy, the center of mass, and (ultimately) the principle that interactions transfer momentum. Finding and bringing to light such hidden consequences is one of the main tasks (and joys) of doing theoretical physics.

Third step: summing over all particles

The final step: showing that the middle term in equation C9.21 is zero

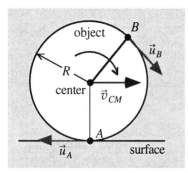

Figure C9.11: An object rolling along a surface. The gray arrows show the velocities of particles at A and B due to the rotation of the sphere alone: $u_A = u_B = R\omega$. The total velocities of these particles will be the sum of this velocity due to rotation and the velocity of the object's center of mass.

The relationship between a rolling object's angular speed and CM speed

Solving the puzzle from section C9.2

C9.8 ROLLING WITHOUT SLIPPING

Consider now an object with circular cross-section (such as a sphere, hoop, cylinder, or disk) that rolls without slipping along a surface. How can we compute the total kinetic energy (both rotational and translational) of this object?

Assume that the object has a mass M, that its circular cross section has a radius R, and that its center of mass moves with a velocity $\vec{v}_{CM}$. Figure C9.11 shows such an object. Note that equation C9.19 implies that the total velocity $\vec{v}_A$ of a point particle A at the object's bottom (where it touches the surface) will be the vector sum of its rotational velocity $\vec{u}_A$ and the velocity $\vec{v}_{CM}$ of the object's center of mass: $\vec{v}_A = \vec{v}_{CM} + \vec{u}_A$. According to equation C9.7, the magnitude of $\vec{u}_A$ will be $u_A = \text{mag}(\vec{u}_A) = R\omega$. Note also that in this particular case, $\vec{u}_A$ and $\vec{v}_{CM}$ point in opposite directions when the particle is at the bottom, so the magnitude of its velocity will be $v_A = \text{mag}(\vec{v}_A) = |v_{CM} - R\omega|$.

But if the object is rolling *without slipping*, then the relative velocity between the particle at this point and the surface upon which the object is rolling should be *zero*. Assuming that the surface itself is not moving, this means that we must have $\vec{v}_A = 0$, which, since $v_A = |v_{CM} - R\omega|$, means that

$$|v_{CM} - R\omega| = 0 \quad \Rightarrow \quad v_{CM} = R\omega \quad \Rightarrow \quad \omega = \frac{v_{CM}}{R} \qquad \text{(C9.26)}$$

The last equation in this sequence is *very important*, because it links a rolling object's angular speed of rotation ω to the speed of its center of mass.

Let's apply this to the case of a ball rolling down an incline. If we model the ball as a solid sphere, then $I = \frac{2}{5}MR^2$. If we ignore the normal (perpendicular) part of the ball's contact interaction with the incline, then conservation of energy implies that $K_i^{\text{cm}} + K_i^{\text{rot}} + V(z_i) = K_f^{\text{cm}} + K_f^{\text{rot}} + V(z_f)$, where the Ks refer to the ball (we ignore the earth's kinetic energy). If the ball starts at rest, then the two initial kinetic energies are zero. If we define the bottom of the ramp to be at $z = 0$ (and take this to be the reference position for gravitational potential energy so that $V(z) = Mgz$), then conservation of energy tells us that

$$0 + 0 + Mgz_i = \tfrac{1}{2}Mv_{CM}^2 + \tfrac{1}{2}I\omega^2 + 0 = \tfrac{1}{2}Mv_{CM}^2 + \tfrac{1}{5}M\cancel{R}^2\left(\frac{v_{CM}}{\cancel{R}}\right)^2 \qquad \text{(C9.27)}$$

where v_{CM} is the *final* speed of the ball's center of mass, and where I have used equation C9.26 in the last step. Multiplying through by $2/M$, we get

$$2gz_i = v_{CM}^2 + \tfrac{2}{5}v_{CM}^2 \quad \Rightarrow \quad v_{CM} = \sqrt{\frac{2gz_i}{7/5}} \qquad \text{(C9.28)}$$

Note that if the rotational term weren't there (as in the case of an object sliding down a ramp, we would get the larger result $v_{CM} = \sqrt{2gz_i}$. This resolves the puzzle discussed in section C9.2 regarding why the ball moves more slowly: indeed, experiments show that equation C9.28 correctly predicts its final speed.

This is one situation where we can handle the frictional part of a contact interaction

Note that it is the *frictional* part of the contact interaction between the ball and the incline that is involved in getting the object rolling. (Ask yourself this question: would the ball roll at all if it were on a *frictionless* incline?) Therefore, we now know how to handle the frictional part of a contact interaction between an object and a surface *if* its sole effect is to keep the object rolling without slipping: we just keep track of the object's rotational kinetic energy! (We will consider more cases where friction is relevant in the next chapter.)

Example C9.4 illustrates how we can solve problems involving rolling using the problem-solving framework discussed in chapter C6. Note that I have made a small addition to the framework in the *conceptual representation* part: we now can handle an interaction (1) by including its potential energy function, (2) by ignoring it, or (3) by *keeping track of rotational kinetic energy.*

EXAMPLE C9.4

OUTLINE OF THE FRAMEWORK

1. Pictorial Representation

a. Draw a picture of the situation that includes:

① (1) sketches of the system in its initial and final states

② (2) reference frame axes

③ (3) labels defining symbols for relevant quantities (in this case, objects' masses, velocities, and separations)

b. List values for all known quantities and specify which quantities are unknown. ④

2. Conceptual Representation

The general task is to construct a conceptual model of the situation and link it to an abstract physics model or principle. In conservation-of-energy problems, we do the following:

⑤ a. Identify the *system* involved. (If it involves the earth, we can ignore the earth's kinetic energy)

⑥ b. Determine whether it is *approximately* isolated, *functionally* isolated, or involved in a *collision* (as defined in chapter C5). Support your conclusions briefly. ⑦

⑦ c. Identify the interactions between objects in the system and for each interaction, determine whether we can handle it by

(1) keeping track of its potential energy (if so, define the reference separation)

(2) ignoring it (because it is very weak or for another reason)

(3) keeping track of rotational kinetic energy

⑧ d. Do we have to make any approximations or assumptions to solve the problem? (If so, describe.)

3. Mathematical Representation

⑨ a. Apply the mathematical equation that appropriately describes the situation (equation C6.16 here)

⑩ b. Solve for unknowns symbolically

⑪ c. Plug in numbers and units and calculate the result and its units.

4. Evaluation

Check that the answer makes sense:

⑫ a. Does it have the correct units?

⑬ b. Does it have the right sign?

⑭ c. Does it seem reasonable?

Problem: A cylindrical hoop with a mass of 2.5 kg and a radius of 0.50 m rolls from rest down a hill 25 m tall. How fast is the hoop rotating (in rev/s) when it reaches the bottom? How fast is the hoop's center of mass moving at this point?

Solution: Let's take the hoop's initial position to define the origin of our reference frame so that the hoop's center of mass has an initial vertical position of $z_i = 0$. I will also use the symbol $\vec{v}$ to refer to the velocity of the hoop's *center of mass* throughout. Initial and final situations then look as follows:

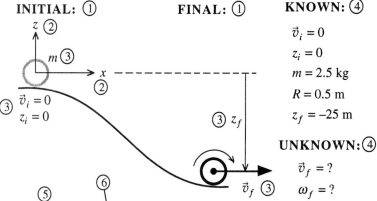

The system here is the earth and the hoop, so we can consider the system to be approximately isolated. The hoop participates in two interactions with the earth: a gravitational interaction and a contact interaction. We can write a potential energy function for the gravitational interaction: taking the $z = 0$ to be the reference position, $V(z) = mgz$. We can ignore the normal part of the hoop's contact interaction with the earth, and (assuming that the hoop rolls without slipping)⑧ we will correctly handle the frictional part of that interaction as long as we keep track of the hoop's rotational kinetic energy. (We will ignore any air friction.)⑧   Conservation of energy then implies that

$$K_i^{cm} + K_i^{rot} + V(z_i) = K_f^{cm} + K_f^{rot} + V(z_f) \quad ⑨$$

In this case, the hoop is at rest initially, so $K_i^{cm} = K_i^{rot} = 0$. Moreover, the hoop's initial vertical position is $z_i = 0$, so $V(z_i) = 0$. Therefore, in this particular situation, the equation above reads:

$$0 + 0 + 0 = \tfrac{1}{2}mv_f^2 + \tfrac{1}{2}I\omega_f^2 + mgz_f$$

where ω_f is the hoop's final angular speed. According to table C9.1, $I = MR^2$ for a hoop. Also, $\omega_f = v/R$ if the hoop rolls without slipping (see equation C9.26). Plugging this stuff in, we get

$$0 = \tfrac{1}{2}mv_f^2 + \tfrac{1}{2}mR^2\left(\frac{v_f}{R}\right)^2 + mgz_f = mv_f^2 + mgz_f \;\Rightarrow\; v_f^2 = -gz_f$$

$$⑩ \;\Rightarrow\; v_f = \sqrt{-gz_f} = \sqrt{-(9.8\text{ m/s}^2)(-22\text{ m})} = 14.7\text{ m/s} \;⑪$$

The object's final angular speed of rotation ω_f is then

$$⑩ \quad \omega_f = \frac{v_f}{R} = \frac{14.7\text{ m/s}}{0.5\text{ m}} = \frac{29.4\text{ rad}}{\text{s}}\left(\frac{1\text{ rev}}{2\pi\text{ rad}}\right) = 4.7\text{ rev/s} \;⑪$$

$$⑬ \qquad\qquad\qquad\qquad\qquad ⑫$$

Both are positive (as appropriate for speeds) and have appropriate units. The magnitudes don't seem outrageous (15 m/s ≈ 33 mi/h). ⑭

MATH SKILLS: Summation Notation

We will be using summation notation extensively in this chapter, chapter C13, and later in the course as well. Since this is the first chapter to use such notation, it is appropriate to discuss its conventions here.

Summation notation is useful when we want to write an equation that involves adding a large number of terms. In this chapter, for example, we compute an object's *moment of inertia* by multiplying the mass of each particle in the object by the square of its distance from the axis of rotation and then summing over all particles in the object. Since there are very roughly 10^{25} elementary particles in a macroscopic object that you could hold in your hand, writing out this sum explicitly would be clearly impossible. We need a more compact notation.

Index notation

The first step in using summation notation is to give each quantity to be summed a number or **index**, which is indicated by a subscript attached to the quantity's symbol. For example, if we number the N particles in a given object 1, 2, 3, ... , N, their masses would be written $m_1, m_2, m_3, \dots, m_N$, their distances from the axis of rotation would be $r_1, r_2, r_3, \dots, r_N$, and so on.

When we want to describe a typical (but arbitrary) particle in this list, we refer to the "*i*th" particle, which has mass m_i and is a distance r_i from the axis. The i subscript stands for any number between 1 and N that you might substitute for the i: any equation or statement that you write involving a symbol with an i subscript should be true no matter what number you might substitute for i.

Notation for a sum

If we want to sum the quantity mr^2 for all N particles in the object, we could write the sum using summation notation as follows:

$$\sum_{i=1}^{N} m_i r_i^2 \equiv m_1 r_1^2 + m_2 r_2^2 + \dots + m_N r_N^2 \qquad \text{(C9.29)}$$

The large Σ (the Greek letter *sigma*) indicates that one is summing the quantity whose symbolic representation follows the Σ: in this case, $m_i r_i^2$ describes the quantity being summed. The items above and below the Σ specify the limits of the sum: we start with the index i being 1 and continue substituting successive integer values for i until we reach $i = N$.

Distributive property

Because of the distributive property of addition and multiplication, any quantity whose value is known to be the *same* for all terms in the sum may be factored out in front of the sum. For example, if all of the particles in an object are the *same* distance R from the axis of rotation, then

$$\sum_{i=1}^{N} m_i R^2 = R^2 \sum_{i=1}^{N} m_i \qquad \text{(distributive property)} \qquad \text{(C9.30)}$$

This simply says that

$$m_1 R^2 + m_2 R^2 + \dots + m_N R^2 = R^2(m_1 + m_2 + \dots + m_N) \qquad \text{(C9.31)}$$

On the other hand, a quantity with an i subscript almost always has a different value for each value for i, and so cannot be factored out of a sum this way:

$$\sum_{i=1}^{N} m_i r_i^2 \neq m_i \sum_{i=1}^{N} r_i^2 \qquad \text{(doesn't make any sense!)} \qquad \text{(C9.32)}$$

The kind of notation used on the right side of equation C9.29 is a clear but more lengthy alternative to the summation notation on the left. If you are ever in doubt about whether you can legally factor out a quantity (or perform any other operation on a sum), you can always check it by writing out the sum explicitly (as we did in equation C9.31).

I. A PUZZLE
   A. Consider two objects with equal masses moving down an incline; one that rolls without slipping and one that slides without friction
      1. Both convert the same amount of gravitational potential energy into kinetic energy, so both *should* have the same final speed
      2. But experimentally the rolling object's speed is slower (!?)
   B. A possible resolution: is there kinetic energy associated with rotation?

II. MEASURING ANGLES
   A. One approach to quantifying the angle between two line segments:
      1. Superimpose a circle centered on the segments' intersection
      2. Divide the circle's circumference into n equally spaced units
      3. Count how many units are bracketed by the two line segments
   B. A more basic approach: if r is the circle's radius and s is the arclength bracketed by the angle on the circle's circumference, then $\theta \equiv s/r$
      1. This is *unitless*, which is appropriate for trig functions like $\sin\theta$
      2. This makes a number of physics equations easier as well
   C. We say that an angle defined this way is expressed in *radians*
      1. But the radian is not a normal unit: according to the definition of angle $\theta = s/r$, 1 rad = 1 m/m = 1! This means that it can be supplied or removed from an equation's units at will
      2. We commonly *supply* the unit of radians when we either
         a) want to emphasize that an *angle* is involved in a quantity, or
         b) when we want to *convert* angular units (in the conversion, we treat radians, degrees, and/or revolutions as ordinary units)
      3. Conversion equations: $360° = 1$ rev $= 2\pi$ rad
   D. We will assume that θ is in radians in all abstract equations that follow

III. THE CONCEPTS OF ANGULAR SPEED AND ANGULAR VELOCITY
   A. A particle's or object's *angular speed* is $\omega \equiv |d\theta/dt|$ (SI units: rad/s)
   B. Its *angular velocity* vector $\vec{\omega}$ has a magnitude of $\omega \equiv |d\theta/dt|$ and a direction that points along the axis of rotation along one's right thumb when one's right fingers curl with the rotation
   C. A particle's *ordinary* speed along a circular path of radius r is $v = r\omega$ (in a rotating object, this is the particle's *rotational speed*)

IV. AN OBJECT'S MOMENT OF INERTIA I
   A. The definition of I (see equation C9.8): $I \equiv \sum_{i=1}^{N} m_i r_i^2$
      1. m_i is the mass of the ith particle
      2. r_i is its distance from the axis of rotation
   B. An object's I depends on its mass, its shape, and the axis of rotation
   C. An object's kinetic energy due to its rotation is $K^{\text{rot}} = \frac{1}{2}I\omega^2$

V. CALCULATING MOMENTS OF INERTIA
   A. The basic procedure:
      1. Divide the object into n pieces such that each piece contains particles that are nearly the same distance from the axis of rotation
      2. Express the mass of each piece as a fraction of the object's mass
      3. Divide terms inside the sum and multiply outside the sum by the square of a characteristic length or radius (makes the sum unitless)
      4. Sum over all n pieces (can use calculus if desired)
   B. Values for I for various objects are listed in Table C9.1.

VI. SEPARATING TRANSLATION AND ROTATION
   A. $K = K^{\text{cm}} + K^{\text{rot}} = \frac{1}{2}Mv_{CM}^2 + \frac{1}{2}I\omega^2$ if an object both rotates and moves
   B. It is not obvious that this should work (but see proof in section C9.7)

VII. AN OBJECT OF RADIUS R THAT IS ROLLING WITHOUT SLIPPING
   A. A bit of analysis shows that $\omega = v_{CM}/R$
   B. This implies that if $I = \frac{1}{2}bMR^2$, then $K^{\text{rot}} = \frac{1}{2}bMv_{CM}^2 = bK^{\text{cm}}$
   C. This resolves the puzzle in a manner consistent with experiment

GLOSSARY

degree, revolution, radian: different possible units for expressing angles: 1 rev = 2π rad = $360°$. The radian is the preferred SI unit. All of these "units" are unusual since an angle as defined by the equation $\theta = s/r$ is really unitless. We can treat these as unitless as long as we recognize that the radian (and *only* the radian) can be removed from or added to a quantity's units at will.

angular speed ω: the rate $|d\theta/dt|$ that a particle's angular position changes with time. *Angular position* here means the angle (in some specified plane) between the particle's position vector and some specified direction. The angular speed of a rigid extended object rotating around some axis is the angular speed of any particle in the object around that axis. The SI units of angular speed are rad/s, and most equations involving ω will not come out correctly if ω is not expressed in rad/s.

angular velocity $\vec{\omega}$: a vector describing an object's rotational motion whose magnitude is the object's angular speed and whose direction is along the axis of rotation in the direction indicated by your right thumb when your fingers curl in the direction of the rotation.

rotational kinetic energy K^{rot}: the part of an extended object's total kinetic energy that is associated with its rotation about some axis. $K^{\text{rot}} = \frac{1}{2}I\omega^2$.

translational kinetic energy K^{cm}: the part of an extended object's total kinetic energy K associated with the motion of its center of mass. Previously, we have assumed that $K^{\text{cm}} = K$, which is true if the object is not rotating.

moment of inertia I (around a given axis): the quantity mr^2 summed over every particle in a rigid extended object, where m is the particle's mass and r is its distance from the axis of rotation.

index: a numerical subscript that we attach to each member of a list of quantities to be summed. The value of the index conventionally ranges from 1 to N, where N is the number of entries in the list.

TWO-MINUTE PROBLEMS

C9T.1 A particle moving along a circular path 10 cm in radius moves at a speed of 50 cm/s. Its angular speed is
A. 50 rad/s
D. 1.26 rad/s
B. 5 rad/s
E. $900°\ \text{s}^{-1}$
C. 0.2 rad/s
F. other (specify)

C9T.2 A merry-go-round makes a complete revolution once every 6.28 s. What is the speed (in m/s) of a horse 5 m from the merry-go-round's center?
A. 0.80 m/s
D. 5.0 m/s
B. 1.0 m/s
E. 31.4 m/s
C. 1.26 m/s
F. other (specify)

C9T.3 A cylindrical barrel is rolling on the ground toward you. Its angular velocity points
A. to your right
C. toward you
B. to your left
D. away from you
E. Toward you at the top, away from you on the bottom
F. other (specify)

C9T.4 A bicyclist passes in front of you, moving from your left to your right. The angular velocity of the bike's wheels point roughly
A. to your right
C. toward you
B. to your left
D. away from you
E. to your right at the top, to your left on the bottom
F. other (specify)

C9T.5 Four point particles, each with mass $\frac{1}{4}M$, are connected by massless rods so that they form a square whose sides have length L. What is the moment of inertia I of this object if it is spun around an axis going through the center of the square perpendicular to the plane of the square?
A. $\frac{1}{16}ML^2$
C. $\frac{1}{4}ML^2$
E. ML^2
B. $\frac{1}{8}ML^2$
D. $\frac{1}{2}ML^2$
F. other (specify)

C9T.6 What would be the moment of inertia I of the square described in the previous problem if it were spun around an axis going through one particle and its diagonal opposite?
A. $\frac{1}{16}ML^2$
C. $\frac{1}{4}ML^2$
E. ML^2
B. $\frac{1}{8}ML^2$
D. $\frac{1}{2}ML^2$
F. other (specify)

C9T.7 Two wheels have the same total mass M and radius R. One wheel is a uniform disk. The other is like a bicycle wheel, with lightweight spokes connecting the rim to the hub. Which has the larger moment of inertia?
A. the solid disk
C. the wheel with spokes
B. insufficient information for meaningful answer

C9T.8 A solid ball and a hollow ball are released from rest at the top of an incline and roll without slipping to the bottom. Which reaches the bottom first?
A. the solid ball
B. The hollow ball
C. both balls arrive at the same time
D. it depends on the masses of the balls

C9T.9 A 10-kg sphere with a radius of 10 cm spinning at 10 rotations per second has a rotational kinetic energy of
A. 5 J
C. 31 J
E. 500 J
B. 10 J
D. 63 J
F. other (specify)

HOMEWORK PROBLEMS

BASIC SKILLS

C9B.1 A roughly spherical asteroid whose radius is 50 km rotates once every 1.5 h. What is its angular speed in rad/s?

C9B.2 A child's top, which has a diameter of 5 cm, spins about 5 times a second. What is its angular speed in rad/s?

C9B.3 An airplane flies clockwise around an airport control tower at a speed of 130 m/s. If that control tower is 8 km from the airplane at all times, what is the plane's angular velocity (magnitude and direction)?

C9B.4 A car travels at a speed of 20 m/s around a circular transition ramp between two freeways. If the car is turning to its right as it goes around the ramp, and the ramp has a radius of 300 m, what is the car's angular velocity (magnitude and direction) in rad/s around the center of the ramp?

C9B.5 A solid cylinder of iron with a radius of 20 cm, a height of 20 cm, and a mass of 200 kg, rotates at a rate of 10 rev/s. What is its rotational kinetic energy?

C9B.6 A hoop whose mass is 2.0 kg and radius is 40 cm rotates at a rate of 2 rev/s. What is its rotational kinetic energy?

C9B.7 Repeat the calculation shown in equation C9.14 for a rod divided into 20 equal pieces. Show that you get a value between 1/12.1 and 1/12. Repeat for 50 pieces (r_j/L = 0.49, 0.47, 0.45, etc.) and show that the result is even *closer* to 1/12.

C9B.8 Evaluate the quantity in brackets in equation C9.16 for $n = 20$ and show that its value is even closer to 1/2 than 0.4975.

SYNTHETIC

C9S.1 A 6-kg bowling ball whose radius is 12 cm rolls away from you without slipping at 4 m/s. What is its angular velocity (magnitude and direction)? What is its total kinetic energy (including rotational kinetic energy)?

C9S.2 A 20-kg piece of steel pipe that is 20 cm in diameter, 80 cm long, and 1 cm thick is rolling toward you without slipping at a speed of 3.0 m/s. What is its angular velocity (magnitude and direction)? What is its total kinetic energy (including rotational kinetic energy)?

C9S.3 In the calculation of the moment of inertia of a rod in section C9.6, it is important to assume that the rod is "thin." Explain why. How would the calculation be inaccurate if the rod were, say, as thick as it is long?

C9S.4 Using a method similar to that used in Example C9.2, find the moment of inertia of a thin rod of mass M and length L being rotated around an axis perpendicular to the rod but going through one end of the rod instead of through its center. Compare with the theoretical result $I = \frac{1}{3}ML^2$. (You may evaluate any sum that you might need using calculus if you can: otherwise divide the rod into 10 pieces, calculate the value of each of the 10 terms in the sum for the moment of inertia, and then sum the terms.)

C9S.5 Using an approach similar to that used in Example C9.3, find the moment of inertia of a disk just like the one shown in Figure C9.7 except that it has a hole in the center of radius $R/2$. Assume that the total mass of the modified disk is still M, and its outer radius is still R, and it still rotates around the same axis as before. Compare to the theoretical result $I = \frac{5}{8}MR^2$. (You may evaluate any sum that you might need using calculus if you can; otherwise, divide the disk into 10 pieces and sum over the pieces.)

C9S.6 Calculate the moment of inertia of a wheel constructed as shown in Figure C9.12 for rotations around an axis perpendicular to the drawing and going through the wheel's center. Assume that both the spokes and the circumference are constructed out of the same kind and thickness of iron rod. (*Hint*: Break the wheel down into three parts that all rotate around the same axis: two rods and one hoop. What fraction of the mass of the whole is the mass of the hoop? The mass in the two rods?)

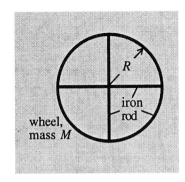

Figure C9.12: The wheel considered in problem C9S.6.

C9S.7 (a) Estimate the rotational kinetic energy of the earth, treating it as a uniform sphere. (b) The earth is actually not a uniform sphere, but is more dense at its center than it is at its edge. Does this make the estimate that you made in part *a* somewhat too large or somewhat too small? Explain.

C9S.8 A typical neutron star (what is left behind when a star goes supernova) has a mass of 1.4 solar masses and a radius of roughly 12 km. Just after formation, a neutron star can be spinning at a rate of 500 turns/s or so. Estimate the total rotational kinetic energy of the neutron star (describe any approximations or assumptions you make). If this energy were somehow converted to other forms of energy at the same rate as the sun radiates energy, how long would it take to bring the neutron star to zero angular speed?

C9S.9 A piece of concrete pipe being stored at a construction site is shaken loose in an earthquake and rolls down a hill. The pipe is a cylindrical shell 2.0 m in diameter, 3.2 m long, and 5 cm thick. Concrete has a density of roughly 2300 kg/m^3. When the pipe reaches the street after descending a vertical distance of 45 m, how fast is it going?*

C9S.10 Imagine holding one end of the thread on a spool of thread, and then releasing the spool from rest. What is the spool's vertical speed after it has fallen a distance h? You may assume that the thread is essentially massless compared to the spool; describe any other approximations that you make.*

C9S.11 A cylindrical section of a tree trunk 50 cm in diameter and 75 cm long is seen rolling down a road below a sawmill at a speed of 12 m/s. (Wood has a density of about 750 kg/m^3.) Assuming that the road has an incline of 5% (meaning that if you travel 100 m along the road, you go up 5 m), at least how far up the road is the sawmill? Describe any assumptions or approximations that you make. *

C9S.12 A length of thread is wrapped many times around a steel disk of mass M and radius R, which is free to rotate around a fixed, frictionless, horizontal axle. The end of the thread is connected to a small object of mass m. If this small mass is held at rest and then released, how fast is it moving after it has fallen through a vertical distance h? Express your answer in terms of M, R, m, g, and h (and be sure to check that your answer makes sense in the extreme limits $m \gg M$ or $M \gg m$ at least).*

---

*Please write your solution to a starred problem using the problem-solving framework illustrated by Example C9.4.

RICH-CONTEXT

C9R.1 Imagine that you are replacing a tire on your car on a steep hill in San Francisco, and somehow your spare tire gets away and rolls down the hill. If the hill has an incline of 14°, about how fast is the tire moving when it reaches the intersection 85 m away (as measured down the slope)? Will this tire likely represent a hazard to pedestrians? Describe any approximations that you make.

C9R.2 Two kids enter unpowered homemade carts in a soapbox derby race. The carts both have masses of 36 kg and four wheels that each have a mass of 3.0 kg. The racetrack is an incline 100 m long. The only significant difference between the carts is that one has solid, disk-like wheels and the other has bicycle-like wheels where most of the mass is on the rim. Other things being equal, which cart will win, and how much longer will it take the other to reach the finish? (*Hint:* Show that at every point along the track, the carts' speeds are related by a fixed factor.)

ADVANCED

C9A.1 Find the moment of inertia of a uniform sphere of radius R and mass M, for rotations around any axis through its center by dividing the sphere into disks of equal thickness Δx, each perpendicular to the axis of rotation. Compare your result to the theoretical result $I = \frac{2}{5}MR^2$. (*Hints:* Draw a picture. Note that the squared radius of the jth disk is $r_j^2 = R^2 - x_j^2$, where x_j is the position of the center of that disk along the axis of rotation, assuming that $x = 0$ is the center of the sphere. Argue that $m_j / M = 3r_j^2 \Delta x / R^3$. You may evaluate any sum that you need using calculus if you can; otherwise, divide the sphere into 20 disks.)

C9A.2 Find the moment of inertia of a thin, uniform spherical shell of radius R, mass M, and thickness $\Delta R \ll R$, for rotations around any axis through its center, by dividing the shell up into n thin hoops, each perpendicular to the axis of rotation and each having angular width $\Delta \theta = \pi/n$ (one such hoop is illustrated in Figure C9.13). Compare your result to the theoretical result $I = \frac{2}{3}MR^2$. (*Hints:* Argue that the distance that the particles in the jth hoop are away from the axis is approximately $r_j = R\sin\theta_j$. Also argue that the mass of the jth hoop is given by the expres-

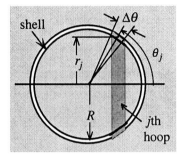

Figure C9.13: Evaluating the moment of inertia of a thin shell.

sion $m_j = M\frac{1}{2}r_j^2 \Delta\theta / R^2$. You may evaluate any sum that youneed using calculus if you can: otherwise divide the sphere up into 20 hoops with equal angular widths.)

C9A.3 We can use integral calculus to evaluate moments of inertia *exactly* and with less work than the method described in the chapter. To do this, we go through exactly the same process outlined in the examples up to the point of actually doing the sum. Then we define a new unitless variable $u \equiv r/L$ or r/R and convert the sum to an integral instead of calculating the sum by hand.

For example, in the case of a rod of length L, we can rewrite the sum in equation C9.14 as follows:

$$\sum_{j=1}^{n} \left(\frac{r_j}{L}\right)^2 \frac{\Delta L}{L} = \sum_{j=1}^{n} u_j^2 \Delta u \qquad (C9.33)$$

where $u_j = r_j / L$, and $\Delta u \equiv \Delta r/L = \Delta L/L = 1/n$. Note that as n goes to infinity, Δu will go to zero, so in this limit the sum becomes an integral

$$\lim_{n \to \infty} \sum_{j=1}^{n} u_j^2 \Delta u = \int_0^{1/2} u^2 du + \int_0^{1/2} u^2 du \qquad (C9.34)$$

(The first integral in this case corresponds to the part of the sum from the center to one end of the rod at $r = L/2$, and the other to summing from the center to the other end.) Show that the sum of these two integrals is 1/12. Then use the same technique to evaluate the moment of inertia of a disk, and also a disk with a hole of radius $R/2$ in the middle (see problem C9S.5).

ANSWERS TO EXERCISES

C9X.1 *Away* from the north pole. (The earth rotates toward the east, since the sun rises in the east. If we look at the earth from above the north pole, the earth thus rotates counterclockwise. The right hand rule then implies that the angular velocity points toward us.)

C9X.2 kg·m^2.

C9X.3 3.9 J. (Remember to convert the rotational speed to rad/s before you calculate the energy!)

C9X.4 (This is just a straightforward calculation.)

C9X.5 (This is just a straightforward calculation.)

C9X.6 Divide the object up into three parts (two particles and the rod) and sum the moments of inertia for each part around the central axis (remembering that each particle is a

distance of $L/2$ from the axis of rotation). The result is $I = \frac{1}{4}mL^2 + \frac{1}{4}mL^2 + \frac{1}{12}mL^2 = \frac{7}{12}mL^2 = \frac{7}{36}ML^2$, where $M = 3m$.

C9X.7 According to equation C9.20

$$K_i = \frac{1}{2}m_i(\vec{v}_i \cdot \vec{v}_i) = \frac{1}{2}m_i(\vec{v}_{CM} + \vec{u}_i) \cdot (\vec{v}_{CM} + \vec{u}_i)$$

$$= \frac{1}{2}m_i(\vec{v}_{CM} \cdot \vec{v}_{CM} + \vec{v}_{CM} \cdot \vec{u}_i + \vec{u}_i \cdot \vec{v}_{CM} + \vec{u}_i \cdot \vec{u}_i) \qquad (C9.35)$$

Since the dot product is commutative, we can combine the two middle terms. Since the dot product of a vector with itself is the squared magnitude of the vector, the first and last terms become v_{CM}^2 and u_i^2 respectively. Once we actually multiply out the m_i factor, the result is equation C9.21.

C10

THERMAL ENERGY

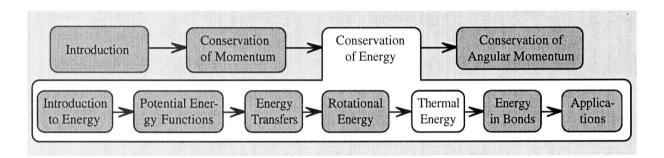

C10.1 OVERVIEW

In the past few chapters, we have learned how to apply conservation of energy to a variety of physical interactions. However, there are processes and interactions that we cannot yet understand using conservation of energy. In particular, the friction part of contact interactions remains troublesome, since such interactions clearly remove kinetic energy from the objects involved, and yet it is not clear where this energy goes.

This destruction of energy turns out to be only apparent. The macroscopic objects of daily life can store energy internally in various ways that are hidden to the eye of a macroscopic observer. Our task in the next two chapters is to learn about these various forms of hidden energy, which we will call *internal energy*. We begin in this chapter by studying *thermal energy*, which is the most common form in which we encounter internal energy. This chapter will provide essential background for discussing the more subtle forms of internal energy that we will encounter in the next chapter.

Here is an overview of the sections of this chapter.

C10.2 *THE CASE OF THE DISAPPEARING ENERGY* looks at examples of processes that seem to destroy energy.

C10.3 *CALORIC IS ENERGY* discusses the historical steps that people took to recognizing that hot objects contain internal energy.

C10.4 *THERMAL ENERGY* presents a contemporary model for understanding how such energy is stored in an object and how it is related to temperature. This section also discusses the absolute (kelvin) temperature scale.

C10.5 *FRICTION AND THERMAL ENERGY* shows how we can explain the mystery of the disappearing energy using the idea of thermal energy.

C10.6 *HEAT AND WORK* defines the technical terms *heat* and *work* and how they are related to (but are distinct from) thermal energy.

C10.7 *SPECIFIC HEAT* shows how we can calculate the change in an object's thermal energy in terms of the change in its temperature.

C10.8 *KEEPING TRACK OF INTERNAL ENERGIES* illustrates how we can modify the problem-solving framework to more easily solve conservation of energy problems involving internal energy.

C10.2 THE CASE OF THE DISAPPEARING ENERGY

Many natural processes seem to destroy energy

Newton himself recognized that *momentum* was conserved when he proposed his theory of mechanics in 1686. However, it took a century and a half longer for the physics community to realize that *energy* was also conserved. Why did this take so long? The main problem was that many everyday physical processes involving macroscopic objects *seem* to destroy (or occasionally create) energy.

Processes involving *friction* provide a vivid illustration of this problem. Consider a book sliding along a flat, horizontal tabletop. Under normal circumstances, the contact interaction between the book and the table has a frictional aspect that (in a given time interval dt) delivers to the book a momentum transfer $d\vec{p}$ opposite to its direction of motion. Since the angle between the book's velocity $\vec{v}$ and the momentum transfer $d\vec{p}$ is $180° = \pi$, $dK = \vec{v} \cdot d\vec{p}$ is negative, meaning that this part of the interaction drains the book's kinetic energy. This energy is presumably transformed to some other kind of energy, but what?

There is no potential energy function for friction

Might it go to some form of frictional potential energy? An interaction's potential energy, by definition, depends only on the separation of the interacting objects. In this case, the book is interacting with the table, and the separation between the book and table does not change during the interaction. So, whatever potential energy the book/table system has must remain constant in this process. Moreover, the amount of energy transformed by friction as the book slides a given distance depends on variables like the book's speed: an interaction's potential energy should depend *only* on separation, not on variables like the speed. The bottom line is that *we cannot describe the frictional part of a contact interaction using a potential energy function.*

So if friction does not transform the book's kinetic energy to potential energy, to what form of energy *is* the kinetic energy transformed? Superficially, the energy seems to disappear!

Elastic and inelastic collisions

There are other contact interactions that seem to make kinetic energy disappear. If we drop a book on the floor, gravitational potential energy is converted to kinetic energy as the book falls, but when the book hits the floor, that energy seems to vanish. Similarly, when you catch a baseball or hammer a nail or collide with a wall, kinetic energy seems to disappear. We call an impact process (like the ones just described) that transforms kinetic energy to something else an **inelastic** impact process.

Processes that involve either friction or inelastic collisions therefore *superficially* seem to destroy energy. This was the problem that kept physicists from realizing that energy really *was* conserved in spite of what these processes *look* like. The insights needed to move past this barrier came from scientists working in an area of physics that seemed at first to be completely unrelated.

C10.3 CALORIC IS ENERGY

Powerful as Newton's theory of mechanics was, it did not seem to have anything to say about physical processes involving heat and temperature change. Physicists studying such problems of **thermal physics** therefore had to create their own models to explain the nature of heat and temperature.

The caloric model

Prior to the 1840s, the accepted model of thermal physics (proposed by Joseph Black in 1770) was that hot objects contained an abundance of a fluid called **caloric**. In this model, an object feels hot because of the caloric it holds in much the same way as a sponge feels wet because of the water it holds. When we bring hot and cold objects in contact, caloric flows from the hot one to the cold one just as water flows from a wet sponge into a dry sponge. (Caloric was imagined to be made up of particles that repelled each other: this explained why the caloric in a hot object would spontaneously flow into the cold object.)

The calorie

Caloric was measured in **calories**, where 1 calorie was defined to be the amount of caloric required to increase the temperature of 1 g of water by 1°C. Just as squeezing two equally damp sponges yields twice as much water as

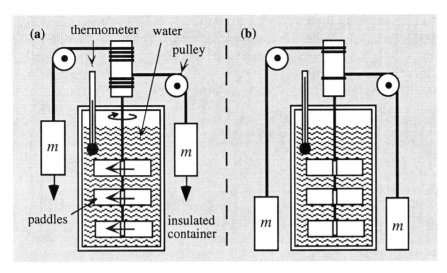

Figure C10.1: A simplified diagram of the apparatus used by James Joule to demonstrate that adding mechanical energy to water was equivalent to adding caloric. Joule was able to use this apparatus to show that there was a fixed relationship between caloric and mechanical energy.

squeezing either sponge separately, if the temperature of 2 g of water changes by 1°C, the water releases or absorbs 2 calories of caloric. Moreover, experiments showed that increasing the temperature of a substance by 2°C required almost exactly twice as much caloric as increasing by 1°C. So the caloric absorbed or released by an amount of water with mass M undergoing a given (relatively small) temperature change ΔT is given by the equation:

$$\text{caloric absorbed/released} = cM \,\Delta T, \text{ where } c = 1.00 \text{ cal} \cdot \text{g}^{-1} \cdot (\text{C}°)^{-1} \qquad \text{(C10.1)}$$

In general, this equation was found to apply to almost any kind of substance undergoing a (relatively small) change in temperature as long as the value of c quoted above was replaced with a value appropriate to the substance in question.

The caloric model is intuitive, vivid, and works very well in most common circumstances. Starting in the late 1700s, though, physicists began to uncover significant weaknesses. The first steps toward a new theory were taken by the American-born physicist Benjamin Thompson. Thompson emigrated to Europe during the Revolutionary War (because of his loyalist sympathies), and later became director of the Bavarian Arsenal (and was given the title Count Rumford for his services). While supervising the boring of cannons, Thompson began to wonder about why the drilling bit became so hot. So much caloric seemed to be released that water used to cool the bit boiled away and had to be continuously replaced. The model of this process at the time was that grinding up the metal released the caloric inside it. On the basis of his experience, however, Thompson determined that there seemed to be no limit to the caloric that could be released from a finite amount of iron. This seemed absurd, so Thompson proposed that caloric is not really a substance at all but rather a form of motion created by the motion of the tool. Thompson later showed that the caloric generated by such a tool is approximately proportional to the mechanical energy supplied to the tool.

By the 1830s, a number of physicists were thinking about this general problem. In 1843, the British physicist James Prescott Joule provided a crucial piece of evidence by demonstrating experimentally that the effects of adding caloric to an object could be both qualitatively and quantitatively duplicated by transferring mechanical energy to the object (using friction as the agent of energy transfer). The apparatus Joule used is schematically illustrated in Figure C10.1. In this experiment, water in a thermally insulated container is stirred by a paddlewheel driven by falling weights. The gravitational potential energy released as the weights move downward has got to go somewhere: Joule reasoned that the energy had to be absorbed by the water. What he showed was that adding energy this way caused the *same* kind of temperature increase that adding caloric would.

In order to appreciate the full significance of Joule's work, we need to remember that the calorie and the joule are *independently* defined. The calorie is

The demise of the caloric model of thermal physics

an amount of caloric defined in terms of the temperature increase observed when the caloric is transferred to a known amount of water. The joule, on the other hand, is a unit of *energy* that is defined in terms of purely mechanical variables: $1 \text{ J} = 1 \text{ kg} \cdot \text{m}^2/\text{s}^2$. There is no obvious reason why there should be *any* connection between these two quantities. Yet Joule showed that

$$1 \text{ calorie } = 4.186 \text{ J} \qquad\qquad (C10.2)$$

consistently in a wide variety of circumstances: that is, putting a given amount of mechanical energy (4.186 J in modern units) into an object always had exactly the same effect on its temperature as putting 1 calorie of caloric into it. Joule also linked the calorie to units of chemical and electrical forms of energy.

Conservation of energy

By the end of the 1840s, the physics community understood that Joule's results (supplemented and supported by the work of other physicists) meant that the caloric model was incorrect: what had been called caloric was in fact a previously unknown form of *energy*, and that the energy of an isolated system was *conserved*. It is hard to say who first thought of this idea in its full generality: various physicists at various times expressed working versions of the idea in very different terms. Unlike some "discoveries" in physics, this extremely important and powerful idea (one of the greatest intellectual triumphs of the 19th century!) seems to have occurred gradually to a number of people at roughly the same time. In any case, by the end of the decade, the caloric model was dead and the principle of conservation of energy had become firmly established.

Exercise C10X.1: Performing the experiment shown in Figure C10.1 is not easy. Assume that the two weights have masses of 2.0 kg each and are able to drop a distance of 0.5 m. If there are 4 kg of water in the container (about 1 gallon) what would be its approximate change in temperature?

C10.4 THERMAL ENERGY

The contemporary model of internal energy storage

In the middle of the 19th century, it was still unclear *how* an object could absorb and hold energy and what this had to do with temperature. Since the early 1900s, though, physicists have understood that (1) all objects are constructed of a huge number of tiny molecules, (2) these molecules are in ceaseless random motion, and (3) an object's **temperature** is a measure of the violence of this motion. We will discuss the definition of *temperature* more fully in Unit T, but for gases and simple solids under everyday conditions, the temperature T of a substance (measured in the SI unit of **kelvins**) turns out to be directly proportional to the average *kinetic* energy per molecule of its molecules' random motions in the substance (treating the molecule like a point particle)

$$K_{avg} \text{ (per molecule) } = \tfrac{3}{2} k_B T \qquad\qquad (C10.3)$$

where $k_B = 1.38 \times 10^{-23}$ J/K is called **Boltzmann's constant**.

The absolute temperature scale and absolute zero

This kind of simple statement is possible only if temperature is defined in such a way that an object whose molecules are all at rest has a temperature of *zero*. Since a substance's molecules cannot have negative kinetic energy, this is the lowest possible temperature an object can have: we therefore call this temperature **absolute zero**. The Kelvin temperature scale is defined so that 0 K corresponds to absolute zero and so that a *difference* in temperature of 1 K is the same as a difference in temperature of 1°C (= 0.01 times the temperature difference between freezing and boiling water). With these definitions, the temperature of freezing water (0°C) turns out to be 273.15 K, and other Celsius temperatures can be converted to kelvins by adding 273.15 K. (Note that while we read 0°C as "zero degrees Celsius," you should read 273.15 K as "273.15 kelvins." You should *not* say "degrees kelvin" or write K with a degrees symbol. The SI unit of kelvins is treated exactly like any other unit in the SI system.)

If there are N molecules in an object, equation C10.3 would *seem* to imply that an object's total **thermal energy** due to these microscopic motions is

$$\text{thermal energy} = \tfrac{3}{2} N k_B T \quad (???) \tag{C10.4}$$

However, an object's thermal energy includes not only the kinetic energy associated with the random translational motion of its molecules but also any energy associated with the rotation or vibration of atoms within molecules, the potential energy of (ordinarily fairly weak) interactions between molecules and so on. Even so (as the name suggests), an object's total thermal energy depends on (and is indirectly indicated by) its temperature.

Now, the total thermal energy that gets stored in the potential energy of intermolecular interactions and the rotation and vibration of molecules can depend in very complicated ways on the average motion of the molecules (and thus the temperature) of a substance. Therefore, while equation C10.3 applies quite generally to many substances, equation C10.4 applies only to rarefied monatomic gases (like helium), whose molecules are single atoms (which cannot vibrate or rotate) and are spaced so far apart that any interactions between them are negligibly weak. In more general situations, one can only say that the average thermal energy per molecule in a given substance is (virtually always) a monotonically increasing (but maybe quite complicated) function of its temperature T. This energy is usually in the range $k_B T < \text{thermal energy} / \text{molecule} < 10\,k_B T$.

Exercise C10X.2: A cubic foot of helium gas at atmospheric pressure and room temperature ($22°C = 295$ K) contains roughly 7.5×10^{23} molecules. Estimate the total thermal energy contained in this cubic foot of gas. How fast would *you* have to be traveling to have this much *kinetic* energy?

C10.5 FRICTION AND THERMAL ENERGY

Now we are in a position to understand how friction transforms kinetic energy to thermal energy. Consider again the book sliding on the table. When two surfaces are in contact and one moves past the other, their molecules often become momentarily entangled (see Figure C10.2). As the book's moving surface continues to push ahead, the entangled molecules are stretched away from their normal positions. Their interaction transforms a tiny bit of the book's kinetic energy to potential energy in the bonds between molecules (represented by springs here). At a certain point, the molecules suddenly become unstuck and snap back toward their initial positions, where they oscillate wildly.

This energy of the wildly oscillating surface molecules is eventually transmitted to the rest of the molecules in the solid through the interactions between molecules. The net effect is that the macroscopic kinetic energy of the book is converted to energy associated with molecular vibrations. From a microscopic point of view, this energy is simply ordinary kinetic and potential energy. Even so, we cannot see these vibrations with our eyes: the only sign at the macroscopic level that this has happened is that the temperature of the surface increases. *The interaction has thus transferred kinetic energy to thermal energy.*

Figure C10.2: A schematic illustration of a book's molecules sliding past atoms on a table. In **(a)**, two molecules become entangled. In **(b)**, these molecules are pulled and twisted out of position by the motion of the book. In **(c)**, the molecules snap back and oscillate wildly. (This scenario has been greatly simplified.)

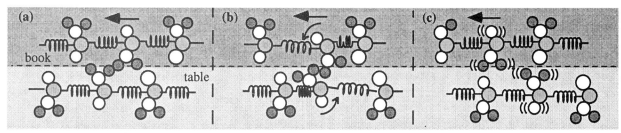

Collisions also transform kinetic to thermal energy

Similarly, when an object collides with another object, the complicated interaction between the surface molecules that touch tends to set them oscillating wildly at the expense of the kinetic energy of the colliding objects. This doesn't *always* happen; if a substance is especially *elastic*, then molecules that are pushed out of position by the collision simply return to their normal positions during the rebound without much random oscillation. Most collisions, however, transfer at least *some* of the objects' kinetic energy to thermal energy.

This model thus resolves the mystery of the disappearing energy: the kinetic energy apparently lost in friction and collision interactions actually is transformed to *thermal energy*. Understanding this, as Joule and his contemporaries first saw, makes conservation of energy credible as a universal law of physics.

We can quantify the energy transformed to thermal energy using methods discussed in previous chapters. Linking thermal energy changes to temperature changes will be our focus in the next few sections.

Exercise C10X.3: A 3.0-kg book experiences a constant 20-N rearward friction force as it slides along a tabletop. If it comes to rest after sliding 2 m, how much energy has the frictional part of the book's contact interaction converted to thermal energy in the book and tabletop? (*Hint:* Use equation C8.17.)

C10.6 HEAT AND WORK

Keeping track of *U* by watching the boundaries

In many practical situations, we have no way of knowing how much thermal energy an object contains at a given temperature. However, since an object's thermal energy resides entirely *inside* it, we can determine how that thermal energy *changes* by keeping careful track of the amount of energy that crosses the object's boundaries. The total amount of the thermal energy in an object is usually irrelevant to understanding and predicting its thermal behavior.

Let me give you an analogy. You don't need to know how much oil is in your car's engine to keep it running. You can keep track of the oil level using the dipstick. If the oil is low, you put in enough to get you back to the correct level. If you see a greasy spot under the car, then you know that there will be less oil in the engine. If no such spot appears but the oil level goes down anyway, then you can guess that your engine is burning oil. My point is that you can tell a lot about how the total amount of oil in your engine changes without knowing that amount, and it is these *changes* that are important in practice.

Similarly, in thermodynamics we are often interested less in the total amount of thermal energy in an object than in how that energy changes under certain conditions. Knowing how that energy changes involves watching the amount of energy that crosses the objects' boundaries. The crucial thermodynamic concepts *heat* and *work* therefore are both defined to describe *energy transfer across a system boundary.*

Definition of *heat*

When a hot object is placed in contact with a cold object, energy spontaneously flows across the boundary between them (for reasons we will discuss in Unit *T*) until both objects come to have the same temperature. As a result, the thermal energy of the hot object decreases and the thermal energy of the cold object increases. In physics, **heat** is any energy that crosses the boundary between the two objects *because* of the temperature difference between them. Let me emphasize that to be *heat*, the energy in question *must*

1.   be flowing across some kind of boundary between systems, AND
2.   do so as a direct result of a temperature difference across that boundary.

Definition of *work*

We define **work** to be any *other* kind of energy flowing across the boundary of a system. For example, if I stir a cup of water vigorously and it gets warm as a result, I have not "heated" the water, I have done *work* on it; in other words, the mechanical energy that flows across the boundary of the water flows not because of a temperature difference but because of my stirring effort.

Note that both *heat* and *work* refer to energy in transit across a boundary. This sharply distinguishes both from **internal energy**, which refers to energy *inside* the system boundary. Both heat and work flows can contribute to changes in the thermal energy. In fact, conservation of energy implies that

$$\Delta U = Q + W \qquad (C10.5)$$

where ΔU is the change in a system's internal energy in a given process, Q is the heat energy added in the process, and W is the work energy that has flowed into the system in the process. In words, this equation says that the change in a system's internal energy in a given process is equal to the sum of the heat and work energy that flows into it during the process. Note that Q and W are considered negative if energy flows *out* of the system: see Figure C10.3.

Thermal energy U^{th} is *one form* of internal energy: it is the part that changes when the system's temperature changes (and the only form we will consider in this chapter). The superscript "th" in U^{th} is not an exponent: it just distinguishes thermal energy from internal energy U in general.

The definitions here make it clear that *heat is not the same as thermal energy* in physics. A hot object does *not* contain heat, it contains internal energy. Heat is always energy in transit across a system boundary, never energy inside the boundary. Keeping these terms straight is essential in order to avoid confusion when studying thermal physics. Unfortunately, the word "heat" is used in colloquial English (and even in some science books) in ways incompatible with its meaning in physics. Be careful to avoid using language (like "friction converts energy to heat in the object") that confuses heat with internal energy.

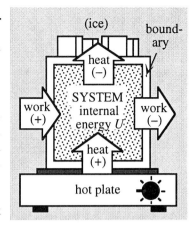

Figure C10.3: An illustration of the definitions of heat and work.

Heat is not the same as thermal energy

Exercise C10X.4: In each process described below, energy flows from object A to object B. Is the energy flow involved heat or work? 　　　heat or work?
a. The water (B) in a pan sitting on an electric stove (A) gets hot. 　____
b. The brake shoes (B) of your car (A) get hot when they are used. 　____
c. Electricity flowing from a battery (A) makes a wire (B) warm. 　____
d. A cup of water (B) in a microwave oven (A) gets hot. 　____
e. Your ice cream (B) melts on a warm summer day (A). 　____

C10.7 SPECIFIC HEAT*

In section C10.4, we discussed how the average thermal energy per molecule in a given substance $U^{th}_{mol} \equiv U^{th}/N$ (where N is the number of molecules) was generally some complicated function $U^{th}_{mol}(T)$ of temperature T. Figure C10.4 illustrates what a graph of $U^{th}_{mol}(T)$ might look like for a hypothetical substance. This graph makes it clear that while temperature and thermal energy are clearly related, they are *not* equivalent. Temperature is to thermal energy roughly what the *depth* of water in a jar is to the *volume* of water in the jar. Just as the shape of a jar influences how the volume of water it holds is related to its depth, so the microscopic physics of a substance influences how the thermal energy in a sample of that substance is related to its temperature. Also, just as two jars may have the same water depth and yet hold different amounts of water, so two objects may have the same temperature and yet contain different amounts of thermal energy. Temperature *indicates*, but is not *equivalent to,* thermal energy.

Even though the average thermal energy per molecule $U^{th}_{mol}(T)$ may be a complicated function of temperature T, over sufficiently small ranges of temperature, U^{th}_{mol} often increases fairly linearly with temperature (this is also illustrated in Figure C10.4), meaning that

$$dU^{th}_{mol} \propto dT \quad \Rightarrow \quad \frac{dU^{th}_{mol}}{dT} = \text{some constant} \quad \text{(for small } dT) \qquad (C10.6)$$

*The point of this asterix is explained at the end of the section.

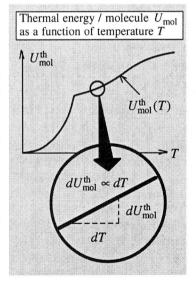

Figure C10.4: When viewed on the large scale, the average thermal energy per molecule in a substance may be a complicated function of temperature, but over a sufficiently small range, it will look linear (except possibly near a temperature where the substance's phase changes).

where the constant of proportionality between dU_{mol}^{th} and dT depends on the type of substance and on the approximate temperature. Thus, for a small temperature change dT, we can write the change in the thermal energy of a block of mass m of a substance made up of N molecules each having mass m_{mol} as follows:

The defining equation for *specific heat*

$$dU^{th} = N dU_{mol}^{th} = \left(\frac{m}{m_{mol}}\right) dU_{mol}^{th} = m\left(\frac{1}{m_{mol}} \frac{dU_{mol}^{th}}{dT}\right) dT = mc\, dT \quad (C10.7)$$

(assuming that there are no chemical or nuclear changes in the substance). We call $c \equiv (dU_{mol}^{th}/dT)/m_{mol} = (dU^{th}/dT)/m$ the substance's **specific heat.*** The value of c can be significantly different for different substances and even for different **phases** (that is, solid, liquid, or gas) of the same substance. The specific heat may also depend weakly on its temperature and the surrounding pressure. Specific heats* for various substances are listed in Table C10.1.

Table C10.1: Specific heats* of some common substances (evaluated at ≈ 20°C)	
Substance	Specific Heat* (in $J \cdot kg^{-1} \cdot K^{-1}$)
Water	4186
Alcohol	2400
Ice (−5°C)	2100
Wood	≈1700
Aluminum	900
Granite	790
Air	≈ 740
Iron	450
Copper	387
Silver	234
Gold	129
Lead	128

The specific heat* of water provides a concrete example of how c depends on temperature and phase. Precise measurements (using very small values of dT) indicate that the specific heat* of liquid water at normal atmospheric pressure ranges from a high of about 4217 $J \cdot kg^{-1} \cdot K^{-1}$ near the freezing and boiling points to a low of about 4178 $J \cdot kg^{-1} \cdot K^{-1}$ at about 34°C (a total variation of less than 1%). The value of c for liquid water is usually quoted as 4186 $J \cdot kg^{-1} \cdot K^{-1}$ (its value at about 15°C and 65°C). The actual value of c for water is within about 0.2% of 4186 $J \cdot kg^{-1} \cdot K^{-1}$ unless the water is within a few degrees of the freezing and boiling points, so c depends only *very* weakly on temperature over the entire range from about 3°C to 97°C. The specific heat* of *ice*, on the other hand, is about 2100 $J \cdot kg^{-1} \cdot K^{-1}$, less than half that of water only a few degrees warmer. This illustrates that a substance's phase can make a big difference.

Equation C10.7 is therefore accurate as long as dT is sufficiently small that c is almost constant over the range in temperatures involved ("sufficiently small" in this context can be tens and even hundreds of degrees for some substances). Note also that since a kelvin is defined to be the same size as a degree on the Celsius scale, temperature *differences* in kelvins have the same numerical value as temperature differences in °C.

The meaning of the asterisk in *specific heat*

You are probably wondering why I attach an asterisk to the end of "specific heat" whenever I refer to it. This is to draw our attention to a conceptual problem with this conventional technical term. *Specific* is fine: it is often used in physics and chemistry to mean a quantity defined in such a way that it depends on the specific *type* but not the *amount* of substance we are studying. However, *heat* is misleading: c actually expresses the change in *thermal energy* per unit mass per unit temperature, not the "change in *heat*" (whatever that might mean). You *could* cause an object's thermal energy to change by adding heat but you could add energy in other ways as well. An object's specific heat* therefore has essentially nothing to do with *heat*. Think of the asterisk as referring to an automatic (but unwritten) footnote: "What we really mean is specific thermal energy change per unit change in temperature." (The term became conventional in the 19th century before *heat* and *thermal energy* had become firmly distinguished.)

EXAMPLE   C10.1

Problem: How much thermal energy do we have to add to the water in a 10-gallon aquarium to raise its temperature by 2°C? (10 gallons ≈ 38 kg of water.)

Solution: A temperature difference of 2°C is the same as 2 K. The specific heat* of water is going to be almost exactly constant (≈ 4186 $J \cdot kg^{-1} \cdot K^{-1}$) over this small a temperature range, so it should be fine to use equation C10.7:

$$dU^{th} = mc\, dT = (38\ \cancel{kg})(4186\ J \cdot \cancel{kg}^{-1} \cdot \cancel{K}^{-1})(2\ \cancel{K}) \approx 320{,}000\ J \quad (C10.8)$$

This is a lot of energy! To increase the tank's *kinetic* energy by this amount, we'd have to increase its speed from zero to about 130 m/s (290 mi/h)!

Exercise C10X.5: How much thermal energy has to be removed from a glass of milk ($\approx$ water) to cool it from room temperature ($\approx 20°C$) to refrigerator temperature ($\approx 5°C$)? (*Hint:* 1 cup $\approx$ 0.25 liter $\approx$ 250 cm^3 $\approx$ 250 g of water.)

C10.8 KEEPING TRACK OF INTERNAL ENERGIES

Consider an isolated system involving various extended objects that interact with each other. The total energy E of such a system involves not only the kinetic energies of all objects in the system and the potential energies of their interactions but their *thermal* energies as well. Imagine that this system evolves from some initial state to some final state. Conservation of energy implies that the system's total energy in its initial state is the same as that in its final state:

$$K_i + V_i + U_i \;=\; K_f + V_f + U_f \qquad\qquad (C10.9)$$

where i and f mean *initial* and *final* respectively, and each term on a given side is meant to represent the total amount of that type of energy in the system. The only problem with this is that while we can usually calculate well-defined values for K and V in the initial and final states, U is generally a very complicated function of temperature, so we rarely have a simple formula that we can use to calculate its initial and final values. The same problem arises when we consider other forms of internal energy in the next chapter.

How can we handle this problem? If we subtract the right side of equation C10.9 from the left side, we can express conservation of energy as follows:

$$0 \;=\; (K_f - K_i) + (V_f - V_i) + (U_f - U_i) \;=\; \Delta K + \Delta V + \Delta U \qquad (C10.10)$$

This version of the conservation-of-energy equation is completely equivalent to the original version given by equation C10.9; instead of stating that the initial total energy is equal to the final total energy, though, this version simply states that there is no *change* in the system's total energy during a process.

This version is more useful than equation C10.9 when internal energies are involved, because it never asks for the actual values of U_i and U_f: we only need to supply the *change* in internal energy $\Delta U = U_f - U_i$. We can usually measure and calculate ΔU much more easily than U.

The trick in applying equation C10.10 is that we must be very careful with the *signs* of the quantities ΔK, ΔV, and ΔU. Remember that the change in each quantity is *its final value minus its initial value*. This means that the change in a given energy category is *positive* if the process in question *increases* the energy in that category. Keep both of these things in mind as you use equation C10.10.

We need make only two small adjustments to the problem-solving framework discussed in chapter C9. In the *Conceptual Representation section*, we must examine each interaction between objects in our system and decide whether we can handle it by (1) keeping track of its potential energy, (2) ignoring it, or (3) keeping track of rotational energies *or internal energies* (the last is the new part). In the *Math Representation* part, we use equation C10.10 instead of equation C6.16 (taking lots of care with the signs!) when internal energies are involved. Examples C10.2 and C10.3 illustrate the application of this adjusted framework in situations involving thermal energy.

Note, by the way, that if $U_i = U_f$ (that is, the internal energy does *not* change in a given process), then U_i and U_f cancel out of equation C10.9, meaning that we can ignore the internal energy altogether. This justifies what we have done in previous chapters, where we have applied conservation of energy without including any internal energy: as long as it doesn't *change*, we can ignore it.

Applying conservation of energy when thermal energies are involved

A new version of the conservation of energy equation

Some useful adjustments to the problem-solving framework when internal energies are involved

EXAMPLE C10.2

OUTLINE OF THE FRAMEWORK

1. Pictorial Representation

  a. Draw a picture of the situation that includes:

    ① (1) sketches of the system in its initial and final states

    ② (2) reference frame axes

    ③ (3) labels defining symbols for relevant quantities (in this case, objects' masses, velocities, and separations)

  b. List values for all known quantities and specify which quantities are unknown. ④

2. Conceptual Representation

The general task is to construct a conceptual model of the situation and link it to an abstract physics model or principle. In conservation-of-energy problems, we do the following:

  ⑤ a. Identify the *system* involved. (If it involves the earth, we can ignore the earth's kinetic energy)

  ⑥ b. Determine whether it is *approximately* isolated, *functionally* isolated, or involved in a *collision* (as defined in chapter C5). Support your conclusions briefly.

  ⑦ c. Identify the interactions between objects in the system and for each interaction, determine whether we can handle it by

    (1) keeping track of its potential energy (if so, define the reference separation)

    (2) ignoring it (because it is very weak or for another reason) ⑧

    (3) keeping track of rotational or internal energies

  d. Do we have to make any approximations or assumptions to solve the problem? (If so, describe.) ⑧

3. Mathematical Representation

  ⑨ a. Apply the mathematical equation that appropriately describes the situation (equation C10.10 here)

  ⑩ b. Solve for unknowns symbolically

  ⑪ c. Plug in numbers and units and calculate the result and its units.

4. Evaluation

Check that the answer makes sense:
  ⑫ a. Does it have the correct units?
  ⑬ b. Does it have the right sign?
  ⑭ c. Does it seem reasonable?

Problem: Imagine that we drop a bag of lead shot (small lead spheres) from rest at the top of a 10-story building. When the bag of shot hits the ground, almost all of its kinetic energy of motion will go to banging the lead spheres against each other inside the bag, and thus eventually to thermal energy in the lead (very little thermal energy will be deposited on the ground. If this model is accurate, about how much warmer should the lead shot be after it hits the ground?

Solution: We will define our reference frame so that its z axis is vertical and take $z = 0$ to be at the ground. Since a story on a building is roughly 3 m (10 ft) tall, the building's height is about 30 m. So our initial and final situations look something like this:

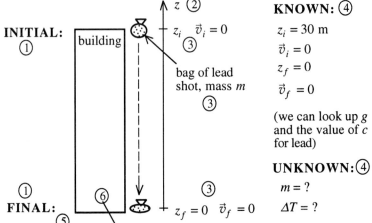

KNOWN: ④

$z_i = 30$ m
$\vec{v}_i = 0$
$z_f = 0$
$\vec{v}_f = 0$

(we can look up g and the value of c for lead)

UNKNOWN: ④

$m = ?$
$\Delta T = ?$

The system here is the bag interacting with the earth, so we will take the system to be approximately isolated. The bag interacts with the earth (1) gravitationally during its fall and (2) via a contact interaction when it hits the ground. We can describe the gravitational interaction here using the potential energy formula $V(z) = mgz$ (defining $z = 0$ to be the reference separation). We cannot ignore the contact interaction, because it clearly has an effect on the bag's kinetic energy, so we will handle it by keeping track of internal energies (thermal energies) here. We will assume (as postulated in the problem statement) that all of the energy transferred by the contact interaction goes from the bag's kinetic energy to its thermal energy, with none going to the ground. We will also ignore interactions with the air. The difference form of the law of conservation of energy (equation C10.10) then tells us that

$$0 = \Delta K + \Delta V + \Delta U^{\text{th}} \quad ⑨$$

where ΔK is the change in the bag's kinetic energy (we are ignoring the earth's kinetic energy). Since the bag is at rest initially and finally, $\Delta K = 0$ in this case. $\Delta V \equiv V(z_f) - V(z_i) = mgz_f - mgz_i = -mgz_i$, since $z_f = 0$. We also know that $\Delta U^{\text{th}} = mc\,\Delta T$ (where c is the specific heat* of lead) as long as ΔT is "sufficiently small" so that the value of $c \approx$ constant. Plugging all this into the equation above, we get:

$$0 = 0 - mgz_i + mc\,\Delta T \implies \Delta T = \frac{\cancel{m}gz_i}{\cancel{m}c} = \frac{gz_i}{c} \quad ⑩$$

(Note that the unknown mass of the shot cancels: this is good!) So:

$$\Delta T = \frac{(9.80 \text{ m/s}^2)(30 \text{ m})}{128 \text{ J} \cdot \text{kg}^{-1} \cdot \text{K}^{-1}}\left(\frac{1 \text{ J}}{1 \text{ kg} \cdot \text{m}^2/\text{s}^2}\right) = 2.3 \text{ K} \quad ⑪$$

⑬ ΔT is positive (the lead gets warmer) as we would expect, and it has the ⑫ right units. Its magnitude is plausible. ⑭

EXAMPLE C10.3

OUTLINE OF THE FRAMEWORK

1. Pictorial Representation

   a. Draw a picture of the situation that includes:

     ① (1) sketches of the system in its initial and final states

     ② (2) reference frame axes

        (3) labels defining symbols for relevant quantities (in this case, objects' masses, specific heats*, temperatures)
     ③

   b. List values for all known quantities and specify which quantities are unknown.
     ④

2. Conceptual Representation

The general task is to construct a conceptual model of the situation and link it to an abstract physics model or principle. In conservation-of-energy problems, we do the following:

   ⑤ a. Identify the *system* involved. (If it involves the earth, we can ignore the earth's kinetic energy)

   ⑥ b. Determine whether it is *approximately* isolated, *functionally* isolated, or involved in a *collision* (as defined in chapter C5). Support your conclusions briefly.

   ⑦ c. Identify the interactions between objects in the system and for each interaction, determine whether we can handle it by

     (1) keeping track of its potential energy (if so, define the reference separation)

     (2) ignoring it (because it is very weak or for another reason)

     (3) keeping track of rotational or internal energies

   d. Do we have to make any approximations or assumptions to solve the problem? (If so, describe.)
   ⑧

3. Mathematical Representation

   ⑨ a. Apply the mathematical equation that appropriately describes the situation (equation C10.10 here)

   ⑩ b. Solve for unknowns symbolically

   ⑪ c. Plug in numbers and units and calculate the result and its units.

4. Evaluation

   Check that the answer makes sense:
   ⑫ a. Does it have the correct units?
   ⑬ b. Does it have the right sign?
   ⑭ c. Does it seem reasonable?

Problem: Imagine that we place a 50-g block of aluminum with an initial temperature of 100°C into an insulating styrofoam cup containing 250 g of water at 22°C. Heat will flow from the aluminum to the water until both are at the same temperature. What is that temperature?

Solution: Setting up a reference frame is irrelevant here, ② since the objects involved do not change position or have velocities. The initial and final situations thus look like this:

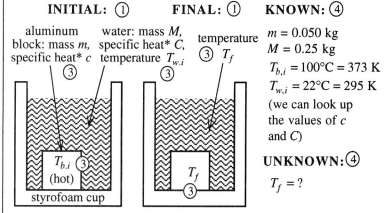

INITIAL: ①   **FINAL:** ①   **KNOWN:** ④

aluminum block: mass m, specific heat* c ③

water: mass M, specific heat* C, temperature $T_{w,i}$ ③

temperature ③ T_f

$m = 0.050$ kg
$M = 0.25$ kg
$T_{b,i} = 100°C = 373$ K
$T_{w,i} = 22°C = 295$ K
(we can look up the values of c and C)

$T_{b,i}$ ③ (hot)

T_f ③

styrofoam cup

UNKNOWN: ④
$T_f = ?$

The system here is the block and the water. Since the objects do not move, $dK = \vec{v} \cdot d\vec{p} = 0$, which means that neither the objects' contact interaction with the cup nor their gravitational interaction with the earth transfer any macroscopic potential energy to kinetic energy, making the system *functionally* isolated with regard to these external interactions. The styrofoam cup is also described as being "insulating", which (we assume) means it isolates the system with regard to external transfers of heat. (We will ignore heat exchanges with the air.) The only significant internal interaction involved in this system is the contact interaction between the block and the water, which allows them to exchange energy at the microscopic level. We will handle this by keeping track of internal energies. Conservation of energy then implies that

$$0 = \Delta K_b + \Delta K_w + \Delta V + \Delta U_b^{th} + \Delta U_w^{th} \quad ⑨$$

where the "b" and "w" subscripts refer to the block and water, respectively. Since the block and water remain at rest and do not change position, $\Delta K_b = \Delta K_w - \Delta V = 0$ here. If the temperature changes are small enough so that the specific heats* c and C are essentially constant, then $\Delta U_b^{th} = mc\,\Delta T_b = mc(T_f - T_{b,i})$ and $\Delta U_w^{th} = MC\,\Delta T_w = MC(T_f - T_{w,i})$. So the equation above becomes

$$0 = 0 + 0 + 0 + mc(T_f - T_{b,i}) + MC(T_f - T_{w,i})$$
$$\Rightarrow mcT_{b,i} + MCT_{w,i} = (mc + MC)T_f$$
$$\Rightarrow T_f = \frac{mcT_{b,i} + MCT_{w,i}}{mc + MC} \quad ⑩$$

In this case, we have $mc = (0.050 \text{ kg})(900 \text{ J·kg}^{-1}\text{·K}^{-1}) = 45$ J/K and $MC = (0.25 \text{ kg})(4186 \text{ J·kg}^{-1}\text{·K}^{-1}) = 1050$ J/K, so

$$T_f = \frac{(45 \text{ J/K})(373 \text{ K}) + (1050 \text{ J/K})(295 \text{ K})}{45 \text{ J/K} + 1050 \text{ J/K}} = 298 \text{ K } (= 25°C) \quad ⑪$$
$$③$$

This final temperature is positive (necessary for an absolute temperature!) and has the right units of kelvins. ⑫ It is also between the initial temperatures of the block and water, which seems right. ⑭

SUMMARY

I. DISAPPEARING ENERGY

A. Some interactions seem to destroy energy. Examples: (1) the frictional part of a contact interactions (2) inelastic collisions

B. We cannot define sensible potential energies for such interactions

C. The key to resolving this puzzle comes from thermal physics

II. CALORIC IS REALLY ENERGY

A. The caloric model for thermal physics:

    1. Caloric is a fluid composed of particles that repel each other

    2. Hot objects contain lots of caloric, cold objects contain less

    3. Caloric spontaneously flows from hot to cold like water from a wet sponge flows to a dry one.

B. 1 calorie $\equiv$ the caloric that raises the temperature of 1 g of water by 1°C

C. The demise of the caloric theory and the rise of conservation of energy

    1. Thompson finds that hole-drilling can release infinite caloric (!?)

    2. Joule shows that adding 4.186 J of energy consistently has the same effect as adding 1 calorie of heat (implying that caloric = energy)

    3. Many others also contribute to the energy model in the 1840s

III. THERMAL ENERGY

A. The contemporary model of thermal energy

    1. All objects are built of molecules in ceaseless motion

    2. An object's temperature $\propto$ its molecule's average kinetic energy

    3. This implies that temperature has an absolute zero where $K_{avg} = 0$

    4. The kelvin temperature scale is defined as follows

        a) $T \equiv 0$ at absolute zero

        b) 1 kelvin of temperature change = 1 K $\equiv$ 1°C of change

B. Thermal energy U^{th} in addition to molecular kinetic energy includes:

    1. molecular rotational and vibrational energy

    2. possibly the potential energy between molecules

    3. other forms of energy that are linked to molecular motion

C. This complexity means that U^{th} can be a complicated function of T

D. Friction and inelastic collisions can convert kinetic energy to thermal energy: complex interactions between molecules on the surfaces in contact convert an object's bulk motion to microscopic random motions

IV. HEAT AND WORK

A. Thermal energy U^{th} is a special case of internal energy U

B. Internal energy in general is hard to calculate directly

C. But we can keep track of U by watching the object's boundaries

D. The definition of heat Q: energy that flows

    1. across the object's boundary

    2. driven by a temperature difference alone

E. The definition of work W: any *other* energy flow across that boundary

F. Conservation of energy implies that $\Delta U = Q + W$.

V. SPECIFIC HEAT*

A. Thermal energy is related to (but is not the same as) temperature

B. If dT is sufficiently small, then $dU^{th} = mc\,dT$, where m is the object's mass and c is a constant called the substance's *specific heat**

    1. Values of c are strikingly different for different substances, phases

    2. But c only depends weakly on temperature and surrounding pressure

C. The asterisk indicates this automatic footnote: "technically, the specific *change in thermal energy* per unit temperature change (instead of *heat*)."

VI. KEEPING TRACK OF INTERNAL ENERGIES

A. Let U stand for *internal energy* in general (thermal energy is one type)

B. The usual conservation of energy equation $E_i = E_f$ is hard to use when internal energies change because it is hard to calculate U_i and U_f.

C. The equivalent equation $0 = \Delta K + \Delta V + \Delta U$ is much easier to use.

GLOSSARY

inelastic (impact): an impact or interaction in which *some* kinetic energy is converted to thermal energy.

thermal physics: the study of phenomena having to do with heat and temperature.

caloric: A hypothetical fluid, self-repelling fluid that fills hot objects (according to the caloric model, which was accepted between the 1770s and the 1840s).

calorie: the amount of caloric required to raise the temperature of a gram of water by 1°C. (1 cal = 4.186 J.)

temperature T: a quantity that reflects the average kinetic energy associated with the random motion of the molecules in a substance.

absolute zero: the temperature where all random molecular motion ceases.

kelvin: the SI unit of temperature, defined so that a temperature *change* of 1 K is equal to a change of 1°C. The zero of the kelvin scale is defined to be absolute zero, which is –273.15°C. (Therefore to convert a temperature in Celsius to one in kelvins, we simply need to add 273.15 K.)

internal energy U: the energy that an object contains within its boundaries in various hidden (microscopic) forms. We will consider various types of thermal energy in this chapter and chapters C11 and C12.

thermal energy U^{th}: the part of an object's internal energy that depends on its *temperature* (as opposed to changes in its chemical or nuclear composition). It includes the kinetic and potential energies of random translational, rotational, and vibrational molecular motions.

Boltzmann's constant k_B: a constant equal in value to 1.38×10^{-23} J/K. The average molecular translational kinetic energy in a substance (if T is expressed in kelvins) is about $\frac{3}{2}k_B T$. Total thermal energies per molecule at a given temperature T typically range between $k_B T$ and $10 k_B T$.

heat: hidden energy that flows across the boundary between two objects driven by a temperature difference alone.

work: any *other* energy flowing across that boundary.

phase (of a substance): any one of a number of qualitatively different ways that a substance's molecules can be organized: solid, liquid, or gas are different possible *phases* for a typical substance.

specific heat* c: the ratio $(dU/dT)/m$, which has a fairly constant value for a substance in a given phase (c only weakly depends on temperature). Since *specific heat** doesn't talk about *heat*, the asterisk is meant to indicate an automatic (unwritten) footnote saying "actually this refers to the *specific thermal energy change* per unit temperature change."

TWO-MINUTE PROBLEMS

C10T.1 Two railroad cars collide and lock togther. What kind of impact is this?
A. elastic   B. inelastic
C. we need more information to tell for sure

C10T.2 The *root-mean-square* (rms) speed of a molecule's motion is the speed that the molecule would have if its actual kinetic energy were equal to its average kinetic energy K_{avg}. The rms speed of random motion of a nitrogen molecule in a container of air at room temperature is about 510 m/s. The mass of a hydrogen molecule is about 14 times smaller. What is *its* rms speed of random motion at the same temperature? Select the closest response.
A. 35 m/s   C. 510 m/s   E. 7,100 m/s
B. 140 m/s   D. 1,910 m/s

C10T.3 Say that the rms speed of random motion of helium gas molecules at room temperature (22°C) is v. If the temperature "doubles" (to 44°C) what is this speed now? Select the closest response. (*Hint:* why the " " marks?)
A. about the same   C. $2v$
B. $\sqrt{2}\,v$ D. $4v$

C10T.4 If you rub your hands together, they get warmer (try it!). Rubbing therefore heats your hands (T or F).

C10T.5 Is the change in the following objects' thermal energies due to a flow of heat (A) or work (B)?

(a) a hot cup of tea on a table becomes cooler with time.
(b) A meteorite entering the atmosphere glows white-hot.
(c) Liquid nitrogen poured on a slab of ice boils furiously. (Liquid nitrogen boils at 77 K.)
(d) A drill bit gets hot as it drills a hole in a metal slab.

C10T.6 The specific heat* of water is roughly constant (within 0.2%) over a range from 5°C to 95°C. Considering this, a change in temperature from 98°C to 102°C will likely be "sufficiently small" so that one can use equation $dU = mcdT$ to calculate accurately the thermal energy change of a certain amount of water (T or F).

C10T.7 Objects A and B are made of the same substance but object A is twice as massive as B. Originally, object A has a temperature of 100°C and B has a temperature of 0°C. If these objects are placed in contact they will eventually come to a common final temperature T_f. Assuming that these objects are isolated from everything else,
A. $T_f = 100$°C   C. $T_f = 50$°C   E. $T_f = 0$°C
B. $T_f > 50$°C   D. $T_f < 50$°C

C10T.8 Which do you think is larger, the energy E_A required to increase a 1000-kg car's speed from 0 to 23 m/s (about 50 mi/h) or the energy E_B required to increase the temperature of a gallon ($\approx$ 3.8 kg) of lemonade from refrigerator temperature ($\approx$ 5°C) to room temperature?
A. $E_A \gg E_B$ B. $E_B \gg E_A$ C. $E_A \approx E_B$

HOMEWORK PROBLEMS

BASIC SKILLS

C10B.1 You can convert temperatures from °F to kelvins by adding 460°F and then multiplying by 5 K/9°F. Human body temperature is about 98°F. What is this in kelvins?

C10B.2 You can convert temperatures from kelvins to °F by multiplying by 9°F/5 K and then subtracting 460°F. Show using this that the freezing water (whose temperature is 273.15 K) has a temperature of 32°F. Also verify that the boiling point of water is 212°F.

C10B.3 You can convert temperatures from °F to °C by subtracting 32°F and multiplying by 5°C/9°F. To convert from °C to °F, you can multiply by 9°F/5°C and add 32°F. If the temperature during a Wisconsin winter night is –40°F, what is this in °C? The temperature during extremely hot day in the desert might be about 55°C. What is this in °F?

C10B.4 The space shuttle enters the atmosphere traveling at a speed of roughly 8 km/s, but by the time it lands, its speed has decreased to about 100 m/s. The gravitational potential energy of the earth-shuttle system has also decreased. Where does all this energy go? Explain.

C10B.5 Estimate how much energy it would take to increase the temperature of a 500-g horseshoe from room temperature to about 1000°C. What assumption(s) do you have to make to calculate this?

C10B.6 Compare the thermal energy that a cup (250 g) of tea loses in going from 95°C (nearly boiling) to room temperature (22°C) to the kinetic energy that your body would lose if you ran into a brick wall at 5 m/s (11 mi/hr).

C10B.7 A hot bath can require 40 gallons of water whose temperature has been increased from about 55°F (13°C) to 140°F (60°C). Estimate the energy that this requires. If electrical energy costs about $1 per 25 MJ, how much does this bath cost if you have an electrical water heater?

C10B.8 An average residential swimming pool might contain 15,000 gal. About how much energy would it take to heat such a pool from 63°F (about 17°C) to a comfortable swimming temperature of 75°F (about 24°C). If electrical energy costs about $1 per 25 MJ, what does this cost if you use electrical energy to do this?

SYNTHETIC

C10S.1 Imagine that in the Joule experiment shown in Figure C10.1, the weights each have a mass of 10 kg and there are 8 kg (≈ 2 gallons) of water in the insulated container. About how far would the weights have to drop to increase the water's temperature by 0.5°C?

C10S.2 A 22-kg block of iron drops out of the back of a pickup truck traveling at 55 mi/h. The block slides on the road for 150 m before coming to rest. By roughly how much has the temperature of the iron increased? (Assume that it gets about half of the thermal energy produced by its interaction with the road.)*

C10S.3 A 65-kg stunt person climbs to the top of a tower 65 m tall and dives into a tank of water shaped like a cube 3.0 m on a side. The initial temperature of the water is about the same as body temperature. After the splash and wave energy gets converted to thermal energy, by about how much has the temperature of the water increased in this process? (Assume the water gets 90% of the thermal energy produced.)*

C10S.4 A 180-g granite stone is given an initial temperature of 100°C and then is placed in an insulated tub holding 850 g of water at 0°C. What is the final common temperature of the stone and water?*

C10S.5 Imagine that we slowly pour a gallon of water (≈ 3.8 kg) from a pitcher into an insulated bucket 75 cm below the lip of the pitcher. If the temperature of the water is exactly 22°C before it is poured, what is the temperature of water in the bucket after everything settles down?*

C10S.6 Starting from rest, a railroad car rolls down a hill 20 m high and hits another identical car at rest. The cars couple together after the collision. What fraction of the first car's change in potential energy is converted to thermal energy in the collision? (*Hint:* this collision conserves *momentum* as well as energy).*

C10S.7 Assume that the brake shoes in your car have a mass of about 3.0 kg per wheel. Let's also assume that your car has a mass of 1500 kg. Very roughly estimate the final temperature of your brake shoes if you go down a 300-m hill while braking to maintain a constant speed.*

> *Write your solution to the starred problems following the problem-solving framework discussed in section C10.8.

RICH-CONTEXT

C10R.1 A meteorite enters the earth's atmosphere at an altitude of 200 km traveling at about 40 km/s. If air friction slows it down so that it is traveling at only 120 m/s when it hits the ground, and the meteorite retains even 1% of the energy that friction converted to thermal energy (the rest being carried away by the air), what is its final temperature? Why do you think meteors are visible at night? Is the meteorite's initial kinetic, potential, or thermal energy most important in this problem? What assumptions did you make to do this problem? Seeing your answer, which assumptions were valid and which not, do you think? (*Hint:* Rock would glow pretty brightly at ≈ 2000 K and would vaporize at ≈ 3000 K.)

C10R.2 Imagine that in 2021, a practical teleportation device is invented. Its only problem is that it converts any difference in gravitational potential energy between an object's starting position and its final position to thermal energy in the object. Roughly how great an elevation change could you experience during teleportation and still survive? (Make appropriate estimates.)

ANSWERS TO EXERCISES

C10X.1 0.0012°C. (Joule probably cycled the weights a number of times to get a measurable ΔT.)

C10X.2 about 4600 J (*U* for helium *is* given by equation C10.4). If you have a mass of 55 kg, you'd have to move at about 13 m/s (28 mi/hr) to have this much kinetic energy.

C10X.3 According to $dK = \vec{F} \cdot d\vec{r}$, the sliding book loses 40 J of kinetic energy, which goes to thermal energy.

C10X.4 heat, work, work, work, heat. (The whole point of a microwave oven is that it uses microwaves, not a temperature difference, to increase an object's *U*.)

C10X.5 about 15,700 J.

C11

ENERGY IN BONDS

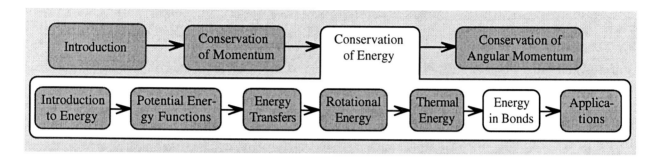

C11.1 OVERVIEW

In the last chapter, we discussed *thermal energy*, which describes the energy that an object contains by virtue of the random microscopic motion of its molecules and the interactions between them. Thermal energy turns out to be just one of many forms of *internal energy*, which generally describes the energy stored *inside* an object in any number of ways.

This chapter explores how energy can be stored in *bonds* between molecules, especially bonds between atoms, and bonds between protons and neutrons in atomic nuclei. Understanding how bonds work will enable us to understand not only how and why a substance's thermal energy changes when its phase changes, but also the nature of *latent, chemical,* and *nuclear energy*, which are forms of internal energy distinct from thermal energy.

This chapter will prepare us for studying a broad range of applications of the conservation of energy concept in the next chapter. We will also use ideas from section C11.2 often in what follows (especially in Unit *Q*).

Here is an overview of the sections of this chapter.

C11.2 *POTENTIAL ENERGY DIAGRAMS* explores how we can learn about how a system of two objects with a given energy will move by simply looking at a graph of the potential energy function of the interaction between the objects.

C11.3 *BONDS* uses the concepts developed in the previous section to discuss the nature of bonds between particles, how such bonds are formed, and why processes that make bonds release energy while those that break bonds absorb energy.

C11.4 *LATENT HEAT* explores how the weak interactions between molecules in a substance make it possible for molecules to form bonds that allow the substance to condense from gas to liquid or liquid to solid and what these phase changes mean for the internal energy of a substance.

C11.5 *CHEMICAL AND NUCLEAR ENERGY* are forms of internal energy associated with changes in an object's chemical and nuclear composition. This section discusses how changes in these forms of energy are related to making or breaking bonds at the atomic and/or nuclear levels.

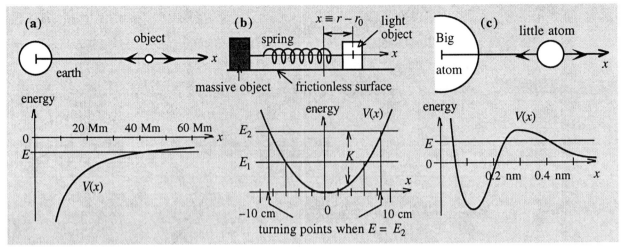

Figure C11.1: Examples of potential energy diagrams.

What is a potential energy diagram?

First simplification: motion in one dimension

Second simplification: one object is very massive

Representing a system's total energy on a PE diagram

Reading the light object's KE from the diagram

C11.2 POTENTIAL ENERGY DIAGRAMS

A **potential energy diagram** is simply a graph of the potential energy $V(r)$ of the interaction of two isolated objects as a function of their separation. A potential energy diagram provides a powerful tool for illustrating the implications of conservation of energy in a given situation. We can often make a variety of qualitative statements about how objects will move in a given context simply by looking at its potential energy diagram.

While there are ways of constructing and interpreting potential energy graphs for *any* system of two objects, it helps at first to restrict our attention to pairs of objects that move directly toward or away from each other along a line, which we will define to be the x axis. Figure C11.1 shows potential energy diagrams for three different kinds of systems fitting this description. The vertical scale in each diagram is not marked and is not really important: we'll see the *shape* of the potential energy curve is what contains the important information.

We will also limit ourselves at present to cases where we have a light object interacting with a very massive object that is initially essentially at rest in our reference frame. Then, for the same reasons that we can ignore the earth's motion and kinetic energy (see section C8.5), we can ignore the massive object's motion and kinetic energy, even though it does respond *slightly* to the interaction. The objects' separation is then essentially determined by the light object's x-position.

If an isolated system is set up initially so that it has total energy E, then conservation of energy implies that the system (once it is isolated) *always* has that total energy E, no matter what the separation between its objects might be. Since the system's total E is independent of separation, we represent it by a *horizontal line* on a potential energy diagram at a vertical position determined using the same energy scale used to plot $V(x)$. This is illustrated in Figure C11.1.

Note that how we initially set up a system fixes its total energy E. For example, if we hold the light object at *rest* at some x-position, then the system's total energy E is *equal* to the interaction's potential energy $V(x)$ when the object is at that position. We can vary this by moving the object. When we release the object, the system becomes isolated, and during its subsequent evolution, E remains equal to the value $V(x)$ had when the object was released. For example, the system shown in Figure C11.1b will have total energy E_1 if the light object is released from rest at $x = \pm 6$ cm and energy E_2 if it is released at $x = \pm 8.5$ cm.

As long as the energy in a system is only transferred between kinetic and potential forms, then $E = K + V(x)$, where K is the kinetic energy of the light object (the kinetic energy of the massive object ≈ 0). Thus

$$K \text{ (at } x) = E - V(x) \qquad\qquad \text{(C11.1)}$$

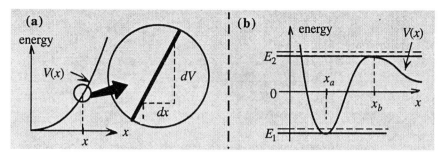

Figure C11.2: (a) dV/dx evaluated near a point x is the slope of the graph of $V(x)$ at that point. (b) $F_x = 0$ at x_a and x_b (since $dV/dx = 0$). If we place the light object at rest at one of these points (which means it will have energy E_1 or E_2 respectively), it will remain at rest. If we increase its energy a bit (dotted lines), it will oscillate back and forth near x_a but fly away from x_b.

We can thus read the light object's kinetic energy at a given position x directly from the diagram: it corresponds to the difference between the total energy E and the system's potential energy $V(x)$ at that x, as shown in Figure C11.1b.

We can also read from the diagram the x-force F_x that the interaction exerts on the light object at any position. If the particle moves only along the x axis, then $dy = dz = 0$, and the dK for this interaction is simply

Reading the x-force F_x acting on the light object from slope of $V(x)$

$$dK = \vec{F} \cdot d\vec{r} = F_x dx + F_y dy + F_z dz = F_x dx \qquad \text{(C11.2)}$$

Any gain in kinetic energy here comes at the expense of potential energy, so

$$-dV = dK = F_x dx \quad \Rightarrow \quad F_x = -\frac{dV}{dx} \qquad \text{(C11.3)}$$

As shown in Figure C11.2a, dV/dx evaluated at a given position corresponds to the *slope* of the potential energy function at that position. So the x-force on the light object at any given point is -1 times the slope of $V(x)$ at that point.

In Figure C11.1b, there are two positions where the potential energy curve crosses a given energy line (these positions are at $x = \pm 6.0$ cm when $E = E_1$). As the light object approaches either of these critical positions from closer to the origin it will slow down (since $K = E - V$ becomes smaller) until it comes to *rest* exactly at the critical point (since $K = E - V = 0$ there). The object cannot *remain* at rest there, though: the slope of $V(x)$ is nonzero, so $F_x \neq 0$, meaning that the interaction is still transferring momentum to the object. In fact, you can see from the graph that F_x is *negative* at $x = +6.0$ cm (because dV/dx is positive there) and *positive* at $x = -6.0$ cm, so in both cases the interaction will turn the object around and push the object back toward the origin. These critical positions where $E = V(x)$ are thus called **turning points.** If the system in Figure C11.1b has energy E_1, the light object will then move back and forth between the turning points at $x = \pm 6.0$ cm.

Turning points

The light object can never be found where $V(x) > E$ (since it would have to have $K < 0$ there, which is absurd); we call such regions **forbidden regions.** Regions where $V(x) < E$ are **allowed regions.** For the energy E_1 in Figure C11.1b, the forbidden regions are $x > +6.0$ cm and $x < -6.0$ cm.

Forbidden and allowed regions

Equation C11.3 implies that the x-force on the light object will be zero at any position where $dV/dx = 0$ (that is, where the graph of $V(x)$ is horizontal): such a position is called an **equilibrium position**. The slope of $V(x)$ will always be zero at the exact bottom of a "valley" (local minimum) and the exact top of a "hill" (local maximum) in the graph of $V(x)$. In principle, an object placed at rest at one of these positions *could* remain at rest when we release it. Imagine that we place the object at rest at a position corresponding to the bottom of a valley. If some external influence jostles the object (increasing the system's energy slightly), then the object will oscillate back and forth between turning points close to the equilibrium position (see Figure C11.2b). On the other hand, if we set it at rest at the top of a potential energy *hill*, jostling it enables it to move away from that point with increasing speed, possibly never to return. We thus call an equilibrium position where $V(x)$ has a local minimum a **stable equilibrium position**; all other equilibrium positions are **unstable.**

Stable and unstable equilibrium positions

EXAMPLE C11.1

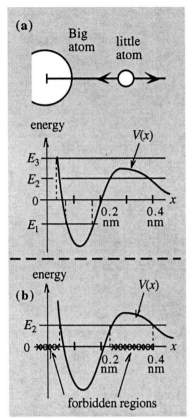

Figure C11.3: (a) Graph of a possible potential energy function for a system of two interacting atoms. **(b)** The system's forbidden regions when $E = E_2$.

Problem: Consider the hypothetical potential energy graph for an isolated system of two atoms (one much more massive than the other) shown in Figure C11.3a. What are the possible motions for this system if it has energy E_1? If it has energy E_2? If it has energy E_3?

Solution If the system has energy E_1, the only allowed region for the little atom's position x is the region between the turning points at roughly 0.07 nm and 0.17 nm. This means that the lighter atom will oscillate back and forth within this range of separations from the big atom. As long as the system has this energy, the little atom cannot escape from the big atom: the two are bound together as a molecule.

If the system has energy E_3, there is only one turning point at roughly $x = 0.03$ nm. If the little atom is initially approaching the big atom, it will slow down as it approaches the bump in the potential energy function at $x = 0.30$ nm, speed up as it passes the valley centered at about $x = 0.12$ nm, and finally bounce off the big atom, getting no closer than $x = 0.03$ nm. The little atom will then return to large separations without forming a molecule.

If the system has energy E_2, two qualitatively different kinds of motion are possible. If the little atom is initially within the allowed region between about $x = 0.04$ nm and $x = 0.22$ nm, it will oscillate between these two turning points. In this case, the system is a molecule (though it oscillates a bit more wildly than it would if its energy were E_1). If the little atom is initially in the allowed region where $x > 0.40$ nm and is approaching the big atom, it will be turned back when it reaches the turning point at $x = 0.40$ nm: the atom will thus bounce off the big atom without forming a molecule.

The only way for a little atom to come in from very large x and then form a molecule with the big atom is for the energy of the system to be reduced (say, from E_3 to E_2) while the little atom is in the neighborhood of $x \approx 0.15$ nm. In a real chemical reaction, there must be some mechanism for doing this: the system might emit the extra energy in the form of a photon of light or somehow transfer it to a third atom. A molecule cannot be formed unless some energy is removed from the system.

The main point to understand here is that we can extract a lot of information about how the light object in a system will move simply by studying a graph of the system's potential energy.

Exercise C11X.1: Where are the stable equilibrium positions (if any) for the potential energy graphs shown in Figure C11.1a and C11.1b?

Exercise C11X.2: Where are the turning points and forbidden regions for the system shown in Figure C11.1b when $E = E_2$?

Exercise C11X.3: "As the total energy of the system in Figure C11.1b increases, the amplitude of oscillation increases." Is this true? Explain.

Exercise C11X.4: For separations greater than 0.30 nm, is the interaction between the atoms in Figure C11.3a attractive or repulsive? Explain.

C11.3 BONDS

Steps for forming a bond

Figure C11.3 illustrates a typical potential energy curve for a **bond**. In general a *bond* between two interacting objects will form whenever (1) there is a valley (local minimum) in the potential energy function $V(x)$ that describes their interaction, (2) at a certain time, the separation between the objects is within this valley, and (3) at that time, some external interaction lowers the system's energy so that it has an allowed region in the valley bounded by turning points on either side (for example, as in the system shown in Figure C11.3 when $E = E_1$). After such a bond forms, the system will oscillate between the turning points, meaning that the two objects maintain a roughly fixed separation.

Such an interaction between two atoms is caused by imperfectly canceled electromagnetic interactions between their charged parts. Here is a simplified model for understanding the shape of the potential energy function caused by such interactions. When the separation r between the atoms is much larger than the atoms themselves, the atoms seem to each other like uncharged particles, and the interaction between them is very weak: this means that slope of $V(r)$ goes to zero as the separation becomes large. As the atoms get closer, there is usually some initial repulsion between the atoms' negative electron clouds, which begin to overlap while the atoms' nuclei are still far apart: this means that $V(r)$ increases with decreasing separation for a while. As the atoms get still closer, their electron clouds can sometimes rearrange themselves into new configurations with a lower potential energy, leading to a valley in the potential energy function. As the atoms get closer yet, the electrostatic repulsion between the nuclei (and other effects) causes an increase in $V(r)$ that overwhelms any decrease due to electron rearrangement, so the potential energy sharply rises again.

The real potential energy functions between atoms look pretty much like the graph shown in Figure C11.3, except that the hill in the potential energy function is commonly much lower than shown there (its height is often 10 or more times smaller than the valley is deep). This varies, though. For certain pairs of atoms, there may be essentially no hill; for others, there may be no valley.

The potential energy function for the interaction between two protons is qualitatively similar: the electrostatic repulsion between the protons at large separations provides the hill in the potential energy function, while the attractive strong nuclear interaction (which kicks in only at small separations) provides the valley (a quantum effect provides the repulsion at very small separations). For protons or neutrons interacting with neutrons, there is no electrostatic repulsion, so the potential energy function has essentially only a valley.

All of these $V(r)$ functions have this much in common: the force between the objects goes to zero as r becomes large, meaning that the slope of $V(r)$ goes to zero, meaning that $V(r)$ flattens out toward an asymptotic value as r becomes large. The reference separation for such an interaction is invariably chosen to be at $r = \infty$ so that this asymptotic value is *zero* ($V(r) \to 0$ as $r \to \infty$).

This means that if the two interacting objects initially have a very large separation and nonzero kinetic energy, then their total energy $E > 0$. An isolated system under these circumstances is *not* bonded: there will be a turning point either on the outer side of the hill (if $E < V_{hill}$, where V_{hill} is the potential energy at the top of the hill) or at very small r (if $E > V_{hill}$), and if the objects approach each other, they simply bounce off this turning point and go back out to infinity. To get the objects close enough to bond, the system's initial energy has to be greater than V_{hill}. To then actually form the bond, we have to reduce the system's energy from its initial energy to some $E < V_{hill}$, trapping the system in the valley. So two atoms initially separated by a large distance can only form a bond if there is some mechanism (for example, an interaction with a third object or emission of a photon) that enables them to release energy while they are close together. Thus *when bonds form, energy is released,* which often goes (at least at first) to increasing the thermal energy of the surroundings.

On the other hand, consider a system that is already bonded and thus whose initial energy $E < V_{hill}$. To *break* this bond (that is, to cause the objects to split apart to large separations), we have to *add* energy to make $E > V_{hill}$. Therefore, *when bonds break, energy is absorbed,* again often from the thermal energy in the system's surroundings (at least at first).

A simplified model for the interaction between atoms

Making bonds releases energy

Breaking bonds absorbs energy

EXAMPLE C11.2

Problem: A mixture of hydrogen and oxygen gas will not burn at room temperature. Assuming that the potential energy of interaction between a hydrogen molecule and an oxygen molecule looks like that shown in Figure C11.3, estimate the minimum height of the hill in the potential energy function.

Solution The average kinetic energy of a hydrogen molecule at room temperature will be *very* roughly $k_B T \approx (1.4 \times 10^{-23} \text{ J/K})(300 \text{ K}) = 4 \times 10^{-21}$ J. Since the atoms are presumably not bonding because they do not get past the hill in the potential energy function, the hill must have at least this height.

C11.4 LATENT HEAT*

Definition of latent heat*

One of the macroscopic consequences of the issues discussed in the last section is that when a substance undergoes a phase change (for example, from solid to liquid or liquid to solid) it usually either absorbs or releases energy. The energy a given substance absorbs or releases per kilogram during a given change of phase is called the **latent heat*** for that substance undergoing phase change. In this section, we will see that this energy flow is a consequence of the making or breaking of microscopic bonds between molecules. (The word "heat" is as inappropriate here as it is in "specific heat*": the asterisk reminds us that again we are really talking about a transfer to or from a form of internal energy.)

Microscopic models for phase changes

The molecules of almost every kind of substance attract each other weakly, making it possible to form weak bonds between molecules. At high temperatures, the molecules have so much kinetic energy that the total energy of interaction between any two molecules is typically much greater than zero, implying that the molecules are unbound. A substance whose molecules are unbound is a **gas**: gas molecules thus bounce freely and randomly back and forth between the walls of whatever container holds the gas, completely filling its volume.

As the temperature of gas decreases, though, the collisions between molecules become less and less violent, allowing them eventually to form weak bonds with each other. As such bonds form, the substance condenses to form a **liquid**. In a liquid, the bonds are not so much between two individual molecules but between each molecule and the rest of the liquid. This means that molecules are reasonably free to move around *within* the liquid but cannot easily escape it.

As the temperature of the substance decreases further, the kinetic energy of each molecule becomes so small that it can begin to form tight bonds with specific neighboring molecules. As these specific bonds form, molecules become essentially locked into specific locations relative to their neighbors in a more or less rigid lattice: the substance is now a **solid**. The molecules will still vibrate about these positions, but they are no longer free to roam around.

As a substance condenses from a gas to a liquid, intermolecular bonds are being formed: this releases a certain amount of energy. Conversely, to convert a liquid to a gas, we need to supply the same amount of energy to break those bonds. The energy that we need to supply (usually in the form of thermal energy) to vaporize a kilogram of a given kind of substance in liquid form is called its **latent heat* of vaporization**. The latent heat* of vaporization for water is 2256 kJ/kg, meaning that we have to supply 2256 kilojoules of energy to vaporize one kilogram of water. This is a lot of energy: if we could supply this much energy to a kilogram of water *without* vaporizing it, its temperature would increase by 539 K! The energy involved in making and breaking the intermolecular bonds associated with phase changes is much greater than that associated with small changes in a substance's temperature.

Exercise C11X.5: Verify that supplying 2256 kJ of thermal energy to a kilogram of water would increase its temperature by 539 K if it didn't vaporize.

Similarly, when a liquid freezes to become a solid, new, tighter intermolecular bonds are being formed, which releases a certain amount of energy. The energy released per kilogram of a freezing substance is called its **latent heat* of fusion.** We have to supply the same amount of energy to break these bonds and melt the substance. The latent heat* of fusion of water is 333 kJ/kg, meaning that we have to supply 333 kilojoules of energy to melt a kilogram of ice.

So when we boil a pan of water on a stove, the thermal energy supplied by the stove is used to break the bonds that hold water molecules in the liquid. It turns out that breaking these bonds soaks up all the energy that you might supply during the phase change. If you attempt to raise the temperature of a substance undergoing a phase change by supplying more energy, the extra energy you supply gets channeled instead to breaking more bonds, making the phase change more rapid without increasing the substance's temperature. So the temperature of boiling water in a pan maintains a constant temperature of 373 K (that is, 100°C) until all of the water is boiled away. Similarly, a glass of ice water has a constant temperature of 273 K (0°C) until the ice completely melts.

Phase changes take place at a constant temperature

We often take advantage of these characteristics of phase changes in our daily lives. Human beings keep cool by sweating: as the sweat evaporates, it absorbs thermal energy from the skin, leaving the skin cool. Placing an ice cube in a cold drink cools it better than putting in an equal amount of water at 0°C would: as the ice melts, it absorbs an enormous amount of thermal energy from the drink. Refrigerators operate by forcing a liquid to boil in cooling coils inside the refrigerator (thus making the liquid absorb thermal energy from the contents of the refrigerator) and then forcing it to condense in coils on the outside of the refrigerator (thus releasing this energy into the environment). Fruit growers sometimes spray water on the fruit trees to protect the fruit from a cold snap: the temperature of the fruit will not drop below freezing until all of the water on the outside has frozen (and this may take longer than the cold snap lasts).

Table C11.1: Latent heats* of various substances

Substance and phase change	Latent Heat* in kJ/kg
melting O_2	13.8
melting H_2	58.6
melting Al	105
melting Cu	205
melting H_2O	333
boiling O_2	213
boiling H_2	452
boiling H_2O	2256
boiling Cu	4730
boiling Al	11400

Finally, the fixed temperature of boiling water makes predictable cooking possible. Cooking food by boiling in a pan (at sea level) exposes the food to a constant temperature of 373 K whether the pan is on an electric stove, on a gas stove, or over a fire, no matter how hot the stove or fire might be.

We call the internal energy that a substance has in the form of broken intermolecular bonds its **latent energy** U^{la} (*latent* because absorbing or releasing this energy does not manifest itself in a change in temperature, so the energy transfer is thus even more hidden than usual).

Latent energy

When a substance condenses or freezes, this latent energy is converted to thermal energy; when it melts or vaporizes, thermal energy is converted to latent energy. The energy released or absorbed by a unit mass of a given substance during a phase change is called its **latent heat* of transformation** L:

$$\Delta U^{th} = +mL, \quad \Delta U^{la} = -mL \quad \text{(for condensation or freezing)}$$
$$\Delta U^{th} = -mL, \quad \Delta U^{la} = +mL \quad \text{(for vaporization or melting)} \qquad \text{(C11.4)}$$

where m is the object's mass and L is the latent heat* associated with the phase transformation. Latent heats* for various substances are listed in Table C11.1.

Problem: If thermal energy from burning natural gas costs about 2¢ per MJ, how much does it cost to completely boil a gallon of water already at 100°C?

EXAMPLE   C11.3

Solution One gallon = 4 quarts ≈ 4 liters ≈ 4 kg of water. Vaporizing this much water, even if it is already at the boiling point, involves increasing its latent energy by $\Delta U^{la} = +mL = (4 \text{ kg})(2.256 \text{ MJ/kg}) = 9.0$ MJ. If this comes at the expense of thermal energy at a cost of 2¢ per MJ (and no energy is wasted), then it will cost 18¢.

EXAMPLE C11.4

Problem: Imagine that you put a 60-g ice cube (at 0°C) into a glass holding 250 g (roughly 8 oz) of water at 15°C. What is the water's final temperature?

Solution The increase in latent energy required to melt $m = 60$ g of ice is:

$$\Delta U_{ice}^{la} = +mL = (0.060 \ \text{kg})(333,000 \ \text{J/kg}) = 20,000 \ \text{J} \qquad \text{(C11.5)}$$

This energy comes at the expense of the thermal energy of the rest of the drink:

$$\Delta U_{ice}^{la} = -\Delta U_{drink}^{th} \qquad \text{(C11.6)}$$

But $\Delta U_{drink}^{th} = Mc\,\Delta T$, where M is the mass of the drink, c is its specific heat*, and ΔT is its change in temperature. So $Mc\,\Delta T = -\Delta U_{ice}^{la}$, which implies that

$$\Delta T = \frac{-\Delta U_{ice}^{la}}{Mc} = \frac{-20,000 \ \text{J}}{(0.25 \ \text{kg})(4190 \ \text{J} \cdot \text{kg}^{-1} \cdot \text{K}^{-1})} = -19 \ \text{K} \qquad \text{(C11.7)}$$

where I have assumed that the drink is composed essentially of water. Since the drink was initially at 15°C, if its temperature were really to decrease by 19 K, we'd end up with a drink at –4°C (remember that a temperature difference in K is the same as a temperature difference in °C). But this is absurd: how can ice cool the drink below the temperature of the ice?

What really happens is that the drink cools to 0°C, releasing thermal energy that melts some (but not all) of the ice: if no energy comes in from outside, the water and ice will then be in equilibrium and no further change will take place. As the water cools to 0°C, the change in the ice's latent energy is

$$\Delta U_{ice}^{la} = -\Delta U_{drink}^{th} = -Mc\,\Delta T \qquad \text{(C11.8)}$$

where ΔT in this case is –15 K. Using $\Delta U_{ice}^{la} = +mL$, we find that the amount of ice melted will be

$$m = \frac{\Delta U_{ice}^{la}}{L} = \frac{-Mc\,\Delta T}{L} = \frac{-(0.25 \ \text{kg})(4190 \ \text{J} \cdot \text{kg}^{-1} \cdot \text{K}^{-1})(-15 \ \text{K})}{333,000 \ \text{J/kg}}$$

$$= 0.047 \ \text{kg} = 47 \ \text{g} \qquad \text{(C11.9)}$$

At the end, then, we have 297 g of drink and 13 g of ice, all at 0°C.

Exercise C11X.6: How much ice would you need to cool a 500 g drink of water from room temperature (about 22°C) to 0°C?

C11.5 CHEMICAL AND NUCLEAR ENERGY

Typical energies released by a chemical reaction

The bonds between molecules of a substance are generally much weaker than the bonds between the atoms in a given molecule. Chemical reactions, which make and break atomic bonds, can therefore absorb or release much more energy per kilogram of substance than is absorbed or released in a phase change. For example, burning a kilogram of gasoline releases roughly 46 MJ of thermal energy, roughly 20 times the thermal energy released by a kilogram of condensing water. Burning a kilogram of natural gas releases about 55 MJ.

Nuclear energy

In turn, the protons and neutrons in an atomic nucleus form bonds that are much stronger than the bonds between atoms, mostly because the strong nuclear interactions between the protons and neutrons are much stronger than the electromagnetic interactions between atoms. Nuclear reactions can rearrange these bonds to form more tightly bound nuclei, releasing enormous amounts of energy.

For example, a *deuterium* (^{2}H) nucleus contains a proton bound to a neutron. A *tritium* (^{3}H) nucleus consists of a proton bound to two neutrons. If we force these nuclei together, we can create a helium (^{4}He) nucleus (two protons and two neutrons) and a free neutron (this type of nuclear reaction, which creates a more massive nucleus from lighter nuclei, is called a **fusion** reaction). The formation of new bonds in this process releases 340 TJ (340×10^{12} J) of energy per kilogram of ^{2}H-^{3}H mixture. This is roughly 7×10^6 times the energy released by burning a kilogram of gasoline, and represents enough energy to supply the electrical needs of about 10,000 average U.S. households for a year. Nuclear **fission** reactions (which involve breaking apart large nuclei into smaller but more tightly-bound fragments) produce roughly 70 TJ per kilogram of fuel.

The enormous amounts of energy produced by nuclear reactions make nuclear reactions an attractive source of energy, but it is not easy to produce this energy safely. All currently-operating nuclear reactors are fission reactors, which produce large amounts of intensely radioactive waste. No one knows how to store this waste safely for the millennia required to render it harmless, and so no one wants it stored in their back yards. Fission plants also produce nuclear fuel that can be used to make atomic bombs. Finally, the most common designs for fission plants can (under unusual circumstances) fail catastrophically releasing large amounts of radioactive substances into the environment. For these reasons and others, utilities in the U.S. are no longer building nuclear power plants.

Fusion reactors would produce far more energy per kilogram of fuel, use fuel that is much more readily obtainable, produce much less (but not zero) radioactive waste, would not produce materials that can be used to make bombs, and cannot "melt down" the way that fission reactors can. However, commercially viable fusion reactors are still decades away (though progress is made every year).

Thermal, latent, chemical, and *nuclear* energy are all subcategories of the general category of internal energy, since in each case energy is stored in the microscopic motions and/or interactions inside the substance. An object's **chemical energy** U^{ch} changes if and only if its chemical composition changes as a result of internal chemical reactions. Similarly, an object's **nuclear energy** U^{nu} changes as the result of internal nuclear reactions. An object's latent energy changes U^{la} during phase changes. An object's **thermal energy** U^{th} changes if its temperature changes. Thermal energy often is the common currency for internal energy changes. For example, a decrease in an object's chemical energy usually shows up first as an increase in its thermal energy; likewise if an object's chemical energy increases, this almost always comes at the expense of its thermal energy (at least at first).

In many, cases, in fact, thermal energy is the *only* form of internal energy involved in a physical process. In such cases, it is conventional to use U *without* a superscript to refer to thermal energy (I will do this in unit T).

As in the case of thermal energy, it is difficult to attach a specific value to the *total* chemical, nuclear, or latent energy in a given object but easier to specify *changes* in these energies. Therefore, when we do conservation of energy problems involving changes in any of these internal (hidden) energies, it is best to express the law of conservation of energy in difference form:

$$0 = \Delta K + \Delta V + \Delta U^{\text{th}} + \Delta U^{\text{la}} + \Delta U^{\text{ch}} + \Delta U^{\text{nu}} \qquad \text{(C11.10)}$$

Symbols for chemical and nuclear energy

As usual, when we do this, we have to be *very* careful with signs: a difference is always positive when the final amount of energy in a given category has increased in the process (and so is greater at the end than it was in the beginning).

Example C11.5 on the next page illustrates the solution of a conservation of energy problem involving internal energies using the problem-solving framework that we have been developing.

EXAMPLE C11.5

OUTLINE OF THE FRAMEWORK

1. Pictorial Representation

   a. Draw a picture of the situation that includes:

①   (1) sketches of the system in its initial and final states

②   (2) reference frame axes

③   (3) labels defining symbols for relevant quantities (in this case, objects' masses, specific heats*, temperatures)

   b. List values for all known quantities and specify which quantities are unknown.

④

2. Conceptual Representation

The general task is to construct a conceptual model of the situation and link it to an abstract physics model or principle. In conservation-of-energy problems, we do the following:

⑤ a. Identify the *system* involved. (If it involves the earth, we can ignore the earth's kinetic energy)

⑥ b. Determine whether it is *approximately* isolated, *functionally* isolated, or involved in a *collision* (as defined in chapter C5). Support your conclusions briefly.

⑦ c. Identify the interactions between objects in the system and for each interaction, determine whether we can handle it by

   (1) keeping track of its potential energy (if so, define the reference separation)

   (2) ignoring it (because it is very weak or for another reason)

   (3) keeping track of rotational or internal energies

   d. Do we have to make any approximations or assumptions to solve the problem? (If so, describe.)

⑧

3. Mathematical Representation

⑨ a. Apply the mathematical equation that appropriately describes the situation (equation C10.10 here)

⑩ b. Solve for unknowns symbolically

⑪ c. Plug in numbers and units and calculate the result and its units.

4. Evaluation

Check that the answer makes sense:
⑫ a. Does it have the correct units?
⑬ b. Does it have the right sign?
⑭ c. Does it seem reasonable?

Problem: Beth, whose mass is 52 kg, climbs up a hill 400 m high. She evaporates 0.5 kg (about a pint) of water from her skin and lungs during the process. Roughly how much food energy does she have to "burn" in this process? Express your answer in food calories. [One **food calorie** = 1 Cal (with a capital C) is defined to be 1000 physics calories = 1000×4.186 J = 4186 J.]

Solution: The drawing below shows the initial and final situations:

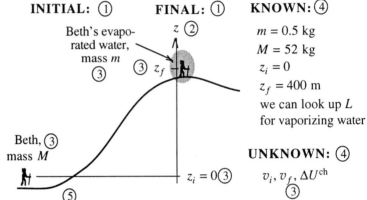

INITIAL: ①   **FINAL:** ①   **KNOWN:** ④

Beth's evaporated water, mass m ③

Beth, ③ mass M

$z_i = 0$ ③

⑤

KNOWN: ④
$m = 0.5$ kg
$M = 52$ kg
$z_i = 0$
$z_f = 400$ m
we can look up L for vaporizing water

UNKNOWN: ④
$v_i, v_f, \Delta U^{ch}$ ③

⑥ The system here is Beth, the earth (including the environment), and the water that gets evaporated. This system is isolated (it floats in space). Beth interacts gravitationally with the earth and participates in contact interactions with the water and the earth. We can handle the gravitational interaction by keeping track of its potential energy, which (if we define $V \equiv 0$ at $z = 0$) is $V(z) = Mgz$. We will handle her contact interactions with the water by keeping track of internal energies. We will *ignore* both the frictional and normal parts of her contact interaction with the hill, and any other energy exchanges with the earth (this is probably a bad approximation, but what else can we do?). We will assume that Beth's kinetic energy is negligible (it will be about the same at the top of the hill as at the bottom anyway). We will assume that Beth's temperature ≈ constant throughout. We will also treat Beth's mass as constant, even though she loses 0.5 kg in the process. All of these approximations mean that our answer is going to be a rough estimate at best!

⑦

⑧

Conservation of energy implies that

⑨ $0 = \Delta K + \Delta V + \Delta U^{th}_{Beth} + \Delta U^{ch}_{Beth} + \Delta U^{la}_{water} + \Delta U^{th}_{env}$

Since Beth's change in kinetic energy is negligible and her temperature remains the same, $\Delta K = \Delta U^{th}_{Beth} = 0$. $\Delta V = Mg(z_f - z_i) = Mgz_f$ here, and the water's latent energy increase is $\Delta U^{la}_{water} = +mL$, where L is 2256 kJ/kg. We are also assuming that the environment's thermal energy doesn't change much as Beth interacts with it, so $\Delta U^{th}_{earth} = 0$. Plugging all this in to the above and solving for ΔU^{ch}_{Beth}, we get

$$\Delta U^{ch}_{Beth} = -\Delta V - \Delta U^{la}_{wa} = -Mgz_f - mL \quad ⑩$$

$$= -(52 \text{ kg})(9.8 \text{ m/s}^2)(400 \text{ m})\left(\frac{1 \cancel{J}}{1 \text{ kg} \cdot \text{m}^2/\text{s}^2}\right)\left(\frac{1 \text{ MJ}}{10^6 \cancel{J}}\right)$$

$$- (2.256 \text{ MJ/kg})(0.5 \text{ kg}) = -0.2 \text{ MJ} - 1.1 \text{ MJ} = -1.3 \text{ MJ}$$

$$= -(1.3 \times 10^6 \cancel{J})\left(\frac{1 \text{ Cal}}{4186 \cancel{J}}\right) = -310 \text{ Cal} \quad ⑪$$

So Beth has to use up 310 Cal of food energy (at least) to accomplish the climb (note that evaporating water requires the most energy!). The
⑫ units and sign are right (Beth is *losing* chemical energy here). The mag-
⑬ nitude is plausible (a normal daily diet supplies about 2000 Cal).
⑭

I. POTENTIAL ENERGY DIAGRAMS
A. A potential energy diagram for a system of two objects consists of
    1. A graph of its potential energy as a function of object separation
    2. A horizontal line representing the system's total energy
B. PE diagrams are valuable for predicting the system's possible motions
C. Simplifying assumptions that we are making:
    1. Both objects move only along a line we take to be the x axis
    2. One object is much more massive than the other (we ignore its KE)
D. How to read a potential energy diagram
    1. The KE of the light object at a given position x is $K = E - V(x)$
    2. The x-force on that object is $F_x = -dV/dx = -[\text{slope of } V(x)]$
    3. The light object has *turning points* where $E = V(x)$
        a) It comes to rest when reaching such points, as $K = E - V(x) = 0$
        b) Since $F_x = -dV/dx \neq 0$, the object does not *remain* at rest
        c) The object in fact reverses direction upon reaching such a point
    4. The light object's *forbidden regions* are where $V(x) > E$ (it cannot be in such a region because its K would be < 0, which is absurd)
    5. The light object's allowed regions are where $E > V(x)$.
    6. The light object's *equilibrium positions* are where $F_x = -dV/dx = 0$
        a) The object *could* remain at rest if placed at such a position
        b) Such an equilibrium position is *stable* if it is at a local minimum of $V(x)$; it is *unstable* otherwise (an object initially at rest at an equilibrium position will oscillate around a stable equilibrium position if jostled, but fly away from an unstable position)

II. BONDS
A. A *bond* can form between two objects if:
    1. There is a region where $V(x)$ for their interaction has a valley
    2. The objects' separation x is within the valley just as an external interaction removes energy from the system
B. A model for the interaction between two electrically neutral atoms
    1. At large separations, $V(r) \approx$ constant (interaction force $\approx$ zero)
    2. As the atoms get closer, their electron clouds repel, so $V(r)$ increases
    3. As atoms get still closer, the electron clouds rearrange and $V(r)$ drops
    4. At very close separations, various effects cause $V(r)$ to grow rapidly
    5. We always take the reference separation to be ∞, so $V(\infty) = 0$
    6. See Figure C11.3 for a qualitative graph of such a function
C. Nuclear bonds are qualitatively similar
D. Making bonds releases energy, breaking them requires energy

III. LATENT HEAT*
A. Interactions between molecules are usually weakly attractive
    1. In a *gas*, molecular kinetic energies are too high to form bonds
    2. At lower temperatures, bonds can form, creating *liquids* or *solids*
B. An object's *latent energy* U^{la} is a form of internal energy that describes how much energy we have stored in the form of broken bonds
C. A phase change transfers latent energy to or from thermal energy
    1. $\Delta U^{th} = +mL$, $\Delta U^{la} = -mL$ (for condensation or freezing)
    2. $\Delta U^{th} = -mL$, $\Delta U^{la} = +mL$ (for vaporization or melting)
    where $L =$ energy transferred per unit mass by a phase change
        a) We call L the *latent heat** of the phase transformation
        b) L is typically in the range of 0.1 MJ/kg to 10 MJ/kg
D. A substance's temperature remains $\approx$ constant during a phase change

IV. CHEMICAL AND NUCLEAR ENERGY
A. Analogous internal energies associated with broken chemical and nuclear bonds are chemical energy U^{ch} and nuclear energy U^{nu}, respectively
B. For chemical reactions, ΔU^{ch} per mass ranges from 10 to 100 MJ/kg
C. For nuclear reactions, ΔU^{nu} per mass ranges from 50 to 500 TJ/kg

GLOSSARY

potential energy diagram: A graph of the potential energy curve for a given interaction between two objects as a function of their separation, with a horizontal line indicating the system's total energy. Such a diagram is simplest to interpret if the system involves a very massive object interacting with a light object that moves in only one dimension (which we can take to be the x axis). Subsequent definitions will assume this situation.

turning point: any position x for a light object where the system's potential energy is equal to the system's total energy: $V(x) = E$. As the light object approaches a turning point, it slows down, comes instantaneously to rest exactly at the turning point, and then turns around and starts moving in the opposite direction.

forbidden region: any continuous range of light object positions where the system's potential energy would exceed its total energy. Such a position is *forbidden* because the kinetic energy of a light object would have to be negative there, but $K = \frac{1}{2}mv^2$ cannot possibly be negative.

allowed region: any continuous range of light object positions where the system's potential energy is less than its total energy. Such a positions is *allowed* because the kinetic energy of light object is positive there.

equilibrium position: any light object position where it would experience zero force due to interaction with the massive object. The slope of the potential energy curve is zero at such a position.

stable equilibrium position: the equilibrium position at the lowest point of a valley (local minimum) in the system's potential energy function. If the light object is placed at rest at such a position, it will remain at rest. If it is then jostled slightly, its position will undergo small oscillations around the equilibrium position.

unstable equilibrium position: any equilibrium position that is not at the bottom of a valley in the system's potential energy function. If the light object is placed at rest at such a position, it will remain at rest, but if it is then jostled slightly, it will move a large distance away from the equilibrium position and may never return.

bond: an interaction between two objects such that they remain bound together, maintaining a roughly constant separation. Making a bond releases energy; breaking the bond requires energy.

gas, liquid, solid: possible **phases** for many substances. The molecules of a gas are not bound to each other. The molecules of a liquid are bound to each other in a way that permits some freedom of movement. The molecules of a solid are strongly bound into a relatively rigid lattice.

latent heat* (of transformation): the energy per unit mass released or absorbed by a substance undergoing a phase transformation. The latent heat* involved in a phase transformation from a solid to liquid or vice versa is called the **latent heat* of fusion,** while that involved in a transformation from liquid to gas or vice versa is called the **latent heat* of vaporization.** The asterisk indicates again that "heat" is not quite the correct term here: we are really talking about thermal energy here, not heat. We call the part of an object's internal energy associated with phase transitions its **latent energy** U^{la}: the object's energy in this form changes when latent heat* is released or absorbed.

chemical energy U^{ch}: the part of an object's internal energy that changes if the object undergoes an internal chemical reaction.

nuclear energy U^{nu}: the part of an object's internal energy that changes if the object undergoes a nuclear reaction.

thermal energy U^{th}: the part of an object's internal energy that changes when its temperature changes.

fission, fusion: types of nuclear reactions. *Fission* involves splitting large nuclei to create more tightly bound medium-sized nuclei, while *fusion* reactions involve combining very small nuclei to create more tightly bound medium-sized nuclei.

food calorie (Cal): 1 Cal = 1000 cal = 4186 J. This unit is typically used to express the energy content of foods.

TWO-MINUTE PROBLEMS

C11T.1 An object is free to move along the x axis. It is connected through two identical springs to two points $\pm y_0$ on the y axis. When the object is at $x = 0$, both springs are equally compressed. What kind of position is $x = 0$?
A. unstable equilibrium   B. stable equilibrium
C. not an equilibrium position

C11T.2 If your stove burner provides thermal energy at a rate of 4,500 J/s, about how much water can you boil in a minute?   B. 120 kg   D. 0.12 kg
A. 2 kg   C. 0.002 kg   E. other (specify)

C11T.3 A 300-g hunk of ice at 0°C is placed in a thermos bottle containing 1 kg of water at 20°C. If the thermos perfectly insulates the ice-water system from the outside world, what will be the final temperature of the system?
A. Below 0°C   D. very roughly 10°C
B. almost exactly 0°C   E. somewhat below 20°C
C. somewhat above 0°C   F. almost exactly 20°C

C11T.4 The thermal energy of a block of ice at 0°C melting to a puddle of water at 0°C
A. increases   B. decreases   C. doesn't change

C11T.5 An egg will not cook any faster in furiously boiling water than it will in gently simmering water (T or F).

C11T.6 A 100-g sample of a certain substance undergoes a transformation of some kind that releases about 20,000 J of energy. What kind of transformation is this likely to be?
A. a temperature change   D. a nuclear reaction
B. a phase change   E. it is impossible to guess
C. a chemical reaction

C11T.7 If you were to climb about 10 stories-worth of stairs, roughly what is the *minimum* number of food calories that you would have to burn? (Select the closest)
A. 70,000 Cal   D. 4 Cal
B. 4000 Cal   E. less than 1 Cal
C. 70 Cal

Situation for probs. CT11.8 through CT11.11: Two atoms interacting with each other have the potential energy shown in Figure C11.4 below. You may assume that the massive atom's mass is much larger than the light atom's mass, the light atom can only move along the x axis, and $V(x) \to 0$ smoothly as $x \to \infty$.

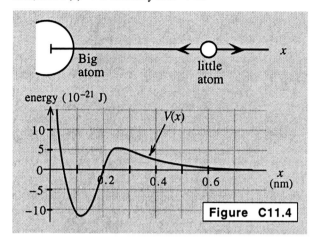

Figure C11.4

C11T.8 Imagine that the little atom approaches the big atom from infinity with an initial $K = 5 \times 10^{-21}$ J. How close to the big atom does it get?
A. $x = 0$ D. $x = 0.2$ nm
B. $x = 0.04$ nm   E. $x = 0.3$ nm
C. $x = 0.11$ nm   F. other (specify)

C11T.9 Imagine that at $t = 0$, the little atom is at position $x = 0.11$ nm and has a kinetic energy of 5×10^{-21} J. About how much energy would we have to add to break the bond?
A. 1×10^{-21} J   C. 12×10^{-21} J
B. 6×10^{-21} J   D. none: bond is already broken

C11T.10 Imagine that at $t = 0$, the little atom is at rest at $x = 0.20$ nm. What is the closest that it will ever get to the big atom subsequently (in the absence of external effects)?
A. 0.03 nm   C. 0.20 nm
B. 0.05 nm   D. other (specify)

C11T.11 If this system has a total energy of $+ 3 \times 10^{-21}$ J and the little atom is at $x = 0.11$ nm at $t = 0$, the atoms are
A. bound   B. unbound
C. it depends on little atom's initial direction of motion
D. depends on little atom's initial speed

HOMEWORK PROBLEMS

BASIC SKILLS

C11B.1 Assume that the two-atom system shown in Figure C11.4 has a total energy of $- 5 \times 10^{-21}$ J. Where are the turning points and what are the allowed and forbidden regions in this case?

C11B.2 Assume that the two-atom system shown in Figure C11.4 has a total energy of $+ 5 \times 10^{-21}$ J. Where are the turning points and what are the allowed and forbidden regions in this case?

C11B.3 Assume that the two-atom system shown in Figure C11.4 has a total energy of zero. Where are the turning points and what are the allowed and forbidden regions in this case?

C11B.4 Imagine that at $t = 0$ the little atom shown in Figure C11.4 is at $x = 0.11$ nm, has a kinetic energy of about 7×10^{-21} J, and is moving away from the big atom. Describe its subsequent motion in as much detail as you can.

C11B.5 Imagine that at $t = 0$ the little atom shown in Figure C11.4 is at very large x, has a kinetic energy of about 2×10^{-21} J, and is moving toward the big atom. Describe its subsequent motion in as much detail as you can.

C11B.6 Imagine that at $t = 0$ the little atom shown in Figure C11.4 is at rest at $x = 0.20$ nm. Describe its subsequent motion in as much detail as you can.

C11B.7 Imagine that at $t = 0$ the little atom shown in Figure C11.4 is at very large x, has a kinetic energy of about 10×10^{-21} J, and is moving toward the big atom. About how much energy must be removed from the system (at the appropriate time) for the atoms to become bound?

C11B.8 Imagine that at $t = 0$ the little atom shown in Figure C11.4 is at $x = 0.11$ nm, has a kinetic energy of about 10×10^{-21} J. About how much energy must be added to the system for the atoms to become unbound?

C11B.9 Imagine that a stove burner provides thermal energy at a rate of 4500 J/s. What is the minimum time that it would take to melt a quart (about 800 g) of ice in a pan placed on that burner?

C11B.10 A natural gas furnace produces 20,000 J of thermal energy per second. How much gas does it use per hour?

C11B.11 The current *total* energy consumption of the United States is on the order of magnitude of 10^{20} J/yr. If we could produce all of this energy by nuclear fusion, how many kilograms of deuterium/tritium mix would we need per year?

SYNTHETIC

C11S.1 A light object that is free to move along the x axis interacts with a massive object at $x = 0$. Figure C11.5 shows the potential energy function for their interaction. Draw a quantitatively accurate graph of the x component of the force acting on the light object as a function of x.

C11S.2 Imagine a plastic bead with a charge of $+1$ nC sliding along a wire that defines the x axis. Two fixed beads with the same charge are placed at $x = 0$, $y = \pm 5$ cm. Draw a quantitatively accurate graph of the potential energy of this system as a function of the position of the sliding bead. Is there an equilibrium position for this bead? Is it stable? Explain your answer.

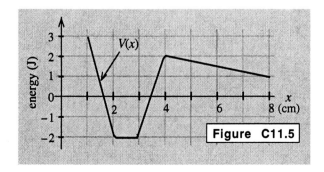

Figure C11.5

C11S.3 People whose feet are wet can walk on hot coals for a short while (DO NOT TRY THIS AT HOME!) Why is it important that the feet be wet? Why does this offer protection only for a limited time?

C11S.4 A standard hair dryer produces about 2500 J of thermal energy per second. What is the maximum amount of ice that you could melt in a minute?

C11S.5 A 120-g block of ice at 0°C is placed in an insulated thermos containing 420 g of water at 22°C. What is the final temperature of the water? Is there any ice left? If so, how much?*

C11S.6 A 12-g block of ice at 0°C is placed in an insulated thermos containing 450 g of water at 22°C. What is the final temperature of the water? Is there any ice left? If so, how much?*

C11S.7 What is the minimum amount of ice that would cool a 15-kg container of lemonade from 27°C to 0°C?*

C11S.8 Imagine that a person whose mass is 60 kg burns 1600 food calories while climbing a mountain 1300 m high. What fraction of the food energy is converted into thermal energy and/or latent energy in the environment?*

C11S.9 A certain solid-propellant model rocket engine releases a total of 6000 J of energy as it burns. If this engine carries a model rocket having a mass of 320 g to an altitude of 270 m, what fraction of the chemical energy released by the engine is wasted in the form of thermal energy in the air?*

C11S.10 Imagine that you were to eat a kilogram of snow. Your body will burn whatever food energy resources it has to maintain your internal temperature at 37°C. How many food calories will your body have to burn as a consequence of your meal of snow? (Note: This is NOT recommended as a diet plan.)*

> *Please follow the outline of the problem-solving framework when writing solutions to the starred problems.

C11S.11 Icebergs present real hazards to shipping, so many ways have been considered to destroy them. Why not just melt them? Estimate the energy required to melt a small iceberg with a volume of 1 km^3 (the density of ice is about 0.91 g/cm^3). Compare to the energy released by an atom bomb ($\approx 4\times10^{14}$ J).

C11S.12 If your car gets 25 mi/gallon when driven on the highway at 55 mi/h, about how many joules of chemical energy does the engine convert to other forms per second? Please show all of your work and estimates.

RICH-CONTEXT

C11R.1 You are preparing for a 5-day backpacking trip where you plan to use a gasoline cook stove for about 30 minutes each morning and night. The description of your cook stove brags that the stove can warm a liter of water to boiling in about 12 minutes. Estimate the *minimum* amount of gasoline you should take on your trip.

C11R.2 Imagine that your car can travel 25 mi on a gallon of gas when traveling on a level road at 55 mi/h. Estimate your gas mileage while going up an incline that gains 3 m in elevation for every 100 m forward (such an incline is called a 3% incline). Assume that your car (including passengers) has a mass of 1500 kg.

ADVANCED

C11A.1 Imagine that two objects with masses m and M interact only with each other, and that their potential energy is given by $V(r)$, where r is their separation. Imagine that the two objects move only along the x axis. Let us also choose our reference frame so that the center of mass of this isolated system is at rest at the origin. If x is the position of the object with mass m some time later, show that the definition of the center of mass implies that the other object's position at that time is $X = -mx/M$ and that $r = bx$, where $a \equiv (1+m/M)$. Show also that the system's total kinetic energy is bK, where K is the kinetic energy of the lighter object. If I were to draw a graph of $V(x)$, how would it be related to a graph of $V(r)$? How is the difference $E - V(x)$ related to the kinetic energy of the lighter object at the position x? Do you get the expected results when M becomes very large compared to m? (These results would help you interpret a potential energy diagram for a system whose interacting objects have comparable masses instead of very different masses.)

ANSWERS TO EXERCISES

C11X.1 There are no equilibrium positions at all for the potential energy curve shown in Figure C11.1a. The potential energy curve shown in Figure C11.1b has a single stable equilibrium point at $x = 0$.

C11X.2 The turning points are at about $x = \pm8.5$ cm. The forbidden regions are values of x such that $|x| > 8.5$ cm.

C11X.3 This is true: as the system's total energy increases, the line corresponding to that energy on the diagram gets higher and the turning points move outward.

C11X.4 The slope of $V(x)$ is *negative* for $x > 0.30$ nm, so the x-force F_x is *positive*, meaning that it pushes the little atom in the $+x$ direction. This is *away* from the big atom, so the interaction is repulsive.

C11X.5 (The calculation is straightforward, as long as you remember that 2256 kJ is 2,256,000 J.)

C11X.6 138 g.

C12

APPLICATIONS

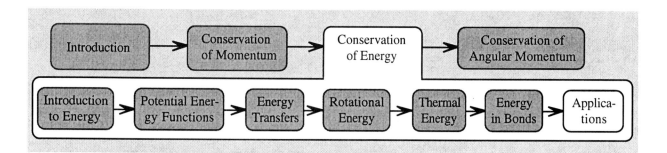

C12.1 OVERVIEW

This is the final chapter in the subunit on conservation of energy. In this subunit, we have (in a step-by-step manner) broadened our ability to understand interactions in terms of conservation of energy, starting with simple interactions that we could describe with potential energy functions, to more complicated contact interactions where we have to keep track of rotational and/or thermal energy, and finally to processes involving other forms of hidden (internal) energy. In this final chapter, we will learn a bit about several more forms of hidden energy and then look at a series of interesting applications of energy concepts. The final section brings both energy and momentum concepts to bear on understanding collision processes. The concepts presented in this chapter will provide a rich background for our future work throughout the course.

Here is an overview of the sections in this chapter

C12.2 *POWER* defines what the technical term *power* means in physics.

C12.3 *ELECTRICAL ENERGY* discusses what this form of hidden energy is, how it is transported, and what units we use to measure it.

C12.4 *ENERGY IN LIGHT AND SOUND* describes how we can quantify the energy carried by sound waves and light.

C12.5 *BUOYANCY* shows that we can understand why an object floats with the help of energy concepts.

C12.6 *FLYWHEEL POWER* discusses a way of storing energy that may prove to be the path to an emission-free car.

C12.7 *ELASTIC AND INELASTIC COLLISIONS* looks at processes that require us to apply what we know both about conservation of energy *and* conservation of momentum (a fitting close to this last chapter on conservation of energy).

Active Agent	Power	Energy Transfer Involved
The sun	3.9×10^{26} W	nuclear energy $\rightarrow$ electromagnetic waves
A large electrical power plant	≈ 1000 MW	nuclear or chemical energy $\rightarrow$ electrical energy
A gas-guzzling car	≈ 140 kW	chemical energy $\rightarrow$ thermal, kinetic, and/or potential
A large radio station	≈ 10 kW	electrical energy $\rightarrow$ electromagnetic waves
A typical home furnace	≈ 10 kW	chemical energy $\rightarrow$ thermal energy
A typical toaster	≈ 1500 W	electrical energy $\rightarrow$ thermal energy
One horsepower	≈ 746 W	
Resting human metabolism	≈ 60 W	chemical energy $\rightarrow$ thermal energy (mostly)
A commonly-available He-Ne laser	≈ 1 mW	electrical energy $\rightarrow$ electromagnetic waves

Table C12.1:
Power benchmarks.

The definition of *power*

C12.2 POWER

In physics, **power** is a technical term that expresses the rate at which an interaction transfers energy. At the fundamental level, such a transfer is always to or from some form of kinetic energy, so $P \equiv dK / dt$ (note that this formula is the energy counterpart to the formula $\vec{F} \equiv d\vec{p} / dt$), but at the macroscopic level, power can describe a transfer of any kind of energy to any other kind of energy. The SI unit of power is the **watt**:

$$1 \text{ W} \equiv 1 \text{ J/s} \qquad (C12.1)$$

So a 100 W light bulb converts 100 J of electrical energy to light and thermal energy (mostly the latter) every second. See Table C12.1 for some benchmarks for the power involved in various physical processes.

The power associated with the energy transfer mediated by an interaction that exerts a force $\vec{F}$ on a moving object given instant is given by

$$\text{power} \equiv P = \frac{dK}{dt} = \vec{F} \cdot \frac{d\vec{r}}{dt} = \vec{F} \cdot \vec{v} = F_x v_x + F_y v_y + F_z v_z \qquad (C12.2)$$

EXAMPLE C12.1

Problem: A 1200-kg car descends a 5% incline with its brakes on, maintaining a constant speed of 11 m/s ($\approx$ 24 mi/h). (A 5% incline means that the distance an object goes up or down as it travels along the incline is 5% of the distance that it goes along the incline.) At what rate is energy being transformed to thermal energy in the car's brakes? (Ignore air friction.)

Solution Every second, the car moves forward 11 m, so its vertical displacement every second $\Delta z = -0.05(11 \text{ m}) = -0.55$ m. The gravitational force on the car is downward, so $F_x = F_y = 0$, $F_z = -mg$ (see equation C8.22). Therefore, the amount of energy per second that the gravitational interaction on the car converts from gravitational potential energy to the common currency of kinetic energy is

$$\frac{dK}{dt} = \vec{F}_g \cdot \vec{v} = 0 + 0 - mg v_z = (-1200 \text{ kg})(9.8 \text{ m/s}^2)(-0.55 \text{ m/s})$$

$$= 6500 \frac{\text{kg-m}^2}{\text{s}^3} \left(\frac{1 \text{ J}}{1 \text{ kg-m}^2/\text{s}^2} \right) \left(\frac{1 \text{ W}}{1 \text{ J/s}} \right) = 6500 \text{ W} \qquad (C12.3)$$

Since the kinetic energy of the car does not actually change, the friction interaction in the car's brakes must immediately channel this to thermal energy at the same rate of 6500 W. While this is a credibly small fraction of the total power involved in automobile travel (see the benchmarks), it is still the thermal power of more than four toasters, so it is easy to see why the brake shoes get hot!

Exercise C12X.1: A bicyclist produces about 0.2 hp of mechanical power while pushing a bike at a constant speed of 15 m/s against air friction. What is the approximate magnitude of the force of air friction on the bike?

C12.3   ELECTRICAL ENERGY

I have delayed speaking more than superficially about **electrical energy** until this chapter, partly because it is easier to talk about electrical energy in the language of *power*. A power company produces electrical energy essentially by creating an electrical field in the wires leading from the power company's generators to your home. Electrons flowing through an appliance gain kinetic energy from this electric field (which is analogous to a gravitational field except that it affects only charged particles) and then convert their kinetic energy to other forms of energy depending on the nature of the appliance: thermal and light energy in light bulbs, mechanical energy in motors, thermal energy in toasters. We will discuss electrical circuits in much more detail in Unit *E*.

A qualitative definition of *electrical energy*

Since electrical energy is really a hidden form of energy associated with the microscopic motion of electrons, we will treat it as an internal energy associated with the electron flow (symbol: U^{el}) in conservation of energy problems.

Electrical power, even in everyday life, is measured in the SI unit of watts: when you read the labels on common appliances you often see a statement of the electrical power that they use in watts. Electrical energy, on the other hand, is commonly measured in the unit of **kilowatt-hours** instead of joules. A kilowatt-hour is defined to be the total electrical energy transferred during 1 hour if it is used at the rate of 1000 W: therefore 1 kW·h = (1000 J/s)(3600 s) = 3.6 MJ. Since a typical household of four uses about 700 kW·h of electrical energy per month, this is a conveniently large unit of energy, appropriate for use in power company bills. According to my recent bills, electrical energy in the Los Angeles area costs between 11¢ and 15¢ per kilowatt-hour.

Electrical energy is often measured in *kilowatt-hours*

Problem: Imagine that you wanted to construct a fountain that was able to shoot 12 gallons/min of water in a stream that goes 30 ft high. What should the minimum power of the electrical pump motor be?

EXAMPLE   C12.2

Solution Since 1 gallon ≈ 3.8 kg of water, the rate at which water flows is

$$\frac{12 \text{ gal}}{\text{min}}\left(\frac{1 \text{ min}}{60 \text{ s}}\right)\left(\frac{3.8 \text{ kg}}{1 \text{ gal}}\right) = 0.76 \text{ kg/s} \qquad \text{(C12.4)}$$

Let $m = 0.76$ kg be the mass of the "chunk" of water that goes through the pump during a given second. Initially, the system consists of this chunk of water essentially at rest at ground level ($z_i = 0$), the pump, the earth, and some incoming electrical energy. The final state of the system has everything the same except that the electrons that have flowed through the pump have given up their electrical energy and the chunk of water is again at rest but now at the top of the fountain trajectory ($z_f = h = 30$ ft ≈ 10 m). The change in the chunk's gravitational potential energy is $\Delta V = mg(z_f - z_i) = mgh$. Conservation of energy (ignoring friction and the kinetic energy of the earth) then implies that

$$0 = \Delta K + \Delta V + \Delta U^{el} = 0 + mgh + \Delta U^{el} \Rightarrow \Delta U^{el} = -mgh$$

A negative ΔU^{el} simply means that electrical energy is being converted to something else (ultimately gravitational potential energy in this case). We are simply interested in the magnitude of the electrical energy needed, so

$$\left|\Delta U^{el}\right| = +mgh = (0.76 \text{ kg})(9.8 \text{ m/s}^2)(10 \text{ m})\left(\frac{1 \text{ J}}{1 \text{ kg} \cdot \text{m}^2/\text{s}^2}\right) = 75 \text{ J} \quad \text{(C12.5)}$$

Since this energy transformation happens every second, the pump motor must draw *at least* 75 J/s = 75 **W** of electrical power. Allowing for friction will only make this result larger.

The preceding example illustrates one way of handling a continuous flow of material like water in the fountain: you can treat the flow as if it were a series of isolated "chunks" of material. We can use conservation of energy to analyze the behavior of each chunk as we would any discrete object, and at the end translate what we have learned about each chunk to a statement about the flow.

Exercise C12X.2: Roughly what does it cost you to leave a 100-W lamp on overnight? How much does this cost per month if you do this every night?

C12.4 ENERGY IN LIGHT AND SOUND

Analogy between sound and water waves

Just as a stone thrown in a pool of water generates concentric ripples of water waves that move radially away from the splash, so a mechanical disturbance in almost any kind of medium can radiate **sound waves** that radiate away from the disturbance. Just as a passing water wave momentarily displaces atoms of water from their normal positions near the surface of the undisturbed pool, a sound wave passing through a medium physically displaces atoms away from their normal positions in the medium. Since such displacements involve motion of the medium's atoms, such waves will carry energy (mostly in the form of kinetic energy in the displacing atoms).

Light as a wave

As we will see in Unit E, we can consider **light** to be an electromagnetic wave moving through a vacuum in much the same way that sound is a wave moving through a medium. Even though there is nothing in the vacuum that is physically moving, electromagnetic waves *do* carry energy, which is stored in the oscillating electromagnetic fields the waves create (we'll discuss this more in Unit E). Radio and television signals are carried by electromagnetic waves whose frequency of oscillation are out of the visible range. Similarly, microwaves, infrared light (which carry radiant heat), ultraviolet light, and X-rays are all electromagnetic waves that are outside the visible range.

When doing conservation of energy problems, we can think of a burst or pulse of sound or electromagnetic waves as an "object" in the system with its own internal energy U^{sw} or U^{em}, respectively. For example, if 100 J of light energy falls on a surface and is absorbed, we would say that $\Delta U^{em} = -100$ J.

Definition of *intensity*

The **intensity** I of an energy-carrying wave is defined to be the *power per unit area* that the wave delivers to a surface that is perpendicular to the wave's direction of travel. The intensity of direct sunlight at noon on a clear day, for example, is about 1000 W/m^2, meaning that the sunlight delivers about 1000 J per second to every square meter of surface facing the sun. A panel of perfectly-efficient photovoltaic cells facing the sun would produce 1000 W of electrical power for every square meter of cell surface (actual photovoltaic cells, unfortunately, are only about 10% efficient). If the solar energy falling on a home roof that is 30 ft × 60 ft could be converted entirely into electrical energy and appropriately stored, it would supply more than 20 times the electrical needs of an average household (even if one counts on only an average of three hours of sunlight per day!).

The intensity of sound waves is commonly expressed in **decibels**, where

Expressing sound wave intensities in *decibels*

$$\text{sound level in decibels} = 10 \log_{10}\left(\frac{I}{I_0}\right) \tag{C12.6}$$

where I_0 is the intensity of barely audible sound $\approx 10^{-12}$ W/m^2. This definition implies that when the sound level increases by 10 db, the intensity of the sound increases by a *factor* of 10. The sound level during a normal conversation is about 50 db ($I \approx 10^{-7}$ W/m^2), in busy traffic is about 80 db ($I \approx 10^{-4}$ W/m^2), near a power mower is about 100 db ($I \approx 0.01$ W/m^2), and at a rock concert (roughly the level of pain and ear damage) is about 120 db ($I \approx 1$ W/m^2).

Problem: Imagine that you are facing a 100-W incandescent light bulb about   **EXAMPLE C12.3**
30 m ($\approx$ 100 ft) away (such a bulb converts about 5% of the electrical energy it
consumes into actual light). What is the intensity of the bulb's light at your location? About how much light energy enters each of your eyes every second?

Solution According to the problem description, the bulb radiates about 5 J of
actual light energy every second. Imagine a sphere with a radius $r = 30$ m centered on the bulb. Every second, 5 J of light energy crosses this sphere. Every
bit of area on this sphere directly faces the bulb, so if the bulb's light energy is
radiated uniformly in all directions, then the light's intensity at $r = 30$ m will be
the total light energy going through the sphere per second divided by the area of
the sphere. This sphere has a surface area of $4\pi r^2 = 4\pi(30\text{ m})^2 = 11{,}000$ m², so

$$I = \frac{\text{energy radiated/time}}{\text{area facing light}} = \frac{5\text{ J/s}}{11{,}000\text{ m}^2}\left(\frac{1\text{ W}}{1\text{ J/s}}\right) = 4.5\times10^{-4}\text{ W/m}^2 \quad \text{(C12.7)}$$

(Note that this is about 2 million times less intense than direct sunlight!) Now,
light enters the eye through its pupil, which in reasonably dim conditions is
about 6 mm in diameter (3 mm in radius). If we treat each pupil as a flat circle,
the area that it presents to the light is thus $\pi r^2 = \pi(0.003\text{ m})^2 = 2.8\times10^{-5}$ m².
So the energy entering the pupil per second is about

$$\text{power} = \frac{\text{power}}{\text{unit area}}\cdot\text{area} = I\pi r^2 = (4.5\times10^{-4}\text{ W/m}^2)(2.8\times10^{-5}\text{ m}^2)$$

$$= 1.3\times10^{-8}\text{ W}\left(\frac{1\text{ J/s}}{1\text{ W}}\right)\left(\frac{1\text{ nJ}}{10^{-9}\text{ J}}\right) = 13\text{ nJ/s} \quad \text{(C12.8)}$$

Exercise C12X.3: The sound level near a jet engine is about 150 db. What is
the intensity of the sound waves produced by the jet engine? Compare this intensity to the intensity of bright sunlight.

Exercise C12X.4: The human ear is really remarkably sensitive. Considering
that an eardrum has an area on the order of magnitude of 0.1 cm², estimate the
energy that falls on the eardrum from a barely audible clap that lasts 0.1 s.

C12.5 BUOYANCY

You probably learned in high school that an object in water will sink until   **We can discuss buoyancy**
it has displaced an amount of water whose mass is equal to the object's mass.   **in terms of energy ideas**
We can actually prove this now using energy concepts!

To simplify matters, let's consider a cylindrical object with height h, cross-
sectional area A, and density ρ ; its mass is therefore mass $m = \rho Ah$. We place
this cylinder upright in a large pool of water whose density $\rho_w > \rho$. It turns out
to be convenient to define a unitless constant $\mu \equiv \rho/\rho_w$: then we can write

$$m = \rho_w(\rho/\rho_w)Ah = \rho_w A\mu h \quad \text{(C12.9)}$$

Our system here consists of both the cylinder and the water interacting gravitationally with the earth. Let $V_{cyl}(z)$ and $V_{wa}(z)$ be the potential energies of the
earth's gravitational interaction with the cylinder and the water, respectively. Let
us define $z = 0$ to be the surface of the water, and the reference separation for
both $V_{cyl}(z)$ and $V_{wa}(z)$ to be when the cylinder's bottom is at $z = 0$ (that is,
when it just begins to touch the water: see the dashed outline in Figure C12.1a).

Now imagine that the cylinder sinks to a depth d (so $z = -d < 0$). The potential energy of the earth's gravitational interaction with the cylinder is

$$V_{cyl}(z) = mgz = (\rho_w A\mu h)gz = -(\rho_w Ag\mu h)d \quad \text{(C12.10)}$$

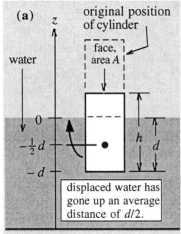

(a)

original position of cylinder

face, area A

water

displaced water has gone up an average distance of $d/2$.

(b)

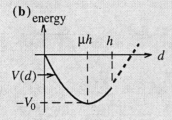

Figure C12.1: (a) When the cylinder is pushed into the water a distance d, water is effectively displaced to the surface. **(b)** A graph of the total potential energy function for this system.

After friction dissipates a bobbing object's kinetic energy, it settles to a depth where it displaces its own mass in water

Wanted: a really great battery!

(This is negative because the cylinder is now below its reference position.) Calculating the potential energy of the earth's interaction with the water is a bit trickier. By sinking to a depth d, the object has displaced a cylinder of water whose volume is Ad and whose mass is therefore $m_w = \rho_w Ad$. Where has this water gone? Since the total volume of water in the pool is always the same, the water level in the pool must rise slightly as the object is pushed down into it. So it is as if the water displaced has been added as a thin film to the pool's surface. (This film will be *very* thin if the pool's surface area is very large.) Since the average initial depth of this water was $\frac{1}{2}d$ and the water is now essentially at $z = 0$, the water has been displaced *upward* by an average distance of $\frac{1}{2}d$. The potential energy of the earth's gravitational interaction with this displaced water has thus *increased* from zero to $m_w g(\frac{1}{2}d)$. The potential energy of the earth's gravitational interaction with the water as a function of depth d is thus

$$V_{wa}(d) = m_w g(\tfrac{1}{2}d) = [\rho_w Ad]g\tfrac{1}{2}d = \tfrac{1}{2}\rho_w Agd^2 \qquad (C12.11)$$

Therefore, when $0 > z > -h$ (that is, the cylinder has not sunk deeper than its height), the total gravitational potential energy for this system is given by:

$$V(d) = V_{cyl}(d) + V_{wa}(d) = -\rho_w Ag\mu hd + \tfrac{1}{2}\rho_w Agd^2$$
$$= [\tfrac{1}{2}\rho_w Ag][d^2 - 2\mu hd] \qquad (C12.12)$$

If we define the constant $V_0 \equiv [\tfrac{1}{2}\rho_w Ag][\mu h]^2$ and add zero to the expression above in the form $0 = V_0 - V_0$, we can express equation C12.12 as follows

$$V(d) = [\tfrac{1}{2}\rho_w Ag][d^2 - 2\mu hd + (\mu h)^2] - V_0 = [\tfrac{1}{2}\rho_w Ag][d - \mu h]^2 - V_0 \quad (C12.13)$$

Note that the total potential energy as a function of depth $V(d)$ is smallest when $d = \mu h$ and increases for depths on either side of this value (see Figure C12.1b). For positions in the range $0 < d < h$, the shape of this potential energy function is like that of a mass on a spring (compare with Figure C7.4), so the cylinder should *behave* pretty much like a mass on a spring: when placed in the water, it will bob up and down for a while. Eventually, though, friction with the water gradually converts kinetic energy to thermal energy until the system's total non-thermal energy is as small as possible ($K = 0$, $V = -V_0$), which corresponds to the object being at rest at depth $d = \mu h$. If we multiply both sides of this expression by $\rho_w A$ and refer to equation C12.9 we find that at this resting depth

$$\rho_w Ad = \rho_w A\mu h \quad \Rightarrow \quad m_w = m \qquad (C12.14)$$

that is, the mass of the water displaced *is* equal to the mass of the object.

In general, *any* object moving in the presence of friction will eventually transform all of its available kinetic energy to thermal energy, coming to rest at the position with the lowest possible potential energy. (We will study more fully *why* this happens in unit *T*.)

C12.6 FLYWHEEL POWER

One of the main problems preventing the efficient generation and use of electrical power is the difficulty of storing electrical energy. For example, electric automobiles are quiet, non-polluting, efficient, and would be ultimately simpler and less expensive than gasoline automobiles IF there were a decent way to store electrical energy with anything approaching the energy density of a tankful of gasoline. With the current battery technology available, electric cars remain overweight, underpowered, and expensive. Recent advances in solar cell technology have made solar-generated electricity cheaper than many other kinds of electricity while the sun is shining, but with current technologies for storing energy (for use during the night or during cloudy days), solar electricity remains too expensive for most applications. The person or people who first provide the world with an electrical storage unit that can hold as much energy per kilogram as gasoline will open whole new vistas in the use of clean, safe, electrical energy (and probably become billionaires in the process).

One of the possible solutions to this problem is the idea of storing energy in a flywheel in the form of rotational kinetic energy. A well-designed electric motor can also be used as an electrical generator. If we were to attach a motor/ generator to an appropriately designed flywheel, we could use it as a motor to *store* electrical energy in the flywheel (by increasing its rotational speed) and as a generator to extract electrical energy from the flywheel's rotational energy.

Can we store energy in the form of rotational energy?

The problem is that as we feed a flywheel more and more energy (making it spin faster and faster), it eventually will fly apart. A steel flywheel, for example, simply cannot be rotated fast enough to even *approach* a battery's energy per mass ratio before it begins to come apart.

So, do we give up? Not yet! High-tech materials have recently become available that are much stronger than steel. Other things being equal, it turns out that the internal stresses in a rotating wheel increase in proportion to the material's density and to the square of its rotation speed (just like the energy stored does). So, to maximize the energy that we can store in a flywheel before it begins to come apart, we want to maximize the ratio of its material's tensile strength (that is, its ability to tolerate stresses) to its density.

Composite materials based on carbon fibers have about 3.5 times more tensile strength than steel while being 4.8 times less dense, so a carbon-fiber flywheel can store almost 17 times more energy than a steel flywheel. Engineers have recently built* a working carbon-fiber flywheel whose mass is 23 kg, radius is 15 cm and which rotates safely at 1,700 rev/s. At this angular speed, the flywheel stores roughly 15 MJ of rotational kinetic energy.

A realistic flywheel for energy storage

Exercise C12X.5: Check that the disk described *does* store about 15 MJ.

At these kinds of rotation speeds, the flywheel has to rotate in a vacuum on magnetic bearings that actually suspend the flywheel in space. Magnets on the flywheel axle interact electromagnetically with coils in the case to convert the flywheel's rotational kinetic energy to electrical energy or vice versa. The complete package has a mass of about 41 kg. Sixteen such flywheel packages (with a total mass of 660 kg) could store 240 MJ, which could give an efficient car an effective range of about 300 mi. This total mass is not too bad considering that the mass of a normal gasoline engine, tank, and all its supporting systems has a mass that is roughly comparable.

The lead-acid batteries used in the General Motors EV1 electric car, by contrast, store only about a third as much energy per kilogram. Moreover, flywheels can both receive and supply energy at much higher rates than batteries, leading to faster recharge times and peppier accelerations. The batteries in the EV1 will also die after 100 to 200 recharge cycles and have to be replaced, while the flywheel system should survive more than 10,000 cycles (about 30 years of driving).

How a flywheel energy storage system compares to batteries

So what is the catch? The high-tech fiber wheel and supporting equipment involved in a flywheel unit mean that, when mass-produced, each unit will cost about $800, putting the total cost of 16 units at about $13,000. The batteries for the EV1, by contrast, cost about $2,000. Flywheels *would* pay for themselves in less than 10 years compared to batteries, but (as is the case with many energy-efficient technologies) one has to make a steep initial investment.

The rub...

Still, there is great promise in the technology, as engineers continue to improve carbon-fiber materials (while basic chemistry sharply limits improvements to batteries). Maybe someday your car will run on flywheels!

---

*Much of the information in this section comes from W. Hively, "Reinventing the Wheel", *Discover*, **17**, 8, p. 58 (August 1996). For a deeper discussion of the physics involved, see Post, et. al., *Scientific American*, **229**, 6 (1973).

C12.7 ELASTIC AND INELASTIC COLLISIONS

Why we can treat a system involved in a collision as if it were isolated

As we have discussed in chapters C5 and C8, the total energy and total momentum of almost *any* system involved in a collision is very nearly conserved (as long as we examine the system *just before* and *just after* the collision), because if the collision process is very short, external interactions have too little time to transfer much momentum or energy to the system.

While the *total* energy of a system involved in a collision might be conserved, collision processes do involve strong internal interactions, and these interactions usually transfer at least *some* of the colliding objects' kinetic energy to internal energy (usually thermal energy). However, there are some kinds of collisions where very little kinetic energy is transformed. For example, colliding rubber balls deform each other during the collision, converting kinetic energy to microscopic forms of potential energy, but this deformation energy is almost entirely converted back into kinetic energy as the balls rebound.

Categories for collisions

We call a collision like this that conserves the colliding objects' total *kinetic* energy an **elastic** collision. Collisions involving macroscopic objects are never *perfectly* elastic, but some are close enough to make it useful as a model. Examples include fairly gentle collisions between rubber balls, steel balls, or billiard balls, and also collisions between objects that interact strongly gravitationally or electromagnetically as they pass close by each other without touching (remember that objects do not have to touch to "collide"). Collisions between microscopic systems like atoms or molecules can be *perfectly* elastic (quantum mechanics often forbids energy transfers to internal energy in such systems).

An **inelastic** collision converts some kinetic energy to internal energy (and thus does not conserve kinetic energy). A collision where the objects remain stuck together is **completely inelastic**: it turns out that such collisions convert as much kinetic energy to internal energy as conservation of momentum allows. An explosion might be considered a collision that converts internal energy to kinetic energy: we might call this a **superelastic** collision. But a normal collision (one that does not somehow trigger an active release of chemical or nuclear energy) will be at best elastic and usually inelastic, never superelastic.

We apply both conservation of momentum and energy in collision problems

The following examples show how we can usefully apply both conservation of energy and conservation of momentum to collision problems. Since I imagine that you know the problem-solving framework pretty well by now, I have not included the framework outline in the margin for these solutions (though you can see that I am still *following* that outline). The only real modification we need to make to the framework is to use *both* the law of conservation of momentum and the law of conservation of energy in the solution.

You also might enjoy reading problem C12S.15, which discusses asteroid impacts (an interesting application of collision physics)!

EXAMPLE C12.4

Problem: Imagine that a ball with mass m_1 is moving at a speed v_0 in a direction we define to be the $+x$ direction just before it collides elastically with another ball of mass m_2 at rest. After this head-on collision, both balls move along the $\pm x$ axis. What is the x-velocity of the first ball just after the collision?

Solution Figure C12.2 shows a diagram of the initial and final states of the system. We do not actually know yet whether the ball with mass m_1 moves in the $+x$ direction or the $-x$ direction after the collision (the diagram arbitrarily shows the latter case). In this problem, what we "know" are the balls' masses, that the first ball's initial velocity is v_0 in the $+x$ direction, that the other ball's initial velocity is zero, and that the velocities of both balls after the collision have components only in the x direction. We don't know v_{1x} or v_{2x}.

The system here is the two colliding balls. We can apply both conservation of both momentum and energy (pretty much no matter what their external interactions might be) because they are involved in a collision and we are looking at their velocities just before and just after that collision.

Conservation of momentum tells us that $\vec{p}_{1i} + \vec{p}_{2i} = \vec{p}_{1f} + \vec{p}_{2f}$. Since this elastic collision conserves *kinetic* energy we also have $K_{1i} + K_{2i} = K_{1f} + K_{2f}$. In this particular case, these two equations become, respectively

$$\begin{bmatrix} +m_1 v_0 \\ 0 \\ 0 \end{bmatrix} + \begin{bmatrix} 0 \\ 0 \\ 0 \end{bmatrix} = \begin{bmatrix} m_1 v_{1x} \\ 0 \\ 0 \end{bmatrix} + \begin{bmatrix} m_2 v_{2x} \\ 0 \\ 0 \end{bmatrix} \qquad \text{(C12.15a)}$$

$$\tfrac{1}{2} m_1 v_0^2 + 0 = \tfrac{1}{2} m_1 v_1^2 + \tfrac{1}{2} m_2 v_2^2 \qquad \text{(C12.15b)}$$

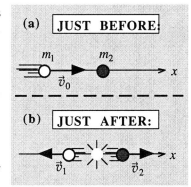

Figure C12.2: A drawing showing our system **(a)** just before the collision, and **(b)** just after the collision.

Only the top line of equation C12.15a has anything useful to tell us. Since only the x components of the object velocities in this problem are nonzero, $v_1^2 = v_{1x}^2$ and $v_2^2 = v_{2x}^2$. Therefore equations C12.15 in this case boil down to:

$$m_1 v_0 = m_1 v_{1x} + m_2 v_{2x} \quad \text{and} \quad \tfrac{1}{2} m_1 v_0^2 = \tfrac{1}{2} m_1 v_{1x}^2 + \tfrac{1}{2} m_2 v_{2x}^2 \qquad \text{(C12.16)}$$

We have here two independent equations in the two unknowns v_{1x} and v_{2x} that we have to solve simultaneously. We can do this by solving the first for v_{2x} :

$$v_{2x} = \frac{m_1}{m_2}(v_0 - v_{1x}) \qquad \text{(C12.17)}$$

and use this to eliminate v_{2x} in the other equation. Multiplying both sides of that equation by 2, subtracting $m_1 v_{1x}^2$ from both sides, and plugging in our result for v_{2x}, we get:

$$m_1(v_0^2 - v_{1x}^2) = m_2\left(\frac{m_1}{m_2}\right)^2 (v_0 - v_{1x})^2 = \frac{m_1^2}{m_2}(v_0 - v_{1x})^2 \qquad \text{(C12.18)}$$

Since $(v_0^2 - v_{1x}^2) = (v_0 - v_{1x})(v_0 + v_{1x})$, we can divide both sides of this equation by $m_1(v_0 - v_{1x})$ to get

$$v_0 + v_{1x} = \frac{m_1}{m_2}(v_0 - v_{1x}) \quad \Rightarrow \quad m_2 v_0 + m_2 v_{1x} = m_1 v_0 - m_1 v_{1x}$$

$$\Rightarrow \quad (m_1 + m_2)v_{1x} = (m_1 - m_2)v_0 \quad \Rightarrow \quad v_{1x} = \left(\frac{m_1 - m_2}{m_1 + m_2}\right)v_0 \qquad \text{(C12.19)}$$

(Note that when we divide by $v_0 - v_{1x}$, we are assuming that $v_0 \neq v_{1x}$. If we did have $v_0 = v_{1x}$, equation C12.17 would say that $v_{2x} = (m_1 / m_2)(v_0 - v_{1x}) = 0$: this means that *neither* ball is affected by the collision, which is absurd.)

Exercise C12X.6: Use equation C12.19 to find a similar formula for v_{2x}.

How might we check a *symbolic* answer like this? There are at least *three* general things we can do. (1) *We can check that the units make sense.* In this case, the quantity in parentheses is a unitless ratio of masses, so both sides of this equation should have units of speed. (2) *We can consider extreme cases* to see whether the formula yields results that makes sense. What if m_2 was very large, for example? Intuitively, we might think that the lighter ball m_1 should just bounce off such a nearly immovable object. Indeed, if $m_2 \gg m_1$, the ratio in parentheses in equation C12.19 becomes ≈ -1, implying that the lighter ball *does* just bounce off, reversing its direction but rebounding with the same speed. (3) *We can test the formula in simpler cases where we already know the answer.* We saw in Figure C2.2 that when a moving cart hits an identical cart at rest, a "sufficiently springy" collision causes the first one coming to a dead stop. This is consistent with equation C12.19: if $m_2 = m_1$, then v_{1x} is indeed zero after the collision. Checks like these can build our confidence in equation C12.19.

Three ways to check a symbolic formula for accuracy

EXAMPLE C12.5

(a) ┌─────────────┐
│ JUST BEFORE │
└─────────────┘

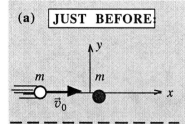

(b) ┌─────────────┐
│ JUST AFTER: │
└─────────────┘

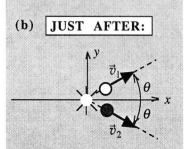

(c) ┌─────────┐
│ KNOWN: │
└─────────┘

$m = 0.30$ kg

$$\vec{v}_0 = \begin{bmatrix} +v_0 \\ 0 \\ 0 \end{bmatrix} = \begin{bmatrix} 1.0 \text{ m/s} \\ 0 \\ 0 \end{bmatrix}$$

The gray ball's initial velocity is zero.

$$\vec{v}_1 = \begin{bmatrix} +v_1 \cos\theta \\ +v_1 \sin\theta \\ 0 \end{bmatrix}$$

$\vec{v}_2$ makes an angle of $\theta = 30°$ with the +x direction

┌───────────┐
│ UNKNOWN: │
└───────────┘

v_1, anything else about $\vec{v}_2$, the change in the system's internal energy ΔU.

Figure C12.3: (a) The system (two wooden balls) just before the collision. **(b)** The system just after the collision. **(c)** Knowns and unknowns for this problem.

Problem: A 0.30-kg wooden ball moving at a speed of 1.0 m/s in the +x direction glancingly collides with a wooden ball with the same mass at rest. Just after the collision, the velocities of *both* balls make a 30° angle with the +x direction. What *fraction* of the system's original kinetic energy has been converted to internal energy in this collision?

Solution Let's orient our reference frame so the first ball's final velocity collision lies in the xy plane. We will shortly see that the second ball's final velocity must then lie in the xy plane as well. Figure C12.3 shows the initial and final states of the system in this situation assuming this. The diagram also lists knowns and unknowns.

The system here consists of the two wooden balls. We are not told anything about external interactions, but since we are looking at the velocities just before and just after a *collision*, we can treat this system as if it were isolated. Conservation of momentum tells us that $\vec{p}_{1i} + \vec{p}_{2i} = \vec{p}_{1f} + \vec{p}_{2f}$, which in this case reads

$$\begin{bmatrix} +mv_0 \\ 0 \\ 0 \end{bmatrix} + \begin{bmatrix} 0 \\ 0 \\ 0 \end{bmatrix} = \begin{bmatrix} mv_1\cos\theta \\ mv_1\sin\theta \\ 0 \end{bmatrix} + \begin{bmatrix} mv_{2x} \\ mv_{2y} \\ mv_{2z} \end{bmatrix} \qquad \text{(C12.20)}$$

We can see immediately from the third line of this equation that v_{2z} must be zero. $\vec{v}_2$ *does* therefore lie in the xy plane, and since makes an angle of $\theta = 30°$ with the +x axis, we must have $v_{2x} = v_2\cos\theta$ and $v_{2y} = \pm v_2\sin\theta$. The second line of equation C12.20 only makes sense if v_{2y} is negative (so it can cancel the first term on the right), so $v_{2y} = -v_2\sin\theta$ (this is consistent with I have drawn in Figure C12.3b). Then the second line of equation C12.20 reads

$$0 = mv_1\sin\theta - mv_2\sin\theta \quad \Rightarrow \quad v_1 = v_2 \qquad \text{(C12.21)}$$

Plugging this into the first line, we get

$$mv_0 = 2mv_1\cos\theta \quad \Rightarrow \quad v_1 = \frac{v_0}{2\cos\theta} \quad \left(= \frac{1.0 \text{ m/s}}{2\cos 30°} = 0.58 \text{ m/s} \right) \qquad \text{(C12.22)}$$

Now, this problem involves internal energies, so we will use the difference version of the conservation of energy formula: $0 = \Delta K + \Delta V + \Delta U$, where ΔK, ΔV, and ΔU are the changes in the system's total kinetic energy, internal potential energy, and internal energy, respectively. The gravitational interaction between these balls is insignificant, and "just before" and "just after" the collision, they are not participating in any *other* internal interactions, so $\Delta V = 0$. So conservation of energy in this case implies that $0 = \Delta K + \Delta U$, which means that

$$\Delta U = -\Delta K = -(\tfrac{1}{2}mv_1^2 + \tfrac{1}{2}mv_2^2 - \tfrac{1}{2}mv_0^2) = m(\tfrac{1}{2}v_0^2 - v_1^2)$$
$$= m\left(\frac{v_0^2}{2} - \frac{v_0^2}{4\cos^2\theta} \right) = \tfrac{1}{2}mv_0^2\left(1 - \frac{1}{2\cos^2\theta}\right) \qquad \text{(C12.23)}$$

The system's original kinetic energy was $\tfrac{1}{2}mv_0^2$, so the fraction of this energy that ΔU represents is

$$\frac{\Delta U}{\tfrac{1}{2}mv_0^2} = \frac{\tfrac{1}{2}mv_0^2}{\tfrac{1}{2}mv_0^2}\left(1 - \frac{1}{2\cos^2\theta}\right) = 1 - \frac{1}{2\cos^2 30°} = 0.33 \qquad \text{(C12.24)}$$

This is unitless (as a ratio of energies should be). It is also *positive*, which is very important (normal collisions do not *decrease* a system's internal energy). The magnitude is also less than 1, which makes sense (we would not expect this collision to convert more energy than was available in the first place!).

I. POWER
   A. Definition: $P \equiv dK / dt$ is the *rate* that an interaction transfers energy
      1. The SI unit of power is the watt: 1 W = 1 J/s
      2. This formula is the energy counterpart of $\vec{F} \equiv d\vec{p} / dt$
   B. $P = \vec{F} \cdot \vec{v}$ is the power of the energy transferred by an interaction that exerts a force $\vec{F}$ on an object that is moving with velocity $\vec{v}$

II. ELECTRICAL ENERGY
   A. How a power plant delivers energy to an electrical appliance
      1. It sets up an "electric field" in the wires leading to the appliance
      2. Electrons going through the appliance pick up dK from this field
      3. The appliance converts this dK to other forms of energy
   B. Since this energy is associated with the motion of microscopic particles, we will treat it as an internal energy U^{el}
   C. The common unit of electrical energy is the *kilowatt-hour* (this is the energy transferred during 1 h at a rate of 1000 W = 1000 J/s)
      1. 1 kW·h = 3.6 MJ costs about $0.11 to $0.16 in Los Angeles
      2. a typical household of four uses roughly 700 kW·h per month

III. ENERGY IN SOUND AND LIGHT WAVES
   A. A *sound wave* moving through a medium disturbs (wiggles) that medium's atoms as it passes by. These atoms thus have a kinetic energy that moves along with the wave disturbance.
   B. *Light* is an electromagnetic wave that we can think of as analogously "disturbing" the vacuum through which it moves
      1. There is energy associated with this disturbance (see Unit E)
      2. Radio waves, microwaves, infrared radiation, ultraviolet radiation, and X-rays are also electromagnetic waves (that we just cannot see).
   C. Treat the energy carried by such waves as internal energy U^{sw} or U^{em}
   D. The intensity of a sound or light wave
      1. Definition: *intensity* the power delivered by the wave per area per time to a surface that directly faces the wave (SI unit: W/m^2)
      2. Sound wave intensities are often expressed in *decibels*:
         a) Definition: the "sound level in db" $\equiv 10 \log_{10}(I / I_0)$, where $I_0 = 10^{-12}$ W/m^2 = a barely audible sound.
         b) Note that a 10-db increase means a *factor* of 10 increase in I!

IV. APPLICATION: BUOYANCY
   A. A basic principle: frictional interactions in a system will transfer kinetic energy to internal energy until it reaches a configuration where its kinetic energy is zero and its potential energy is a minimum
   B. The potential energy associated with an object floating in a pool is minimized when the object displaces its own mass in water

V. APPLICATION: FLYWHEEL POWER (This section illustrates one practical application of the ideas of rotational kinetic energy and electrical power.)

VI. APPLICATION: COLLISIONS
   A. We can treat a system involved in a collision as if it were *isolated*
      1. A *collision* is any short-duration but strong internal interaction
      2. If we look at the system just before and just after this short collision, there will not be enough time for external interactions to transfer significant amounts of momentum or energy to the system
      3. So both its energy and momentum are conserved
   B. Categories of collisions
      1. *elastic*: kinetic energy is conserved (none is transferred to internal)
      2. *inelastic*: some kinetic energy is transferred to internal energy
      3. *completely inelastic*: the objects stick together after the collision
      4. *superelastic*: a collision where internal energy is released
   C. Collision problems often involving several equations simultaneously

GLOSSARY

power: the rate at which energy is transformed from one form to another in a process (that is, the amount of energy transformed per unit time).

watt: the SI unit of power. 1 W = 1 J/s.

electrical energy: the term for energy delivered to a system in the form of electrons flowing through a circuit. We can treat this as a form of internal energy U^{el}.

kilowatt-hour: a unit of energy commonly used by power companies, equal to the total amount of energy used in an hour if it is used at the rate of 1 kW. 1 kW·h = 3.6 MJ.

sound wave: a disturbance that moves through a medium (solid, liquid, or gas). The passing disturbance jiggles atoms momentarily away from their normal positions as it passes, and thus effectively carries kinetic energy along with it. We treat this as an internal energy U^{sw}.

light: an electromagnetic wave (a disturbance in an electromagnetic field) that can travel through a vacuum and carries energy (see unit E for more details about how this is possible). We treat the energy carried by an electromagnetic wave as an internal energy U^{em}. Radio waves, microwaves, infrared radiation, ultraviolet radiation, and X-rays are electromagnetic waves that are not visible.

intensity (of a wave): the power (energy per time) per unit area delivered by the wave to a surface directly facing the oncoming wave.

decibel: a unit that expresses the intensity of sound waves on a logarithmic scale, where an increase of 10 decibels implies that the sound intensity has increased by a *factor* of 10. 120-db sound has an intensity of 1 W/m^2, 110-db sound an intensity of 0.1 W/m^2, and so on.

elastic (collision): a collision where the kinetic energy of the colliding objects is conserved: no energy is converted to internal energy.

inelastic (collision): a collision where some of the kinetic energy of the colliding objects is converted to internal energy (usually thermal energy).

completely inelastic (collision): a collision where the colliding objects stick together afterward. Such a collision converts the maximum possible amount of a system's original kinetic energy to internal energy.

superelastic (collision): a collision where internal energy is converted to kinetic energy. This *doesn't happen* with ordinary passive collisions: the collision must trigger an explosion that releases chemical or nuclear energy.

TWO-MINUTE PROBLEMS

C12T.1 A trained bicyclist in excellent shape might be able to convert food energy to mechanical energy at a rate of 0.25 hp for a reasonable length of time. Imagine such a person pedaling a stationary bike connected to a perfectly efficient electrical generator. Could such a person generate enough electrical power to run a toaster (T = yes, F = no)? How about a single ordinary light bulb (T = yes, F = no)?

C12T.2 An object moving with a speed of 5 m/s in the $-x$ direction is acted on by a force with a magnitude of 5 N acting in the $+x$ direction. At what rate does the interaction exerting this force transform this object's kinetic energy to some other form of energy (or vice versa)?
A. +25 W   C. −25 W   E. zero
B. −25 W   D. −1 W   F. other (specify)

C12T.3 An object moving with a velocity whose components are [4 m/s, −1 m/s, 3 m/s] is acted on by a force whose components are [−5 N, 0, +5 N]. What is the rate $P = dK / dt$ of energy transfer mediated by this interaction?
A. −35 W   C. zero   E. +35 W
B. −5 W   D. +5 W   F. other (specify)

C12T.4 You are standing 10 m from a light bulb on a dark night. Your friend is standing 40 m from the same bulb. How many times more intense is the light from the bulb at your location than at your friend's location?
A. 2 times   D.   64 times
B. 4 times   E.   the *intensity* is the same
C. 16 times   F.   other (specify)

C12T.5 How many times more intense is a 100-db sound wave than a 50-db sound wave?
A. 0.2 times   C. 20 times   E. 100,000 times
B. 2 times   E. 50 times   F. other (specify)

C12T.6 The shuddering of the earth during an earthquake is an example of a sound wave (T or F).

C12T.7 An object with mass m moving in the $+x$ direction collides head-on with an object of mass $3m$ at rest. After this elastic collision, the first object
A. moves in the $+x$ direction   B.   is at rest
C. moves in the $-x$ direction
D. (the answer depends on moving object's initial speed)

C12T.8 An object moving with speed v_0 collides head-on with an object at rest that is very much more massive. If the collision is elastic, how does the lighter object's speed v *after* the collision compare with its original speed v_0?
A. v is about equal to v_0 D. v is very small
B. v is noticeably less than v_0 E. v is exactly zero
C. v is half of v_0 F. $v \approx -v_0$

C12T.9 If two moving objects collide, we can *always* orient our reference frame so that the collision takes place entirely in the xy plane (T or F).

C12T.10 A object of mass m (object A) moving in the $+x$ direction collides with another object at rest (object B) whose mass is unknown. After the collision, object B is observed moving in the $+y$ direction. This collision *cannot* be elastic (T or F).

HOMEWORK PROBLEMS

BASIC SKILLS

C12B.1 Imagine that Leslie (whose mass is 55 kg) climbs a rope at a speed of about 0.5 m/s. How is energy being transformed in this process? What is the power associated with this energy transformation?

C12B.2 A bicyclist produces energy at the rate of 0.30 hp with her legs, which keeps her bike traveling at a constant speed of 12 m/s on a level road against a headwind. What is the approximate magnitude of the air friction force on the bike? (Assume that friction in the wheels is negligible.)

C12B.3 An electric motor uses 300 W of electrical power. If this motor is attached to a winch, what is the maximum rate at which it could lift a person whose mass is 60 kg?

C12B.4 A typical refrigerator uses about 350 W of power. If the refrigerator actually runs for an average of 8 hours every day, about how much does the electricity used by the refrigerator cost per month?

C12B.5 Does it cost more to leave a 100-W light bulb on all the time or run a 4000-W electric clothes dryer an average of about 45 minutes a day? Explain your response.

C12B.6 How many times brighter (that is, how many times more intense) is the light from a star 25 light-years away than that from an identical star 80 light-years away?

C12B.7 Imagine that you are standing 5 m from a chain saw and the sound level at your ears is an uncomfortable 120 db. How far would you have to move away from the chain saw to reduce the sound level at your ears to 100 db?

C12B.8 A rubber ball with mass m moving at a speed of 1.0 m/s in the $+x$ direction hits another rubber ball of mass $2m$ at rest. If the collision is elastic, what are the speeds and directions of motion of the two balls afterward?

C12B.9 A 6-kg bowling ball moving at 2.0 m/s elastically collides with a bowling pin of mass 1.5 kg head-on. What is the speed of the bowling pin after the collision?

C12B.10 Your lab partner writes the following on a lab report: "Since the collision was inelastic, neither energy nor momentum was conserved." Is this statement correct? If not, how might it be corrected? Explain your reasoning.

SYNTHETIC

C12S.1 In the last chapter, I claimed that the 340 TJ of energy released in the nuclear fusion of one kilogram of deuterium/tritium mixture was enough to supply the energy needs of roughly 10,000 households for a year. Using the information provided in section C12.3, verify this claim.

C12S.2 Imagine that you drive a 2000-kg truck up a 3% slope at a roughly constant speed of 16 m/s. If your truck engine is converting chemical energy to other forms of energy at a rate of 100 kW, roughly what fraction of the engine's energy ultimately goes to increasing the system's gravitational potential energy?

C12S.3 A car with a mass of 920 kg travels down an incline that makes an angle of 7° with the horizontal. The driver applies the brakes to hold the car's speed at a constant 18 m/s (40 mi/h). If air friction at this speed is not very significant, what is the approximate power going to thermal energy in the car's brake shoes?

C12S.4 Jenny knows that she can produce no more than about 0.12 hp of mechanical power indefinitely while riding a mountain bike. If her mass plus the mass of the bike is 63 kg, what is the *minimum* time that she should allow for a trip to the top of a 6500-ft mountain if the bike trail starts at an elevation of 1200 ft?

C12S.5 As we will see in unit N, an object falling in air will eventually reach a *terminal speed*, at which the rate at which air friction removes the downward momentum of the object is exactly equal to the rate at which gravity adds downward momentum. Consider a 62-kg skydiver falling at a terminal speed of 56 m/s. Energy is being transformed in this process: from what form to what form? What is the power associated with this transformation?

C12S.6 Imagine that you plan to generate electrical power for your 60-W study lamp by raising an object of mass 32 kg (70 lbs) a vertical distance of 2.5 m (about 8 ft) with a rope, wrapping the rope around the axle of an electrical generator, and then allowing the object to sink slowly back to the floor (unwrapping the rope and thus turning the generator). About how long will it take the mass to sink to the floor if the generator is to produce electrical power at a roughly constant rate of 60 W? (Assume that the generator is roughly 100% efficient.)

C12S.7 Approximately 3.3×10^5 m³ of water every minute drops roughly 50 m as it flows over Niagara Falls. If you could convert 80% of the change in gravitational potential energy involved into electrical energy using a hydroelectric power plant, how much power could you produce? If you sold this power at $0.06 a kilowatt-hour, what would be your annual gross income?

C12S.8 Verify the claim that I made in section C12.4 that an average of three hours of sunlight a day falling on a roof approximately 30 ft by 60 ft (when averaged over the day) is equivalent to about 20 times the electrical power used by a typical household of four.

C12S.9 An iron manhole cover is dropped from a height of 3.0 m onto an identical manhole cover lying on the ground. There is a dreadful clang and some bouncing around, but after everything settles down, we find that the temperature of both covers has increased by 0.029 K. Estimate the fraction of the original gravitational potential energy that has been converted to sound energy.*

C12S.10 A 1.0-kg cart with frictionless wheels moving along the $+x$-axis at an initial speed of 1.5 m/s collides elastically with another cart of mass 0.75 kg moving in the $-x$ direction with a speed of 2.0 m/s. If the carts continue to move along the x axis after the collision, what are their x-velocities afterwards?*

C12S.11 A 7.2-kg bowling ball traveling at a speed of 3.5 m/s collides with a 1.2-kg bowling pin at rest. After the collision, the pin moves with a speed of 3.0 m/s at an angle of 60° with respect to the original direction of motion of the bowling ball. What is the final velocity of the ball (magnitude and direction)? Is the collision approximately elastic?*

C12S.12 A 7.2-kg bowling ball traveling at a speed of 3.5 m/s collides elastically with a 1.2 kg bowling pin at rest. After the collision, the pin moves an angle of 30° with respect to the original direction of motion of the bowling ball. What are the final speeds of both the ball and the pin after the collision?*

C12S.13 A 230-g hockey puck originally sliding on ice in the $+x$ direction with a speed of 0.50 m/s collides with another puck of equal mass at rest. After the collision, the first puck is seen to move with a speed of 0.20 m/s in a line that makes an angle of 37° with the x axis (cos 37° ≈ 4/5, sin 37° ≈ 3/5). What is the velocity of the other puck? Is this collision approximately elastic?*

C12S.14 In a certain physics experiment, a helium atom traveling at a speed of 240 km/s hits an oxygen atom at rest. If the helium atom rebounds elastically from the oxygen atom at an angle of 90° with respect to its original direction of motion, what are the final velocities of both atoms (magnitude and direction)? (*Hint*: the mass of the oxygen atom ≈ four times that of the helium atom.)*

---

*Please follow the problem-solving framework as you write solutions to the starred problems.

C12S.15 (Asteroid impacts) Many scientists currently believe that the dinosaurs became extinct due to consequences of an asteroid hitting the earth 65 million years ago. This asteroid, which dug a crater about 175 km across in the Caribbean, probably had a diameter of 10 km, had a mass of about 10^{15} kg, and was likely moving with a speed of about 40 km/s relative to the earth when it hit. What might such an impact do to the earth?

It might be hard to *comprehend* the enormous amounts of energy released in such an impact, but it is not hard to calculate it. Using a floating frame where the earth is initially at rest, estimate the energy converted to internal energy in this completely inelastic collision. If a typical atomic bomb releases about 4×10^{14} J of energy, how many hundreds of millions of atomic bomb explosions would it take to release this much energy?

This energy will be converted into a variety of forms (such as kinetic energy of fragments thrown into space, thermal energy of vaporized rock, and so on). Much of the energy, though, will be converted to thermal energy in the rock below the impact site, creating a hot spot on the ocean floor that will boil the sea water over it for months.

To look at just *one* of the many devastating consequences of this kind of energy release, let's focus on the last issue and ask a simple question: roughly how much seawater would an asteroid like this hitting the Caribbean vaporize? To estimate this, we have to first guess the fraction of the asteroid's energy that goes to boiling sea water. We cannot know this precisely without a lot of research, so let's just make a guess. It will probably be less than 50% of the energy of impact and more than 0.1%, so let's estimate that 10% of the energy goes to boiling seawater. Deep ocean water has a temperature of about 4 °C. Show that this amount of energy would boil away about 2×10^{15} kg of water starting at this temperature, and show that a cube holding this much water would be about 13 km on a side.

Since the *total* amount of water vapor in the earth's atmosphere is only about 10^{16} kg, very suddenly adding 2×10^{15} kg more in a relatively small region could have dramatic effects. For one thing, it might increase global cloud cover (certainly over the region involved), which would reduce the energy the earth receives from the sun and lower the earth's temperature globally (and especially locally). Water vapor also carries energy that is released when the water condenses: the energy released by condens-ing water provides much of the energy that drives hurricanes. (Recent computer models suggest that "hypercanes" 10 miles in diameter with 500-mi/h winds might form over a strike site). In short, just the *water* boiled by an asteroid impact can be expected to have disastrous global effects!

RICH-CONTEXT

C12R.1 On an icy road one day, a car with mass m (car A) traveling due east hits another car of mass $2m$ (car B) in the center of an intersection. After the accident, marks in the ice show that car A skidded at an angle of 60° south of east, while car B skidded at an angle of 60° north of east. The driver of car A claims in court to have been traveling the speed limit of 40 mi/h, but car B ran the stoplight and was moving northward at 20 mi/h at the time of the accident. The driver of car B does not dispute that car A was traveling at 40 mi/h but claims that car B was stalled in the center of the intersection at the time of the accident, so car A should have had plenty of time to stop. You are the judge. Which story is more consistent with the physical facts? (*Hints*: Can this collision be superelastic? It also may help you to know that $\cos(60°) = 1/2$, $\sin(60°) = \sqrt{3}/2$. Work with these *fractions*, not their decimal equivalents!)

C12R.2 Everyone knows that bullets bounce off Superman's chest. If bad guys shoot 180 rounds a minute of 3-g bullets with a speed of 620 m/s, will the average force exerted by this stream of bullets require super strength to resist, or could an ordinary person (with a similarly impervious chest) resist being bowled over? (*Hint:* Remember that $\vec{F} = d\vec{p}/dt$.) (Adapted from Halliday, D. and Resnick, R., *Fundamentals of Physics*, 3/e, New York: Wiley.)

ADVANCED

C12A.1 Prove that if an originally moving object of mass m collides elastically with an object of equal mass at rest, the angle between the objects' velocities after the collision is 90°. (*Hint:* Assume that the final velocities lie in the xy plane, and then show that $v_{1x}v_{2x} + v_{1y}v_{2y} = 0$.)

C12A.2 In the situation described in problem C12R.1, find the *range* of northward speeds that car B might have had before the collision that would be consistent with the physical evidence and the idea that the collision should be inelastic.

ANSWERS TO EXERCISES

C12X.1 About 10 N ($\approx$ 2 lbs!).

C12X.2 Leaving a 100-W lamp on overnight ($\approx$ 8 h) consumes about (0.1 kW)(8 h) = 0.8 kW·h, which costs between 9¢ and 12¢. If you do this for thirty days, though, the costs add up to between $2.70 and $3.60.

C12X.3 120 db is 1 W/m², so 130 db is 10 W/m², 140 db is 100 W/m², and 150 db is 1000 W/m², which is about the same intensity as direct sunlight!

C12X.4 Barely audible sound has an intensity of about 10^{-12} W/m², and there are 10^4 cm² in 1 m², so the power falling on a surface of area 0.1 cm² will be about 10^{-17} W, and the power accumulated during 0.1 s is thus $\approx 10^{-18}$ J!

C12X.5 The moment of inertia of a disk is $I = \frac{1}{2}mR^2$, where m is the disk's mass and R is its outer radius. The energy stored in a disk with $m = 23$ kg and $R = 0.15$ m that is rotating at $\omega = 1700$ rev/s is thus

$$
\begin{aligned}
K^{\text{rot}} &= \tfrac{1}{2}I\omega^2 = \tfrac{1}{4}mR^2\omega^2 \\
&= \tfrac{1}{4}(23\text{ kg})(0.15\text{ m})^2\left(\frac{2\pi\text{ rad}}{\cancel{\text{rev}}}\right)^2\left(\frac{1700\ \cancel{\text{rev}}}{\text{s}}\right)^2 \\
&= 1.48\times10^7\ \frac{\text{kg}\cdot\cancel{\text{m}}^2}{\cancel{\text{s}}^2}\left(\frac{1\text{ J}}{1\ \cancel{\text{kg}\cdot\text{m}^2/\text{s}^2}}\right)\left(\frac{1\text{ MJ}}{10^6\ \cancel{\text{J}}}\right) = 15\text{ MJ}
\end{aligned}
$$

C12X.6 Plugging equation C12.19 into C12.17 yields

$$
\begin{aligned}
v_{2x} &= \frac{m_1}{m_2}\big[v_0 - v_{1x}\big] = \frac{m_1}{m_2}\left[v_0 - \left(\frac{m_1 - m_2}{m_1 + m_2}\right)v_0\right] \\
&= \frac{m_1 v_0}{m_2}\left[\frac{\cancel{m_1} + m_2 - (\cancel{m_1} - m_2)}{m_1 + m_2}\right] = \frac{m_1 v_0}{\cancel{m_2}}\left[\frac{2\cancel{m_2}}{m_1 + m_2}\right] \\
&= \left[\frac{2m_1}{m_1 + m_2}\right]v_0
\end{aligned}
$$

ANGULAR MOMENTUM

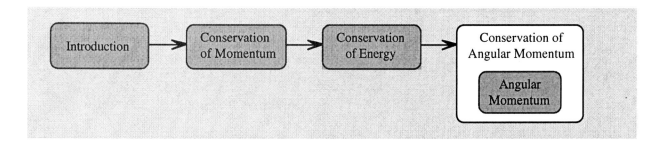

C13.1 OVERVIEW

In the last chapter, we concluded our discussion of conservation of energy. We now turn our attention to the third great conservation law of our unit, the law of *conservation of angular momentum* (which arises from the symmetry principle that the laws of physics are independent of one's orientation in space).

This chapter defines and explores the concept of angular momentum (using and extending the concepts of rotational motion developed in chapter C9), describes the law of conservation of angular momentum, and ends with several examples where that law is applied.

Here is an overview of this chapter's sections.

C13.2 *INTRODUCTION TO ANGULAR MOMENTUM* looks at a few experiments that illustrate the nature of angular momentum and why it might be a useful concept.

C13.3 *THE CROSS PRODUCT* defines a new kind of vector product called the *cross product* and discusses its properties. This section provides essential background for unit *E* as well as for this chapter.

C13.4 *THE ANGULAR MOMENTUM OF A PARTICLE* shows how we can use the cross product to define the angular momentum of a particle.

C13.5 *THE ANGULAR MOMENTUM OF A RIGID OBJECT* explores how we can compute the total angular momentum of a symmetrical rotating object. It turns out that the total angular momentum of such an object is $\vec{L} = I\vec{\omega}$, directly analogous to $\vec{p} = m\vec{v}$.

C13.6 *CONSERVATION OF ANGULAR MOMENTUM* illustrates how one can solve conservation of angular momentum problems using a worksheet that is virtually identical to the one used for linear momentum.

C13.7 *APPLICATION: NEUTRON STARS* discusses how conservation of angular momentum helps us understand why neutron stars spin at incredible rates (as they are observed to do).

This chapter concludes this unit on conservation laws. I hope that you have seen how these simple laws powerfully illuminate a broad range of physical phenomena, enabling us to make confident predictions even about the behavior of complex and poorly-understood systems. The way that these laws cover so much territory with a few simple ideas illustrates physics at its best.

Conservation of energy, momentum, and angular momentum are not the only conservation laws used in physics. We will discuss *conservation of* (electrical) *charge* in Unit *E*, and physicists use other conservation laws in other contexts. Because conservation laws are both powerful and easy to use, physicists are always looking for good conservation laws!

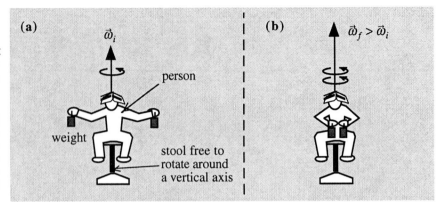

Figure C13.1: An experiment that illuminates the nature of angular momentum. **(a)** A person on a stool that is free to rotate around a vertical axis rotates slowly around that axis while holding two weights with extended arms. **(b)** If the person now draws the weights in closer to the axis of rotation, the person's angular velocity increases dramatically in magnitude.

C13.2 INTRODUCTION TO ANGULAR MOMENTUM

Some experiments that illuminate the nature of angular momentum

Imagine a person sitting on a stool that is free to rotate around a vertical axis. Such a person is isolated from external effects as far as rotations around that axis are concerned. If the stool's bearings are almost frictionless and we set the person rotating, that person will continue to rotate essentially indefinitely. Just as the linear velocity $\vec{v}$ of an isolated object's center of mass remains constant, independent of its internal interactions because its total translational momentum $\vec{p}$ is conserved, so an isolated object's *angular* velocity $\vec{\omega}$ appears to remain constant. Could this (by analogy) because some rotational version of momentum (which we might call **angular momentum** $\vec{L}$) is conserved?

Let's assume for the sake of argument that this is so. How might this quantity be defined? The following experiment (which you may have seen demonstrated) gives us a clue. Imagine that the person sitting on the rotating stool now holds two weights (one in each hand) with arms outstretched. If that person is initially rotating slowly on the stool with arms outstretched, then drawing the weights in closer to the axis of rotation causes the person's angular velocity $\vec{\omega}$ to increase dramatically. Re-extending the arms restores the person's angular velocity $\vec{\omega}$ to its initial value. (See Figure C13.1.)

If you have watched or participated in a diving competition, you know that divers take advantage of this effect to change their rotation rate. A diver whose body is extended after leaving the diving board may be initially rotating only very slowly around his or her center of mass, but tucking into a compact ball causes the diver to rotate rapidly. Divers will then generally extend their bodies at the very end so that they are again only slowly rotating as they hit the water.

We can see from these experiments that if an isolated person's angular momentum is conserved, angular momentum cannot be simply equal to angular velocity $\vec{\omega}$ or even $m\vec{\omega}$, since the values of these quantities can change for an isolated person who is changing the way that his or her mass is distributed. So if an isolated system really does have a conserved angular momentum, it must depend somehow on the *distribution* of mass within the system.

A tentative definition of angular momentum

In chapter C9, we found that an object's rotational kinetic energy was given by $K^{\text{rot}} = \frac{1}{2}I\omega^2$. Comparing this to the formula $K = \frac{1}{2}mv^2$ for the kinetic energy of an object's translational motion, we see that in the rotational formula the angular speed ω plays the role of the center-of-mass speed v and the moment of inertia I plays the role of mass. Note that $I = \sum m_i r_i^2$ depends not only on an object's mass but also on how that mass is distributed. If an object's total translational momentum is defined by $\vec{p} \equiv m\vec{v}$, might its angular momentum be defined by $\vec{L} \equiv I\vec{\omega}$ (with $\vec{\omega}$ again playing the role of velocity and I of mass)? Would this explain what we observe in these two experiments?

This definition satisfies experimental data

We can see that qualitatively, at least, this definition does seem to work. In both cases, the people increase their angular velocity by rearranging mass to be closer to the axis of rotation. This has the effect of *reducing* the moment of inertia I involved in the rotating system. If angular momentum $\vec{L} \equiv I\vec{\omega}$ is conserved, then this means that the person's angular velocity $\vec{\omega}$ must then *increase* to keep $\vec{L}$ constant, which is just what we observe! Indeed, this offers a straightforward and simple explanation of the mystery of how an isolated person can change their angular speed at all without pushing on (or being pushed by) something external.

But could what we are observing be a consequence of conservation of rotational kinetic energy $K^{\mathrm{rot}} = \frac{1}{2}I\omega^2$ instead? More quantitative experiments support the idea of a conserved angular momentum $\vec{L} \equiv I\vec{\omega}$ by showing that an isolated object's angular speed depends inversely on the object's moment of inertia I and not on the square root of I (as conservation of kinetic energy would predict). We see, therefore, that we can nicely explain the experiment shown in Figure C13.1 with the help of a completely new conservation law, a law stating that angular momentum $\vec{L} \equiv I\vec{\omega}$ is *conserved*.

Experimental results also show that we are *not* talking about conservation of rotational kinetic energy

Exercise C13X.1: Verify that if it were rotational kinetic energy that was conserved for an isolated system, then experiments would show that $\omega \propto I^{-1/2}$ instead of $\omega \propto I^{-1}$.

Exercise C13X.2: Two children of mass m riding on a disk-shaped playground merry-go-round of mass $2m$ are initially both standing on opposite sides of the the merry-go-round rim: each is a distance R from its center. The children move in toward the center until they are a distance $\frac{1}{2}R$ from the center. Show that this decreases the system's moment of inertia by a factor of 2. By what factor should its angular speed increase? By what factor does each child's rotational speed $v = r\omega$ increase? (Recall from section C9.2 that an object's *rotational speed* is its ordinary speed due to its rotational motion around some axis.)

C13.3 THE CROSS PRODUCT

The last section states the two most important ideas of this chapter: (1) that we can define a system's angular momentum to be $\vec{L} \equiv I\vec{\omega}$ and (2) that an isolated object's angular momentum is conserved. We might be therefore tempted to end the chapter right here. But it turns out that there are some limitations on the definition $\vec{L} \equiv I\vec{\omega}$ that we should know about, and there are also some nice things that we can prove about a system's angular momentum. In order to learn about these things, we need to develop a formal and careful definition of the angular momentum of a *particle*, and to do this, we first need to define a new kind of product of two vectors, which we call the *cross product*.

The **cross product** $\vec{u} \times \vec{w}$ of two arbitrary vectors $\vec{u}$ and $\vec{w}$ is defined to be a *vector* having a magnitude

$$\mathrm{mag}(\vec{u} \times \vec{w}) = uw\sin\theta \qquad (C13.1a)$$

where θ is the angle measured from the direction of $\vec{u}$ to the direction of $\vec{w}$. (The vector $\vec{w}$ is just an arbitrary vector here, and is *not* the same as an object's angular velocity $\vec{\omega}$.) As Figure C13.2 shows, this product can be interpreted as either being the magnitude of $\vec{u}$ times the absolute value of the component of $\vec{w}$ that is perpendicular to $\vec{u}$ or vice versa:

$$\mathrm{mag}(\vec{u} \times \vec{w}) = u_{\perp}w = w_{\perp}u \qquad (C13.1b)$$

Unlike the dot product (which is a *scalar*), the cross product of two vectors is another *vector*. The direction of $\vec{u} \times \vec{w}$ is defined to be perpendicular to both $\vec{u}$ and $\vec{w}$ in the sense defined by the following right-hand rule: if you point your right fingers first in the direction of $\vec{u}$, and then curl them in the direction of $\vec{w}$, your thumb points in the direction of the cross product (this is illustrated in Figure C13.3).

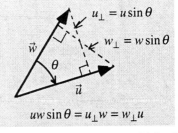

$$uw\sin\theta = u_{\perp}w = w_{\perp}u$$

Figure C13.2: We can think of the magnitude of $\vec{u} \times \vec{w}$ as being the magnitude of $\vec{u}$ times the perpendicular component of $\vec{w}$ or vice versa.

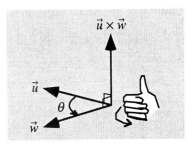

Figure C13.3: The right-hand rule that defines the direction of $\vec{u} \times \vec{w}$.

Mathematical properties of the cross product

Note that the definition of the direction of the cross product implies that:

$$\vec{u} \times \vec{w} = -\vec{w} \times \vec{u} \qquad \text{(C13.2)}$$

Try it! If you point your right fingers first in the direction of $\vec{w}$ and then curl them in the direction of $\vec{u}$, your thumb points the opposite direction than it does if you point them first in the direction of $\vec{u}$ and curl them in the direction of $\vec{w}$. Because the cross product of two vectors changes sign when you reverse the order of the vectors, we say that the cross product is **anticommutative**.

One can also see from the definition of the cross product that

$$(q\vec{u}) \times \vec{w} = \vec{u} \times (q\vec{w}) = q(\vec{u} \times \vec{w}) \qquad \text{(C13.3)}$$

Why? Multiplication by a *positive* scalar q only changes the *magnitude* of a vector, not its direction, so the directions of all three products will remain the same and the magnitudes of all three will be $quw\sin\theta$, with θ being the same in each case. Multiplication by a *negative* scalar is equivalent to multiplying by a positive scalar and then reversing the direction of the vector multiplied. You can check with your right hand that flipping either $\vec{u}$ or $\vec{w}$ flips the direction of the cross product as a whole. Thus the directions of the three products are consistent even when c is negative, and the magnitudes are all equal to $|q|uw\sin\theta$.

Perhaps the most important property of the cross product for how we will use it in what follows is the *distributive* property:

$$\vec{u} \times (\vec{w} + \vec{c}) = \vec{u} \times \vec{w} + \vec{u} \times \vec{c} \qquad \text{(C13.4)}$$

This property also follows directly from the definition, though its proof is more difficult than the others (see Problem C13A.1 for a limited proof).

Table C13.1 summarizes the definition and properties of the cross product (and compares them with those of the dot product).

Exercise C13X.3: The hour and minute hands on a clock are 8 cm and 10 cm long, respectively. Let $\vec{u}$ be the displacement vector from base to tip of the hour hand, and let $\vec{w}$ be the displacement vector from base to tip of the minute hand. At exactly 10 o'clock, what is the magnitude and direction of $\vec{u} \times \vec{w}$?

The cross product in terms of vector components

The cross product in component form is

$$\text{If } \vec{c} = \vec{u} \times \vec{w}, \text{ then } \begin{bmatrix} c_x \\ c_y \\ c_z \end{bmatrix} = \begin{bmatrix} u_y w_z - u_z w_y \\ u_z w_x - u_x w_z \\ u_x w_y - u_y w_x \end{bmatrix} \qquad \text{(C13.5)}$$

This follows directly from the distributive, commutative, and linear properties of the cross product (see problem C13A.2 for details).

How to remember this formula

This formula looks horribly complicated, but in fact there is a very simple way to remember it. First of all, note that all three rows of equation C13.5 have the same basic form: a component of the cross product is equal to a product of a component of $\vec{u}$ times a component of $\vec{w}$ minus another such product. Then, consider the circle in Figure C13.4, which has the subscripts x, y, z arranged in alphabetical order clockwise around the circle. Note that in each line, the subscripts of c and the *first* product of $\vec{u}$ and $\vec{w}$ components follow the order that they appear as you go *clockwise* around the circle, and the subscripts of c and the *second* product of $\vec{u}$ and $\vec{w}$ components follow the order that the subscripts appear as you go *counterclockwise* around the circle. For example, in the second row, the subscript on the c is y. We thus find the subscripts for the first product of $\vec{u}$ and $\vec{w}$ components by going clockwise around the circle from y: the subscripts are thus z and x and the first product is $u_z w_x$. We find the subscripts for the second product by going counterclockwise from y: the subscripts

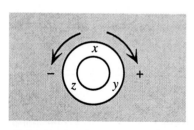

Figure C13.4: Memory aid for equation C13.5.

	DOT PRODUCT	CROSS PRODUCT
Symbolic representation	$\vec{u} \cdot \vec{w}$	$\vec{u} \times \vec{w}$
Type of quantity produced	*scalar*	*vector*
Definition	$\vec{u} \cdot \vec{w} = uw \cos\theta$	$\vec{u} \times \vec{w} = uw \sin\theta$ direction: $\perp$ to $\vec{u}$ and $\vec{w}$, use RH rule
Product of a vector with itself	$\vec{u} \cdot \vec{u} = u^2$	$\vec{u} \times \vec{u} = 0$
Product is zero when:	vectors are perpendicular	vectors are parallel
Commutative or anticommutative?	$\vec{u} \cdot \vec{w} = +\vec{w} \cdot \vec{u}$	$\vec{u} \times \vec{w} = -\vec{w} \times \vec{u}$
Linear property	$(q\vec{u}) \cdot \vec{w} = \vec{u} \cdot (q\vec{w}) = q(\vec{u} \cdot \vec{w})$	$(q\vec{u}) \times \vec{w} = \vec{u} \times (q\vec{w}) = q(\vec{u} \times \vec{w})$
Distributive property	$\vec{c} \cdot (\vec{u} + \vec{w}) = \vec{c} \cdot \vec{u} + \vec{c} \cdot \vec{w}$	$\vec{c} \times (\vec{u} + \vec{w}) = \vec{c} \times \vec{u} + \vec{c} \times \vec{w}$
Component form	$\vec{u} \cdot \vec{w} = u_x w_x + u_y w_y + u_z w_z$	$\vec{u} \times \vec{w} = \begin{bmatrix} u_y w_z - u_z w_y \\ u_z w_x - u_x w_z \\ u_x w_y - u_y w_x \end{bmatrix}$

Table C13.1: A comparison of the properties of the dot and cross products.

are x and z and thus the second product is $u_x w_z$. You can check for yourself that this mnemonic trick works for the other two lines as well.

Exercise C13X.4: Two displacement vectors $\vec{u}$ and $\vec{w}$ have components given by $\vec{u} = [3\text{ m}, -2\text{ m}, 0]$ and $\vec{w} = [-2\text{ m}, 5\text{ m}, 0\text{ m}]$. What are the components of $\vec{u} \times \vec{w}$? Does the direction of your result make sense, considering that both $\vec{u}$ and $\vec{w}$ happen to lie in the xy plane in this case?

C13.4 THE ANGULAR MOMENTUM OF A PARTICLE

A particle's **angular momentum** around point O when it is at position $\vec{r}$ relative to O and moving with velocity $\vec{v}$ can be written very easily using the cross product as follows

$$\vec{L} \equiv m(\vec{r} \times \vec{v}) = \vec{r} \times m\vec{v} = \vec{r} \times \vec{p} \quad \text{(for any particle)} \qquad \text{(C13.6)}$$

The definition of a particle's angular momentum

Note that this quantity will have SI units of $\text{kg} \cdot \text{m}^2/\text{s}$.

According to equation C13.1b, the magnitude of $\vec{L}$ will be

$$\text{mag}(\vec{L}) \equiv L = mrv_\perp \qquad \text{(C13.7)}$$

where $v_\perp$ is the component of the particle's velocity $\vec{v}$ that is perpendicular to $\vec{r}$. Thus the magnitude of $\vec{L}$ depends on the particle's mass, the distance it is from the point O and the part of its velocity that is causing it to go "around" O (as opposed to directly toward or away from O).

Indeed, if the particle happens to be moving in a *circle* around O, $v_\perp$ is *equal* to its speed (because, since the distance between the particle and O is not changing, the particle's velocity $\vec{v}$ has *no* component toward or away from O). According to equation C9.7, the particle's speed under these circumstances is $v = r\omega$, where ω is its angular speed, and the particle's angular momentum has

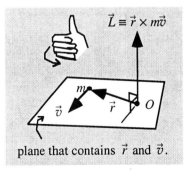

plane that contains $\vec{r}$ and $\vec{v}$.

Figure C13.5: The definition of a particle's angular momentum around a point O.

a magnitude of $L = mr(r\omega) = mr^2\omega$. Moreover, you can see from Figure C13.5, the particle's angular momentum $\vec{L}$ around O points along the axis of the particle's rotation around O in the direction indicated by the right-hand rule, which is the *same* way that we defined the direction of the particle's angular velocity $\vec{\omega}$ in chapter C9. Therefore, in the case of circular motion around O, we can write a particle's angular momentum as follows:

This coincides (for circular motion) to the hypothetical definition in section C13.2

$$\vec{L} = mr^2\,\vec{\omega} \quad \text{(for circular motion at least)} \tag{C13.8}$$

Since mr^2 is the particle's moment of inertia I for rotations around O, so this definition (for circular motion at least) coincides with the hypothetical definition of $\vec{L}$ that we came up with in section C13.2, which is nice. However, the definition of a particle's angular momentum as $\vec{L} \equiv \vec{r} \times m\vec{v}$ is more general (because we can easily calculate it no matter how the particle is moving) and more powerful (because the nice mathematical properties of the cross product make it easier to work with mathematically).

An object's angular momentum depends on one's choice of origin O

One thing that you need to understand about a particle's angular momentum is that it depends not only on the particle's mass and velocity, but also on its radius vector $\vec{r}$ from some origin O. The magnitude and direction of the particle's angular momentum therefore *depends on our choice of O*. As a consequence, we must be sure to carefully specify the location of O whenever we work with angular momentum. You may have noticed how I keep saying "the particle's angular momentum *about O*" as a way of emphasizing this.

Exercise C13X.5: A 0.5-kg particle is moving once every 2.0 s around a circle with radius 2.0 m. What is the magnitude of its angular momentum?

Exercise C13X.6: At a given instant of time, a 2.0-kg particle is 3.0 m away from a point O in the $+y$ direction and is moving with a velocity whose x, y, and z components are [0, 3 m/s, 4 m/s]. What is the magnitude and direction of the particle's angular momentum around O at that instant?

C13.5 THE ANGULAR MOMENTUM OF A RIGID OBJECT

What we mean by a symmetrical object

Consider now a rigid object whose center of mass is at rest and which is rotating around a certain fixed axis. Imagine that this object is also symmetrical around this axis of rotation in the sense that for *every* particle A on one side of the axis there is a corresponding particle B, lying in the same plane and having the same mass and distance from the axis, but lying directly *across* the axis from A (see Figure C13.6).

The angular momentum $\vec{L}_i$ around a given point O along the object's axis of any *one* of that object's particles does *not* generally point in the direction of the object's angular velocity $\vec{\omega}$ (unless that particle and O both happen to lie in a plane that is perpendicular to the rotation axis). This can be seen in Figure C13.6. The velocity of particle A in that diagram points directly *out* of the plane of the diagram. By definition of the cross product, its angular momentum $\vec{L}_A \equiv \vec{r}_A \times m\vec{v}_A$ has to be perpendicular to *both* $\vec{r}_A$ and $\vec{v}_A$, so it must point in the direction indicated by the gray arrow. Note that this is definitely not parallel to $\vec{\omega}$! This means that a sum of all the angular momenta $\vec{L}_i$ for the particles in a rotating object will *not* generally end up being parallel to the object's angular velocity $\vec{\omega}$.

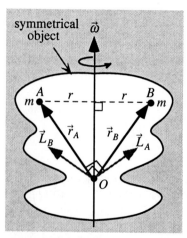

Figure C13.6 A *symmetrical* rotating object. Note that the velocities of particles A and B are directly *out of* and *into* the plane of the drawing respectively.

However, if the object happens to be symmetrical as described, this sum *does* end up being parallel to $\vec{\omega}$. Consider the total angular momentum $\vec{L}_A + \vec{L}_B$ of the pair of symmetrically opposite but identical particles A and B shown in Figure C13.6. Because their positions $\vec{r}_A$ and $\vec{r}_B$ are symmetrical with respect to the axis, $\vec{L}_A$ and $\vec{L}_B$ are also symmetrical, and when we add them, their components perpendicular to the axis cancel and the result is parallel to the axis, as shown in Figure C13.7. Since every particle has such an opposite in a symmetrical object, the sum over all particles is indeed parallel to $\vec{\omega}$.

The *magnitude* of the resulting sum is

$$\mathrm{mag}(\vec{L}_A + \vec{L}_B) = 2L_B \sin \alpha \qquad (C13.9)$$

Now, as you can see from the diagram, $\alpha + \theta = 90°$ and $\theta + \phi = 90°$, so $\alpha = \phi$. Therefore,

$$\sin \alpha = \sin \phi = \frac{r}{r_B} \qquad (C13.10)$$

Since $\vec{v}_B$ is perpendicular to $\vec{r}_B$, the magnitude of $\vec{L}_B$ is $L_B = mr_Bv_B$. Also note that $v_B = r\omega$. Putting this all together, we find that

$$\mathrm{mag}(\vec{L}_A + \vec{L}_B) = 2mr^2\omega \qquad (C13.11)$$

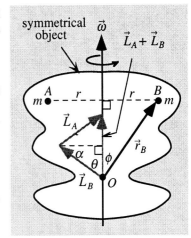

Figure C13.7: Another version of Figure C13.6 showing the sum of the angular momenta of A and B and related quantities.

Exercise C13X.7: Verify equation C13.11.

In short, we see that $\vec{L}_A + \vec{L}_B = 2mr^2\vec{\omega}$ in both magnitude and direction. So when we add the angular momenta of all symmetrically opposite *pairs* of particles in the object, we get the same result we *would* have gotten if we added $mr^2\vec{\omega}$ for each particle. Therefore, when we sum over all particles in an object that is symmetrical about its axis of rotation, we get (for *symmetrical* objects):

$$\vec{L} \equiv \sum_{i=1}^{N} \vec{L}_i = \sum_{i=1}^{N} m_ir_i^2\,\vec{\omega} = \left[\sum_{i=1}^{N} m_ir_i^2\right]\vec{\omega} = I\vec{\omega} \qquad (C13.12)$$

The total angular momentum of a *symmetrical* rotating rigid object

as we had guessed in section C13.2. Note that this result is independent of the exact location of the point O relative to which we are determining the objects angular momentum as long as O lies *somewhere* along the rotation axis.

What do we learn from this? Two things. The first is that our definition of the angular momentum $\vec{L} \equiv \vec{r} \times m\vec{v}$ of a *particle* is consistent with the idea that $\vec{L} = I\vec{\omega}$. The second, though, is that this *only* works if the object is symmetrical. If it is not, the off-axis components of the angular momenta of its particles will *not* generally cancel in the nice way they do here. This often leads to a total $\vec{L}$ for the object that is not parallel to the object's angular velocity $\vec{\omega}$! This kind of situation has some very interesting consequences that are often explored in a sophomore or junior-level course in classical mechanics (we will only deal with symmetrical objects in this course).

What we learn from this proof

Exercise C13X.8: Is a rectangular book (approximately) symmetric around an axis perpendicular to its face and going through its center of mass? Is it symmetric around an axis going diagonally from one corner to the other?

Exercise C13X.9: What is the angular momentum of a 5.0-kg bowling ball with a radius of 12 cm that is spinning at a rate of 5 turns per second?

What if an object is rotating around its axis and also is moving as a whole around some origin point O? As was the case with kinetic energy, it turns out that we can divide the angular momentum of an object rotating *and* moving around any point O into the sum of two parts

A useful theorem about objects that are rotating *and* moving as a unit

$$\vec{L} = \vec{L}^{\,\mathrm{cm}} + \vec{L}^{\,\mathrm{rot}} \qquad (C13.13)$$

where $\vec{L}^{\,\mathrm{rot}}$ is the angular momentum around O associated with the rotation of the object around its axis and $\vec{L}^{cm}$ is the angular momentum around O associated with the translational motion of the object's center of mass around the point O (computed as if the object were a particle located at its center of mass).

A proof of this theorem

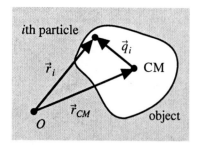

Figure C13.8: The relationship between $\vec{r}_i$, $\vec{r}_{CM}$, and $\vec{q}_i$.

We can prove this fairly easily using the nice properties of the cross product. Let $\vec{r}_i$ be the position of the object's ith particle relative to O, $\vec{r}_{CM}$ be the position of the object's center of mass relative to O, and $\vec{q}_i$ be the position of the ith particle relative to the center of mass. These are related as follows:

$$\vec{r}_i = \vec{r}_{CM} + \vec{q}_i. \qquad (C13.14)$$

as shown in Figure C13.8. From this, it also follows that

$$\vec{v}_i = \vec{v}_{CM} + \vec{u}_i \qquad (C13.15)$$

where $\vec{v}_i$ is the ith particle's velocity relative to O, $\vec{u}_i$ is its velocity relative to the object's center of mass, and $\vec{v}_{CM}$ is the velocity of the center of mass relative to O. The definition of the center of mass and the fact that the object's total momentum is equal to the object's total mass M times the velocity of its center of mass, state (respectively) that

$$M\vec{r}_{CM} = \sum_{i=1}^{N} m_i \vec{r}_i \quad \text{and} \quad M\vec{v}_{CM} = \sum_{i=1}^{N} m_i \vec{v}_i \qquad (C13.16)$$

Using these three equations, you can fairly easily show that

$$0 = \sum_{i=1}^{N} m_i \vec{q}_i \quad \text{and} \quad 0 = \sum_{i=1}^{N} m_i \vec{u}_i \qquad (C13.17)$$

Exercise C13X.10: Verify equation C13.17.

Using the distributive property of the cross product, we see that the object's total angular momentum around the point O is given by

$$\vec{L} \equiv \sum_{i=1}^{N} \vec{r}_i \times m_i \vec{v}_i = \sum_{i=1}^{N} \left[(\vec{r}_{CM} + \vec{q}_i) \times m_i (\vec{v}_{CM} + \vec{u}_i) \right]$$

$$= \sum_{i=1}^{N} \left[\vec{r}_{CM} \times m_i \vec{v}_{CM} + \vec{r}_{CM} \times m_i \vec{u}_i + \vec{q}_i \times m_i \vec{v}_{CM} + \vec{q}_i \times m_i \vec{u}_i \right] \qquad (C13.18)$$

After some rearrangement using the distributive and linear properties of the cross product and the idea that we can pull a factor out of a sum if the factor is the same in every term, this equation boils down to:

$$\vec{L} = \vec{r}_{CM} \times M\vec{v}_{CM} + \vec{r}_{CM} \times \left[\sum_{i=1}^{N} m_i \vec{u}_i \right]$$

$$+ \left[\sum_{i=1}^{N} m_i \vec{q}_i \right] \times \vec{v}_{CM} + \sum_{i=1}^{N} \left[\vec{q}_i \times m_i \vec{u}_i \right] \qquad (C13.19)$$

Exercise C13X.11: Verify equation C13.19.

Equations C13.17 immediately imply that the middle two terms in this expression are zero. The first term is the angular momentum of the center of mass around O computed as if it were a particle, and the last is the angular momentum of the object, calculated as if it were only rotating around its center of mass. Therefore we do indeed have $\vec{L} = \vec{L}^{cm} + \vec{L}^{rot}$, as claimed in equation C13.13.

C13.6 CONSERVATION OF ANGULAR MOMENTUM

The law of conservation of angular momentum simply says that the total angular momentum of an isolated system around *any* arbitrary origin point O is conserved. "Isolated" here means the same thing that it did when we were talking about conservation of *linear* momentum: a system can be *approximately* or *functionally* isolated, and we can apply conservation of angular momentum to a system that is not isolated if it is undergoing a short-duration collision and if we look at the system's angular momentum just before and just after the collision.

EXAMPLE C13.1

Problem: Consider an isolated particle of mass m moving at a constant velocity $\vec{v}$ along a straight line that passes within distance b of a point O. What is the object's angular momentum about O? Is it constant?

Solution For the sake of argument, let's set up a coordinate system whose origin is at O and whose x axis is parallel to the direction of the object's constant velocity $\vec{v}$. At a given instant of time, let the particle's position be $\vec{r}$, and let θ be the angle that $\vec{r}$ makes with the x axis (see Figure C13.9). According to the cross-product definition of the angular momentum,

$$\vec{L} = \vec{r} \times m\vec{v} \qquad (C13.20)$$

The direction of $\vec{L}$ will be perpendicular to both $\vec{r}$ and $\vec{v}$ in the direction specified by the right hand rule. This will always be perpendicular to the plane of the drawing in Figure C13.9 going directly *into* the drawing, no matter where the particle is on its trajectory. The *direction* of $\vec{L}$ is thus constant.

According to the definition of the cross product, the *magnitude* of $\vec{L}$ is

$$L = mrv\sin\theta = mv(r\sin\theta) = mvb \qquad (C13.21)$$

since as you can see on the diagram, $r\sin\theta = b$, no matter where the particle is along its trajectory. Since m and v are also constant, the *magnitude* of $\vec{L}$ is also constant. Since the particle is "isolated," its $\vec{L}$ *should* be constant. (Note that a particle can have a meaningful angular momentum around a point O even if its motion is a straight line!)

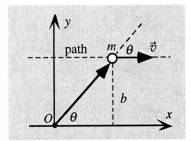

Figure C13.9: Angular momentum of an isolated particle moving with a constant velocity past the point O.

We can adapt our general problem-solving framework for conservation of angular momentum by making slight modifications in the framework that we used for conservation of ordinary momentum. The main differences are as follows: (1) In the *Pictorial representation* section, you should specify symbols for the quantities you need to calculate *angular momenta* (such as masses, radii, angular velocities, and so on). (2) In the *Mathematical representation* use the the fundamental conservation of angular momentum equation

$$\vec{L}_{1i} + \vec{L}_{2i} + \ldots = \vec{L}_{1f} + \vec{L}_{2f} + \ldots \qquad (C13.22)$$

(where the numerical subscripts refer to the various objects in our system and i and f mean "initial" and "final") as the starting point for your calculation. (3) In the same section, you should also specify the origin O (or at least the axis) around which you are calculating the angular momentum (and then make sure that you *do* calculate *all* angular momenta with reference to that origin or axis).

In most of the problems you will encounter, we will consider systems that are described as being "free to rotate" around some axis. This phrase implies that the system is *approximately* isolated at least with regard to rotations around the particular axis in question. Such systems are usually *functionally isolated* with regard to rotations around other axes (the angular momentum around other axes is trivially conserved because rotations around those axes are not permitted!). Such issues should be discussed in the *Conceptual representation* section.

Examples C13.2 and C13.3 illustrate the use of the modified framework.

EXAMPLE C13.2

OUTLINE OF THE FRAMEWORK

1. Pictorial Representation

　a. Draw a picture of the situation that includes:

　　① (1) sketches of the system in its initial and final states

　　② (2) reference frame axes

　　　(3) labels defining symbols for relevant quantities (in this case, masses, radii, angular velocities, and so on)
　　③

　b. List values for all known quantities and specify which quantities are unknown.
　④

2. Conceptual Representation

The general task is to construct a conceptual model of the situation and link it to an abstract physics model. In conservation-of-angular-momentum problems, we do the following:

　⑤ a. Identify the *system* involved.

　⑥ b. Decide if conservation of angular momentum applies to this system: is it

　　(1) *approximately* isolated, because external interactions are weak?

　　(2) *functionally* isolated, because external interactions that might transfer angular momentum cancel out?

　　(3) involved in a *collision* of short duration so that we can ignore external interactions?

　⑦ c. Do we have to make any approximations or assumptions to solve the problem? (If so, describe.)

3. Mathematical Representation

　⑧ a. Apply the mathematical equation that appropriately describes the situation (equation C13.22 here)

　⑨ b. Specify the origin or axis around which all $\vec{L}$s will be calculated

　⑩ c. Solve for unknowns symbolically

　⑪ d. Plug in numbers and units and calculate the result and its units.

4. Evaluation

　Check that the answer makes sense.

　⑫ a. Does it have the correct units?

　⑬ b. Does it have the right sign?

　⑭ c. Does it seem reasonable?

Problem: A cat is sitting on the rim of a wooden turntable that is free to turn around a vertical axis. The turntable's mass is three times the cat's mass and it is initially at rest. The cat then starts walking around the rim at a speed of 0.6 m/s relative to the ground. What is the cat's walking speed relative to the turntable?

Solution: We will define the z axis of our reference frame to coincide with the turntable's axis of rotation and point vertically upward. Top-view initial and final diagrams of this situation then look like this:

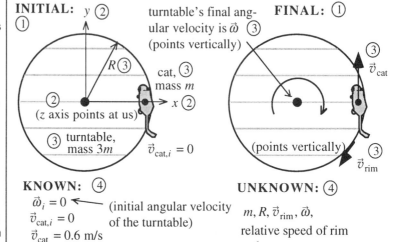

KNOWN: ④

$\vec{\omega}_i = 0$ ← (initial angular velocity of the turntable)
$\vec{v}_{cat,i} = 0$
$\vec{v}_{cat} = 0.6$ m/s
turntable mass is $3m$　⑤

UNKNOWN: ④

$m, R, \vec{v}_{rim}, \vec{\omega}$, relative speed of rim and cat.　⑥

The system here is the cat and the turntable: it is *approximately* isolated for rotations around the z axis (since it is "free to rotate" around this axis) and *functionally* isolated (with rotations forbidden) around the x and y axes. We will model the turntable by a disk, so that its moment of inertia is $I = \frac{1}{2}MR^2 = \frac{3}{2}mR^2$. We will also model the cat by a point particle (what else can we do?) and *assume* that its center of mass is roughly R from the turntable's center. Conservation of angular momentum in this case implies that $\vec{L}_{cat,i} + \vec{L}_{ttb,i} = \vec{L}_{cat,f} + \vec{L}_{ttb,f}$. We will take the origin O to be the center of the turntable. Both the turntable and the cat are initially at rest, so $\vec{L}_{cat,i} + \vec{L}_{ttb,i} = 0$. The magnitude of the cat's angular momentum after it starts walking (treating the cat as a particle) is $\text{mag}(\vec{L}_{cat,f}) = mRv_{cat}$ (note that $\vec{v}_{cat}$ is always perpendicular to its position $\vec{r}$ from the turntable's center, so $\sin\theta = 1$). Since $\vec{v}_{cat}$ and $\vec{r}$ both lie in the xy plane, $\vec{L}_{cat,f}$ must point along the z axis: the right-hand rule indicates the *positive z* direction. The turntable's final angular momentum is given by $\vec{L}_{ttb,f} = I\vec{\omega} = \frac{3}{2}mR^2\vec{\omega}$, and $\vec{\omega}$ points along the z axis. So conservation of $\vec{L}$ implies that

$$\vec{L}_{cat,i} + \vec{L}_{ttb,i} = \vec{L}_{cat,f} + \vec{L}_{ttb,f} \Rightarrow \begin{bmatrix} 0 \\ 0 \\ 0 \end{bmatrix} + \begin{bmatrix} 0 \\ 0 \\ 0 \end{bmatrix} = \begin{bmatrix} 0 \\ 0 \\ +mRv_{cat} \end{bmatrix} + \begin{bmatrix} 0 \\ 0 \\ \frac{3}{2}mR^2\omega_z \end{bmatrix}$$
⑧

Only the bottom line has any meaning here: after dividing through by m and R it implies that $0 = v_{cat} + \frac{3}{2}R\omega_z \Rightarrow R\omega_z = -\frac{2}{3}v_{cat}$. Since this means that $\vec{\omega}$ points in the $-z$ direction, the right hand rule implies that the turntable rotates clockwise, as shown in the picture. Note also that $R\omega = R|\omega_z|$ is just the speed v_{rim} of a point on the rim, so $v_{rim} = \frac{2}{3}v_{cat} = 0.4$ m/s. Since the cat is walking forward at 0.6 m/s relative to the ground, and the rim is moving backward at 0.4 m/s, the cat must be moving at 0.6 m/s + 0.4 m/s = 1.0 m/s forward relative to the rim. The direction table's rotation *should* be clockwise to conserve $\vec{L}$, the units are right, and 1.0 m/s seems reasonable.

EXAMPLE C13.3

OUTLINE OF THE FRAMEWORK

1. Pictorial Representation

ⓐ a. Draw a picture of the situation that includes:

① (1) sketches of the system in its initial and final states

② (2) reference frame axes

③ (3) labels defining symbols for relevant quantities (in this case, masses, radii, angular velocities, and so on)

b. List values for all known quantities and specify which quantities ④ are unknown.

2. Conceptual Representation

The general task is to construct a conceptual model of the situation and link it to an abstract physics model. In conservation-of-angular-momentum problems, we do the following:

⑤ a. Identify the *system* involved (by circling it on the sketches)

⑥ b. Decide if conservation of angular momentum applies to this system: is it

(1) *approximately* isolated, because external interactions are weak?

(2) *functionally* isolated, because external interactions that might transfer angular momentum cancel out?

(3) involved in a *collision* of short duration so that we can ignore external interactions?

⑦ c. Do we have to make any approximations or assumptions to solve the problem? (If so, describe.)

3. Mathematical Representation

⑧ a. Apply the mathematical equation that appropriately describes the situation (equation C13.22 here)

⑨ b. Specify the origin or axis around which all $\vec{L}$s will be calculated

⑩ c. Solve for unknowns symbolically

⑪ d. Plug in numbers and units and calculate the result and its units.

4. Evaluation

Check that the answer makes sense:

⑫ a. Does it have the correct units?
⑬ b. Does it have the right sign?
⑭ c. Does it seem reasonable?

⑬ The units are right and the magnitude
⑭ (≈ 2.2 s/rev) seems reasonable.

Problem: A student with a moment of inertia of 0.72 kg·m² around a vertical axis sits (initially at rest) on a stool that is free to rotate around the vertical axis. The student is holding a bicycle wheel with a mass of 1.0 kg and a moment of inertia of 0.10 kg·m² that is rotating counterclockwise around a vertical axis at a rate of 2 rev/s. The axle of the wheel is about 0.40 m from the axis of the student. If the student turns the wheel over, what happens? Be as descriptive as you can!

Solution: Let's define our reference frame so the z axis corresponds to the rotation axis of the stool and points vertically upward. Initial and final drawings of this situation look like this:

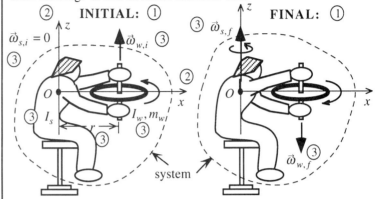

④ **KNOWN:** $r = 0.40$ m $I_s = 0.72$ kg·m², $I_w = 0.10$ kg·m²

$\vec{\omega}_{s,i} = 0$, $\vec{\omega}_{w,f} = -\vec{\omega}_{w,i}$, $m_w = 1.0$ kg,

④ **UNKNOWN:** $\vec{\omega}_{w,f}$ $\vec{\omega}_{w,i} = \dfrac{2\ \text{rev}}{\text{s}}\left(\dfrac{2\pi\ \text{rad}}{\text{rev}}\right)$ upward

The system here is the student, the stool, and the bicycle wheel. We are told that the stool is "free to rotate" around the z axis, so we will take the system to be approximately isolated for rotations around that axis. We will assume that the student is symmetric (though this is clearly only an approximation!). We will also assume that the mass of the rotating part of the stool is so small its angular momentum can be ignored (what else can we do?). Conservation of angular momentum in this case then tells us that $\vec{L}_{s,i} + \vec{L}_{w,i} = \vec{L}_{s,f} + \vec{L}_{w,f}$. ⑧ We will use the point O shown on the diagram as our origin: it lies along the student's axis of rotation and is placed vertically so that the wheel's center of mass lies in the xy plane. To find the wheel's total angular momentum around this point, we have to use equation C13.13:

$$\vec{L}_w = \vec{L}_w^{\text{cm}} + \vec{L}_w^{\text{rot}} = mr^2\vec{\omega}_s + I_w\vec{\omega}_w = mr^2\vec{\omega}_s + I_w\vec{\omega}_w$$

I have used equation C13.8 to find the $\vec{L}_w^{\text{cm}}$ since the wheel's center of mass moves in a circle around point O at the angular velocity of the student. So the equation describing conservation of angular momentum becomes $\vec{L}_{s,i} + \vec{L}_{w,i}^{\text{cm}} + \vec{L}_{w,i}^{\text{rot}} = \vec{L}_{s,f} + \vec{L}_{w,f}^{\text{cm}} + \vec{L}_{w,f}^{\text{rot}}$, or more specifically, (recognizing that $\vec{\omega}_{s,i} = 0$), we have

⑧ $$0 + 0 + I_w\vec{\omega}_{w,i} = (I_s + mr^2)\vec{\omega}_{s,f} + I_w\vec{\omega}_{w,f}$$ ⑩

In this case, though, $\vec{\omega}_{w,f} = -\vec{\omega}_{w,i}$. Plugging this into the above and solving for $\vec{\omega}_{s,f}$, we get $\vec{\omega}_{s,i} = +2I_w\vec{\omega}_{w,i}/(I_s + mr^2)$. We see from this that the student's final angular velocity points in the same direction (the $+z$ direction) as the wheel's does initially, so the student will turn counterclockwise. Taking the magnitude of both sides of this, we get

⑫

$$\omega_{s,f} = +\frac{2I_w\omega_{w,i}}{I_s + mr^2} = \frac{2(0.10\ \text{kg·m}^2)(4\pi\ \text{rad/s})}{0.72\ \text{kg·m}^2 + (1.0\ \text{kg})(0.40\ \text{m})^2} = 2.9\ \frac{\text{rad}}{\text{s}}$$ ⑪

C13.7 APPLICATION: NEUTRON STARS

Why stars go supernova

A normal star supports itself against its own gravitational field because thermonuclear interactions keep its core hot, and a hot gas has a high pressure that resists compression. As the star ages, "ashes" from the thermonuclear reactions begin to build up in the core. Since these ashes cannot produce thermal energy to keep pressure in the core high, the core begins to contract. If the star is fairly massive, the core will eventually accumulate about 1.4 solar masses of "ashes" within a radius of about 10,000 km (with a density $> 10^9$ g/cm^3 !).

Up to this point, the pressure of electrons rattling around the core keeps it from shrinking too quickly. But at this density, electrons mingle so closely with atomic nuclei that electrons start to react with protons to form neutrons and neutrinos ($p + e^- \rightarrow n + v$). This nuclear reaction destroys the very electrons that support the core against collapse. The core thus begins to shrink: this squeezes electrons into yet closer proximity to protons, which encourages the reaction, which increases the rate of contraction, and so on.

So this contraction quickly develops into a catastrophic collapse. Once the reaction begins, the core's radius goes from about 10,000 km to about 12 km within about 0.3 s. At this radius, the star is completely comprised of neutrons, and the density is so high ($\approx 10^{14}$ g/cm^3) that the neutrons touch, making the core strongly resistant to further collapse. As material outside the core crashes down on the suddenly solid core, a shock wave is formed that blows much of that material away in a gigantic explosion. This is a supernova.

Neutron stars and pulsars

After the explosion dissipates, what is left behind is a tiny, rapidly rotating **neutron star**. Such objects usually have an intense magnetic field that is swept around with the star as it rotates. This radiates radio waves that pulse in step with the neutron star's rotation. A neutron star emitting detectable pulses of radio waves in this manner is called a **pulsar**.

Estimating the rotation speed of a neutron star

How fast should a pulsar spin? The sun (whose radius is 700,000 km) rotates about once every month (≈ 2.6 Ms). Assume that when the core (which contains 1.4 solar masses) had this radius, it also rotated once every 2.6 Ms. Since the star is an isolated object, conservation of angular momentum implies that the core's L *after* collapse should be the same as its L originally.

Assuming that the core is essentially a sphere at all sizes, the magnitude of its angular momentum will be $L = I\omega = \frac{2}{5}MR^2\omega$. During the contraction and collapse of the core, M remains the same, but R decreases by a factor of about 60,000. Therefore, ω must increase by a factor of $(60,000)^2 = 3.6 \times 10^9$ to keep L the same. This reduces the rotation period of the core by the same factor, from 2.6×10^6 s to about 0.7 ms (0.7×10^{-3} s).

Astronomers have indeed observed a handful of pulsars with rotation periods on the order of 1 ms. Most have periods 10 to 1000 times longer. This is probably because the pulsar sweeps an intense magnetic field around thousands of times a second. Interactions between this magnetic field and gas surrounding the pulsar slowly drain energy from the pulsar, which comes at the expense of its rotational kinetic energy. Over hundreds of millions of years, this gradually slows the neutron star's spin rate: pulsars with long periods are thus ones that have been around for quite a while. But consistent with this model, no pulsars have been observed with periods much *less* than 1 ms.

In 1987, a supernova was detected in the Large Magellanic Cloud: this was the nearest supernova to the earth in several centuries. Consistent with the supernova model described above, a burst of neutrinos was detected just before the explosion became visible. After the debris from the explosion clears, we should see a neutron star remnant rotating with a period of about 1 ms.

Pulsars as clocks

Incidentally, the huge moment of inertia of a neutron star and its excellent isolation mean that its rotation rate is *very* constant. This makes pulsars excellent clocks, better by orders of magnitude than anything available on earth (even taking account of the slowing discussed above).

I. AN INTRODUCTION TO ANGULAR MOMENTUM
  A. An experiment: an isolated object set rotating will continue to do so
    1. An isolated object's constant $\vec{v}$ is due to conservation of $\vec{p}$
    2. Could an isolated object's constant $\vec{\omega}$ reflect a conservation law?
  B. Clues about the conserved quantity
    1. The angular velocity of an isolated rotating person *increases* as mass is pulled in closer to the axis (causing his/her I to *decrease*)
    2. The rotational analog to $K = \frac{1}{2}mv^2$ is $K^{\text{rot}} = \frac{1}{2}I\omega^2$
  C. Both suggest that the conserved quantity is $\vec{L} = I\vec{\omega}$ (cp. with $\vec{p} = m\vec{v}$)

II. THE CROSS PRODUCT
  A. The definition of the cross product: $\vec{u} \times \vec{w}$ is a *vector* whose
    1. magnitude is $uw\sin\theta = u_{\perp}w = w_{\perp}u$, where
       a) θ is the angle from the direction of $\vec{u}$ to that of $\vec{w}$
       b) $u_{\perp}$ is the absolute value of the component of $\vec{u}$ that is perpendicular to $\vec{w}$ and so on
    2. direction is perpendicular to $\vec{u}$ and $\vec{w}$ in the sense specified by your right thumb when you point right fingers in the direction of $\vec{u}$, and curl them in the direction of $\vec{w}$ (right-hand rule)
  B. For a component definition of the cross product, see equation C13.5.
  C. Important properties of the cross product
    1. It is *anticommutative*: $\vec{u} \times \vec{w} = -\vec{w} \times \vec{u}$
    2. It is *linear*: $(q\vec{u}) \times \vec{w} = \vec{u} \times (q\vec{w}) = q(\vec{u} \times \vec{w})$
    3. It is *distributive*: $\vec{c} \times (\vec{u} + \vec{w}) = \vec{c} \times \vec{u} + \vec{c} \times \vec{w}$
  D. For others (and comparisons to the dot product), see Table C13.1

III. THE ANGULAR MOMENTUM OF A PARTICLE
  A. Definition: $\vec{L} \equiv \vec{r} \times m\vec{v} = \vec{r} \times \vec{p}$
    1. $\vec{r}$ is the particle's position from some specified origin O (note that the angular momentum depends crucially on where O is!)
    2. SI units are $\text{kg} \cdot \text{m}^2/\text{s}$
  B. This becomes $\vec{L} = I\vec{\omega}$ if the particle moves in a circle around with O at the center (this actually applies more generally, but I did not show this)

IV. THE ANGULAR MOMENTUM OF A RIGID OBJECT
  A. $\vec{L}$ is not necessarily parallel to $\vec{\omega}$ for general objects
  B. But $\vec{L} = I\vec{\omega}$ for a symmetrical rotating object
    1. Here, *symmetrical* means that for every particle, there is an identical particle directly across the rotation axis and same distance from it
    2. Proof involves showing that the off-axis components of $\vec{L}$ cancel for such particle pairs
    3. Proof applies for any origin O along the axis
  C. The total angular momentum (AM) around a point O of an object that is both rotating and translating is $\vec{L} = \vec{L}^{\text{cm}} + \vec{L}^{\text{rot}}$
    1. $\vec{L}^{\text{rot}}$ is the AM of the object computed as if its CM were at rest
    2. $\vec{L}^{\text{cm}}$ is the AM associated with the translational motion of its CM calculated as if its CM were a particle
    3. Proof involves use of nice cross-product properties

V. CONSERVATION OF ANGULAR MOMENTUM
  A. The total angular momentum of an isolated system is conserved:
     $\vec{L}_{1i} + \vec{L}_{2i} + \ldots = \vec{L}_{1f} + \vec{L}_{2f} + \ldots$
  B. Modifications to our problem-solving framework
    1. Use the equation above as starting point in *Math representation*
    2. Be sure to specify origin or axis and use it to calculate *all* $\vec{L}$s
    3. A system that is "free to rotate" around some axis is approximately isolated around that axis and are usually *functionally* isolated around other axes (because rotation is not permitted)
  C. The spin rate of neutron stars is one contemporary application

GLOSSARY

cross product $\vec{u} \times \vec{w}$ (of two vectors $\vec{u}$ and $\vec{w}$): a vector whose *magnitude* is $uw\sin\theta$ (where θ is the angle from the direction of $\vec{u}$ to that of $\vec{w}$) and whose *direction* is perpendicular to both $\vec{u}$ and $\vec{w}$ in the sense indicated by your right thumb when your right fingers curl from $\vec{u}$ to $\vec{w}$.

angular momentum $\vec{L}$ (around a given point O): For a particle, $\vec{L}$ is defined to be $\vec{L} = \vec{r} \times \vec{p}$, where $\vec{r}$ is the particle's position relative to O, and $\vec{p}$ is its ordinary momentum. If the particle is moving in a circle around O, $\vec{L} = mr^2 \vec{\omega}$, where $\vec{\omega}$ is the particle's angular velocity in its circular trajectory. For a symmetric extended object rotating around any O lying along its axis of rotation, $\vec{L} = I\vec{\omega}$ where $\vec{\omega}$ is the object's angular velocity. The total

angular momentum of an isolated system around any arbitrary origin O will be conserved.

anticommutative: a product (like the cross product) is anticommutative if changing the order of factors in the product changes its sign: $\vec{u} \times \vec{w} = -\vec{w} \times \vec{u}$.

neutron star: the compact "cinder" left behind after a star goes supernova. Such objects have a typical mass of 1.4 solar masses, a radius of 12 km, are composed essentially entirely of neutrons, and rotate from once to 1000 times a second.

pulsar: a rotating neutron star whose intense rotating magnetic field interacts with nearby gas to create detectable radio signals that pulse at the same rate as the star rotates.

TWO-MINUTE PROBLEMS

C13T.1 A child swings a 0.1-kg ball on a string around in a horizontal circle of radius 2.0 m once every 0.63 s. The ball's angular momentum around the child is
A. 0.63 kg·m²/s   D. 10 kg·m²/s
B. 2.0 kg·m²/s   E. 20 kg·m²/s
C. 4.0 kg·m²/s   F. other (specify)

C13T.2 If you are standing 30 m due east of a car traveling at 25 m/s southwest, what is the direction of the car's angular momentum relative to you?
A. southwest   D. west
B. northeast   E. up
C. east   F. down

C13T.3 You are standing 30 m due east of a 50-kg person who is running at a speed of 2.0 m/s due west. What is the magnitude of that person's angular momentum around you?
A. 3000 kg·m²/s   D. 100 kg·m²/s
B. 1000 kg·m²/s   E. zero
C. 300 kg·m²/s   F. other (specify)

C13T.4 The lengths of the hour and minute hands of a clock are 4 cm and 6 cm respectively. If the vectors $\vec{u}$ and $\vec{w}$ represent the hour and minute hands respectively, then $\vec{u} \times \vec{w}$ at 5 o'clock is
A. 24 cm² up   D. 21 cm² down
B. 24 cm² down   E. 12 cm² up
C. 21 cm² up   F. 12 cm² down

C13T.5 A diatomic molecule (like an O_2 or N_2 molecule) can be modeled by two spheres that somewhat overlap each other, as shown in Figure C13.10. This molecule is symmetric (in the sense discussed in section C13.5) around the axis shown in that drawing (T or F). Assume that the axis goes through the molecule's geometrical center.

C13T.6 The letter "N" is symmetric (in the sense discussed in section C13.5) for rotations around an axis pointing in which of the directions listed below?
A. →   D. A and B   F. A, B, and C
B. ↑   E. A and C
C. perpendicular to the plane of the letter

C13T.7 A disk with a mass of 10 kg and a radius of 0.1 m rotates at a rate of 10 turns a second. The magnitude of the disk's total angular momentum is
A. 63 kg·m²/s   D. 6.3 kg·m²/s   T. other (specify)
B. 31 kg·m²/s   E. 3.1 kg·m²/s
C. 10 kg·m²/s   F. 1.0 kg·m²/s

C13T.8 If global warming proceeds during the next century as anticipated it is possible that the polar ice caps will melt, substantially raising sea levels around the world (and flooding coastal cities like New York, etc.). Would this shorten, lengthen, or have strictly no effect on the duration of the day?
A. lengthen the day slightly   B. shorten it slightly
C. have strictly *no* effect on the length of the day

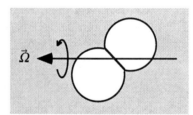

Figure C13.10

HOMEWORK PROBLEMS

BASIC SKILLS

C13B.1 A 1200-kg car turns left around a curve with a radius of 130 m at a speed of 22 m/s. What is the car's angular momentum around the center of the curve (magnitude and direction)?

C13B.2 At a certain time, a 55-kg person is 25 m due north of you and is walking at a speed of 1.2 m/s exactly southwest. What is the magnitude and direction of this person's angular momentum around you?

C13B.3 At a certain instant of time, a 0.25-kg soccer ball is 18 m exactly southwest of you, traveling at 8.1 m/s due north. What is the magnitude and direction of the ball's angular momentum around you?

C13B.4 A simplistic model of the hydrogen atom imagines the electron to be in a circular orbit around the proton. The electron's orbital radius in this model is 0.053 nm, and its speed is about $c/137$, where c is the speed of light. What is the magnitude of this electron's orbital angular momentum? Compare your answer to $h/2\pi$, where h is Planck's constant = 6.63×10^{-34} kg·m²/s.

C13B.5 The lengths of the hour and minute hands of a clock are 8 cm and 12 cm respectively. If the vectors $\vec{u}$ and $\vec{w}$ represent the hour and minute hands respectively, what is $\vec{u} \times \vec{w}$ at 7:30 PM (magnitude and direction)?

C13B.6 Displacement vector $\vec{u}$ = [3 m, 0, –2 m] and displacement vector $\vec{w}$ = [–1 m, 5 m, 2 m]. Find the components of the cross product of these vectors.

C13B.7 Displacement vector $\vec{u}$ = [0 , –1 m, –2 m] and displacement vector $\vec{w}$ = [0, 5 m, 4 m]. Find the components of the cross product of these vectors.

C13B.8 Imagine that you throw a 1.5-kg steel rod that is 1.0 m long in the air, flipping it so that it spins end for end around its center of mass about 1.3 times per second. What is the magnitude of its *rotational* angular momentum?

C13B.9 A 7-kg bowling ball whose radius is 0.13 m is rolling directly toward you, turning 3 times a second. What is the magnitude and direction of its rotational angular momentum?

SYNTHETIC

C13S.1 Prove that the magnitude of $\vec{u} \times \vec{w}$ is the same as the area of the parallelogram whose sides are $\vec{u}$ and $\vec{w}$.

C13S.2 A 0.15-kg baseball is hit at a speed of 52 m/s in a horizontal line 1.4 m above the ground. When the baseball is 12 meters from home plate, what is its angular momentum around home plate?

C13S.3 Many subatomic particles (including the electron) behave as if they were spinning around their axis. Measurements indicate that the electron has a spin angular momentum of $h/4\pi$, where h is Planck's constant. A simplistic model imagines the electron to be a spinning spherical ball of uniform density. Other measurements indicate that if the electron is a spherical ball, its radius must be less than 10^{-18} m. Show that if the simplistic model were true, the speed of the surface of the electron would be much faster than light. (A more sophisticated quantum-mechanical model of electron spin avoids this paradox.)

C13S.4 A Frisbee™ has a mass of about 165 g and a radius of about 13 or 14 cm. *Estimate* the magnitude of its angular momentum when it is thrown normally, and describe the reasoning behind your estimate. (*Hint:* A Frisbee™ is somewhere between a hoop and a disk; a significant part of its mass is on its rim. Performing some experiments might help improve your estimate, but an estimate good to within a factor of three or so is fine.)

C13S.5 A 280-kg cylindrical piece of concrete pipe 1.0 m in diameter, 1.3 m long, and 3 cm thick is rolling toward you at a speed of 5 m/s. What is its approximate rotational angular momentum (magnitude and direction)?

C13S.6 A 6-kg bowling ball with a radius of 12 cm rolls in a straight line past you at a speed of 3 m/s. At its point of closest approach, it is 3 m away from you. Say that we define our coordinate system centered on you so that the ball rolls parallel to the $+y$ direction and the z direction is vertically upward. What are the components of the ball's total angular momentum around your position?

C13S.7 When our sun runs out of fuel, it will eventually become a white dwarf star with about the same radius as the earth. Estimate the time that it will take the sun to rotate once when it is that size. (The sun's current radius is about 700,000 km, and its current period of rotation is roughly 2.6 Ms.)*

C13S.8 A certain playground merry-go-round is essentially a 80-kg iron disk 2.0 m in radius. Two children, each with a mass of 44 kg, are originally standing on opposite sides of the disk near its outer edge. The merry-go-round is turning essentially without friction around a vertical axis once every 5 seconds. The children then clamber toward each other so that they are only 1.0 m from the center. How long does it take the merry-go-round to complete a revolution now?*

C13S.9 Two astronauts of roughly equal mass are floating in space. They both hold onto a light rod 20 m long and the whole system is rotating about the center of the rod about once every 30 s. What is the ordinary speed of each astronaut? Now imagine that the astronauts pull themselves along the rod until they are 10 m apart. What is their ordinary speed now? Where do you think that their increased kinetic energy came from?*

C13S.10 A 60-kg person stands at rest near the rim of a 150-kg metal disk 4.0 m in radius. The disk is supported 0.25 m above the ground and is free to turn around a vertical axis but is initially at rest. The person then starts walking around the rim at 1.5 m/s relative to the surface of the disk. What is the person's speed relative to the ground?*

C13S.11 A dining table has a 3.0-kg turntable in the middle for serving food. The turntable is a wooden disk 0.8 m in diameter. It is rotating at a rate of 5 seconds per turn when someone puts a 0.25-kg coffee cup on it near its edge. What is its rotation rate now?*

*Please follow the problem-solving framework discussed in section C13.6 when writing solutions for the starred problems.

RICH-CONTEXT

C13R.1 A person holds a 5-kg weight in each hand with arms outstretched while standing at rest on a lightweight platform that is free to turn around a vertical axis. Other people then set the person turning at a rate of one turn per 7.2 seconds. The person then lowers the weights until they are alongside the person's legs. At this point, the person is spinning once every 1.2 s. Estimate the person's moment of inertia. (You may find that following the problem-solving framework to be helpful.)

C13R.2 When jumping from a platform, a high diver initially holds his or her body essentially extended and straight and rotates slowly while falling. The diver then tucks into a compact shape and tumbles rapidly. As the diver nears the water, he or she straightens out again and again rotates only slowly while entering the water. Roughly estimate how much faster you would tumble when compacted in a ball than you would when your body is extended and straight. (*Hints:* The gravitational interaction between the diver and the earth does not transfer any rotational angular momentum to the diver, and thus can be ignored. Think of simple shapes that you can use as models for your body in both configurations.)

ADVANCED

C13A.1 We can show that the cross product is distributive

$$\vec{c} \times (\vec{u} + \vec{w}) = \vec{c} \times \vec{u} + \vec{c} \times \vec{w} \qquad (C13.23)$$

fairly easily if $\vec{c}, \vec{u}$ and $\vec{w}$ happen to lie in the same plane. Study the analogous proof for the distributive property of the dot product discussed in problem C8S.1 and adapt it for the cross product.

C13A.2 Here is a way to derive the component equation for the cross product (equation C13.5) from its definition C13.1. Imagine that $\vec{e}_x, \vec{e}_y,$ and $\vec{e}_z$ are three vectors, each having length equal to 1, that point in the x, y, and z directions, respectively. Convince yourself that an arbitrary vector $\vec{u}$ can be written $\vec{u} = u_x \vec{e}_x + u_y \vec{e}_y + u_z \vec{e}_z$. Take the cross product of two vectors written this form and show that equation C13.5 follows from this and the properties of the cross product listed in Table C13.1. (*Hint:* Use the definition of the cross product to argue that $\vec{e}_x \times \vec{e}_x = 0$, $\vec{e}_x \times \vec{e}_y = +\vec{e}_z$, $\vec{e}_x \times \vec{e}_z = -\vec{e}_y$, and so on. Find these products for all pairs of e-vectors before doing anything else.)

ANSWERS TO EXERCISES

C13X.1 If it were rotational kinetic energy that was conserved, then $K^{rot} = \frac{1}{2}I\omega^2$ would be constant when I and ω change. This means that

$$2K^{rot} \cdot I^{-1} = \omega^2 \Rightarrow \omega = [2K^{rot}]^{1/2} I^{-1/2} \qquad (C13.24)$$

So the prediction would be that $\omega \propto I^{-1/2}$.

C13X.2 Treat the children as point particles. Since the total moment of inertia of the merry-go-round plus children is the sum of the moments of inertia of its parts, initially the system's total moment of inertia is

$$I_i = \frac{1}{2}(2m)R^2 + mR^2 + mR^2 = 3mR^2 \qquad (C13.25)$$

remembering that the moment of inertia of a disk of mass M and radius R is given by $\frac{1}{2}MR^2$. When the children move in to radius $\frac{1}{2}R$, the system's moment of inertia becomes

$$I_f = \frac{1}{2}(2m)R^2 + \frac{1}{4}mR^2 + \frac{1}{4}mR^2 = \frac{3}{2}mR^2 \qquad (C13.26)$$

Since the system's moment of inertia has gone down by a factor of two, if its total angular momentum $\vec{L} = I\vec{\omega}$ is to be conserved, then the system's angular velocity $\vec{\omega}$ must increase by a factor of two. Each child's speed remains the same in this case.

C13X.3 69 cm² directly into and perpendicular to the clock face. (*Hint:* The angle between the hands is 60°.)

C13X.4 The x and y components of $\vec{u} \times \vec{w}$ are zero, the z component is +11 m². Since both vectors lie in the xy plane, it makes sense that $\vec{u} \times \vec{w}$ points in the z direction, since it is perpendicular to both vectors by definition.

C13X.5 6.28 kg·m²/s.

C13X.6 24 kg·m²/s in the +x direction (only the velocity component perpendicular to the y-direction is relevant).

C13X.7 Putting together all of the pieces, we have:

$$2L_B \sin\alpha = 2mr_A v_A \frac{r}{r_A} = 2mrv_A = 2mr^2\omega \qquad (C13.27)$$

C13X.8 Yes. No.

C13X.9 0.90 kg·m²/s. (Remember that the moment of inertia of a sphere is of mass M and radius R is $I = \frac{2}{5}MR^2$.)

C13X.10 According to equation C13.14, we have

$$\sum_{i=1}^N m_i \vec{q}_i = \sum_{i=1}^N m_i (\vec{r}_i - \vec{r}_{CM})$$

$$= \sum_{i=1}^N m_i \vec{r}_i - \sum_{i=1}^N m_i \vec{r}_{CM} \qquad (C13.28)$$

The first of these two sums is the definition of $M\vec{r}_{CM}$. In the second, pull out the common factor of $\vec{r}_{CM}$ to get:

$$\sum_{i=1}^N m_i \vec{r}_{CM} = \vec{r}_{CM} \sum_{i=1}^N m_i = \vec{r}_{CM} M \qquad (C13.29)$$

Therefore, we have

$$\sum_{i=1}^N m_i \vec{q}_i = M\vec{r}_{CM} - M\vec{r}_{CM} = 0 \qquad (C13.30)$$

The proof for the sum involving $m_i\vec{u}_i$ is almost identical.

C13.11 First, break up the sum of the four products in equation C13.18 into four separate sums:

$$\vec{L} = \sum_{i=1}^N \vec{r}_{CM} \times m_i \vec{v}_{CM} + \sum_{i=1}^N \vec{r}_{CM} \times m_i \vec{u}_i$$

$$+ \sum_{i=1}^N \vec{q}_i \times m_i \vec{v}_{CM} + \sum_{i=1}^N \vec{q}_i \times m_i \vec{u}_i \qquad (C13.31)$$

In the first sum, use linearity to pull the factor m_i out in front of the cross product, and then pull the common factor of the cross product out of the sum:

$$\sum_{i=1}^N \vec{r}_{CM} \times m_i \vec{v}_{CM} = \sum_{i=1}^N m_i (\vec{r}_{CM} \times \vec{v}_{CM})$$

$$= (\vec{r}_{CM} \times \vec{v}_{CM}) \sum_{i=1}^N m_i = (\vec{r}_{CM} \times \vec{v}_{CM}) M \qquad (C13.32)$$

We can then put the M back in front of $\vec{v}_{CM}$ to get the first term in equation C13.19. In the second sum, simply pull the common factor of $\vec{r}_{CM}$ out in front of the sum to get the second term in equation C13.19. In the third sum, use the linearity of the cross product to associate the mass m_i with the $\vec{q}_i$ factor rather than the $\vec{v}_{CM}$, and then pull the common factor of $\vec{v}_{CM}$ out the back of the sum (since the cross product is not commutative, we don't want to change the order of any products!). The last sum is fine as it stands.

INDEX TO UNIT *C*